Lecture Notes in Computer Science   12070

More information about this series at http://www.springer.com/series/7407

Irek Ulidowski · Ivan Lanese ·
Ulrik Pagh Schultz · Carla Ferreira (Eds.)

Reversible Computation: Extending Horizons of Computing

Selected Results of the COST Action IC1405

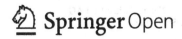

Editors
Irek Ulidowski
University of Leicester
Leicester, UK

Ivan Lanese
University of Bologna
Bologna, Italy

Ulrik Pagh Schultz
University of Southern Denmark
Odense, Denmark

Carla Ferreira
NOVA University Lisbon
Caparica, Portugal

ISSN 0302-9743   ISSN 1611-3349   (electronic)
Lecture Notes in Computer Science
ISBN 978-3-030-47360-0   ISBN 978-3-030-47361-7   (eBook)
https://doi.org/10.1007/978-3-030-47361-7

LNCS Sublibrary: SL1 – Theoretical Computer Science and General Issues

Acknowledgement and Disclaimer
This publication is based upon work from COST Action IC1405 Reversible Computation: Extending Horizons of Computing, supported by COST (European Cooperation in Science and Technology).
The book reflects only the authors' views. Neither the COST Association nor any person acting on its behalf is responsible for the use, which might be made of the information contained in this publication. The COST Association is not responsible for external websites or sources referred to in this publication.

This Springer imprint is published by the registered company Springer Nature Switzerland AG
The registered company address is: Gewerbestrasse 11, 6330 Cham, Switzerland

European Cooperation in Science and Technology (COST)

This publication is based upon work from COST Action IC1405 Reversible Computation - Extending Horizons of Computing, supported by COST (European Cooperation in Science and Technology).

COST is a funding agency for research and innovation networks. Our Actions help connect research initiatives across Europe and enable scientists to grow their ideas by sharing them with their peers. This boosts their research, career, and innovation.

www.cost.eu

Funded by the Horizon 2020 Framework Programme of the European Union

Preface

Reversible Computation (RC) is a new paradigm that extends the traditional forwards-only mode of computation with the ability to execute in reverse, so that computation can run backwards as easily as forwards. It aims to deliver novel computing devices and software, and to enhance existing systems by equipping them with reversibility. There are many potential applications of RC, including languages and software tools for reliable and recovery-oriented distributed systems and revolutionary reversible logic gates and circuits, but they can only be realised and have lasting effect if conceptual and firm theoretical foundations are established first. This state-of-the-art survey presents the main recent scientific outcomes in the area of RC, focusing on those that have emerged during COST Action IC1405 Reversible Computation - Extending Horizons of Computing, a European research network that operated from May 2015 to April 2019.

Action IC1405 was organised into four Working Groups. The members of Working Group 1 concentrated their efforts on establishing Foundations of RC. Working Groups 2 and 3 focused on specific technical challenges and potential application areas of reversibility in Software and Systems and in Reversible Circuit Design respectively. The purpose of Working Group 4 was to validate and explore application of Action's research results via practical case studies.

Working Groups 1–3 produced yearly scientific reports during the life of the Action, and these reports have been developed further into four comprehensive chapters surveying the main conceptual, theoretical, and technical achievements of the RC Action. Seven of the case studies from Working Group 4 were selected for presentation in this book. They show that RC techniques can form essential parts of solutions to many difficult practical problems as can be seen, for example, in the success of reversible debugging software tools. Overall, there are 40 co-authors of the book, which represents a substantial proportion of around 110 active members of the RC Action. This survey is a result of collaborative work that was carried out in part during regular Action meetings and Short-Term Scientific Missions (STSMs) supported by COST.

The content of the survey is structured as follows:

- Chapter 1 presents many new theoretical developments in the foundations of RC. It is worth noting the work on reversing Petri nets and on categorical characterisation of reversibility which was carried out as a direct result of the members of the respective communities participation in IC1405. Results obtained by Working Group 1 on reversibility in programming languages, term rewriting, membrane systems, process calculi, automata, and quantum formal verification are also given here.
- The main results obtained in the area of reversible software and systems are described in Chapter 2. They span from the definition of imperative and reversible object-oriented languages to the impact of reversibility on analysis techniques based on behavioural types, and to the application of reversibility for recovery, efficient

simulation, and wireless communications. The outcomes of Working Group 2 have been mostly of practical nature, hence some of the topics above are further discussed in the chapters of the book devoted to case studies.

- Chapter 3 covers simulation and design techniques for quantum circuits. Quantum circuits are inherently reversible and have received significant attention in the recent years. Simulating and designing them in a proper fashion is however a non-trivial task. The chapter provides an overview of solutions for these tasks which utilise expertise on efficient data structures and algorithms gained in the design of conventional circuits and systems.
- An overview of recent results towards a new classification of reversible functions, which would be useful in the synthesis of reversible circuits, is presented in Chapter 4. Firstly, theoretical results on properties of component functions of reversible functions are given. Then, the results of recent research on the existence of Boolean reversible functions of any number of variables (with all component functions belonging to different equivalence classes) are described. Finally, results on the existence of Boolean reversible functions with specified properties of all component functions are reported.
- Chapter 5 focuses on the application of reversibility to debugging. This is a quite natural application, since debugging aims at finding bugs (that is, wrong lines of code) causing visible misbehaviours, and to do that it is quite natural to execute backward from the misbehaviour. The chapter focuses on debugging of concurrent systems, where the use of reversibility is more recent, and considers both a standard imperative language and a subset of the functional language Erlang. Notably, the results described in this section are practical, but obtained as a direct application of theoretical investigations in the area of process calculi and semantics.
- The combination of reversibility and run-time monitoring of distributed systems is advocated in Chapter 6. It considers Erlang programs as an instance of the implementation of a model-driven methodology which can also be applied to other message-passing frameworks. Reversible choreographies are introduced to abstractly represent message-passing software and are used to specify adaptation and recovery strategies. These specifications are then used to generate monitors that govern the recovery and run-time adaptation of the execution according to the specified recovery policies.
- Chapter 7 give an overview of process calculi and Petri nets techniques for the modeling and reasoning about reversibility of systems, including out-of-causal-order reversibility as in chemical reactions. As an example, the autoprotolysis of water reaction is modeled in the Calculus of Covalent Bonding, the Bonding Calculus, and in Reversing Petri Nets.
- A robotic assembly case study is presented in Chapter 8. It investigates to what extent program inversion of a robotic assembly sequence can be considered to derive a reverse behaviour, and to what extent changing the execution direction at runtime (namely backtracking and retrying) using program inversion can be used as an automatic error handling procedure. The programming model is used to reversibly control industrial robots and demonstrates reversible control of industrial robots in real-world scenarios.

- Chapter 9 presents practical results in the field of optimistic parallel discrete event simulation (PDES). Optimistic PDES requires reversibility to perform a distributed roll-back in case conflicts are detected due to the optimistic execution approach. Two approaches to reversibility are compared: one based on the reversible programming language Janus, the other based on a variant of checkpointing, also called incremental state saving. For the purpose of comparing the performance of the two approaches, a benchmark simulation model is presented which is specifically designed for evaluating the performance of approaches to reversibility in PDES.
- A case study on applications of RC in wireless communications is given in Chapter 10. A communication system has an inherent link with RC. It is demonstrated that the communication channel can be modeled using reversible paradigms such as reversible cellular automata, that the hardware conducting communications based on wave time reversal has a natural, simple implementation in terms of reversible gates, and, lastly, that optimisation for large antenna arrays can be efficiently done in real time using reversible computational models such as Reversing Petri Nets.
- Finally, Chapter 11 provides an overview of key reconciliation techniques in quantum key distribution protocols with a focus on communication and computing performance. Different ways to identify errors in establishing symmetric cryptographic keys are investigated, with a focus on recursivity and reversibility. This is particularly noticeable with the Cascade Protocol, while other protocols focus on achieving one-sided processing which is of great importance for satellite quantum communications. Also, a new approach to key reconciliation techniques based on artificial neural networks is introduced.

We are grateful to all the contributors of this book, who worked tirelessly preparing the chapters and improving them greatly following a review process. Our thanks are due to many reviewers who helped to improve the scientific quality of the book. We would like to thank Veroniva Gaspes, the STSM Coordinator of Action IC1405, for dealing efficiently with over 80 STSM visits. We also thank Jovanka Pantović for taking care of ICT conference grants.

We would like to express our appreciation to Ralph Stübner, the Scientific Officer of the Action, for the support and advice received over the four years of the Action. Our administrative and financial affairs were looked after very effectively by Olga Gorczyca from COST. Our special thanks also go to Alfred Hofmann, Anna Kramer and Elke Werner, and other members of the editorial team at Springer, for their efficient and patient editorial assistance.

March 2020

Irek Ulidowski
Ivan Lanese
Ulrik Pagh Schultz
Carla Ferreira

Organization

Action IC1405 Committee

Action Scientific Officer

Ralph Stübner   COST Association, Belgium

Action Chair

Irek Ulidowski   University of Leicester, UK

Action Vice-chair

Ivan Lanese   Focus Team, University of Bologna/Inria, Italy

Working Group (WG) Leaders and Co-leaders

WG1 Leader
Iain Phillips   Imperial College London, UK

WG1 Co-leader
Michael Kirkedal Thomsen University of Copenhagen, Denmark

WG2 Leader
Claudio Antares Mezzina University of Urbino, Italy

WG2 Co-leader
Rudolf Schlatte   University of Oslo, Norway

WG3 Leader
Robert Wille   Johannes Kepler University, Austria

WG3 Co-leader
Paweł Kerntopf   Warsaw University of Technology, Poland

WG4 Leader
Ulrik Pugh Schultz   University of Southern Denmark, Denmark

WG4 Co-leader

Carla Ferreira   University of Lisbon, Portugal

STSM Coordinator

Veronica Gaspes   University of Halmstad, Sweden

ITC Conference Grants Coordinator

Jovanka Pantović   University of Novi Sad, Serbia

COST Action Equality Chair

Anna Philippou   University of Cyprus, Cyprus

COST Action Website Chair

Michael Kirkedal Thomsen   University of Copenhagen, Denmark

Additional Reviewers

Aman, Bogdan   Niemann, Philipp
Ciobanu, Gabriel   Philippou, Anna
Di Giusto, Cinzia   Podlaski, Krzysztof
Francalanza, Adrian   Schlatte, Rudolf
Giunti, Marco   Schordan, Markus
Glück, Robert   Tuosto, Emilio
Hoey, James   Vidal, German
Kerntopf, Pawel   Wille, Robert
Krivine, Jean   Worsch, Thomas
Mehic, Miralem   Yokoyama, Tetsuo
Mezzina, Claudio

Contents

Foundations of Reversible Computation

Bogdan Aman[1,2], Gabriel Ciobanu[1,2], Robert Glück[3], Robin Kaarsgaard[3], Jarkko Kari[4], Martin Kutrib[5], Ivan Lanese[6], Claudio Antares Mezzina[7], Łukasz Mikulski[8], Rajagopal Nagarajan[9], Iain Phillips[10(✉)], G. Michele Pinna[11], Luca Prigioniero[5,12], Irek Ulidowski[13], and Germán Vidal[14]

[1] Romanian Academy, Institute of Computer Science, Iaşi, Romania
`baman@iit.tuiasi.ro`
[2] A.I. Cuza University, Iaşi, Romania
`gabriel@info.uaic.ro`
[3] University of Copenhagen, Copenhagen, Denmark
`{glueck,robin}@di.ku.dk`
[4] University of Turku, Turku, Finland
`jkari@utu.fi`
[5] University of Giessen, Giessen, Germany
`kutrib@informatik.uni-giessen.de`
[6] Focus Team, University of Bologna/Inria, Bologna, Italy
`ivan.lanese@gmail.com`
[7] Università di Urbino, Urbino, Italy
`claudio.mezzina@uniurb.it`
[8] Folco Team, Nicolaus Copernicus University, Toruń, Poland
`mikulskilukasz@gmail.com`
[9] Middlesex University, London, England
`R.Nagarajan@mdx.ac.uk`
[10] Imperial College London, London, England
`i.phillips@imperial.ac.uk`
[11] Università di Cagliari, Cagliari, Italy
`gmpinna@unica.it`
[12] Università degli Studi di Milano, Milan, Italy
`prigioniero@di.unimi.it`
[13] University of Leicester, Leicester, England
`iu3@leicester.ac.uk`
[14] MiST, VRAIN, Universitat Politècnica de València, Valencia, Spain
`gvidal@dsic.upv.es`

Abstract. Reversible computation allows computation to proceed not only in the standard, forward direction, but also backward, recovering past states. While reversible computation has attracted interest for its multiple applications, covering areas as different as low-power computing, simulation, robotics and debugging, such applications need to be supported by a clear understanding of the foundations of reversible computation. We report below on many threads of research in the area of foundations of reversible computing, giving particular emphasis to the results obtained in the framework of the European COST Action IC1405, entitled "Reversible Computation - Extending Horizons of Computing", which took place in the years 2015–2019.

I. Ulidowski et al. (Eds.): RC 2020, LNCS 12070, pp. 1–40, 2020.
https://doi.org/10.1007/978-3-030-47361-7_1

1   Introduction

Reversible computation allows computation to proceed not only in the standard, forward direction, but also backward, recovering past states, and computing inputs from outputs. Reversible computation has attracted interest for multiple applications, covering areas as different as low-power computing [113], simulation [37], robotics [122] and debugging [129]. However, such applications need to be supported by a clear understanding of the foundations of reversible computation. Over the years, a number of theoretical aspects of reversible computing have been studied, dealing with categorical foundations of reversibility, foundations of programming languages and term rewriting, considering various models of sequential (automata, Turing machines) and concurrent (cellular automata, process calculi, Petri nets and membrane computing) computations, and tackling also the challenges posed by quantum computation, which is in a large part naturally reversible. We report below on those threads of research, giving particular emphasis to the results obtained in the framework of the European COST Action IC1405 [78], titled "Reversible Computation - Extending Horizons of Computing", which took place in the years 2015–2019 and involved researchers from 34 different countries.

The contents of this chapter are as follows. Section 2 covers category theory, Sect. 3 reversible programming languages, Sect. 4 term rewriting, and Sect. 5 membrane computing. We then discuss process calculi (Sect. 6), Petri nets (Sect. 7), automata (Sect. 8), and quantum verification and machine learning (Sect. 9). The chapter ends with a brief conclusion (Sect. 10).

2   Category Theory

Category theory is a framework for the description and development of mathematical structures. In category theory mathematical objects and their relationships within mathematical theories are abstracted into primal notions of *object* and *morphism*. Despite being a staple of the related field of quantum computer science for years (see, *e.g.*, [3, 79, 174]), category theory has seen comparatively little use in modelling reversible computation, where operational methods remain the standard. While the present section aims to give an overview of the use of categorical models in providing categorical semantics for reversible programming languages, categorical models have also been studied for other reversible computing phenomena, notably reversible event structures [65].

2.1   Dagger Categories

One approach to categorical models of reversible computation is given by dagger categories, *i.e.*, categories with an abstract notion of inverse given by assigning to each morphism $X \xrightarrow{f} Y$ an *adjoint* morphism $Y \xrightarrow{f^\dagger} X$, such that $(g \circ f)^\dagger = f^\dagger \circ g^\dagger$ and $\mathrm{id}_X^\dagger = \mathrm{id}_X$ (that is, composition is respected) and $f^{\dagger\dagger} = f$ for all compatible morphisms f and g. Note that this definition says nothing about how f and $f^\dagger$

ought to interact. As such, $f^\dagger$ is not required to "undo" the behaviour of f in any way, but can be *any* morphism with the appropriate signature, so long as the above constraints are met.

A useful specialisation of dagger categories, in connection with reversible computation, is dagger traced symmetric bimonoidal (or *rig*) categories, *i.e.*, dagger categories equipped with two symmetric monoidal tensors (usually denoted $-\oplus-$ and $-\otimes-$), interacting through a distributor and an annihilator, yielding the structure of a *rig* (*i.e.*, a ring without additive inverses). Iteration is modelled by means of a trace operator Tr (see [1,85,175]) such that $(\mathrm{Tr}f)^\dagger = \mathrm{Tr}(f^\dagger)$. These categories are strongly related to the dagger compact closed categories [3,174] that serve as the model of choice for the Oxford school of quantum computing.

The use of dagger traced symmetric bimonoidal categories to model reversible computations goes back at least as far as to the works by Abramsky, Haghverdi and Scott (see, *e.g.*, [2,4]) on (reversible) combinatory algebras, though its applications in reversible programming were perhaps best highlighted by the development of the Π and Π^0 calculi [34,83]. In addition, the reversible functional programming language Theseus [82] exhibits a correspondence with the Π^0 calculus. However, dagger traced symmetric bimonoidal categories are not strictly enough to model Π^0, as such categories fail to account for the recursive data types formed using $-\oplus-$, $-\otimes-$, and their units. In his recent thesis, Karvonen [94] describes precisely the categorical features necessary for such a correspondence, which he calls traced ω-continuous dagger rig categories.

Another notable application of this line of research is found in [167], where a reversible Π^0-like language is extended to describe quantum computations without measurement, but with support for (necessarily terminating) primitively recursive functions.

2.2 Inverse Categories

Another approach to model reversible computation is inverse categories [95] (see [40] for a more modern presentation), a specialisation of dagger categories in which morphisms are required to be partial isomorphisms. More precisely, each morphism $X \xrightarrow{f} Y$ may be *uniquely* assigned a *partial inverse* $Y \xrightarrow{f^\dagger} X$ satisfying $f \circ f^\dagger \circ f = f$.

The development of inverse categories as models of reversible computation was pioneered in the thesis of B.G. Giles [58], though a concrete correspondence was never provided. This work, combined with the comprehensive account of inverse categories with joins given in the thesis of Guo [67], was exploited in [86] to give an account of reversible recursion in inverse categories with joins.

Much of this theory was then put to use in [87], where the authors managed to show soundness, adequacy, and (under certain conditions) full abstraction for reversible flowchart languages [185] in a class of inverse categories with joins.

2.3   Monads and Arrows for Reversible Effects

The first account of monads pertaining to reversible computing was given in [71] as *dagger Frobenius monads*. Though these arise naturally in quantum computation in the context of measurement, it turns out that they are exceedingly rare in the case of classical reversible computing. A better concept for modelling and programming with reversible effects turns out to be that of *dagger* and *inverse arrows* [70], with examples such as reversible computation with mutable memory, errors and error handling, and more.

3   Foundations of Reversible Programming Languages

Reversible programming languages bridge the gap between the hardware and the specific application, and therefore play a central role in the development of reversible computing. Reversible languages must be expressive and usable in a variety of application domains. Their semantics must be precise and their programs accessible to program inversion, analysis and verification. Additionally, they must have efficient realisations on reversible devices and on standard ones. Recent programming language studies have advanced the foundations and theory of reversible languages in several interrelated directions.

3.1   Language Cores

Reversible languages have been reduced to their computational cores:

R-Core [63] is a structured reversible language consisting of a single command for *reversible store updates*, a single control-flow operator for *reversible iteration*, and data structures built from a single binary constructor and a single symbol. Despite its extreme simplicity, the language is *reversibly universal*, which means it is as computationally powerful as any reversible language can be. Its four-line program inverter is as concise as the one for Bennett's reversible Turing machines. The core language and a recent extension with *reversible recursion* were equipped with a denotational semantics [61,63,64].

R-While [62] adds reversible *rewrite rules* and *pattern matching* as syntactic sugar to R-Core, which makes the family of structured reversible languages more accessible to foundational studies and educational purposes than do reversible Turing machines and other reversible devices. The *procedural extension* [64] draws a distinction between tail-recursion by iteration and general recursion by reversible procedures, a notoriously difficult transformation problem in program inversion [96,151]. The *linear-time self-interpretability* makes the language also suitable for foundational studies of computability and complexity from a programming language perspective [84].

CoreFun [80] is a typed reversible functional language that seeks to reduce reversible functional programming [184] to its essentials so that it can serve as a foundation for modern functional language concepts. The language has a formal semantics and a type system to statically check for reversibility of programs.

3.2   Formal Semantics

Precise semantics is the foundation of every programming language, and formality is from where programming languages derive their usefulness and power.

A program is regarded as reversible if each of its meaningful subprograms is partially invertible. Thus, *reversible programs have reversible semantics* [61]. A foundation of the semantics has been established for structured reversible languages built on inverse categories [59,60]. This class of languages includes Janus, a reversible language that was originally formalised by conventional (irreversible) operational semantics, and the R-Core and R-While languages. For example, predicates and assertions occurring in reversible alternatives and reversible iterations are modelled by decision maps, in contrast to conventional semantics. A benefit of the reversible semantic approach is that program inverters and equivalences of reversible programs can be derived directly from the semantics.

The assumption of countable joins in inverse categories is suitable in a categorical account of reversible recursion [86], which enables modelling of procedures in reversible structured and functional languages. Reversibility of Janus was proved with a proof assistant [153].

3.3   Compilation Principles

High-level languages are more productive in most application domains, but high levels of computational abstractions do not come for free. A clean and effective translation to lower abstraction levels is required and sophisticated optimisations may be necessary to generate high quality implementations.

Dynamic memory management is a central runtime mechanism to support dynamic data structures in reversible machines. Its purpose is to support reversible object-oriented languages as well as the core languages described above. Garbage collectors that use multiple references [142] to overcome linearity requirements and heap manager algorithms have been developed and experimentally evaluated. To ease the analysis and optimisation when translating from a high-level reversible language to the underlying reversible machine, the *reversible single static assignment* (RSSA) form can be a suitable intermediate representation in optimising compilers [141]. Its aim is to allow for advanced optimisations such as register allocation on reversible Von Neumann machines.

The recent languages Joule [173] and ROOPL [68] demonstrated that well-known *object-oriented concepts* can be captured reversibly by extending a Janus-like imperative language. *Reversible data types* [43], that is data structures with all of its associated operations implemented reversibly, are enabled by dynamic allocation of constructor terms on the heap [11]. A reversible dynamic memory management based on the Buddy Memory system [99] has been developed and tested in a compiler targeting the assembly language of a reversible computer [43].

3.4   Reversibilisation Techniques

A separate approach to reversibility is *reversibilisation*, which turns irreversible computations into reversible computations. This can be achieved by extending the semantics of an irreversible language or by instrumenting an irreversible program to continually produce information that ensures reversibility.

Some reversibilisation techniques work without user interaction, while others require annotation of programs. Techniques have been developed in recent years that add tracing to term rewriting systems [150] and instrument C++ programs with incremental state saving [171]. Other investigations have focused on techniques for debugging concurrent programs [121,149] and on extending the operational semantics of an irreversible language with tracing [72], thereby defining the inverse semantics of the language. Hybrid approaches aim to combine reversibilisation and reversible sublanguages [172]. In general, the minimisation of the additional computational resources required for sealing information leaks by reversibilisation remains a central challenge.

4   Term Rewriting

Term rewriting [17,98,178] is a foundational theory of computing that underlies most rule-based programming languages. A *term rewriting system* (TRS) is specified as a set of rewrite rules of the form $l \to r$ such that l is a nonvariable term and r is a term whose variables appear in l. Positions are used to address the nodes of a term viewed as a tree. A *position* p in a term t is represented by a finite sequence of natural numbers, where $t|_p$ denotes the *subterm* of t at position p and $t[s]_p$ the result of *replacing the subterm* $t|_p$ by the term s. *Substitutions* are mappings from variables to terms.

Given a TRS $\mathcal{R}$, we define the associated rewrite relation $\to_\mathcal{R}$ as the smallest binary relation satisfying the following: given terms s, t, we have $s \to_\mathcal{R} t$ iff there exist a position p in s, a rewrite rule $l \to r \in \mathcal{R}$, and a substitution σ such that $s|_p = l\sigma$ and $t = s[r\sigma]_p$. Given a binary relation $\to$, we denote by $\to^*$ its reflexive and transitive closure, i.e., $s \to_\mathcal{R}^* t$ means that s can be reduced to t in $\mathcal{R}$ in zero or more steps. The goal of term rewriting is reducing terms to so-called *normal forms*, where a term t is called *irreducible* or in *normal form* w.r.t. a TRS $\mathcal{R}$ if there is no term s with $t \to_\mathcal{R} s$. Computing normal forms can be seen as the counterpart of computing *values* in functional programming.

We also consider Conditional TRSs (CTRSs) of the form $l \to r \Leftarrow s_1 \twoheadrightarrow t_1, \ldots, s_n \twoheadrightarrow t_n$, with $\twoheadrightarrow$ interpreted as *reachability* ($\to_\mathcal{R}^*$). Roughly speaking, $s \to_\mathcal{R} t$ iff there exist a position p in s, a rewrite rule $l \to r \Leftarrow s_1 \twoheadrightarrow t_1, \ldots, s_n \twoheadrightarrow t_n \in \mathcal{R}$, and a substitution σ such that $s|_p = l\sigma$, $s_i\sigma \to_\mathcal{R}^* t_i\sigma$ for all $i = 1, \ldots, n$, and $t = s[r\sigma]_p$. Consider, e.g., the following CTRS $\mathcal{R}^{\mathsf{fn}}$:

$$\beta_1 : \mathsf{fn}([\,]) \to [\,]$$
$$\beta_2 : \mathsf{fn}(\mathsf{person}(n, l)\!:\!xs) \to n\!:\!ys \Leftarrow \mathsf{fn}(xs) \twoheadrightarrow ys$$
$$\beta_3 : \mathsf{fn}(\mathsf{city}(c)\!:\!xs) \to ys \Leftarrow \mathsf{fn}(xs) \twoheadrightarrow ys$$

where we use "$:$" and $[\,]$ as list constructors. Here, β_1, β_2 and β_3 denote labels that uniquely identify each rewrite rule. Function fn takes a list of persons of the form person($first\_name$, $last\_name$) and cities of the form city($city\_name$) and returns a list of first names. Note that it could be specified in a typical functional language (say, Haskell) as follows:

```
fn [] = []
fn ((Person n l):xs) = n:ys  where ys = fn xs
fn ((City c):xs) = ys  where ys = fn xs
```

4.1   Reversible Term Rewriting

In general, term rewriting is not reversible, even for injective functions; namely, given a rewrite step $t_1 \rightarrow t_2$, we do not always have a decidable method to get t_1 from t_2. One of the first approaches to reversibility in term rewriting is due to Abramsky [2], who considered reversibility in the context of *pattern matching automata*.[1] Abramsky's approach requires a condition called *biorthogonality* (which, in particular, implies injectivity), so that the considered automata are reversible. This work can be seen as a rather fundamental delineation of the boundary between reversible and irreversible computation in logical terms. However, biorthogonality is overly restrictive in the context of term rewriting, since almost no term rewrite system is biorthogonal. Another example of a term rewrite system with both forward and reverse rewrite relations is the *reaction systems for bonding* in [159]. It has been used to model a simple catalytic reaction, polymer construction, by a scaffolding protein and a long-running transaction with a compensation.

In the context of the COST action IC1405, Nishida *et al.* [148, 150] introduced the first generic notion of *reversible rewriting*, a conservative extension of term rewriting based on a so-called *Landauer embedding*. In this approach, for every rewrite step $s \rightarrow_{\mathcal{R}} t$, one should store the applied rule β, the selected position p, and a substitution σ with the values of some variables (e.g., the variables that occur in the left-hand side of a rule but not in its right-hand side). Therefore, reversible rewrite steps have now the form $\langle s, \pi \rangle \rightharpoonup \langle t, \beta(p, \sigma) : \pi \rangle$, where $\rightharpoonup$ is a reversible (forward) rewrite relation and π is a *trace* that stores the sequence of terms of the form $\beta(p, \sigma)$. The dual, inverse relation $\leftharpoonup$ is also introduced, so that its union $\rightleftharpoons$ can be used to perform both forward and backward reductions.

Moreover, [148] also introduces a scheme to *compile* the reversible extension of rewriting into the system rules. Essentially, given a system $\mathcal{R}$, new systems $\mathcal{R}_f$ and $\mathcal{R}_b$ are produced, so that standard rewriting in $\mathcal{R}_f$, i.e., $\rightarrow_{\mathcal{R}_f}$, coincides with the forward reversible extension $\rightharpoonup_{\mathcal{R}}$ in the original system, and analogously $\rightarrow_{\mathcal{R}_b}$ is equivalent to $\leftharpoonup_{\mathcal{R}}$. Therefore, $\mathcal{R}_f$ can be seen as an *injectivisation* of $\mathcal{R}$, and $\mathcal{R}_b$ can be seen as the *inversion* of $\mathcal{R}_f$.

---

[1] Although he did not consider rewriting explicitly, pattern matching automata can also be represented in terms of standard notions of term rewriting.

For instance, the injectivisation $\mathcal{R}_f^{\mathsf{fn}}$ of the previous CTRS $\mathcal{R}^{\mathsf{fn}}$ is as follows:

$$\mathsf{fn}^{\mathsf{i}}([\,]) \rightarrow \langle[\,], \beta_1\rangle$$
$$\mathsf{fn}^{\mathsf{i}}(\mathsf{person}(n,l):xs) \rightarrow \langle n:ys, \beta_2(l, ws)\rangle \Leftarrow \mathsf{fn}^{\mathsf{i}}(xs) \twoheadrightarrow \langle ys, ws\rangle$$
$$\mathsf{fn}^{\mathsf{i}}(\mathsf{city}(c):xs) \rightarrow \langle ys, \beta_3(c, ws)\rangle \Leftarrow \mathsf{fn}^{\mathsf{i}}(xs) \twoheadrightarrow \langle ys, ws\rangle$$

together with the corresponding inversion $\mathcal{R}_b^{\mathsf{fn}}$:

$$\mathsf{fn}^{-1}([\,], \beta_1) \rightarrow [\,]$$
$$\mathsf{fn}^{-1}(n:ys, \beta_2(l, ws)) \rightarrow \mathsf{person}(n,l):xs \Leftarrow \mathsf{fn}^{-1}(ys, ws) \twoheadrightarrow xs$$
$$\mathsf{fn}^{-1}(ys, \beta_3(c, ws)) \rightarrow \mathsf{city}(c):xs \Leftarrow \mathsf{fn}^{-1}(ys, ws) \twoheadrightarrow xs$$

For example, the following rewrite derivation in $\mathcal{R}^{\mathsf{fn}}$:

$$\mathsf{fn}([\mathsf{person}(\mathsf{john}, \mathsf{smith}), \mathsf{city}(\mathsf{london}), \mathsf{person}(\mathsf{ada}, \mathsf{lovelace})]) \rightarrow^* [\mathsf{john}, \mathsf{ada}]$$

is now as follows in $\mathcal{R}_f^{\mathsf{fn}}$:

$$\mathsf{fn}^{\mathsf{i}}([\mathsf{person}(\mathsf{john}, \mathsf{smith}), \mathsf{city}(\mathsf{london}), \mathsf{person}(\mathsf{ada}, \mathsf{lovelace})])$$
$$\rightarrow^* \langle[\mathsf{john}, \mathsf{ada}], \beta_2(\mathsf{smith}, \beta_3(\mathsf{london}, \beta_2(\mathsf{lovelace}, \beta_1)))\rangle$$

where $\beta_2(\mathsf{smith}, \beta_3(\mathsf{london}, \beta_2(\mathsf{lovelace}, \beta_1)))$ is the trace of the computation. Besides proving some fundamental properties of reversible rewriting, Nishida et al. [150] have developed a prototype implementation of the reversibilisation transformations (injectivisation and inversion), which is publicly available through a web interface from http://kaz.dsic.upv.es/rev-rewriting.html.

4.2   Application to Bidirectional Transformations

The framework of *bidirectional transformations* considers two representations of some data and the functions that convert one representation into the other and vice versa (see, e.g., [75] for an overview). Typically, we have a function called "**get**" that takes a *source* and returns a *view*. In turn, the function "put" takes a possibly updated view (together with the original source) and returns the corresponding, updated source. In this context, *bidirectionalisation* [128] aims at automatically producing one of the functions, typically producing a function put from the corresponding function get. For this purpose, a so-called *complement* function is often introduced so that **get** becomes injective (see, e.g., [55]).

In [152], Nishida and Vidal present a bidirectionalisation technique based on the injectivisation and inversion transformations of CTRSs from [150]. They also prove a number of relevant properties which ensure that changes in both the source and the view are correctly propagated and that no undesirable side-effects are introduced.

To be precise, given a **get** function f, the corresponding put can be automatically defined as follows:

$$\mathsf{put}_f(v, s) \rightarrow s' \Leftarrow \mathsf{f}^{\mathsf{i}}(s) \twoheadrightarrow \langle v', \pi\rangle, \mathsf{f}^{-1}(v, \pi) \twoheadrightarrow s'$$

Note that the trace of a computation, π, plays the role of a *complement* (following the terminology in the literature of bidirectional transformations).

For instance, given the previous function fn, the corresponding put function is defined as follows:

$$\mathsf{put}_{\mathsf{fn}}(v, s) \rightarrow s' \Longleftarrow \mathsf{fn}^{\mathsf{i}}(s) \twoheadrightarrow \langle v', \pi \rangle, \mathsf{fn}^{-1}(v, \pi) \twoheadrightarrow s'$$

so that, e.g., $\mathsf{put}_{\mathsf{fn}}([\mathsf{peter}, \mathsf{ada}], \beta_2(\mathsf{smith}, \beta_3(\mathsf{london}, \beta_2(\mathsf{lovelace}, \beta_1))))$ reduces to $[\mathsf{person}(\mathsf{peter}, \mathsf{smith}), \mathsf{city}(\mathsf{london}), \mathsf{person}(\mathsf{ada}, \mathsf{lovelace})]$. Note that the first element has been updated from $\mathsf{person}(\mathsf{john}, \mathsf{smith})$ to $\mathsf{person}(\mathsf{peter}, \mathsf{smith})$.

However, $\mathsf{put}_{\mathsf{f}}$ is only defined for "compatible" view updates. E.g., the function $\mathsf{put}_{\mathsf{fn}}([\mathsf{ada}], \beta_2(\mathsf{smith}, \beta_3(\mathsf{london}, \beta_2(\mathsf{lovelace}, \beta_1))))$ cannot be reduced to a value. In [152], the use of *narrowing* [76,176]—an extension of rewriting that replaces matching with unification—is introduced to precisely characterise *compatible* (also called *in-place*) view updates.

For example, given the trace $\beta_2(\mathsf{smith}, \beta_3(\mathsf{london}, \beta_2(\mathsf{lovelace}, \beta_1)))$, narrowing allows us to compute the *view skeleton* $[x_1, x_2]$. This means that any view update that can be obtained as an instance of $[x_1, x_2]$ is compatible with the trace (and, thus, the put function is well defined).

Finally, [152] also discusses some directions for dealing with view updates that are not compatible.

5   Membrane Computing

Natural computing is a complex field of research dealing with models and computational techniques inspired by nature that helps us in understanding the biochemical world in terms of information processing. Membrane computing [154] and reaction systems [53] are two important theories of natural computing inspired by the functioning of living cells.

Membrane computing deals with multisets of symbols processed in the compartments of a membrane structure according to some multiset rewriting rules; some of the symbols (presented with their multiplicity within the regions delimited by membranes) evolve in parallel according to the rules associated with their membranes, while the others remain unchanged and can be used in the subsequent steps. It is also possible to send multisets of symbols in the neighbouring membranes, the systems being organised in a tree-like fashion. The evolution takes place in a maximal parallel manner: all the instances of the applicable rules have to be applied in order to reach the next state.

The situation is different in reaction systems. These systems represent a qualitative model: they deal with sets rather than multisets. Two major assumptions distinguish the reaction systems from the membrane systems: (i) threshold assumption: reaction systems have actually an infinite multiplicity for their resources; (ii) no permanency assumption: only entities produced at one step will be present in the system at the next step.

The issue of reversibility in various computational paradigms has gained interest in recent years. In one of the earliest papers on reversibility in membrane systems [5], the authors (under the influence of category theory) presented reversibility as a form of duality. A full description of this kind of reversibility in membrane systems is given by Agrigoroaiei and Ciobanu in [6].

In [7], Aman and Ciobanu investigated the reversibility of biochemical reactions in parallel rewriting systems; these systems can easily represent some classes of membrane systems and Petri nets. Formally, a parallel rewriting system is a tuple $(O, \mathcal{R}, w_0)$, where O is a finite alphabet of objects, $\mathcal{R}$ is a set of rewriting rules and w_0 is a multiset of objects over O. For each rule $r \in \mathcal{R}$ there exist the non-empty multisets $lhs(r), rhs(r) \in O^+$ standing for the left-hand side and right-hand side of the rule, respectively, such that $r : lhs(r) \to rhs(r)$. Given a multiset of rules F, then the left-hand side and right-hand side of it can be defined as: $lhs(F) = \sum_{r \in \mathcal{R}} F(r) \cdot lhs(r)$ and $rhs(F) = \sum_{r \in \mathcal{R}} F(r) \cdot rhs(r)$.

A parallel rewriting system $(O, \mathcal{R}, w_0)$ evolves in a maximal parallel manner. This means that a non-empty multiset R of rules is applicable to a multiset w of objects if $lhs(R) \leq w$ and there does not exist $r \in \mathcal{R}$ such that $lhs(r) \leq w - lhs(R)$. By applying a multiset R of rules, a multiset w of objects is transformed into another multiset $w' = w - lhs(R) + rhs(R)$ of objects. If no multiset of rules is applicable, then the computation stops.

The new features of this approach are given by adding an external control specified by using a special symbol $\rho \notin O$ that informs the system that a rollback will be executed, and by constructing two new sets of rules $\overrightarrow{\mathcal{R}} = \{u \to v|_{\neg \rho} \mid u \to v \in \mathcal{R}\}$ and $\overleftarrow{\mathcal{R}}_\rho = \{v \to u|_\rho \mid u \to v \in \mathcal{R}\} \cup \rho \to \lambda$ to mark the rules that will be applied in forward and backward steps, respectively.

Several theoretical results are obtained, including the so-called loop results and the connections between the evolutions of these systems and their reversible extensions. If there exist multisets of rules not competing for the same resources, then the following results hold.

A first result presents the **forward diamond** property:

If $w \xrightarrow{\overrightarrow{\mathcal{R}}} w'$ and $w \xrightarrow{\overrightarrow{\mathcal{R'}}} w''$, where $\overrightarrow{\mathcal{R}}$ and $\overrightarrow{\mathcal{R'}}$ are two valid multisets of rules such that $lhs(\overrightarrow{\mathcal{R}}) \cap lhs(\overrightarrow{\mathcal{R'}}) = \emptyset$, then there exists a multiset w_1 such that $w' \xrightarrow{\overrightarrow{\mathcal{R'}}} w_1$ and $w'' \xrightarrow{\overrightarrow{\mathcal{R}}} w_1$.

The second result presents the **reverse diamond** property:

If $w \xrightarrow{\overleftarrow{\mathcal{R}}_\rho} w'$ and $w \xrightarrow{\overleftarrow{\mathcal{R'}}_\rho} w''$, where $\overleftarrow{\mathcal{R}}_\rho$ and $\overleftarrow{\mathcal{R'}}_\rho$ are two valid multisets of rules such that $lhs(\overleftarrow{\mathcal{R}}_\rho) \cap lhs(\overleftarrow{\mathcal{R'}}_\rho) = \emptyset$, then there exists a multiset w_1 such that $w' \xrightarrow{\overleftarrow{\mathcal{R'}}_\rho} w_1$ and $w'' \xrightarrow{\overleftarrow{\mathcal{R}}_\rho} w_1$.

A forward step performed using the multiset $\overrightarrow{\mathcal{R}}$ of rules can be matched by a backward step performed using the multiset $\overleftarrow{\mathcal{R}}_\rho$ of rules, and vice-versa (**loop**):

$$w \xrightarrow{\overrightarrow{\mathcal{R}}} w' \quad \text{if and only if} \quad \rho w' \xrightarrow{\overleftarrow{\mathcal{R}}_\rho} w.$$

In [8], Aman and Ciobanu investigated reversibility in reaction systems. Reaction systems [53] deal with sets rather than multisets, assuming that each resource is present in the system in a sufficient amount to ensure that several reactions needing such a resource are not in conflict. Formally, a reaction system $\mathcal{A}$ is a tuple (S, A), where S is a finite alphabet and $A \subseteq rac(S)$. The set $rac(S) = \{(R, I, P) \mid R, I, P \subseteq S, R \cap I = \emptyset\}$ is the set of all reactions over S. Given a reaction $a = (R_a, I_a, P_a)$, the sets R_a, I_a and P_a contain the reactants, inhibitors and products of a, respectively. For a set $C \subseteq S$ and a set of reactions $A \subseteq rac(S)$, the result of applying A on C is defined by $res(A, C) = \bigcup_{a \in A} P_a$, and the evolution can be written as $C \xrightarrow{A} res(A, C)$. The set of all reactions from A that are enabled by C is $en(A, C) = \{a \in A \mid R_a \subseteq C, I_a \cap C = \emptyset\}$.

An interactive process is a pair $\pi = (\gamma, \delta)$ such that $\gamma = C_0, \ldots, C_{n-1}$, $\delta = D_1, \ldots, D_n$ with $n \geq 1$, where $C_{j-1}, D_j \subseteq S$ for $1 \leq j \leq n$ are the context and result sets, respectively. The sets D_j are computed using the equalities $D_1 = res(A, W_0)$ and $D_i = res(A, W_{i-1})$, where the sets $W_0 = C_0$ and $W_i = D_i \cup C_i$ for each $2 \leq i \leq n$ represent the states.

In order to have backward computations, we add to each state W_i a register T_i to remember objects no longer available after step i. The reverse of a set A of reactions is the set $\tilde{A} = \{(P_a, I_a, R_a) \mid (R_a, I_a, P_a) \in A\}$. If $\rho \notin W_i$ and $E_i \neq \emptyset$, then a forward computation $(W_i, T_i) \xrightarrow{E_i} (W_{i+1}, T_{i+1})$ takes place, where $T_{i+1} = inc(T_i) \cup \bigcup_{t \in W_i \setminus lhs(E_i)}(t, 0)$, $inc(T) = \bigcup_{(t,i) \in T}(t, i+1)$ and $W_{i+1} = res(E_i, W_i)$. However, if $\rho \in W_i$ and $\tilde{E}_i \neq \emptyset$, then a backward computation $(W_{i+1}, T_{i+1}) \stackrel{\tilde{E}_i}{\rightsquigarrow} (W_i, T_i)$ takes place, where $T_i = dec(T_{i+1})$, $dec(T_d) = \bigcup_{(t,i) \in T_d; i > 0}(t, i - 1)$ and $W_i = res(\tilde{E}_i, W_{i+1}) \cup zero(T_{i+1})$ with $zero(T) = \bigcup_{(t,0) \in T} t$.

If the states satisfy some preconditions, then backward reductions are the inverse of the forward ones, and vice-versa:

- If $W = res(\tilde{E}, W') \cup zero(T')$ and $\rho \in W'$, then

$$(W, T) \xrightarrow{E} (W', T') \text{ implies } (W', T') \stackrel{\tilde{E}}{\rightsquigarrow} (W, T).$$

- If $W' = res(E, W)$ and $\rho \notin W$, then

$$(W', T') \stackrel{\tilde{E}}{\rightsquigarrow} (W, T) \text{ implies } (W, T) \xrightarrow{E} (W', T').$$

An operational correspondence between reaction systems and rewriting theory is also proved. It allows a translation of the reversible reaction systems into some rewriting systems executable in the rewriting engine Maude [39].

In [163] Pinna pursues reversibility in membrane systems from a different perspective. The paper focuses on how to reverse steps in computations of membrane systems, without adding rules to represent the reverse application of the original rules. Just one assumption on rules is made, namely that rules are not allowed to rewrite a multiset of objects into an empty multiset: the application of a rule must have an effect, though this could be not observable. This requirement is driven by the necessity that, in order to reversely apply a rule, this one must produce something. Furthermore, as in most rewriting systems, also in the considered membrane systems a computation step does not register the (multiset of) rules applied. Since this information may be crucial to reversely apply the same (multiset of) rules, one needs some strategies to solve the issue and obtain reversibility.

A solution can be to enrich each object with the information on how the particular object has been produced, namely each object now may carry the name of the rule r used to produce it. Objects are then $O \times R \cup \{\bot\}$ where R is the set of rules $\bigcup_i R_i$, with i ranging over the membranes, and $\bot$ denotes that the object is present in the initial configuration. The unique assumption is that rule names are unique. The drawback of this solution is that once an object is used the information on how it has been produced is lost.

To overcome this problem, the proposed solution is to add to the notion of configuration, previously a vector of multiset of objects, with one element for each membrane, a memory organised as a labelled partial order. Each element of the partial order corresponds to an object and carries also the information on which rule produced it. According to this a memory m is a triple $(X, \preceq, l)$ where $\preceq$ is a partial order and $l : X \to O \times R \cup \{\bot\} \times \{1, \ldots, n\}$ is the labelling associating the object, the name of rule that produced it and the membrane where the object is allocated. A configuration of a membrane system with n membranes is then the pair $\mathcal{C} = (C, \mathsf{m})$, where $C = (w_1, \ldots, w_n)$ is the tuple of multisets over objects O and $\mathsf{m} = (X, \preceq, l)$ is a memory such that for each $i \in \{1, \ldots, n\}$ it holds that $w_i = \mathsf{obj}_i(max(\mathsf{m}))$, where max gives the multiset of maximal elements of the memory and obj_i forgets the information about the rule.

The effect of applying a vector of multisets of rules $\mathcal{R}$ does not consist only in updating suitably the multisets of objects forming a configuration in the classical sense, but also in adding the information on which rule produced a specific object in the memory. This will be denoted with $(C, \mathsf{m})\{\!\![\mathcal{R} > (C', \mathsf{m}')$ where $C \xRightarrow{\mathcal{R}} C'$ is the usual step in membrane systems computation and the new memory m' is obtained adding to m the objects produced by the rules in $\mathcal{R}$ and by updating the partial order so that the produced elements are greater than the ones consumed by these rules.

Then the reverse application of a vector of multisets of rules can be obtained by looking in this memory for the maximal elements, which correspond to the right-hand sides of the rules to be reversely applied. The proper configuration is then computed from the new memory obtained by removing the maximal elements. The reverse application of a vector of multisets of rules $\mathcal{R}$ is denoted with $(C, \mathsf{m}) < \mathcal{R}]\!\!\}(C', \mathsf{m}')$, where the maximal elements of m' corresponding to the right-hand sides of rules in $\mathcal{R}$ are removed obtaining a memory m and a configuration C where each element $w_i = \mathsf{obj}_i(max(\mathsf{m}))$.

The following result has been proved:

Let Π_m be a membrane system with memory, (C, m) a configuration, and $\mathcal{R}$ be a vector of multisets of rules such that $(C, \mathsf{m})\{\!\![\mathcal{R} > (C', \mathsf{m}')$. Then, for all multi-rule vectors $\mathcal{R}'$ such that $(C', \mathsf{m}') < \mathcal{R}']\!\!\}(C, \mathsf{m})$, it holds that $\mathcal{R}' = \mathcal{R}$.

This simple implementation has the advantage of properly realising the causal reversibility. Furthermore the memory allows also to capture the dependencies among objects in a membrane system computation.

6 Process Calculi

Process calculi are a class of algebraic models for concurrent and distributed systems. Process calculi allow one to express the behaviour of a concurrent system in a concise way, abstracting away from implementation details, and focusing on the interaction patterns among the components of the system. Thus, it is possible to express the behaviour of a system in a mathematically precise way and verification techniques can be easily developed on top of it.

Research on reversing process calculi can be perhaps tracked back to the Chemical Abstract Machine [30], a calculus inspired by chemical reactions whose operational semantics defines both forward and reverse reduction relations. The first attempts to reverse existing process calculi can be found in [44,46], where a reversible extension of CCS [140] was presented. A main contribution of [44] was the definition of the notion of *causal-consistent* reversibility: any action can be undone, provided that its consequences, if any, are undone first. This definition is tailored to concurrent systems, where actions may overlap in time, hence saying "undo the last action" is not meaningful. Notably, this definition relates reversibility to causality instead of time, thus it can be applied even in those settings, such as some distributed systems, where no unique notion of time exists. A survey on causal-consistent reversibility can be found in [120].

6.1 Reversing Process Calculi

Following [44], causal-consistent extensions of other and more expressive process calculi have been defined. They can be divided into two families, one dealing with calculi equipped with labelled transition system semantics (describing interactions between the process and the outside world), and one dealing with reduction semantics (describing the evolution of processes in isolation). The former is more general, while the latter is normally simpler and hence more easily applicable to expressive calculi. The first approach extended causal-consistent reversibility from CCS to any calculus defined using a specific SOS format (a subset of the *path* format [146]) [160,161], and to π-calculus [42]. In the second line of research we find extensions of a fragment of CCS with biological relevance [35,36], of the higher-order π-calculus [117,119], of the coordination language Klaim [56], of a π-calculus with sessions [179], and of a CCS with broadcast communications [133]. The instance of the framework in [160] on CCS is called CCSK. CCSK differs from the reversible CCS in [44] in the way history is kept. Indeed, the approach of [160] can be considered static, since the structure of processes does not change during computation, and the minimal history information needed to enable reversibility is kept in the processes themselves, while in [44] the process is consumed during execution (as standard in process calculi) and larger memories are added to store history information. Nonetheless the two methods are equivalent as hinted at by [130] and fully proved by [115], where a mapping from an instance on CCS of [160] to the reversible CCS of [44] and vice versa is presented.

As discussed above, causally-consistent reversibility relates reversibility with causality. In CCS just one main notion of causality exists, and both the reversible variants of CCS above are based on it. In the π-calculus, many relevant notions of causality exist, which differ in the treatment of parallel extrusions of the same name. In [131] a uniform framework to define reversible π-calculi is presented. The framework is parametric w.r.t. a data structure that stores information about extrusions of a name. Different data structures yield different approaches to the parallel extrusion problem, leading to different ways of reversing a name extrusion, thus giving rise to different reversible variants of the π-calculus.

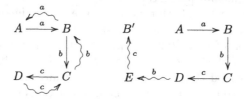

Fig. 1. Example of causal-consistent (left) and out-of-causal order reversibility (right)

6.2   Controlled Reversibility

The line of research described above focused on uncontrolled reversibility, defining how to reverse a process execution (in particular, which history and causal information is needed, and how to manage it), but not specifying when and whether to prefer backward execution over forward execution or vice versa. Uncontrolled reversibility allows one to understand how reversibility works, but not to exploit it into applications. Indeed, different application areas need different mechanisms to control reversibility. For instance, in biological systems the direction of the computation depends on physical conditions such as temperature and pressure, while in reliable systems reversibility is used to recover a consistent state when a bad event occurs. Triggered by these needs different mechanisms for controlling reversibility have been proposed (see the categorisation in [118]). For instance, [45,179] introduced irreversible actions to avoid going backward after a relevant result has been computed. Instead, [56,57,114,116,118,126] proposed an explicit rollback operator undoing a past action inside calculi where normal computation is forward, and a mechanism of alternatives allowing one to avoid trying the same path again and again. As shown in [57], the rollback operator satisfies a simple intuitive specification, namely that it is the smallest causal-consistent sequence of backward moves undoing the target action. Also, [18] let an energy potential drive the direction of computation while [158] introduced a forward monitor controlling the direction of execution of a reversible monitored process. A process calculus with a prefixing operator to model locally-controlled reversibility is introduced in [102,103]. Actions can be undone spontaneously, as in other reversible process calculi, or as pairs of concerted actions, where performing a weak action forces the undoing of a past action. Concerted actions allow one to model out-of-causal order computation, where effects can be undone before their causes, which is forbidden in most other reversible calculi. This form of reversibility is common in biochemical reactions, e.g., in the hydration of formaldehyde in water into methanediol. Such a feature can be disabled by considering a reduced form of concerted actions.

Reversibility, both in causal order and out-of-causal order, can be modelled in reversible event structures [157].

Figure 1 shows the difference between causal-consistent (left) and out-of-causal order reversibility. In both cases, the system performs actions a, b and c to reach state D. On the left, in order to get back to the original state, one has to first undo (in Fig. 1 undoing is represented with squiggly arrows) c then b and finally a. On the right, since causes do not need to be respected, the system can undo b before c, reaching in this way a new state E which may not have been reachable from the initial configuration by just using forward steps. From there, a and c may or may not be undoable. In the example, only c can be undone, leading to B'. If undoing b and undoing c do commute, then $B = B'$.

6.3   Analysis Techniques

Despite the proliferation of calculi for reversibility, when the COST Action IC1405 started, analysis techniques for reversible calculi were very limited, consisting essentially in some limited analysis about behavioural equivalences (in particular, forward-reverse bisimilarity [161]) and a technique for causal compression in CCS with irreversible actions [101]. Thus, the work in the COST Action tackled analysis techniques in depth, considering behavioural equivalences, contracts [77] and session types [77].

Behavioural Equivalences. Understanding which notions of behavioural equivalences are suitable for reversible process calculi is a non-trivial, and still open, problem.

As shown in [119], notions of weak bisimilarity that do not distinguish forward actions from backward actions are very coarse, while notions of strong bisimilarity distinguishing them, such as forward-reverse bisimilarity [161], are very fine-grained, hence other notions are worth exploring.

In [135] Mezzina and Koutavas studied testing preorders, and in particular a safety one and a liveness one, in a reversible CCS where reductions are totally ordered and rollbacks lead systems to past states. Liveness and safety in this setting correspond to the should-testing [166] and inverse may-testing preorders [50] for the underlying forward calculus, respectively. In general, one would expect the models of these preorders to be based on both forward and backward transitions, thus offering complex proof techniques for verification. Instead, in [135] full abstraction of liveness and safety is based only on forward transitions and limited rollback points, giving rise to considerably simpler proof techniques. Moreover, total reversibility allows one to make finer observations w.r.t. liveness, but not w.r.t. safety.

Contracts. (Binary) contracts are a behavioural model [77] to study the interactions between a client and a server. The first investigation of contracts in a reversible setting appeared in [21,22]. There, both the client and the server could rollback to a previous checkpoint at any moment. The main result was that the compliance relation, ensuring that the client and the server can successfully interact, and the sub-behaviour relation, are both decidable, and they remain so also when the possibility of skipping some messages is added.

In retractable contracts [23,24] the client and the server can both get back to previous decision points and take alternative paths only when the interaction is stuck. The main results in [23,24] are that retractable contracts are a conservative extension of contracts, both compliance and the subcontract relation are decidable in polynomial time, and the dual of a contract always exists and has a simple syntactic characterisation. Furthermore, retractable contracts are equivalent to a novel model of contracts featuring a speculative choice: all the options of the choice are explored concurrently, and the computation succeeds if at least one of the options is successful. In [20], a three-party game-theoretic interpretation of retractable session contracts [23] has been proposed. In such an interpretation a client is compliant with a server if and only if there exists a winning strategy for a particular player in a game-theoretic model of contracts. Such a player can be looked at as a mediator, driving the choices in the retractable points.

Session Types. Session types [77] are one of the formalisms that have been proposed to structure interaction and reason over communicating processes and their behaviour. In a series of works [136–138] reversible monitored semantics for binary [136,138] and multiparty [137] session types is investigated. The novelty of the approach is that monitors are derived by types, and they store all the needed information to bring the system back to previous states. This implies that processes of the system are oblivious to reversibility, as they do not store any information about past computations. A deeper discussion on session types and reversibility can be found in [134].

7   Petri Nets

Petri nets [165] are a mathematical formalism for modelling and reasoning on concurrent systems. In most of the cases, Petri nets are four-tuples containing two finite sets, of active (actions/transitions) and static (places) elements, which are connected by a flow function (or relation) with initial state given by tokens scattered on places. In what follows, by Petri net we mean its most common variant, called place-transition net.

Petri nets support both action-based and state-based approaches (via reachability graphs which are equivalent to transition systems). Reversibility in Petri nets was always an important notion, however its meaning changed in time. At first, in the seventies, the notion of reversibility referred to nets where each transition has its inverse [54]. Such a notion of local reversibility is very close to the one currently used in other fields, like programming languages or process calculi. This notion of reversible nets (also called symmetric nets [54]) is still occasionally used to define the inverse net [33]. The time complexity of some decision problems in bounded symmetric Petri nets is lower than in the general case of bounded nets. The other meaning of reversibility in Petri nets, also called cyclicity [33], takes a global approach and requires the initial state of the net to be reachable from any other reachable state [147]. Petri nets are called symmetric also in other situations than the described local notion of reversibility [41].

During the four years of the COST Action IC1045, "Reversible Computation - Extending Horizons of Computing", the notion of local reversibility was investigated. One can divide the proposed contributions into three main threads: two of them consider how to reverse a single transition in a Petri net, allowing one to use, respectively, a single reverse transition or a set of reverses. The last thread focuses on modelling reversible semantics in specific models based on Petri nets.

An approach to invert a single transition using a single (strict) reverse was investigated under both the sequential semantics and the true concurrent semantics. The case of sequential semantics was considered in [28]. The strict reverse is added to the net as a fresh transition with arcs copied from the original one, but with the opposite direction. The problem of checking whether the set of reachable markings in a net changes, when a strict reverse for a single transition is added, was proven to be undecidable. The opposite result was shown for the set of all coverable markings. Another important fact shown in [28] is related to cyclicity: introducing a strict reverse in a cyclic net may change the set of reachable markings.

The above problem of checking whether the set of reachable markings in a net changes by adding a strict reverse for a single transition becomes decidable for the bounded nets. Therefore, one can ask a more general question - is it possible to reverse the specified transition while only requiring the resulting net and the given one to have isomorphic behaviour (i.e., isomorphic reachability graph), but allowing one to change the structure of the net? The question has been answered by using well-known techniques from region theory [19]. There are transition systems which are reachability graphs of a bounded Petri net where transitions cannot be inverted by strict reverses, but one can easily combine separate solutions for different transitions to solve the problem [26]. Even in the special case of linear transition systems over binary sets of actions the transitions cannot be always inverted by strict reverses. In such systems, the time complexity of the problem of checking whether the set of reachable markings changes by adding a strict reverse for a single transition is linear [48]. Another special case of bounded nets are occurrence nets, that is 1-safe and acyclic nets without backward conflicts, where one can always use strict reverses. This property of occurrence nets and their infinite extensions was used as an intermediate step in [132], described later on.

Another line of research on strict reverses considers systems under concurrent semantics of action execution. In such systems one can execute more than one action at the same time, including the situation when a single action is executed multiple times (auto-concurrency). Reversing atomic transitions in such systems is discussed in [49]. In simple cases, where auto-concurrency is excluded, one can reduce reversing under the concurrent semantics to the sequential case. However, in the case of true multisets of actions executed simultaneously, one needs to allow mixed reverses (i.e., steps where both forward and backward actions are present) and true concurrent reversing can be reduced to coping with all spikes (i.e., multisets of actions with singleton support).

In a more general setting, in order to invert a single transition, one can allow to define a set of reverses with the opposite effect, called effect reverses [26]. In such a case, the problem of finding a bounded Petri net where each transition can be reversed and with isomorphic behaviour becomes always solvable [26]. Hence, some systems where inverting transitions using strict reverses was impossible become reversible in this setting. Moreover, the price to make any bounded net ready for inverting by the sets of effect reverses is not high - one needs to transform the original net into its complementary version, which doubles the size of the set of places [26].

A similar attempt for unbounded nets is presented in [139]. There are unbounded nets which cannot be inverted even using infinite sets of effect reverses for their transitions. However, if it is possible, then finite sets are enough. The problem of finding a possibly totally different net with isomorphic behaviour that can be reversed was reduced to extending the existing one by new places which do not disable any transitions in any reachable state and checking whether there exists a pair of problematic states. Those pairs of problematic states are strongly structured, with a natural partial order. The set of all minimal pairs of problematic states for a given system is finite, however, the problem of checking whether two given states form a problematic pair is not elementary, while the problem of checking whether there exists at least one such pair is undecidable [139].

A different line of research considers extensions of Petri nets with causal-consistent local reversibility [132]. Such an extension can be obtained for any place transition net by unfolding it into occurrence nets and folding them back to a coloured Petri net with an infinite number of colours. Those colours are used to encode the content of a stack used to reverse the computation. The price to be paid is that coloured Petri nets with infinitely many colours are in general Turing complete.

Another approach to investigate causal-consistent local reversibility, but also out-of-order local reversibility, is the biologically inspired model of reversing Petri nets [155]. There tokens are persistent bases connected by bonds which are relocated by transitions of the net. The greatest limitation of the approach is the requirement of finiteness and acyclicity of the net modelled in this way. On the other hand, one can encode reversing Petri nets into coloured Petri nets with a finite number of colours [27], hence also into classical bounded place-transition systems. Moreover, reversing Petri nets were successfully applied to the distributed antenna selection problem [156].

Petri net theory has been deeply studied. Cyclic and symmetric systems play quite an important role, however the issue of equipping concurrent systems with reversing mechanisms was not explored. The research conducted as a part of the COST Action IC1405 "Reversible Computation - Extending Horizons of Computing" enriched the theory of Petri nets by exploring some approaches to reverse transitions in existing systems. Although the effect of adding reverses of the actions to the existing system is in general difficult to evaluate (the problem of behaviour preservation is undecidable for place-transition nets), the problem can be solved if one allows unbounded stacks (coloured Petri nets approach) or restricts oneself to bounded models.

8 Automata

Automata theory studies abstract machines, or automata, as mathematical models of computation. They help in understanding limits of computation and the role of various resources – such as time and space – on the computational power. Examples of widely studied classes of automata include finite automata (bounded memory), pushdown automata (infinite memory organised as a stack), counter machine (infinite memory organised as counters), Turing machines (infinite memory tape) and cellular automata (massively parallel regular network of finite automata). These come in several flavours and variations, e.g., with respect to determinism. An automaton is reversible if it preserves information so that its computation can be retraced back in time. All the automata classes above can support reversibility. See [105, 143] for details on computation by various models of reversible automata.

8.1 Finite Automata

Reversibility in finite automata has been widely investigated, e.g., [9, 162]. The class of languages having a reversible one-way automaton is a proper subclass of the regular one. However, different models have been considered, depending on whether automata are required to have only one initial state and/or only one final state. Languages not having any reversible classical automaton have been characterised in terms of a forbidden pattern in the minimum automaton [73]. In the same paper, an NL-complete method to decide whether the language accepted by a given deterministic finite automaton can also be accepted by some reversible deterministic finite automaton has been derived.

In case the language accepted by a deterministic finite automaton is reversible, the size of the smallest reversible automaton may be exponential with respect to the size of the minimal irreversible one [73]. Recently analyses about the descriptional complexity of reversible deterministic finite automata provided some techniques to simulate these devices in an efficient way [123, 125]. Indeed, though converting a deterministic automaton into a reversible one may require an exponential increase in size, the proposed representation allows to limit this cost by concisely representing the reversible automaton rather than explicitly writing down its description.

Based on the forbidden pattern approach, the degree of irreversibility for a regular language has been studied [13]. The degree is defined to be the minimal number of such forbidden patterns necessary in any deterministic finite automaton accepting the language. It is shown that the degree induces a strict infinite hierarchy of language families. The behaviour of the degree of irreversibility under the usual language operations union, intersection, complement, concatenation, and Kleene star, has been studied, showing tight bounds (some asymptotic) on the degree.

Because of the narrowness of the power of reversible finite automata with respect to the irreversible ones, the definition of reversibility has been relaxed, by considering finite automata whose computations can be reversed, at any point, by accessing the last k symbols read from the input, for a fixed k. These devices are said to be "weakly irreversible". Characterisations of languages accepted by weakly irreversible automata and languages not having any weakly irreversible automaton ("strongly irreversible" languages) have been given [124].

Another treatment of a relaxed definition of reversibility concerns nondeterminism. It turned out that reversible nondeterministic finite automata are more powerful compared to their reversible deterministic counterparts, but still cannot accept all regular languages [74]. The two notions of relaxed reversibility have been compared and closure properties of the language family induced by these devices have been derived.

8.2 Pushdown Automata

Reversible classical pushdown automata have been introduced in [107]. Their computational capacity turned out to lie properly in between the regular and deterministic context-free languages. In the same paper, it is shown that a deterministic context-free language cannot be accepted reversibly if more than real-time is necessary for acceptance. Closure properties as well as decidability questions for reversible pushdown automata are studied and it is shown that the problem to decide whether a given nondeterministic or deterministic pushdown automaton is reversible is P-complete, whereas it is undecidable whether the language accepted by a given nondeterministic pushdown automaton is reversible.

One extension of finite automata in order to enlarge the underlying language class as well as to preserve many positive closure properties and decidable questions is represented by input-driven pushdown automata. Such automata share many desirable properties with finite automata, but still are powerful enough to describe important non-regular behaviour. Basically, for such devices the operations on the pushdown store are determined by the input symbols. With respect to reversibility they have been studied in [110]. So, the sub-family of the context-free languages that share the two important properties of being accepted by an input-driven pushdown automaton as well as of being accepted by a reversible pushdown automaton are considered. This intersection can be defined on the underlying language families or on the underlying machine classes. It turned out that the latter class is properly included in the former. The relationships between the language families obtained in this way and to reversible context-free languages as well as to input-driven languages are studied. In general, a hierarchical inclusion structure within the real-time deterministic context-free languages is obtained. Finally, the closure properties of these families under the standard operations are investigated and it turned out that all language families introduced are anti-AFLs (that is, they are not closed under any of the operations required to be an Abstract Family of Languages).

Since reversible finite automata do not accept all regular languages and reversible pushdown automata do not accept all deterministic context-free languages, it is of significant interest both from a practical and theoretical point of view to close these gaps. Therefore these reversible models have been extended by a preprocessing unit which is basically a reversible injective and length-preserving sequential transducer [16]. It turned out that preprocessing the input using such weak devices increases the computational power of reversible deterministic finite automata to the acceptance of all regular languages. On the other hand, for reversible pushdown automata the accepted family of languages lies strictly in between the reversible deterministic context-free languages and the real-time deterministic context-free languages. Moreover, it has been derived that the computational power of both types of machines is not changed by allowing the preprocessing sequential transducer to work irreversibly.

Two-pushdown automata where the input is placed in one pushdown and that perform computations by inspecting and rewriting words at the top of the pushdowns are of particular interest as the deterministic variant is known to characterise the class of Church-Rosser languages when the rewriting is length-reducing. Such reversible two-pushdown automata are studied in [14]. A separation of the deterministic and reversible variants are obtained as well as the incomparability with the (deterministic) context-free languages. However, their properties of emptiness, (in)finiteness, universality, inclusion, equivalence, regularity, and context-freeness are not even semi-decidable.

8.3   Finite State and Pushdown Transducers

Computational models are not only interesting from the viewpoint of accepting some input, but also from the more applied perspective of transforming some input into some output. Transductions that are computed by different variants of transducers are studied in detail in the book of Berstel [31].

Reversibility in transducing devices has been investigated recently in [47, 111] for deterministic finite state transducers. In [111], the families of transductions computed are classified with regard to three types of length-preserving transductions as well as to the property of working reversibly. It is possible to settle all inclusion relations between these families of transductions even with injective witness transductions. Furthermore, the standard closure properties and decidability questions have been investigated. It turned out that the non-closure under almost all operations can be shown, whereas all decidability questions can be answered in polynomial time. Finally, the strict concept of reversibility is relaxed and an infinite and dense hierarchy with respect to the grade of reversibility is obtained.

Deterministic pushdown transducers have also been introduced, and analysed with respect to their ability to compute reversible transductions [66]. Now, the families of transductions computed are classified with regard to four types of length-preserving transductions as well as to the property of working reversibly. It turns out that accurate to one case separating witness transductions can be provided. For the remaining case it is possible to establish the equivalence of both families by proving that stationary moves can always be removed in length-preserving reversible pushdown transductions.

8.4 Queue Automata and Limited Automata

A further natural and well-studied extension of finite automata are queue automata, where the extension is by a storage media of type queue. Their reversible variant has been studied in [109]. In contrast to, for example, finite or pushdown automata, it has been shown that any queue automaton can be simulated by a reversible one. So, reversible queue automata are as powerful as Turing machines. Therefore it is of interest to impose time restrictions on queue automata. Quasi real-time and real-time computations have been considered. It has been shown that every reversible quasi real-time queue automaton can be sped up to real-time. On the other hand, under real-time conditions reversible queue automata are less powerful than general queue automata. Furthermore, a lower bound of $\Omega\left(\frac{n^2}{\log(n)}\right)$ time steps for real-time queue automata witness languages to be accepted by any equivalent reversible queue automaton has been exhibited. The closure properties of reversible real-time queue automata are similar as for reversible deterministic pushdown automata. Moreover, all commonly studied decidability questions such as emptiness, finiteness, or equivalence are not semi-decidable for reversible real-time queue automata. Furthermore, it is not semi-decidable whether an arbitrary given real-time queue automaton is reversible.

A k-limited automaton is a linear bounded automaton that may rewrite each tape square only in the first k visits, where $k \geq 0$ is a fixed constant. It is known that these automata accept context-free languages only. The deterministic k-limited automata have been investigated towards their ability to perform reversible computations [112]. It turned out that, for all $k \geq 0$, sweeping k-limited automata accept regular languages only. In contrast to reversible finite automata, all regular languages are accepted by sweeping 0-limited automata. Then the computational power gained in the number k of possible rewrite operations has been studied. It has been shown that the reversible 2-limited automata accept regular languages only and, thus, are strictly weaker than general 2-limited automata. Furthermore, a proper inclusion between reversible 3-limited and 4-limited automata languages has been obtained. The next levels of the hierarchy are separated between every k and $k + 3$ rewrite operations. Finally, it turned out that all k-limited automata accept Church-Rosser languages only, that is, the intersection between context-free and Church-Rosser languages contains an infinite hierarchy of language families beyond the deterministic context-free languages.

8.5   Cellular Automata

A cellular automaton (CA) is a dynamical system on an infinite grid of cells defined by a local update rule that is applied simultaneously at all cells. More precisely, in the usual rectilinear d-dimensional setting the cells are the elements of $\mathbb{Z}^d$ and each cell stores an element of a finite state set A. The dynamics is specified by a finite neighbourhood $D \subseteq \mathbb{Z}^d$ that gives the relative offsets to neighbours of cells, and a local rule $f : A^D \longrightarrow A$ that gives the new state of a cell based on the previous states in its neighbourhood. A configuration $c : \mathbb{Z}^d \longrightarrow A$, specifying the global state of the system, changes in a single time unit to become the new configuration c' with $c'(\vec{n}) = f(\sigma^{\vec{n}}(c)_{|D})$ for every cell $\vec{n} \in \mathbb{Z}^d$, where $\sigma^{\vec{n}}$ denotes the shift map that translates the configurations so that cell $\vec{n}$ moves to the origin.

By carefully choosing the update rule f, the global dynamics $c \mapsto c'$ can be made information preserving. In this case, an inverse cellular automaton retraces the computation back in time, and the cellular automaton is called reversible (RCA). See [90] for a recent survey on reversible cellular automata. Cellular automata have an important role as providing simple models in microscopic physics, and because of time-reversibility of microscopic dynamics the cellular automata models are also typically reversible [181]. Reversible cellular automata are able to carry out universal computation [180], even in the one-dimensional setting [144].

In the symbolic dynamics nomenclature reversible cellular automata are called automorphisms of the (full) shift. By Hedlund's theorem [69] cellular automata are precisely the transformations $A^{\mathbb{Z}^d} \longrightarrow A^{\mathbb{Z}^d}$ of the configuration space that commute with shifts $\sigma^{\vec{n}}$ and that are continuous under the compact prodiscrete topology on $A^{\mathbb{Z}^d}$. Reversibility then just means that the transformation is a bijection, i.e., a homeomorphism. Automorphisms form a group under composition, and the structure of the automorphism group of the full shift (as well as of its subshifts) is a topic of active research [168]. For example, it is not known if the groups of one-dimensional RCA over two states and over three states are isomorphic with each other.

Decision Problems. Decision problems concerning reversibility and related properties have been extensively studied. There are efficient algorithms to test one-dimensional cellular automata for reversibility [177] while in higher dimensional cases reversibility is undecidable [88]. It is also undecidable, even in the one-dimensional case, whether a given RCA is periodic [92], that is, whether some iteration of the CA amounts to the identity function. Periodicity among one-sided RCA is not known to be decidable or undecidable at this time, where one-sidedness refers to the property that the neighbours to the left of a cell have no influence on its next state, nor on the previous state given by the inverse automaton. Periodicity in the one-sided case remains an active research topic due to its link to the finiteness problem of groups generated by Mealy automata [51].

Two dynamical systems are called conjugate if there is a homeomorphism between them that maps orbits to orbits. Conjugate systems are essentially identical. It is undecidable if two given cellular automata are conjugate [81]. This is true even for one-dimensional cellular automata, but if the considered CA are reversible then the undecidability is known in the two- and higher dimensional cases only.

Physical Universality and Glider Automorphisms. A cellular automaton is called physically universal if it can implement any transformation of patterns on any finite domain of cells by suitably choosing the initial states outside the domain. There are reversible cellular automata that are physically universal [170], even in the one-dimensional setting [169]. These automata (reversibly) break the input pattern into fleets of gliders that scatter out of the finite domain. Symmetrically, the inverse automaton breaks the desired output pattern into fleets of inverse gliders. The task of the surrounding gadget is to change the first fleet into the second fleet to implement the desired transformation.

Glider automorphisms that decompose finite configurations into fleets of gliders have been studied in more general subshifts, and they have found applications in understanding the structure of the automorphism groups [100].

Reversible Cellular Automata and Mahler's Problem in Number Theory. If real numbers are written in base pq for some co-primes p and q then there is no carry propagation when numbers are multiplied by constant p. This means that multiplying by p is a local operation, that is, a reversible cellular automaton. Composing such reversible cellular automata yields, for example, an RCA for multiplying numbers in base 6 by constant $3/2$.

Mahler's problem asks whether there exists some positive real number ξ such that the fractional part of $\xi \left(\frac{3}{2}\right)^n$ is less than 0.5 for all positive integers n [127]. So the fractional part of the number should remain below one half no matter how many times the number is multiplied by $3/2$. The problem is still unsolved. The problem has a very simple interpretation in terms of the RCA that multiplies by $3/2$ in base six [89], and using this link it has been proved that for arbitrarily small $\varepsilon > 0$ there is a number $\xi > 0$ and a finite union $U \subseteq [0, 1)$ of intervals of total length ε such that the fractional parts of all $\xi \left(\frac{3}{2}\right)^n$ are in U [91]. The dynamical property of expansivity of the associated reversible cellular automaton plays a central role in the proof. Conversely, there is also a finite union $V \subseteq [0, 1)$ of intervals of total length $1 - \varepsilon$ that does not contain the fractional parts of all $\xi \left(\frac{3}{2}\right)^n$ for any $\xi > 0$.

Asynchronous Updating. In an asynchronous cellular automaton (ACA) only some cells are updated simultaneously. In the one-dimensional setting, one possibility is that states are updated sequentially during a left-to-right (or right-to-left) sweep across the entire infinite line of cells. Such a setup is studied in [93] where the update performed once in each position is given by a reversible block rule $A^n \longrightarrow A^n$ on n consecutive cells. The authors give a precise characterisation of the one-dimensional cellular automata that can be realised by such a sweep. It turns out that not all reversible CA can be realised, while also some non-reversible ones can be obtained. It is decidable whether a CA can be realised that way or not.

Self-Timed Cellular Automata. *Self-Timed Cellular Automata (STCA)* are a form of Asynchronous Cellular Automata where transitions of cells can take place if they are triggered by transitions of the neighbouring cells. *Delay-Insensitive (DI)* circuits are asynchronous circuits which make no assumption about delays within modules or wires of circuits, and where there is no global clock [97]. As a result, logical gates such as NAND and XOR are not Turing-complete when operated in a DI environment. A lot of research went into finding universal sets of DI modules and [145] contributes a solution for reversible DI circuits in terms of STCAs. Serial and parallel DI circuits are simulated with new STCAs that contain rules for signal movement, right and left turn, memory toggle, merge, fork and join, and parallel crossing of signals. In addition to a number of reversibility and determinism properties, including local determinism and local reversibility, the STCAs exhibit direction-reversibility, where reversing the direction of a signal and running a circuit forwards is equivalent to running the circuit in reverse. Benefits of direction-reversibility are discussed, including garbage-less implementation of reversible functions.

Cellular Automata as Language Acceptors. From the perspective of language recognition, real-time bounded cellular automata which are reversible on the core of computation, that is, from initial configuration to the configuration given by the time complexity, have been studied in [106]. The question whether for a given real-time CA working on finite configurations with fixed boundary conditions there exists a reverse real-time CA with the same neighbourhood has been addressed. It has been shown that real-time reversibility is undecidable, which contrasts the general case, where reversibility is decidable for one-dimensional devices. Moreover, the undecidability of emptiness, finiteness, infiniteness, inclusion, equivalence, regularity, and context-freedom has been proved. First steps towards the exploration of the computational capacity have been done and closure under Boolean operations have been shown.

Similar investigations for real-time one-way cellular automata have been done in [108]. In this case, it turned out that the standard model with fixed boundary conditions is quite weak in terms of reversible information processing, since it accepts exactly the regular languages reversibly. The extension that allows the information to flow circularly from the leftmost cell into the rightmost cell does not increase the computational power in the general case, but does increase it for reversible computations. On the other hand, the model is less powerful than real-time reversible two-way cellular automata. Additionally, it has been derived that the corresponding language class is closed under Boolean operations, and the undecidability of several decidability questions has been proved. Finally, it turned out that the reversibility of an arbitrary real-time circular one-way cellular automaton is undecidable as well.

8.6   Turing Machines

Turing machines (TM) are a classical model of computation where a finite state control unit, the head, moves along a bi-infinite tape of cells, each containing a tape symbol. The head reads and writes symbols on the tape, changes its internal state, and moves to neighbouring cells at discrete time steps as instructed by a fixed transition rule, the program of the TM. A suitable choice of the program makes the machine reversible (RTM). Turing machines are traditionally viewed as language acceptors, but one can also incorporate outputs in the model so that the machine becomes a transducer that computes a (partial) function. In [12] the authors investigate RTM under the strict function semantics that requires that at the end of the computation only the output remains on the tape, and they develop a rigorous foundational theory of reversible computation of functions in this semantics, including the appropriate concept of universality and a design of a universal machine.

Turing machines with bi-infinite tape contents are also discrete dynamical systems (on a compact space) under two possible viewpoints [104]: in the moving tape view (TMT) the position of the head is fixed but the entire tape shifts left or right depending on the current instruction, while in the usual moving head view (TMH) one needs to allow configurations without a head to make the configuration space compact. In [38] the authors present a reversible TMT with the rather surprising property that it has no halting or temporally periodic configurations, thus answering positively a conjecture made in [92]. The machine, dubbed "SMART", is small (4 internal states, 3 tape symbols) and nicely symmetric in both time and space. It possesses the good dynamical properties of transitivity and minimality. The machine is further applied to settle another conjecture made in [92]: it is undecidable whether a given complete reversible Turing machine has a periodic orbit.

The class of RTM dynamical systems becomes more robust if the head is allowed to view and modify locally blocks of several tape symbols at once. In particular, compositions of machines and inverse machines are now in the same class so that reversible Turing machines with any fixed states and tape symbols form a group under composition. The structure of this group and algorithmic questions concerning the group are studied in [25]. The paper also introduces a number of natural subgroups. The model includes multidimensional Turing machines where the tape cells are indexed by $\mathbb{Z}^d$ for dimension d, and both the moving head and the moving tape viewpoints can be taken.

Finally, reversible Turing machines with a working tape and a one-way or two-way read-only input tape are considered as language recognisers [15]. In particular, the classes of languages acceptable by such devices with small time bounds in the range between real time and linear time, that is, with time bounds of the form $n + r(n)$ where $r \in o(n)$ is a sublinear function, have been considered. It has been shown that there exist infinite time hierarchies of separated complexity classes in that range. The question of whether reversible Turing machines in the range of interest are weaker than general ones or not is answered positively by proving that there are languages accepted by irreversible one-way Turing machines in real time that cannot be accepted by any reversible one-way machine in less than linear time.

9   Quantum Formal Verification and Quantum Machine Learning

Large-scale, fault-tolerant quantum computers are still under development and, despite a recent major push for "quantum supremacy" by companies like IBM, Google and Intel, it is not clear when they will become a reality. On the other hand there is much recent interest in using Noisy Intermediate Scale Quantum (NISQ) computers to provide a "quantum advantage". This involves the use of existing or near-term quantum computers to solve valuable problems, faster, cheaper, or more efficiently than any available classical solution. Potential application areas include simulation of many-body physics, quantum chemistry, optimisation and quantum machine learning. Airbus has issued its Quantum Computing Challenge to tackle aerospace flight physics problems using quantum computers. Many companies such as IBM, Microsoft, D-Wave, Rigetti and Xanadu are developing full-stack solutions for implementing quantum algorithms. This typically starts from a high-level programming language and a compiler, down to an assembly language and quantum hardware. These resources are usually accessible via the cloud. Much of these developments will need guarantees regarding security and correctness. Formal verification, which has been used successfully in classical computing for a number of years, could be extremely valuable in increasing confidence in quantum systems.

Quantum cryptography aims to overcome the limitations of classical cryptography by providing unconditional security, which is not dependent on the difficulty of inverting a particular computation. Quantum Key Distribution protocols have been implemented in commercial products by Id Quantique, MagiQ, NEC and Toshiba, amongst others, and have been used in practical applications, e.g. the Geneva election ballot count. Various QKD networks have been built, including the DARPA Quantum Network in Boston, the SeCoQC network around Vienna and the Tokyo QKD Network. China has launched a dedicated satellite "Micius" for quantum communication. On the theoretical side, quantum key distribution protocols such as BB84 [29] have been proved to be unconditionally secure. It is important to understand, however, that this is an information-theoretic proof, which does not necessarily guarantee that *implemented systems* are unconditionally secure. This area is also where approaches such as those based on formal methods could be useful in analysing behaviour of implemented systems.

The paper [32] presents a novel framework for modelling and verifying quantum protocols and their implementations using the proof assistant Coq. It provides a Coq library for quantum bits (qubits), quantum gates, and quantum measurement. As a step towards verifying practical quantum communication and security protocols such as Quantum Key Distribution, it supports multiple qubits, communication and entanglement. These concepts are illustrated by modelling the Quantum Teleportation Protocol, which communicates the state of an unknown quantum bit using only a classical channel. In more recent work, a Quantum IO monad has been implemented in Coq for the specification of the protocols. In addition to quantum operations and measurement, the monad gives us a lightweight process calculus which supports sequencing of operations and keeping of state. This monad has the necessary properties. The process simulation function that gives the QIO monad its semantics has also been written. Current work concerns proving properties of simple quantum protocols.

In [10], the authors present CCSq, a concurrent language for describing quantum systems, and develop verification techniques for checking equivalence between CCSq processes. CCSq has well-defined operational and superoperator semantics for protocols that are functional, in the sense of computing a deterministic input-output relation for all interleavings arising from concurrency in the system. They have implemented QEC (Quantum Equivalence Checker), a tool that takes the specification and implementation of quantum protocols, described in CCSq, and automatically checks their equivalence. QEC is the first fully automatic equivalence checking tool for concurrent quantum systems. For efficiency purposes, the approach is restricted to Clifford operators in the stabiliser formalism, but it is able to verify protocols over all input states. A collection of interesting and practical quantum protocols, ranging from quantum communication and quantum cryptography to quantum error correction, have been specified and verified.

In other recent work, a version of the quantum process calculus CQP has been implemented. The implementation, which has the working title qtpi and is available from github.com/mdxtoc/qtpi, uses symbolic rather than numeric probability calculation. Programs are checked statically, before they run, to ensure that they obey real-world restrictions on the use of qbits (e.g. no cloning, no sharing). Qtpi has been used to simulate some simple protocols such as teleportation, and some more involved ones including QKD. It is early days in the development of the tool, but it can already simulate well over 1M qbit transfers per minute.

Quantum machine learning is the aspect of quantum computing concerned with the design of algorithms capable of generalised learning from labelled training data by effectively exploiting quantum effects. The undertaken work makes various contributions to this emerging area; in particular it has pursued the issue of classification error within a standard quantum computational setting, and explored the congruence of Kernel Methods with the topological quantum computational setting (a congruence that will be developed further in future work).

Specifically, the following have been achieved:

In [52] the authors present a novel approach to computing Hamming distance and its kernelisation within Topological Quantum Computation. This approach is based on an encoding of two binary strings into a topological Hilbert space, whose inner product yields a natural Hamming distance kernel on the two strings. Kernelisation forges a link with the field of Machine Learning, particularly in relation to binary classifiers such as the Support Vector Machine (SVM). This makes our approach of potentially wide interest to the quantum machine learning community.

In [183], the authors set out a strategy for quantising attribute bootstrap aggregation to enable variance-resilient quantum machine learning. To do so, they utilise the linear decomposability of decision boundary parameters in the Rebentrost et al. Support Vector Machine [164] to guarantee that stochastic measurement of the output quantum state will give rise to an ensemble decision without destroying the superposition over projective feature subsets induced within the chosen SVM implementation. It achieves a linear performance advantage, $O(d)$, in addition to the existing $O(\log(n))$ advantages of quantisation as applied to Support Vector Machines. The approach extends to any form of quantum learning giving rise to linear decision boundaries.

Error-correcting output codes (ECOC) are a standard setting in machine learning for efficiently rendering the collective outputs of a binary classifier, such as the support vector machine, as a multi-class decision procedure. Appropriate choice of error-correcting codes further enables incorrect individual classification decisions to be effectively corrected in the composite output. In [182], the authors propose an appropriate quantisation of the ECOC process, based on the quantum support vector machine. They show that, in addition to the usual benefits of quantising machine learning, this technique leads to an exponential reduction in the number of logic gates required for effective correction of classification error.

10 Conclusion

We gave in the previous sections an overview of the status and recent developments of different research threads on the foundations of reversible computation. While many interesting results have been found, we notice that the field is still very heterogeneous. For instance, while process calculi, Petri nets and cellular automata are all models of concurrent systems, they come equipped with different notions of reversibility. Cellular automata are considered reversible if the global dynamics is bijective (similarly to what is done in sequential reversible models), Petri nets if reverse transitions can be added without changing the behaviour of the net, while process calculi are mainly based on the notion of causal-consistent reversibility. Some initial cross-fertilisation results came thanks to the COST Action, e.g. there have been works applying causal-consistent reversibility to Petri nets [132] and related models [27,155]. We also remark that some of the developments described in this chapter have been instrumental to better understand reversibility in programming languages and to advance on a number of application areas, as discussed in the rest of the book.

References

1. Abramsky, S.: Retracing some paths in process algebra. In: Montanari, U., Sassone, V. (eds.) CONCUR 1996. LNCS, vol. 1119, pp. 1–17. Springer, Heidelberg (1996). https://doi.org/10.1007/3-540-61604-7_44
2. Abramsky, S.: A structural approach to reversible computation. Theoret. Comput. Sci. **347**(3), 441–464 (2005)
3. Abramsky, S., Coecke, B.: A categorical semantics of quantum protocols. In: Logic in Computer Science, LICS 2004, pp. 415–425. IEEE (2004)
4. Abramsky, S., Haghverdi, E., Scott, P.: Geometry of interaction and linear combinatory algebras. Math. Struct. Comput. Sci. **12**(5), 625–665 (2002)
5. Agrigoroaiei, O., Ciobanu, G.: Dual P systems. In: Corne, D.W., Frisco, P., Păun, G., Rozenberg, G., Salomaa, A. (eds.) WMC 2008. LNCS, vol. 5391, pp. 95–107. Springer, Heidelberg (2009). https://doi.org/10.1007/978-3-540-95885-7_7
6. Agrigoroaiei, O., Ciobanu, G.: Reversing computation in membrane systems. J. Logic Algebraic Program. **79**(3–5), 278–288 (2010)
7. Aman, B., Ciobanu, G.: Reversibility in parallel rewriting systems. J. Univers. Comput. Sci. **23**(7), 692–703 (2017)
8. Aman, B., Ciobanu, G.: Controlled reversibility in reaction systems. In: Gheorghe, M., Rozenberg, G., Salomaa, A., Zandron, C. (eds.) CMC 2017. LNCS, vol. 10725, pp. 40–53. Springer, Cham (2018). https://doi.org/10.1007/978-3-319-73359-3_3
9. Angluin, D.: Inference of reversible languages. J. ACM **29**(3), 741–765 (1982)
10. Ardeshir-Larijani, E., Gay, S.J., Nagarajan, R.: Automated equivalence checking of concurrent quantum systems. ACM Trans. Comput. Logic **19**(4), 28:1–28:32 (2018)
11. Axelsen, H.B., Glück, R.: Reversible representation and manipulation of constructor terms in the heap. In: Dueck, G.W., Miller, D.M. (eds.) RC 2013. LNCS, vol. 7948, pp. 96–109. Springer, Heidelberg (2013). https://doi.org/10.1007/978-3-642-38986-3_9
12. Axelsen, H.B., Glück, R.: On reversible turing machines and their function universality. Acta Inf. **53**(5), 509–543 (2016)
13. Axelsen, H.B., Holzer, M., Kutrib, M.: The degree of irreversibility in deterministic finite automata. Int. J. Found. Comput. Sci. **28**, 503–522 (2017)
14. Axelsen, H.B., Holzer, M., Kutrib, M., Malcher, A.: Reversible shrinking two-pushdown automata. In: Dediu, A.-H., Janoušek, J., Martín-Vide, C., Truthe, B. (eds.) LATA 2016. LNCS, vol. 9618, pp. 579–591. Springer, Cham (2016). https://doi.org/10.1007/978-3-319-30000-9_44
15. Axelsen, H.B., Jakobi, S., Kutrib, M., Malcher, A.: A hierarchy of fast reversible turing machines. In: Krivine, J., Stefani, J.-B. (eds.) RC 2015. LNCS, vol. 9138, pp. 29–44. Springer, Cham (2015). https://doi.org/10.1007/978-3-319-20860-2_2
16. Axelsen, H.B., Kutrib, M., Malcher, A., Wendlandt, M.: Boosting reversible pushdown machines by preprocessing. In: Devitt, S., Lanese, I. (eds.) RC 2016. LNCS, vol. 9720, pp. 89–104. Springer, Cham (2016). https://doi.org/10.1007/978-3-319-40578-0_6

17. Baader, F., Nipkow, T.: Term Rewriting and All That. Cambridge University Press, Cambridge (1998)
18. Bacci, G., Danos, V., Kammar, O.: On the statistical thermodynamics of reversible communicating processes. In: Corradini, A., Klin, B., Cîrstea, C. (eds.) CALCO 2011. LNCS, vol. 6859, pp. 1–18. Springer, Heidelberg (2011). https:// doi.org/10.1007/978-3-642-22944-2_1
19. Badouel, E., Bernardinello, L., Darondeau, P.: Petri Net Synthesis. TTCSAES. Springer, Heidelberg (2015). https://doi.org/10.1007/978-3-662-47967-4
20. Barbanera, F., de'Liguoro, U.: A game interpretation of retractable contracts. In: Lluch Lafuente, A., Proença, J. (eds.) COORDINATION 2016. LNCS, vol. 9686, pp. 18–34. Springer, Cham (2016). https://doi.org/10.1007/978-3-319-39519-7_2
21. Barbanera, F., Dezani-Ciancaglini, M., de'Liguoro, U.: Compliance for reversible client/server interactions. In: Workshop on Behavioural Types, BEAT 2014. EPTCS, vol. 162, pp. 35–42 (2014)
22. Barbanera, F., Dezani-Ciancaglini, M., de'Liguoro, U.: Reversible client/server interactions. Formal Asp. Comput. 28(4), 697–722 (2016)
23. Barbanera, F., Dezani-Ciancaglini, M., Lanese, I., de'Liguoro, U.: Retractable contracts. In: Workshop on Programming Language Approaches to Concurrency- and Communication-cEntric Software, PLACES 2015. EPTCS, vol. 203, pp. 61–72 (2015)
24. Barbanera, F., Lanese, I., de'Liguoro, U.: Retractable and speculative contracts. In: Jacquet, J.-M., Massink, M. (eds.) COORDINATION 2017. LNCS, vol. 10319, pp. 119–137. Springer, Cham (2017). https://doi.org/10.1007/978-3-319-59746-1_7
25. Barbieri, S., Kari, J., Salo, V.: The group of reversible turing machines. In: Cook, M., Neary, T. (eds.) AUTOMATA 2016. LNCS, vol. 9664, pp. 49–62. Springer, Cham (2016). https://doi.org/10.1007/978-3-319-39300-1_5
26. Barylska, K., Erofeev, E., Koutny, M., Mikulski, Ł., Piątkowski, M.: Reversing transitions in bounded Petri nets. Fund. Inf. 157(4), 341–357 (2018)
27. Barylska, K., Gogolińska, A., Mikulski, Ł., Philippou, A., Piątkowski, M., Psara, K.: Reversing computations modelled by coloured Petri nets. In: Workshop on Algorithms & Theories for the Analysis of Event Data. CEUR Workshop Proceedings, vol. 2115, pp. 91–111. CEUR-WS.org (2018)
28. Barylska, K., Koutny, M., Mikulski, Ł., Piątkowski, M.: Reversible computation vs. reversibility in Petri nets. Sci. Comput. Program. 151, 48–60 (2018)
29. Bennett, C.H., Brassard, G.: Quantum cryptography: public key distribution and coin tossing. In: Conference on Computers, Systems & Signal Processing, CSSP 1984, pp. 175–179 (1984)
30. Berry, G., Boudol, G.: The chemical abstract machine. Theor. Comput. Sci. 96(1), 217–248 (1992)
31. Berstel, J.: Transductions and Context-Free Languages. Teubner, Stuttgart (1979)
32. Boender, J., Kammüller, F., Nagarajan, R.: Formalization of quantum protocols using Coq. In: Workshop on Quantum Physics and Logic, QPL 2015, pp. 71–83 (2015)
33. Bouziane, Z., Finkel, A.: Cyclic Petri net reachability sets are semi-linear effectively constructible. In: Workshop on Verification of Infinite State Systems, INFINITY 1997, ENTCS, pp. 15–24. Elsevier (1997)
34. Bowman, W.J., James, R.P., Sabry, A.: Dagger traced symmetric monoidal categories and reversible programming. In: Reversible Computation, RC 2011, pp. 51–56. Ghent University (2011)

35. Cardelli, L., Laneve, C.: Reversibility in massive concurrent systems. Sci. Ann. Comp. Sci. **21**(2), 175–198 (2011)
36. Cardelli, L., Laneve, C.: Reversible structures. In: Computational Methods in Systems Biology, CMSB 2011, pp. 131–140. ACM (2011)
37. Carothers, C.D., Perumalla, K.S., Fujimoto, R.: Efficient optimistic parallel simulations using reverse computation. ACM Trans. Model. Comput. Simul. **9**(3), 224–253 (1999)
38. Cassaigne, J., Ollinger, N., Torres-Avilés, R.: A small minimal aperiodic reversible Turing machine. J. Comput. Syst. Sci. **84**, 288–301 (2017)
39. Clavel, M., et al.: Maude: specification and programming in rewriting logic. Theor. Comput. Sci. **285**(2), 187–243 (2002)
40. Cockett, J.R.B., Lack, S.: Restriction categories I: categories of partial maps. Theoret. Comput. Sci. **270**(1–2), 223–259 (2002)
41. Colange, M., Baarir, S., Kordon, F., Thierry-Mieg, Y.: Crocodile: a symbolic/symbolic tool for the analysis of symmetric nets with bag. In: Kristensen, L.M., Petrucci, L. (eds.) PETRI NETS 2011. LNCS, vol. 6709, pp. 338–347. Springer, Heidelberg (2011). https://doi.org/10.1007/978-3-642-21834-7_20
42. Cristescu, I., Krivine, J., Varacca, D.: A compositional semantics for the reversible π-calculus. In: Logic in Computer Science, LICS 2013, pp. 388–397. IEEE Computer Society (2013)
43. Cservenka, M.H., Glück, R., Haulund, T., Mogensen, T.Æ.: Data structures and dynamic memory management in reversible languages. In: Kari, J., Ulidowski, I. (eds.) RC 2018. LNCS, vol. 11106, pp. 269–285. Springer, Cham (2018). https://doi.org/10.1007/978-3-319-99498-7_19
44. Danos, V., Krivine, J.: Reversible communicating systems. In: Gardner, P., Yoshida, N. (eds.) CONCUR 2004. LNCS, vol. 3170, pp. 292–307. Springer, Heidelberg (2004). https://doi.org/10.1007/978-3-540-28644-8_19
45. Danos, V., Krivine, J.: Transactions in RCCS. In: Abadi, M., de Alfaro, L. (eds.) CONCUR 2005. LNCS, vol. 3653, pp. 398–412. Springer, Heidelberg (2005). https://doi.org/10.1007/11539452_31
46. Danos, V., Krivine, J.: Formal molecular biology done in CCS-R. In: Workshop on Concurrent Models in Molecular Biology, BioConcur 2003, vol. 180(3) (2003). Electr. Notes Theor. Comput. Sci., 31–49. Elsevier (2007)
47. Dartois, L., Fournier, P., Jecker, I., Lhote, N.: On reversible transducers. In: International Colloquium on Automata, Languages, and Programming, ICALP 2017. LIPIcs, vol. 80, pp. 113:1–113:12. Schloss Dagstuhl - Leibniz-Zentrum für Informatik (2017)
48. de Frutos Escrig, D., Koutny, M., Mikulski, Ł.: An efficient characterization of Petri net solvable binary words. In: Khomenko, V., Roux, O.H. (eds.) PETRI NETS 2018. LNCS, vol. 10877, pp. 207–226. Springer, Cham (2018). https://doi.org/10.1007/978-3-319-91268-4_11
49. de Frutos Escrig, D., Koutny, M., Mikulski, Ł.: Reversing steps in Petri nets. In: Donatelli, S., Haar, S. (eds.) PETRI NETS 2019. LNCS, vol. 11522, pp. 171–191. Springer, Cham (2019). https://doi.org/10.1007/978-3-030-21571-2_11
50. De Nicola, R., Hennessy, M.: Testing equivalences for processes. Theor. Comput. Sci. **34**, 83–133 (1984)
51. Delacourt, M., Ollinger, N.: Permutive one-way cellular automata and the finiteness problem for automaton groups. In: Kari, J., Manea, F., Petre, I. (eds.) CiE 2017. LNCS, vol. 10307, pp. 234–245. Springer, Cham (2017). https://doi.org/10.1007/978-3-319-58741-7_23

52. Di Pierro, A., Mengoni, R., Nagarajan, R., Windridge, D.: Hamming distance kernelisation via topological quantum computation. In: Martín-Vide, C., Neruda, R., Vega-Rodríguez, M.A. (eds.) TPNC 2017. LNCS, vol. 10687, pp. 269–280. Springer, Cham (2017). https://doi.org/10.1007/978-3-319-71069-3_21

53. Ehrenfeucht, A., Rozenberg, G.: Reaction systems. Fund. Inf. **75**(1), 263–280 (2007)

54. Esparza, J., Nielsen, M.: Decidability issues for Petri nets. BRICS Rep. Ser. **1**(8) (1994)

55. Foster, N., Matsuda, K., Voigtländer, J.: Three complementary approaches to bidirectional programming. In: Gibbons, J. (ed.) Generic and Indexed Programming. LNCS, vol. 7470, pp. 1–46. Springer, Heidelberg (2012). https://doi.org/10.1007/978-3-642-32202-0_1

56. Giachino, E., Lanese, I., Mezzina, C.A., Tiezzi, F.: Causal-consistent reversibility in a tuple-based language. In: Parallel, Distributed, and Network-Based Processing, PDP 2015, pp. 467–475. IEEE Computer Society (2015)

57. Giachino, E., Lanese, I., Mezzina, C.A., Tiezzi, F.: Causal-consistent rollback in a tuple-based language. J. Log. Algebr. Meth. Program. **88**, 99–120 (2017)

58. Giles, B.G.: An investigation of some theoretical aspects of reversible computing. Ph.D. thesis, University of Calgary (2014)

59. Glück, R., Kaarsgaard, R.: A categorical foundation for structured reversible flowchart languages. In: Mathematical Foundations of Programming Semantics, MFPS 2018. Electronic Notes in Theoretical Computer Science, vol. 341, pp. 155–171. Elsevier (2018)

60. Glück, R., Kaarsgaard, R.: A categorical foundation for structured reversible flowchart languages: soundness and adequacy. Logical Methods Comput. Sci. **14**(3) (2018)

61. Glück, R., Kaarsgaard, R., Yokoyama, T.: Reversible programs have reversible semantics. In: Reversibility in Programming, Languages, and Automata, RPLA 2019. Lecture Notes in Computer Science. Springer (2019, to appear)

62. Glück, R., Yokoyama, T.: A linear-time self-interpreter of a reversible imperative language. Comput. Soft. **33**(3), 108–128 (2016)

63. Glück, R., Yokoyama, T.: A minimalist's reversible while language. IEICE Trans. Inf. Syst. **E100–D**(5), 1026–1034 (2017)

64. Glück, R., Yokoyama, T.: Constructing a binary tree from its traversals by reversible recursion and iteration. Inf. Process. Lett. **147**, 32–37 (2019)

65. Graversen, E., Phillips, I., Yoshida, N.: Towards a categorical representation of reversible event structures. J. Logical Algebraic Methods Program. **104**, 16–59 (2019)

66. Guillon, B., Kutrib, M., Malcher, A., Prigioniero, L.: Reversible pushdown transducers. In: Hoshi, M., Seki, S. (eds.) DLT 2018. LNCS, vol. 11088, pp. 354–365. Springer, Cham (2018). https://doi.org/10.1007/978-3-319-98654-8_29

67. Guo, X.: Products, joins, meets, and ranges in restriction categories. Ph.D. thesis, University of Calgary (2012)

68. Haulund, T., Mogensen, T.Æ., Glück, R.: Implementing reversible object-oriented language features on reversible machines. In: Phillips, I., Rahaman, H. (eds.) RC 2017. LNCS, vol. 10301, pp. 66–73. Springer, Cham (2017). https://doi.org/10.1007/978-3-319-59936-6_5

69. Hedlund, G.A.: Endomorphisms and automorphisms of the shift dynamical systems. Mathe. Syst. Theor. **3**(4), 320–375 (1969)

70. Heunen, C., Kaarsgaard, R., Karvonen, M.: Reversible effects as inverse arrows. In: Mathematical Foundations of Programming Semantics, MFPS XXXIV. Electronic Notes in Theoretical Computer Science, vol. 341, pp. 179–199. Elsevier (2018)

71. Heunen, C., Karvonen, M.: Monads on dagger categories. Theor. Appl. Categories **31**, 1016–1043 (2016)

72. Hoey, J., Ulidowski, I., Yuen, S.: Reversing parallel programs with blocks and procedures. In: Expressiveness in Concurrency/Structural Operational Semantics. Electronic Proceedings in Theoretical Computer Science, vol. 276, pp. 69–86 (2018)

73. Holzer, M., Jakobi, S., Kutrib, M.: Minimal reversible deterministic finite automata. Int. J. Found. Comput. Sci. **29**(2), 251–270 (2018)

74. Holzer, M., Kutrib, M.: Reversible nondeterministic finite automata. In: Phillips, I., Rahaman, H. (eds.) RC 2017. LNCS, vol. 10301, pp. 35–51. Springer, Cham (2017). https://doi.org/10.1007/978-3-319-59936-6_3

75. Hu, Z., Schürr, A., Stevens, P., Terwilliger, J.F.: Bidirectional transformation "bx" (Dagstuhl Seminar 11031). Dagstuhl Reports **1**(1), 42–67 (2011). http://drops.dagstuhl.de/volltexte/2011/3144/

76. Hullot, J.-M.: Canonical forms and unification. In: Bibel, W., Kowalski, R. (eds.) CADE 1980. LNCS, vol. 87, pp. 318–334. Springer, Heidelberg (1980). https://doi.org/10.1007/3-540-10009-1_25

77. Hüttel, H., et al.: Foundations of session types and behavioural contracts. ACM Comput. Surv. **49**(1), 3:1–3:36 (2016)

78. European COST Action IC1405 on "Reversible Computation - Extending Horizons of Computing". http://www.revcomp.eu/

79. Jacobs, B.: New directions in categorical logic, for classical, probabilistic and quantum logic. Logical Methods Comput. Sci. **11**(3), 1–76 (2015)

80. Jacobsen, P.A.H., Kaarsgaard, R., Thomsen, M.K.: CoreFun: a typed functional reversible core language. In: Kari, J., Ulidowski, I. (eds.) RC 2018. LNCS, vol. 11106, pp. 304–321. Springer, Cham (2018). https://doi.org/10.1007/978-3-319-99498-7_21

81. Jalonen, J., Kari, J.: Conjugacy of one-dimensional one-sided cellular automata is undecidable. In: Tjoa, A.M., Bellatreche, L., Biffl, S., van Leeuwen, J., Wiedermann, J. (eds.) SOFSEM 2018. LNCS, vol. 10706, pp. 227–238. Springer, Cham (2018). https://doi.org/10.1007/978-3-319-73117-9_16

82. James, R.P., Sabry, A.: Theseus: a high level language for reversible computing. In: Work-in-Progress Report Presented at RC 2014. http://www.cs.indiana.edu/~sabry/papers/theseus.pdf

83. James, R.P., Sabry, A.: Information effects. ACM SIGPLAN Not. **47**(1), 73–84 (2012)

84. Jones, N.D.: Computability and Complexity: From a Programming Language Perspective. Foundations of Computing. MIT Press, Cambridge (1997)

85. Joyal, A., Street, R., Verity, D.: Traced monoidal categories. Math. Proc. Cambridge Philos. Soc. **119**(3), 447–468 (1996)

86. Kaarsgaard, R., Axelsen, H.B., Glück, R.: Join inverse categories and reversible recursion. J. Logical Algebraic Methods Program. **87**, 33–50 (2017)

87. Kaarsgaard, R., Glück, R.: A categorical foundation for structured reversible flowchart languages: soundness and adequacy. Logical Methods Comput. Sci. **14**(3), 1–38 (2018)

88. Kari, J.: Reversibility of 2D cellular automata is undecidable. Physica D **45**(1), 379–385 (1990)

89. Kari, J.: Universal pattern generation by cellular automata. Theoret. Comput. Sci. **429**, 180–184 (2012)
90. Kari, J.: Reversible cellular automata: from fundamental classical results to recent developments. New Generation Comput. **36**(3), 145–172 (2018)
91. Kari, J., Kopra, J.: Cellular automata and powers of p/q. RAIRO - Theor. Inf. Applic. **51**(4), 191–204 (2017)
92. Kari, J., Ollinger, N.: Periodicity and immortality in reversible computing. In: Ochmański, E., Tyszkiewicz, J. (eds.) MFCS 2008. LNCS, vol. 5162, pp. 419–430. Springer, Heidelberg (2008). https://doi.org/10.1007/978-3-540-85238-4_34
93. Kari, J., Salo, V., Worsch, T.: Sequentializing cellular automata. In: Baetens, J.M., Kutrib, M. (eds.) AUTOMATA 2018. LNCS, vol. 10875, pp. 72–87. Springer, Cham (2018). https://doi.org/10.1007/978-3-319-92675-9_6
94. Karvonen, M.: The way of the dagger. Ph.D. thesis, School of Informatics, University of Edinburgh (2019)
95. Kastl, J.: Inverse categories. In: Algebraische Modelle, Kategorien und Gruppoide. Studien zur Algebra und ihre Anwendungen, vol. 7, pp. 51–60. Akademie-Verlag (1979)
96. Kawabe, M., Glück, R.: The program inverter LRinv and its structure. In: Hermenegildo, M.V., Cabeza, D. (eds.) PADL 2005. LNCS, vol. 3350, pp. 219–234. Springer, Heidelberg (2005). https://doi.org/10.1007/978-3-540-30557-6_17
97. Keller, R.: Towards a theory of universal speed-independent modules. IEEE Trans. Comput. **23**(1), 21–33 (1974)
98. Klop, J.W.: Term rewriting systems. In: Abramsky, S., Gabbay, D.M., Maibaum, T.S.E. (eds.) Handbook of Logic in Computer Science, vol. I, pp. 1–112. Oxford University Press (1992)
99. Knowlton, K.C.: A fast storage allocator. Commun. ACM **8**(10), 623–625 (1965)
100. Kopra, J.: Glider automorphisms on some shifts of finite type and a finitary Ryan's theorem. In: Baetens, J.M., Kutrib, M. (eds.) AUTOMATA 2018. LNCS, vol. 10875, pp. 88–99. Springer, Cham (2018). https://doi.org/10.1007/978-3-319-92675-9_7
101. Krivine, J.: A verification technique for reversible process algebra. In: Glück, R., Yokoyama, T. (eds.) RC 2012. LNCS, vol. 7581, pp. 204–217. Springer, Heidelberg (2013). https://doi.org/10.1007/978-3-642-36315-3_17
102. Kuhn, S., Ulidowski, I.: A calculus for local reversibility. In: Devitt, S., Lanese, I. (eds.) RC 2016. LNCS, vol. 9720, pp. 20–35. Springer, Cham (2016). https://doi.org/10.1007/978-3-319-40578-0_2
103. Kuhn, S., Ulidowski, I.: Local reversibility in a calculus of covalent bonding. Sci. Comput. Program. **151**, 18–47 (2018)
104. Kurka, P.: On topological dynamics of Turing machines. Theor. Comput. Sci. **174**(1–2), 203–216 (1997)
105. Kutrib, M.: Reversible and irreversible computations of deterministic finite-state devices. In: Italiano, G.F., Pighizzini, G., Sannella, D.T. (eds.) MFCS 2015. LNCS, vol. 9234, pp. 38–52. Springer, Heidelberg (2015). https://doi.org/10.1007/978-3-662-48057-1_3
106. Kutrib, M., Malcher, A.: Fast reversible language recognition using cellular automata. Inf. Comput. **206**, 1142–1151 (2008)
107. Kutrib, M., Malcher, A.: Reversible pushdown automata. J. Comput. Syst. Sci. **78**, 1814–1827 (2012)

108. Kutrib, M., Malcher, A., Wendlandt, M.: Real-time reversible one-way cellular automata. In: Isokawa, T., Imai, K., Matsui, N., Peper, F., Umeo, H. (eds.) AUTOMATA 2014. LNCS, vol. 8996, pp. 56–69. Springer, Cham (2015). https://doi.org/10.1007/978-3-319-18812-6_5

109. Kutrib, M., Malcher, A., Wendlandt, M.: Reversible queue automata. Fund. Inf. **148**, 341–368 (2016)

110. Kutrib, M., Malcher, A., Wendlandt, M.: When input-driven pushdown automata meet reversiblity. RAIRO - Theor. Inf. Applic. **50**, 313–330 (2016)

111. Kutrib, M., Malcher, A., Wendlandt, M.: Transducing reversibly with finite state machines. Theor. Comput. Sci. **787**, 111–126 (2019)

112. Kutrib, M., Wendlandt, M.: Reversible limited automata. Fund. Inf. **155**, 31–58 (2017)

113. Landauer, R.: Irreversibility and heat generated in the computing process. IBM J. Res. Dev. **5**, 183–191 (1961)

114. Lanese, I., Lienhardt, M., Mezzina, C.A., Schmitt, A., Stefani, J.-B.: Concurrent flexible reversibility. In: Felleisen, M., Gardner, P. (eds.) ESOP 2013. LNCS, vol. 7792, pp. 370–390. Springer, Heidelberg (2013). https://doi.org/10.1007/978-3-642-37036-6_21

115. Lanese, I., Medic, D., Mezzina, C.A.: Static versus dynamic reversibility in CCS. Acta Informatica (2019)

116. Lanese, I., Mezzina, C.A., Schmitt, A., Stefani, J.-B.: Controlling reversibility in higher-order Pi. In: Katoen, J.-P., König, B. (eds.) CONCUR 2011. LNCS, vol. 6901, pp. 297–311. Springer, Heidelberg (2011). https://doi.org/10.1007/978-3-642-23217-6_20

117. Lanese, I., Mezzina, C.A., Stefani, J.-B.: Reversing higher-order Pi. In: Gastin, P., Laroussinie, F. (eds.) CONCUR 2010. LNCS, vol. 6269, pp. 478–493. Springer, Heidelberg (2010). https://doi.org/10.1007/978-3-642-15375-4_33

118. Lanese, I., Mezzina, C.A., Stefani, J.-B.: Controlled reversibility and compensations. In: Glück, R., Yokoyama, T. (eds.) RC 2012. LNCS, vol. 7581, pp. 233–240. Springer, Heidelberg (2013). https://doi.org/10.1007/978-3-642-36315-3_19

119. Lanese, I., Mezzina, C.A., Stefani, J.-B.: Reversibility in the higher-order π-calculus. Theor. Comput. Sci. **625**, 25–84 (2016)

120. Lanese, I., Mezzina, C.A., Tiezzi, F.: Causal-consistent reversibility. Bull. EATCS **114** (2014)

121. Lanese, I., Nishida, N., Palacios, A., Vidal, G.: CauDEr: a causal-consistent reversible debugger for Erlang. In: Gallagher, J.P., Sulzmann, M. (eds.) FLOPS 2018. LNCS, vol. 10818, pp. 247–263. Springer, Cham (2018). https://doi.org/10.1007/978-3-319-90686-7_16

122. Laursen, J.S., Schultz, U.P., Ellekilde, L.: Automatic error recovery in robot assembly operations using reverse execution. In: Intelligent Robots and Systems, IROS 2015, pp. 1785–1792. IEEE (2015)

123. Lavado, G.J., Pighizzini, G., Prigioniero, L.: Minimal and reduced reversible automata. J. Automata, Lang. Comb. **22**(1–3), 145–168 (2017)

124. Lavado, G.J., Pighizzini, G., Prigioniero, L.: Weakly and strongly irreversible regular languages. In: Automata and Formal Languages, AFL 2017. EPTCS, vol. 252, pp. 143–156 (2017)

125. Lavado, G.J., Prigioniero, L.: Concise representations of reversible automata. Int. J. Found. Comput. Sci. **30**(6–7), 1157–1175 (2019)

126. Lienhardt, M., Lanese, I., Mezzina, C.A., Stefani, J.-B.: A reversible abstract machine and its space overhead. In: Giese, H., Rosu, G. (eds.) FMOODS/FORTE -2012. LNCS, vol. 7273, pp. 1–17. Springer, Heidelberg (2012). https://doi.org/10.1007/978-3-642-30793-5_1

127. Mahler, K.: An unsolved problem on the powers of 3/2. J. Australian Math. Soc. **8**(2), 313–321 (1968)

128. Matsuda, K., Hu, Z., Nakano, K., Hamana, M., Takeichi, M.: Bidirectionalization transformation based on automatic derivation of view complement functions. In: International Conference on Functional Programming, ICFP 2007, pp. 47–58. ACM (2007)

129. McNellis, J., Mola, J., Sykes, K.: Time travel debugging: root causing bugs in commercial scale software. CppCon talk (2017). https://www.youtube.com/watch?v=l1YJTg_A914

130. Medić, D., Mezzina, C.A.: Static VS dynamic reversibility in CCS. In: Devitt, S., Lanese, I. (eds.) RC 2016. LNCS, vol. 9720, pp. 36–51. Springer, Cham (2016). https://doi.org/10.1007/978-3-319-40578-0_3

131. Medic, D., Mezzina, C.A., Phillips, I., Yoshida, N.: A parametric framework for reversible pi-calculi. In: Workshop on Expressiveness in Concurrency and Workshop on Structural Operational Semantics, EXPRESS/SOS 2018. EPTCS, vol. 276, pp. 87–103 (2018)

132. Melgratti, H., Mezzina, C.A., Ulidowski, I.: Reversing P/T Nets. In: Riis Nielson, H., Tuosto, E. (eds.) COORDINATION 2019. LNCS, vol. 11533, pp. 19–36. Springer, Cham (2019). https://doi.org/10.1007/978-3-030-22397-7_2

133. Mezzina, C.A.: On reversibility and broadcast. In: Kari, J., Ulidowski, I. (eds.) RC 2018. LNCS, vol. 11106, pp. 67–83. Springer, Cham (2018). https://doi.org/10.1007/978-3-319-99498-7_5

134. Mezzina, C.A., et al.: Software and reversible systems: a survey of recent activities. In: Ulidowski, I., et al. (eds.) Reversible Computation. LNCS 12070, pp. 41–59. Springer, Cham (2020)

135. Mezzina, C.A., Koutavas, V.: A safety and liveness theory for total reversibility. In: Theoretical Aspects of Software Engineering, TASE 2017, pp. 1–8. IEEE Computer Society (2017)

136. Mezzina, C.A., Pérez, J.A.: Reversible sessions using monitors. In: Workshop on Programming Language Approaches to Concurrency- and Communication-cEntric Software, PLACES 2016. EPTCS, vol. 211, pp. 56–64 (2016)

137. Mezzina, C.A., Pérez, J.A.: Causally consistent reversible choreographies: a monitors-as-memories approach. In: Principles and Practice of Declarative Programming, PPDP 2017, pp. 127–138. ACM (2017)

138. Mezzina, C.A., Pérez, J.A.: Reversibility in session-based concurrency: a fresh look. J. Log. Algebr. Meth. Program. **90**, 2–30 (2017)

139. Mikulski, L., Lanese, I.: Reversing unbounded Petri nets. In: Donatelli, S., Haar, S. (eds.) PETRI NETS 2019. LNCS, vol. 11522, pp. 213–233. Springer, Cham (2019). https://doi.org/10.1007/978-3-030-21571-2_13

140. Milner, R.: A Calculus of Communicating Systems. LNCS, vol. 92. Springer, Heidelberg (1980). https://doi.org/10.1007/3-540-10235-3

141. Mogensen, T.Æ.: RSSA: a reversible SSA form. In: Mazzara, M., Voronkov, A. (eds.) PSI 2015. LNCS, vol. 9609, pp. 203–217. Springer, Cham (2016). https://doi.org/10.1007/978-3-319-41579-6_16

142. Mogensen, T.Æ.: Reversible garbage collection for reversible functional languages. New Gener. Compu. **36**(3), 203–232 (2018)

143. Morita, K.: Theory of Reversible Computing. Monographs in Theoretical Computer Science. An EATCS Series. Springer, Tokyo (2017). https://doi.org/10.1007/978-4-431-56606-9
144. Morita, K., Harao, M.: Computation universality of one-dimensional reversible (injective) cellular automata. IEICE Trans. **E72**(6), 758–762 (1989)
145. Morrison, D., Ulidowski, I.: Direction-reversible self-timed cellular automata for delay-insensitive circuits. J. Cellular Automata **12**(1–2), 101–120 (2016)
146. Mousavi, M.R., Reniers, M.A., Groote, J.F.: SOS formats and meta-theory: 20 years after. Theor. Comput. Sci. **373**(3), 238–272 (2007)
147. Murata, T.: Petri nets: properties, analysis and applications. Proc. IEEE **77**(4), 541–580 (1989)
148. Nishida, N., Palacios, A., Vidal, G.: Reversible term rewriting. In: Formal Structures for Computation and Deduction, FSCD 2016. LIPIcs, vol. 52. pp. 28:1–28:18. Schloss Dagstuhl - Leibniz-Zentrum für Informatik (2016)
149. Nishida, N., Palacios, A., Vidal, G.: A reversible semantics for Erlang. In: Hermenegildo, M.V., Lopez-Garcia, P. (eds.) LOPSTR 2016. LNCS, vol. 10184, pp. 259–274. Springer, Cham (2017). https://doi.org/10.1007/978-3-319-63139-4_15
150. Nishida, N., Palacios, A., Vidal, G.: Reversible computation in term rewriting. J. Log. Algebr. Meth. Program. **94**, 128–149 (2018)
151. Nishida, N., Vidal, G.: Program inversion for tail recursive functions. In: Rewriting Techniques and Applications, RTA 2011. LIPIcs, vol. 10, pp. 283–298. Schloss Dagstuhl - Leibniz-Zentrum für Informatik (2011)
152. Nishida, N., Vidal, G.: Characterizing compatible view updates in syntactic bidirectionalization. In: Thomsen, M.K., Soeken, M. (eds.) RC 2019. LNCS, vol. 11497, pp. 67–83. Springer, Cham (2019). https://doi.org/10.1007/978-3-030-21500-2_5
153. Paolini, L., Piccolo, M., Roversi, L.: A certified study of a reversible programming language. In: Types for Proofs and Programs, TYPES 2018. LIPIcs, vol. 69, pp. 7:1–7:21. Schloss Dagstuhl - Leibniz-Zentrum für Informatik (2018)
154. Păun, G.: Computing with membranes. J. Comput. Syst. Sci. **61**(1), 108–143 (2000)
155. Philippou, A., Psara, K.: Reversible computation in Petri nets. In: Kari, J., Ulidowski, I. (eds.) RC 2018. LNCS, vol. 11106, pp. 84–101. Springer, Cham (2018). https://doi.org/10.1007/978-3-319-99498-7_6
156. Philippou, A., Psara, K., Siljak, H.: Controlling reversibility in reversing Petri nets with application to wireless communications. In: Thomsen, M.K., Soeken, M. (eds.) RC 2019. LNCS, vol. 11497, pp. 238–245. Springer, Cham (2019). https://doi.org/10.1007/978-3-030-21500-2_15
157. Phillips, I., Ulidowski, I.: Reversibility and asymmetric conflict in event structures. J. Log. Algebr. Meth. Program. **84**(6), 781–805 (2015)
158. Phillips, I., Ulidowski, I., Yuen, S.: A reversible process calculus and the modelling of the ERK signalling pathway. In: Glück, R., Yokoyama, T. (eds.) RC 2012. LNCS, vol. 7581, pp. 218–232. Springer, Heidelberg (2013). https://doi.org/10.1007/978-3-642-36315-3_18
159. Phillips, I., Ulidowski, I., Yuen, S.: Modelling of bonding with processes and events. In: Dueck, G.W., Miller, D.M. (eds.) RC 2013. LNCS, vol. 7948, pp. 141–154. Springer, Heidelberg (2013). https://doi.org/10.1007/978-3-642-38986-3_12
160. Phillips, I., Ulidowski, I.: Reversing algebraic process calculi. In: Aceto, L., Ingólfsdóttir, A. (eds.) FoSSaCS 2006. LNCS, vol. 3921, pp. 246–260. Springer, Heidelberg (2006). https://doi.org/10.1007/11690634_17

161. Phillips, I.C.C., Ulidowski, I.: Reversing algebraic process calculi. J. Log. Algebr. Program. **73**(1–2), 70–96 (2007)

162. Pin, J.-E.: On reversible automata. In: Simon, I. (ed.) LATIN 1992. LNCS, vol. 583, pp. 401–416. Springer, Heidelberg (1992). https://doi.org/10.1007/BFb0023844

163. Pinna, G.M.: Reversing steps in membrane systems computations. In: Gheorghe, M., Rozenberg, G., Salomaa, A., Zandron, C. (eds.) CMC 2017. LNCS, vol. 10725, pp. 245–261. Springer, Cham (2018). https://doi.org/10.1007/978-3-319-73359-3_16

164. Rebentrost, P., Mohseni, M., Lloyd, S.: Quantum support vector machine for big data classification. Phys. Rev. Lett. **113**, 130503 (2014)

165. Reisig, W.: Petri Nets: An Introduction. EATCS Monographs on Theoretical Computer Science, vol. 4. Springer, Heidelberg (1985). https://doi.org/10.1007/978-3-642-69968-9

166. Rensink, A., Vogler, W.: Fair testing. Inf. Comput. **205**(2), 125–198 (2007)

167. Sabry, A., Valiron, B., Vizzotto, J.K.: From symmetric pattern-matching to quantum control. In: Baier, C., Dal Lago, U. (eds.) FoSSaCS 2018. LNCS, vol. 10803, pp. 348–364. Springer, Cham (2018). https://doi.org/10.1007/978-3-319-89366-2_19

168. Salo, V.: Groups and monoids of cellular automata. In: Kari, J. (ed.) AUTOMATA 2015. LNCS, vol. 9099, pp. 17–45. Springer, Heidelberg (2015). https://doi.org/10.1007/978-3-662-47221-7_3

169. Salo, V., Törmä, I.: A one-dimensional physically universal cellular automaton. In: Kari, J., Manea, F., Petre, I. (eds.) CiE 2017. LNCS, vol. 10307, pp. 375–386. Springer, Cham (2017). https://doi.org/10.1007/978-3-319-58741-7_35

170. Schaeffer, L.: A physically universal cellular automaton. In: Innovations in Theoretical Computer Science, ITCS 2015, pp. 237–246. ACM (2015)

171. Schordan, M., Oppelstrup, T., Jefferson, D., Barnes Jr., P.D.: Generation of reversible C++ code for optimistic parallel discrete event simulation. New Gener. Comput. **36**(3), 257–280 (2018)

172. Schordan, M., Oppelstrup, T., Thomsen, M.K., Glück, R.: Reversible languages and incremental state saving in optimistic parallel discrete event simulation. In: Ulidowski, I., et al. (eds.) Reversible Computation. LNCS 12070, pp. 187–207. Springer, Cham (2020)

173. Schultz, U.P., Axelsen, H.B.: Elements of a reversible object-oriented language. In: Devitt, S., Lanese, I. (eds.) RC 2016. LNCS, vol. 9720, pp. 153–159. Springer, Cham (2016). https://doi.org/10.1007/978-3-319-40578-0_10

174. Selinger, P.: Dagger compact closed categories and completely positive maps. In: Workshop on Quantum Programming Languages, QPL 2005. Electronic Notes in Theoretical Computer Science, vol. 170, pp. 139–163 (2005)

175. Selinger, P.: A survey of graphical languages for monoidal categories. New Structures for Physics. Lecture Notes in Physics, vol. 813, pp. 289–355. Springer, Heidelberg (2011). https://doi.org/10.1007/978-3-642-12821-9_4

176. Slagle, J.R.: Automated theorem-proving for theories with simplifiers, commutativity and associativity. J. ACM **21**(4), 622–642 (1974)

177. Sutner, K.: De Bruijn graphs and linear cellular automata. Complex Syst. **5**(1), 19–30 (1991)

178. Terese: Term Rewriting Systems, Cambridge Tracts in Theoretical Computer Science, vol. 55. Cambridge University Press (2003)

179. Tiezzi, F., Yoshida, N.: Reversible session-based pi-calculus. J. Log. Algebr. Meth. Program. **84**(5), 684–707 (2015)

180. Toffoli, T.: Computation and construction universality of reversible cellular automata. J. Comput. Syst. Sci. **15**(2), 213–231 (1977)
181. Toffoli, T., Margolus, N.: Cellular Automata Machines: A New Environment for Modeling. MIT Press, Cambridge (1987)
182. Windridge, D., Mengoni, R., Nagarajan, R.: Quantum error-correcting output codes. Int. J. Quantum Inf. **16**(8), 1840003 (2018)
183. Windridge, D., Nagarajan, R.: Quantum bootstrap aggregation. In: de Barros, J.A., Coecke, B., Pothos, E. (eds.) QI 2016. LNCS, vol. 10106, pp. 115–121. Springer, Cham (2017). https://doi.org/10.1007/978-3-319-52289-0_9
184. Yokoyama, T., Axelsen, H.B., Glück, R.: Towards a reversible functional language. In: De Vos, A., Wille, R. (eds.) RC 2011. LNCS, vol. 7165, pp. 14–29. Springer, Heidelberg (2012). https://doi.org/10.1007/978-3-642-29517-1_2
185. Yokoyama, T., Axelsen, H.B., Glück, R.: Fundamentals of reversible flowchart languages. Theoret. Comput. Sci. **611**, 87–115 (2016)

Software and Reversible Systems: A Survey of Recent Activities

Claudio Antares Mezzina[1]([✉]), Rudolf Schlatte[2], Robert Glück[3], Tue Haulund[4],
James Hoey[5], Martin Holm Cservenka[6], Ivan Lanese[7],
Torben Æ. Mogensen[3], Harun Siljak[8], Ulrik P. Schultz[9], and Irek Ulidowski[5]

[1] Dipartimento di Scienze Pure e Applicate, Università di Urbino, Urbino, Italy
[2] Department of Informatics, University of Oslo, Oslo, Norway
[3] DIKU, Department of Computer Science, University of Copenhagen,
Copenhagen, Denmark
`torbenm@di.ku.dk`
[4] A.P. Moller Maersk, Copenhagen, Denmark
[5] School of Informatics, University of Leicester, Leicester, UK
[6] Practio ApS, Copenhagen, Denmark
[7] Focus Team, University of Bologna/Inria, Bologna, Italy
[8] CONNECT Centre, Trinity College Dublin, Dublin, Ireland
[9] University of Southern Denmark, Odense, Denmark

Abstract. Software plays a central role in all aspects of reversible computing. We survey the breadth of topics and recent activities on reversible software and systems including behavioural types, recovery, debugging, concurrency, and object-oriented programming. These have the potential to provide linguistic abstractions and tools that will lead to safer and more reliable reversible computing applications.

1 Introduction

The notion of reversible computation has a long history [37] which started by studies on the thermodynamic cost of irreversible actions. It was noted that since computation is usually irreversible, information loss causes dissipation of heat. Therefore it could be possible to execute reversible computations in a heat dissipation free way. This was the motivation that gave rise to several reversible computation models such as *reversible Turing machines* [6] and *conservative logic* [22]. Since then there has been a huge effort to introduce reversibility at the level of programming languages and software systems [7,44], where it can bring additional benefits towards reliability, robustness and scalability of conventional software systems. Part of this effort has been carried out by the Working Group (WG) 2: Software and Systems of the COST Action IC1405 Reversible Computation – Extending Horizons of Computing.

This work has been partially supported by COST Action IC1405 on Reversible Computation - Extending Horizons of Computing.

I. Ulidowski et al. (Eds.): RC 2020, LNCS 12070, pp. 41–59, 2020.
https://doi.org/10.1007/978-3-030-47361-7_2

Software plays a central role in all aspects of reversible computing. We survey the breadth of topics and recent activities on reversible software and systems including behavioural types, recovery, debugging, concurrency, and object-oriented programming. These have the potential to provide linguistic abstractions and tools that will lead to safer and more reliable reversible computing applications.

The rest of the chapter is structured as follows: Sect. 2 reports on reversibility and behavioural types; Sect. 3 reports on the interplay between reversibility and recovery for distributed systems; Sect. 4 reports on reversibility and object orientation; Sect. 5 reports on reversing imperative programs with shared memory concurrency and its possible application on reversible debugging; Sect. 6 reports on reversibility and message passing systems, with a special focus on reversible (core) Erlang and its reversible debugger. Section 7 reports on reversibility and control theory. Section 8 concludes the chapter.

2   Behavioural Types

The interest in behavioural types [35] stems from the fact that it is easier to work with a system whose behaviour (in terms of communications) is strongly disciplined by a type theory. Among behavioural types we distinguish: *binary session types* and *contracts*, *multiparty session types* and *choreographies*. Choreographies will be discussed in Sect. 3.

Reversibility and monitored semantics for *binary session types* have been recently studied by Mezzina and Pérez [46,47,49]. In their work, they propose a *monitor as memory* mechanism in which information about the monitor of a process can be used to enable its reversibility. Moreover, by adding *modalities* information at the level of session types, reversibility can be controlled.

In the context of multiparty session types, *global types* describe the message-passing behaviour of a set of participants in a system from a global point of view. A global type can be projected onto each participant so as to obtain local types, which describe individual contributions to the global protocol. The work [48] extends global and local types to keep track of the stage of the protocol that has been already executed; this enables reversible steps in an elegant way. The authors develop a rigorous process framework for multiparty communication, which improves over prior works by featuring asynchrony, decoupled rollbacks and process passing. In this framework, concurrent processes are untyped but their forward and backward steps are governed by monitors. The main technical result is that the developed multiparty reversible semantics is causally-consistent. Finally, [15] proposes a Haskell implementation of the asynchronous reversible operational semantics for multiparty session types proposed in [48]. The implementation exploits algebraic data types to faithfully represent three core ingredients: a process calculus, multiparty session types, and forward and backward reduction semantics. This implementation bears witness to the convenience of pure functional programming for implementing reversible languages.

In a series of works [11,16] *multiparty session types* (aka global types) have been enriched with checkpoint labels on choices that mark points of the protocol where the computations may roll back. In [16], a simple model is developed in which rollback could be done any time after a participant has crossed the checkpointed choice. In [11] a more refined model is presented, in which the programmer can define points where the computation may revert to a checkpointed label, and rollback has to be triggered by the participant that made the decision.

Behavioural contracts are abstract descriptions of expected communication patterns followed by either clients or servers during their interaction. Behavioural contracts come naturally equipped with a notion of *compliance*: when a client and a server follow compliant contracts, their interaction is guaranteed to progress or successfully complete. In [5] two extensions of behavioural contracts are studied: *retractable contracts* dealing with *backtracking* and *speculative contracts* dealing with *speculative execution*. These two extensions give rise to *the same notion of compliance*. As a consequence, they also give rise to the same *subcontract relation*, which determines when one server can be replaced by another while preserving compliance. Moreover, compliance and subcontract relation are both decidable in quadratic time. The above paper also studies the relationship between retractable contracts and calculi for reversible computing.

3 Recovery

Distributed programs are hard to get right because they are required to be open, scalable, long-running, and tolerant to faults. This problem is exacerbated by the recent approaches to distributed software based on (micro-)services where different services are developed independently by disparate teams. In fact, services are meant to be composed together and run in open context where unpredictable behaviours can emerge. This makes it necessary to adopt suitable strategies for monitoring the execution and incorporate recovery and adaptation mechanisms to make distributed programs more flexible and robust. The typical approach that is currently adopted is to embed such mechanisms in the program logic, which makes it hard to extract, compare and debug.

An approach that employs formal abstractions for specifying failure recovery and adaptation strategies has been proposed in [10]. Although implementation-agnostic, these abstractions would be amenable to algorithmic synthesis of code, monitoring and tests. Message-passing programs (à la Erlang, Go, or MPI) are considered, since they are gaining momentum both in academia and industry. In [20] an instance of the framework proposed in [10] is given. More precisely, this approach imbues the communication behaviour of multi-party protocols with minimal decorations specifying the conditions triggering monitor adaptations. It is then shown that, from these extended global descriptions, one can (i) synthesise actors implementing the normal local behaviour of the system prescribed by the global graph, but also (ii) synthesise monitors that are able to coordinate a distributed rollback when certain conditions (denoting abnormal behaviour) are met. The synthesis algorithm produces Erlang code. For each role in the global description, two Erlang actors are generated: one actor implements the normal (forward) behaviour of the system and a second one (the monitor) is in charge of implementing the reversible behaviour of the role. When certain conditions are detected at runtime, the monitors will coordinate with each other in order to bring back the system if possible. One interesting property of this approach is that the two semantics are highly decoupled, meaning that the system is always able to normally execute (i.e., going forward) even in case of a monitor crash.

A static analysis, based on multiparty session types, to efficiently compute a safe global state from which to recover a system of interacting processes has been integrated with the Erlang recovery mechanism in [50]. From a global description of the program communication flow, given in multiparty protocol specification, causal dependencies between processes are extracted. This information is then used at runtime by a recovery mechanism, integrated in Erlang, to determine which process has to be terminated and which one has to be restarted upon a node failure. Experimental results indicate that the proposed framework outperforms a built-in static recovery strategy in Erlang when a part of the protocol can be safely recovered.

In [26] a rollback operator, based on the notion of causal-consistent reversibility, is defined for a language with shared memory. A rollback is defined as the minimal causal-consistent sequence of backward steps able to undo a given action. The paper [69] explores the relationship between the Manetho [17] distributed checkpoint/rollback scheme (based on causal logging) and a reversible concurrent model of computation based on the π-calculus with imperative rollback called roll-π [38]. A rather tight relationship between rollback based on causal logging as performed in Manetho and the rollback algorithm underlying roll-π is shown. The main result is that roll-π can faithfully simulate Manetho under weak barbed simulation, but that the converse only holds if possible rollbacks are restricted.

4   Reversibility and Object-Oriented Languages

Object-oriented (OO) programming uses classes as a means to encapsulate behaviour and state. Classes permit programmers to define new abstractions, such as abstract data types. The key elements of reversible OO languages were initially introduced with a prototype of the Joule language [60] and subsequently formally described for the ROOPL language [29]. Joule and ROOPL demonstrate that well-known object-oriented concepts such as encapsulation, inheritance, and virtual methods can be captured reversibly by extending a base Janus-like imperative language [71] with support for such features.

This approach allows standard OO programming patterns, such as the factory and iterator design patterns [23], to be used reversibly [59], and well-known structures such as an OO-style collection hierarchy (i.e., OO abstract data types but with reversible operations) can similarly be implemented in such languages. Reversible data types [13], that is data structures with all of its associated operations implemented reversibly, are enabled by dynamic allocation of constructor terms in the heap of a reversible machine [1]. Data structures are safe in OO languages because they require no explicit pointer arithmetic in user programs, which is notoriously error prone.

Memory handling is a key concern for reversible object-oriented languages. The original Joule prototype relied on static stack allocation of objects, which does not permit full OO programming: common patterns such as factories are for example not possible [60]. Joule was subsequently extended into Joule^R which uses region-based [24,66] memory management [59]. Regions are sufficient to support the implementation of standard OO programming patterns and a collection hierarchy. The initial presentation of the ROOPL language relied exclusively on stack allocation [29], and was subsequently extended with a reversible heap-based memory manager [13] based on Knuth's Buddy Memory algorithm [36]. With this extension, data structures such as min-heaps and circular buffers can be implemented [13]. The language is reversibly universal (r-Turing complete), which means it has the computational power of reversible Turing machines (cf. [71]). See Figs. 1, 2, and 3 for example programs in Joule and ROOPL, which will be described in the next section.

4.1   Object Orientation and Data Structures

As exemplified by the representation of abstract-syntax trees in the reversible Janus self-interpreter [73], even complex data structures can be expressed in reversible languages with simple type systems including only integers and arrays. However, more effort is required to represent and manipulate the data structures and as the resulting code base grows, the problem exacerbates.

Reversible object-oriented languages allow for easier code reuse and extensibility by encapsulating data and methods in classes, thereby also abstracting from the underlying memory model of the reversible machine. See Figs. 1 and 2 for two classic object-oriented examples in Joule and ROOPL, respectively.

The example in Joule in Fig. 1 models a single point in a two-dimensional space by a class Point with two integer coordinates (x, y) and two methods that translate a point by adding an integer displacement to the respective coordinate (add_to_x, add_to_y). Here, this.x refers to the x-coordinate of the point to which the displacement parameter x is added when add_to_x is applied to a point object.

The example in ROOPL in Fig. 2 illustrates a simple *class hierarchy* of geometric shapes in a two-dimensional space. The two shapes Rectangle and Circle *inherit* the reference point (x, y) from their superclass Shape and *extend* it with the length and width (1, w) in the case of Rectangle and with the radius r in the case of Circle. The two subclasses add a class-specific method getArea that defines how to calculate the area of the respective shape. All methods defined in these three classes are implemented by reversible statements that are similar to those in Janus and reversible flowcharts [71,73]. Methods can also be implemented using reversible control-flow operators (conditionals, iteration) and recursive method calls and uncalls, as illustrated in the next example. It is

```
1   class Point {
2       int x; int y; // private fields, zero-initialised
3
4       Point(int x, int y) { // constructor, runs after allocation
5           this.x += x; this.y += y; // this.x is a field, x a parameter
6       }
7
8       procedure add_to_x(int x) { this.x += x; }
9       procedure add_to_y(int y) { this.y += y; }
10  }
```

Fig. 1. Example Joule class modelling a single point in two-dimensional space, originally from [60]

```
1   class Shape                          // superclass Shape
2       int x, y                         // reference point
3
4       method getArea(int out)          // abstract method
5           skip
6
7       method translate(int dx, int dy) // common method
8           x += dx
9           y += dy
10
11  class Rectangle inherits Shape       // subclass Rectangle
12      int l, w                         // length, width
13
14      method getArea(int out)          // concrete method
15          out ^= l * w
16
17  class Circle inherits Shape          // subclass Circle
18      int r                            // radius
19
20      method getArea(int out)          // concrete method
21          out ^= PI * r * r
```

Fig. 2. Example ROOPL class hierarchy modeling basic geometric shapes in two-dimensional space, originally from [13]

important to note that a *reversible method* cannot overwrite any of the encapsulated data, only perform a *reversible update* [2]. This makes reversible OO languages different from their mainstream counterparts, such as Java or C++, which can perform destructive updates.

The reversible min-heap in Fig. 3 serves as an example of the expressiveness afforded by the richer type systems and memory models of these languages. The `insert` method reversibly inserts a node in the heap, where the only output is the depth of the inserted node, maintaining the min-heap property in the process. This procedure can be used to reversibly extract the minimal value of a data set. The class `Node` recursively defines a binary tree structure by including two nodes, `left` and `right`. The integer v is the value of a node.

The `insert` method makes use of a *reversible conditional* if...fi (lines 5 to 16), which means it contains not only an entry predicate ($v < w$) but also an exit predicate (`counter > 0`). As usual in reversible languages, both predicates are checked at runtime: both must be true when control passes along the then-branch and both must be false when control passes along the else-branch; otherwise, the

```
1    class Node
2        Node left, right /* roots of subtrees */
3        int v           /* value of node     */
4        method insert(int w, int counter) /* counter initially 0 */
5            if v < w then
6                if left = nil then
7                    new Node left
8                    left.v <=> w
9                else call left::insert(w, counter)
10               fi left.right = nil
11               counter += 1 /* counter > 0 */
12           else
13               v <=> w
14               call insert(w, counter)
15               counter -= 1 /* counter = 0 */
16           fi counter > 0
17           left <=> right
18           /* at return, w = 0 and counter = depth of insertion */
```

Fig. 3. Recursive min-heap value insertion implemented in ROOPL using reversible updates and reversible conditionals, originally from [13]

program is undefined (cf. [71,73]). Method calls and uncalls refer to an object. For example, `call left::insert(w, counter)` recursively applies the insert method to the left node `left` with the integer parameters `w` and `counter`. This allows to work with recursively-defined data structures, which in our case are binary trees.

Objects, which are instances of the classes defined in a program, can be allocated and deallocated at runtime in any order using explicit statements. For example, a new object of class node is created by statement `new Node left` where the object's reference is assigned to `left` (line 7). When a new object is created all its fields are initialised with default values, here integer v is initialised with zero and references `left` and `right` with the null pointer `nil`.

Reversible programming demands certain sacrifices compared to mainstream programming because data cannot be overwritten and join points in the control flow require explicit tests (e.g., the exit predicate in `if...fi`), which can also be seen in the case of the insert method. As a consequence, conventional algorithms and data structures need to be rethought in a reversible context regardless of the data structures offered by a reversible language [13,27,28,72]. However, the abstraction and expressiveness of OO reversible data structures ease the task.

With the addition of Joule and ROOPL, reversible programs can now be expressed in a modern programming paradigm like OO programming, with dynamic memory management of variably sized records and programmer-defined recursive data structures that can grow to an arbitrary size at runtime. These new features significantly broaden the applicability of reversible languages and support increased complexity in reversible programs.

5   Reversing Imperative Concurrent Programs

Adding reversibility to irreversible imperative languages has been studied for many years, for example in [9,52,57,58,70]. A proof of correctness is often missing from work in this area. Hoey and Ulidowski introduce a small imperative while language and describe a state-saving approach to reversing executions [33]. This was then extended to support an imperative concurrent language, using identifiers to capture the specific interleaving order and to ensure statements are reversed in the correct order [34]. The proof of correctness provided shows that the reversal is both correct and garbage free. A simulation tool implementing this approach is mentioned in [32] and described in more detail in [30]. Performance evaluation carried out using this simulator indicates that overheads associated with saving and using of reversal information is reasonable. Finally, a link between this simulator and debugging is explored in [32].

5.1 Language and Program State

The imperative language used in this approach contains assignments, conditional statements (branching) and loops (iteration), much like a while language. Details on reversing this imperative while language are available in [33]. This is later extended with block statements containing local variable or procedure declarations, as well as (potentially recursive) procedure calls. With the ability for multiple variables to share a name as a result of local variables, the syntax of this language contains *construct identifiers* (unique names given to complex constructs including block statements) and *paths* (sequence of block names in which a statement resides capturing the position needed for evaluation). Block statements allow the declaration of local variables or procedures, and as such are extended to "clean" up at the end of its execution by "un-declaring" these via *removal statements*. The final addition is that of *interleaving parallel composition*, where the execution of two (or more if nested) programs can be interleaved. The syntax of this language follows.

$$
\begin{aligned}
&\text{P} ::= \varepsilon \mid \text{S} \mid \text{P; P} \mid \text{P par P} \\
&\text{S} ::= \text{skip I} \mid \text{X = E (pa,A)} \mid \text{if In B then P else Q end (pa,A)} \mid \\
&\qquad \text{while Wn B do P end (pa,A)} \mid \text{begin Bn BB end} \mid \\
&\qquad \text{call Cn n (pa,A)} \mid \text{runc Cn P end} \\
&\text{BB} ::= \text{DV; DP; P; RP; RV}
\end{aligned}
$$

DV ::= ε | var X = v (pa,A); DV   DP ::= ε | proc Pn n is P end (pa,A); DP
RV ::= ε | remove X = v (pa,A); RV   RP ::= ε | remove Pn n is P end (pa,A); RP

The program state is represented as a series of environments, including the *variable environment* γ (linking variables to memory locations), the *data store* σ (linking memory locations to values), the *procedure environment* μ (storing multiple copies of procedure bodies being executed in parallel) and the *while environment* β (storing multiple copies of loops being executed in parallel) [34].

5.2 Annotation, Inversion and Operational Semantics

The considered approach is state-saving, where any information required for inversion that is lost during traditional execution is saved [52]. Two versions of an original program are produced. The first, named the *annotated version* and generated via *annotation*, performs the expected forwards execution and saves any required information, named *reversal information*. A design choice made to aid the correctness proof is to store all reversal information in an *auxiliary store* δ separate to the program state. This store is a collection of stacks (ideal for reversal due to their FIFO nature), one for each variable name (all versions share a stack to handle races), two stacks for loops (one for capturing the loop count and one for identifiers), one for conditional statements and one for procedure calls.

The information required depends on the type of statement. Each assignment is destructive as the old value of the variable is lost. This old value is crucial for reversal, thus it is saved into the stack for that variable name on δ prior to each assignment. Conditions are not guaranteed to be invariant, meaning this approach cannot rely on re-evaluation during inversion to behave correctly. For each conditional statement, the result of evaluation is saved onto the stack for conditionals on δ. Loops are handled similarly, with a sequence of booleans saved to capture the number of iterations (onto the first stack for loops). A second design choice made is to save a sequence over implementing a loop counter in order to aid the correctness proof, avoiding modifying the loop code and therefore the behaviour with respect to the program state. Lastly, the final value of a local variable is saved prior to its removal, into the stack for that variable name.

Supporting interleaving parallel composition also requires further information to be saved. Interleaving allows different execution orders to be followed, which must then be correctly inverted. The specific execution order is captured using *identifiers* similarly to Phillips and Ulidowski [55, 56]. The next identifier is assigned to a statement as it executes, stored into a stack of integers associated with each required statement during annotation. Consider the small example shown in Fig. 4 and the executed forwards version shown in Fig. 4a. This is a simple interleaving of three statements, captured via the identifiers 1–3, where the first statement of the right hand side is executed first, before interleaving to the left and finally completing the right. Assuming X and Y are initially 1, this interleaving produces the final state $X = 4$ and $Y = 3$. These identifiers also create a link between a statement and its reversal information, as all entries on δ contain the corresponding identifier. For example, the stack X on δ will contain the pair (2,1) (statement with identifier 2 overwrote the value 1). For loops or procedure calls (potentially multiple copies of the same code in execution across a parallel), identifiers are assigned to the specific copy within μ or β. Since local copies are removed at the end of their execution, the final example of reversal information is the identifiers assigned to such a copy (saved onto the second stack for loops or the stack for calls).

X = Y+2 [2]; **par** Y = X+2 [1];   X = Y+2 [2]; **par** X = 4 [3];
          X = 4 [3];   Y = X+2 [1];

(a) Executed annotated program   (b) Inverted program

Fig. 4. Identifier use example

The execution of an annotated program is defined in terms of small step operational semantics, where each rule performs the expected forwards execution alongside the saving of reversal information and assigning of an identifier [34].

The second version of an original program produced, called the *inverted version*, is generated via *inversion* and has an inverted statement order with all declaration statements changed to removals and vice versa. This forwards-executing program simulates reversal using the saved information and identifiers.

Throughout the inverse execution, the decision of which statement to execute next (that is, invert) is made using the identifiers in descending order to force backtracking order. Returning to the example in Fig. 4, the identifiers are used in the order 3–1, meaning any incorrect inverse execution path cannot be followed. Each statement also uses the identifiers to access the correct reversal information. Assignments will no longer evaluate the expression and instead retrieve the old value from δ. From the example in Fig. 4b, execution of the statement with identifier 2 uses the pair (2,1) to restore the variable to 1. Similarly conditionals and loops retrieve the result of condition evaluation from δ. Declaring a local variable during an inverse execution initialises it to the final value it held during forward execution (retrieved from the stack). Lastly, whenever a copy of a loop or procedure body is made during the inverse execution, it is populated with the required identifiers from δ.

As before, inverse execution is defined by small step semantics, with each rule using identifiers and reversal information to undo the effects of a statement (or step). Complete inverse execution undoes the effects of all statements, producing a state equivalent to that of prior to the forward execution. We refer to the previous property, coupled with the property that all reversal information is consumed (the approach is *garbage free*), as *correct inversion*.

5.3   Correctness of Annotation and Inversion

This approach is proved to perform correct reversal information saving as well as correct and garbage-free inversion. The two results are described in [34] and extended to hold for all programs including parallel composition in [30]. The first, named the *annotation result*, states that an original program and its annotated version executed on the same initial program state will produce equivalent final program states, with the obvious exception of the annotated execution populating the auxiliary store with the required reversal information.

The second result, named the *inversion result*, states that provided an annotated execution has been performed producing the final program state and auxiliary store, then the corresponding inverse execution ran on these final stores will produce a program state and auxiliary store equivalent to that of prior to the forwards execution. This means the inverse execution reverses all effects of the original program, as well as using all of the reversal information saved (the approach is garbage free). These two results together show that no state is reached that was not originally reached in either the forward or reverse execution.

5.4 Simulator and Performance Evaluation

A simulator implementing this approach has been developed, originally for the purposes of testing [30]. The simulator reads a program written in a simplified language (omitting paths, construct identifiers and removal statements as these can be automatically inserted), parses it and sets up the initial program state. Key features include *complete* or *step-by-step* execution, *viewable program state and reversal information* at any point, *random or manual interleaving* and *record mode* (storing further details including interleaving decisions/rule applications).

This simulator has been used for performance evaluation. Design choices (mentioned above) have been made to aid the proof and may not be the most efficient solution, and no optimisation techniques have yet been applied. This analysis concerns the overhead associated with annotation (time required to save reversal information), and the overhead associated with inversion (inverse execution time compared to annotated forward execution time). From figures in [32], the annotated execution experiences a reasonable overhead of between 4.2%–13.4%, while the inverted execution experiences an again reasonable overhead of between -14.7%–1.9%. As expected, the inverse execution is sometimes faster as there is no evaluation (values retrieved from δ).

5.5 Application to Debugging

Many works including [12, 18, 25, 40, 41, 68] have described how reversibility can be beneficial for debugging. The link between this approach to reversibility and debugging is explored in [32], showing that this simulator (not originally developed as a debugger) helps with finding errors. Benefits include bugs being reproducible should a user wish to re-execute a program forwards (for example, a randomly interleaved program experiences a bug that can only be reproduced by luck, with inversion obviously still possible), the ability to pause executions and to view program state at any point. In [32] and [31], this simulator is used to debug an example atomicity violation.

6 Reversible Debugger for Message Passing Systems

A relevant research thread in WG2 has tackled the problem of debugging concurrent message-passing applications using the so called *causal-consistent* approach. Causal-consistent reversibility [14] stems from the observation that in concurrent systems, events (e.g., sending and receive of messages) are not always totally ordered since there may be no unique notion of time. Even if events are totally ordered in principle, such an order is not relevant since it depends on the speed of execution of the various processes, and it is difficult to observe and even more to control. Instead, events naturally form a partial order dictated by causality: causes precede their consequences, while there is no order between concurrent events. The corresponding notion of reversibility, causal-consistent reversibility, allows one to undo any event, provided that its consequences, if any, are undone beforehand. A main property of this notion of reversibility is that states reachable via backward computation are also reachable via forward computation from the initial state, hence reversibility does not introduce new states but only provides different ways of exploring states of forward computations.

This observation led to the development of *causal-consistent reversible debugging* [25], which allows one to explore a concurrent computation backward and forward, looking for the causes of a given misbehaviour, e.g., a wrong value printed on the screen. Indeed, a misbehaviour is due to a bug, that is a wrong line of code, and the execution of the wrong line of code is a cause of the misbehaviour. More precisely, causal-consistent reversible debugging provides primitives to undo past events, including all and only their consequences. For instance, if variable x has a wrong value, one can go back to where variable x has been assigned. If the wrong value is in a message payload, one can go back where the message has been sent. By iterating this technique, one can look for causes of the misbehaviour until the bug is found.

Inside WG2 the research focused on how to apply this approach to a real programming language, and Erlang was the language of choice. Erlang features native primitives for message-passing concurrency, and has been used in relevant applications such as some versions of Facebook chat [45]. For simplicity, the research thread does not deal directly with Erlang, but with Core Erlang [8], which is an intermediate step in Erlang compilation, essentially removing some syntactic sugar from Erlang.

The research thread started with an investigation on the reversible semantics of Core Erlang, aiming at defining a rollback operator to undo a past action in a causal-consistent way [51]. The study was further developed in [42], where relevant properties of the approach were proved, e.g., that the rollback operator indeed satisfies the constraints of causal-consistent reversibility. The focus on debugging started in [41], where CauDEr [40], a Causal-consistent Debugger for (core) Erlang, was described. CauDEr provided the primitives above for causal-consistent reversible debugging, paired with primitives for forward execution and with a graphical interface to show the runtime structure of the program under analysis and the relevant concurrent events in the computation.

A main limitation of CauDEr was that if the user went too far back, there was no automatic way to go forward again with the guarantee to replay the misbehaviour under analysis. This is a relevant problem, since in concurrent systems misbehaviours depend on the scheduling, and of course it is not possible to debug a misbehaviour that does not appear when executing the wrong application inside the debugger. To solve this problem, the research studied techniques for tracing a computation and replay it inside the debugger. This lead to the definition of a new form of replay, called *causal-consistent replay* [43], which allows one to redo a future event of a traced computation, including all and only its causes. One can notice that causal-consistent reversibility and causal-consistent replay are dual, and together they allow one to explore a wrong computation back and forward, always concentrating on events of interest. Also, this approach ensures that if a misbehaviour occurred in the traced computation then the same misbehaviour occurs also in each possible replay (provided that execution goes forward enough). A tracer for Erlang compatible with CauDEr was produced and is available at [39]. An example of application of this framework to a simple Erlang program can be found in [21].

7   Control Theory

The challenge of reversible control is its interaction with the irreversible object of control. Even when the object is reversible, (e.g. motion of a fluid) often the ability to reverse it is not controllable [61]. Disturbance in the system can be fully reversible, but inacessible to the control mechanism. We explored the elements of reversible control in an applied setting of wireless communications, through two different realistic examples, one of resource management in large antenna arrays, and one of wave time reversal in underwater acoustic communications [62].

In the first example [64], we perform antenna selection in a large distributed antenna array which serves as a distributed base station in a next generation cellular network: at any point in time, we want to use n out of m available antennas to serve $k < n$ users in the cell. The subset of antennas to be used is selected so to maximise the Shannon capacity of the communication channel between the base station and the users, which is a non-trivial optimisation task: selecting simply the antennas with the strongest signal does not help as they tend to be correlated and not contributing to the diversity in the channel. We propose a solution using reversing Petri nets [53] with controlled transitions: tokens (indicating antennas that are "on") move between places (antennas) based on simple calculations at the transitions (do the channel sum rates increase with the change of token position, i.e. reconfiguration of the array?) [54]. The results of experiments with varying number of users show that this distributed approach delivers results on par with computationally demanding centralised approaches, and tend to outperform the competition as the number of users increases. The approach we proposed here is not limited to the problem of antenna selection: in the ongoing work, we extend it to general resource management in wireless setting, using the advantages offered by having a reversible control algorithm, namely fault recovery, partial reversal of the system and repetitive motion handling [65].

In the second example, we focus on wave time reversal, the idea of reconstructing a wave (e.g. an acoustic pulse) by measuring the incoming wave at the boundary of a cavity and then re-transmitting the collected samples in reverse, producing a wave that reconverges at the original source [19]. It is straightforward to see how this scheme can be used to establish a communication channel, and hence be used in a communication scheme in e.g. underwater acoustic communications. We selected sound propagation in water as an example of a reversible (but rarely reversed) medium under control, and proposed a reversible hardware architecture for this task [63]. Here we recognised another control challenge: disturbance compensation. If there is a source of disturbance in the medium (e.g. strong stream in the water) the reconstructed pulse will be distorted and hence the quality of communication will degrade. If we cannot remove the source of disturbance, but are in position to control a different part of the environment based on measurements from sensors in the medium, how can we improve the quality of wave time reversal? The more general question we pose here is whether control of a reversible medium is simpler than control of an irreversible one, and the model we chose to work on is one provided by reversible cellular automata. These automata, in the form of lattice gases, have been extensively used for fluid modelling. In cellular automata, the control problem revolves around the question of reaching a certain configuration from an arbitrary initial configuration [3]. In our consideration of reversible cellular automata, instead of observing the question of reaching a microstate, we investigate the problem of reaching a statistical macrostate in a region of the automaton [4]. The idea of reversible automata control being easier than the general automata control stems from the fact that states in reversible automata have unique predecessors, hence minimising the combinatorics of the arc of transition between an initial and a final state, which is an important element of cellular automata control.

8   Conclusions

We have summarised the main results obtained by the Working Group 2 on Software and System of the COST Action IC1405. In these four years the WG was active and produced important results, as witnessed by this document. Research in applying reversibility to software and systems is ongoing, and some of the guidelines and topics indicated in the MOU [67] were not exhaustively investigated during the lifetime of WG2. The interplay between reversibility and the so called recovery patterns deserves to be further investigated. Also, the integration of reversibility in software development is still at an early stage.

Acknowledgement. The WG2 has been led by Claudio Antares Mezzina and Rudolf Schlatte. For both of us, it has been an enormous honour to lead such WG, to organise the WG meetings and to interact with all the people involved in the working group. A witness of the liveness of the working group is the list of authors who happily contributed to this document. We would also thank Irek Ulidowski (chair) and Ivan Lanese (vice-chair) who wisely have led this COST Action and the Management Committee (MC) who appointed us as leader and co-leader (respectively) of this WG.

References

1. Axelsen, H.B., Glück, R.: Reversible representation and manipulation of constructor terms in the heap. In: Dueck, G.W., Miller, D.M. (eds.) RC 2013. LNCS, vol. 7948, pp. 96–109. Springer, Heidelberg (2013). https://doi.org/10.1007/978-3-642-38986-3_9

2. Axelsen, H.B., Glück, R., Yokoyama, T.: Reversible machine code and its abstract processor architecture. In: Diekert, V., Volkov, M.V., Voronkov, A. (eds.) CSR 2007. LNCS, vol. 4649, pp. 56–69. Springer, Heidelberg (2007). https://doi.org/10.1007/978-3-540-74510-5_9

3. Bagnoli, F., Rechtman, R., El Yacoubi, S.: Control of cellular automata. Phys. Rev. E **86**(6), 066201 (2012)

4. Bagnoli, F., Siljak, H.: Control of reversible cellular automata (2019, Manuscript in preparation)

5. Barbanera, F., Lanese, I., de'Liguoro, U.: A theory of retractable and speculative contracts. Sci. Comput. Program. **167**, 25–50 (2018)

6. Bennett, C.H.: Logical reversibility of computation. IBM J. Res. Dev. **17**(6), 525–532 (1973)

7. Bishop, P.G.: Using reversible computing to achieve fail-safety. In: Proceedings the Eighth International Symposium on Software Reliability Engineering, pp. 182–191, November 1997

8. Carlsson, R., et al.: Core Erlang 1.0.3. Language specification (2004). https://www.it.uu.se/research/group/hipe/cerl/doc/core_erlang-1.0.3.pdf

9. Carothers, C.D., Perumalla, K.S., Fujimoto, R.: Efficient optimistic parallel simulations using reverse computation. ACM Trans. Model. Comput. Simul. **9**(3), 224–253 (1999)

10. Cassar, I., Francalanza, A., Mezzina, C.A., Tuosto, E.: Reliability and fault-tolerance by choreographic design. In: Francalanza, A., Pace, G.J. (eds.) Proceedings Second International Workshop on Pre- and Post-Deployment Verification Techniques, PrePost@iFM 2017. EPTCS, vol. 254, pp. 69–80 (2017)

11. Castellani, I., Dezani-Ciancaglini, M., Giannini, P.: Concurrent reversible sessions. In: Meyer, R., Nestmann, U. (eds.) International Conference on Concurrency Theory, CONCUR 2017. LIPIcs, vol. 85, pp. 30:1–30:17. Schloss Dagstuhl - Leibniz-Zentrum fuer Informatik (2017)

12. Chen, S.-K., Fuchs, W.K., Chung, J.-Y.: Reversible debugging using program instrumentation. IEEE Trans. Softw. Eng. **27**, 715–727 (2001)

13. Cservenka, M.H., Glück, R., Haulund, T., Mogensen, T.Æ.: Data structures and dynamic memory management in reversible languages. In: Kari, J., Ulidowski, I. (eds.) RC 2018. LNCS, vol. 11106, pp. 269–285. Springer, Cham (2018). https://doi.org/10.1007/978-3-319-99498-7_19

14. Danos, V., Krivine, J.: Reversible communicating systems. In: Gardner, P., Yoshida, N. (eds.) CONCUR 2004. LNCS, vol. 3170, pp. 292–307. Springer, Heidelberg (2004). https://doi.org/10.1007/978-3-540-28644-8_19

15. de Vries, F., Pérez, J.A.: Reversible session-based concurrency in Haskell. In: Pałka, M., Myreen, M. (eds.) TFP 2018. LNCS, vol. 11457, pp. 20–45. Springer, Cham (2019). https://doi.org/10.1007/978-3-030-18506-0_2

16. Dezani-Ciancaglini, M., Giannini, P.: Reversible multiparty sessions with checkpoints. In: Gebler, D., Peters, K. (eds.) Proceedings Combined 23rd International Workshop on Expressiveness in Concurrency and 13th Workshop on Structural Operational Semantics, EXPRESS/SOS 2016. EPTCS, vol. 222, pp. 60–74 (2016)

17. Elnozahy, E.N., Zwaenepoel, W.: Manetho: transparent rollback-recovery with low overhead, limited rollback, and fast output commit. IEEE Trans. Comput. **41**(5), 526–531 (1992)

18. Engblom, J.: A review of reverse debugging. In: System, Software, SoC and Silicon Debug, pp. 1–6. IEEE (2012)

19. Fink, M.: Time reversal of ultrasonic fields. I. Basic principles. IEEE Trans. Ultrason. Ferroelectr. Freq. Control **39**(5), 555–566 (1992)

20. Francalanza, A., Mezzina, C.A., Tuosto, E.: Reversible choreographies via monitoring in Erlang. In: Bonomi, S., Rivière, E. (eds.) DAIS 2018. LNCS, vol. 10853, pp. 75–92. Springer, Cham (2018). https://doi.org/10.1007/978-3-319-93767-0_6

21. Francalanza, A., Mezzina, C.A., Tuosto, E.: Towards choreographic-based monitoring. In: Ferreira, C., Lanese, I., Schultz, U., Ulidowski, I. (eds.) Reversible Computation: Theory and Applications. LNCS, vol. 12070. Springer, Heidelberg (2020)

22. Fredkin, E., Toffoli, T.: Conservative logic. Int. J. Theor. Phys. **21**, 219–253 (1982)

23. Gamma, E., Helm, R., Johnson, R., Vlissides, J.: Design Patterns: Elements of Reusable Object-Oriented Software. Addison-Wesley, Boston (1995)

24. Gay, D., Aiken, A.: Language support for regions. In: Proceedings of the ACM SIGPLAN 2001 Conference on Programming Language Design and Implementation, PLDI 2001, pp. 70–80. ACM (2001)

25. Giachino, E., Lanese, I., Mezzina, C.A.: Causal-consistent reversible debugging. In: Gnesi, S., Rensink, A. (eds.) FASE 2014. LNCS, vol. 8411, pp. 370–384. Springer, Heidelberg (2014). https://doi.org/10.1007/978-3-642-54804-8_26

26. Giachino, E., Lanese, I., Mezzina, C.A., Tiezzi, F.: Causal-consistent rollback in a tuple-based language. J. Log. Algebr. Methods Program. **88**, 99–120 (2017)

27. Glück, R., Yokoyama, T.: A linear-time self-interpreter of a reversible imperative language. Comput. Softw. **33**(3), 108–128 (2016)

28. Glück, R., Yokoyama, T.: Constructing a binary tree from its traversals by reversible recursion and iteration. Inf. Process. Lett. **147**, 32–37 (2019)

29. Haulund, T., Mogensen, T.Æ., Glück, R.: Implementing reversible object-oriented language features on reversible machines. In: Phillips, I., Rahaman, H. (eds.) RC 2017. LNCS, vol. 10301, pp. 66–73. Springer, Cham (2017). https://doi.org/10.1007/978-3-319-59936-6_5

30. Hoey, J.: Reversing imperative concurrent programs. Ph.D. thesis, University of Leicester (2020)

31. Hoey, J., Lanese, I., Nishida, N., Ulidowski, I., Vidal, G.: A case study for reversible computing: reversible debugging. In: Ferreira, C., Lanese, I., Schultz, U., Ulidowski, I. (eds.) Reversible Computation: Theory and Applications. LNCS, vol. 12070. Springer, Heidelberg (2020)

32. Hoey, J., Ulidowski, I.: Reversible imperative parallel programs and debugging. In: Thomsen, M.K., Soeken, M. (eds.) RC 2019. LNCS, vol. 11497, pp. 108–127. Springer, Cham (2019). https://doi.org/10.1007/978-3-030-21500-2_7

33. Hoey, J., Ulidowski, I., Yuen, S.: Reversing imperative parallel programs. In: Peters, K., Tini, S. (eds.) Proceedings Combined 24th International Workshop on Expressiveness in Concurrency and 14th Workshop on Structural Operational Semantics, EXPRESS/SOS. EPTCS, vol. 255, pp. 51–66 (2017)

34. Hoey, J., Ulidowski, I., Yuen, S.: Reversing parallel programs with blocks and procedures. In: Pérez, J.A., Tini, S. (eds.) Proceedings Combined 25th International Workshop on Expressiveness in Concurrency and 15th Workshop on Structural Operational Semantics, EXPRESS/SOS. EPTCS, vol. 276, pp. 69–86 (2018)

35. Hüttel, H., et al.: Foundations of session types and behavioural contracts. ACM Comput. Surv. **49**(1), 3:1–3:36 (2016)
36. Knuth, D.E.: The Art of Computer Programming: Fundamental Algorithms. Addison-Wesley, Boston (1998)
37. Landauer, R.: Irreversibility and heat generated in the computing process. IBM J. Res. Dev. **5**, 183–191 (1961)
38. Lanese, I., Mezzina, C.A., Schmitt, A., Stefani, J.-B.: Controlling reversibility in higher-order pi. In: Katoen, J.-P., König, B. (eds.) CONCUR 2011. LNCS, vol. 6901, pp. 297–311. Springer, Heidelberg (2011). https://doi.org/10.1007/978-3-642-23217-6_20
39. Lanese, I., Nishida, N., Palacios, A., Vidal, G.: CauDEr tracer website. https://github.com/mistupv/tracer/
40. Lanese, I., Nishida, N., Palacios, A., Vidal, G.: CauDEr website. https://github.com/mistupv/cauder
41. Lanese, I., Nishida, N., Palacios, A., Vidal, G.: CauDEr: a causal-consistent reversible debugger for Erlang. In: Gallagher, J.P., Sulzmann, M. (eds.) FLOPS 2018. LNCS, vol. 10818, pp. 247–263. Springer, Cham (2018). https://doi.org/10.1007/978-3-319-90686-7_16
42. Lanese, I., Nishida, N., Palacios, A., Vidal, G.: A theory of reversibility for Erlang. J. Log. Algebr. Methods Program. **100**, 71–97 (2018)
43. Lanese, I., Palacios, A., Vidal, G.: Causal-consistent replay debugging for message passing programs. In: Pérez, J.A., Yoshida, N. (eds.) FORTE 2019. LNCS, vol. 11535, pp. 167–184. Springer, Cham (2019). https://doi.org/10.1007/978-3-030-21759-4_10
44. Leeman Jr., G.B.: A formal approach to undo operations in programming languages. ACM Trans. Program. Lang. Syst. **8**(1), 50–87 (1986)
45. Letuchy, E.: Erlang at Facebook (2009). http://www.erlang-factory.com/conference/SFBayAreaErlangFactory2009/speakers/EugeneLetuchy
46. Mezzina, C.A., Pérez, J.A.: Reversible semantics in session-based concurrency. In: Proceedings of the 17th Italian Conference on Theoretical Computer 2016, Volume 1720 of CEUR Workshop Proceedings, pp. 221–226 (2016). CEUR-WS.org
47. Mezzina, C.A., Pérez, J.A.: Reversible sessions using monitors. In: Proceedings of the Ninth Workshop on Programming Language Approaches to Concurrency- and Communication-cEntric Software, PLACES 2016. EPTCS, vol. 211, pp. 56–64 (2016)
48. Mezzina, C.A., Pérez, J.A.: Causally consistent reversible choreographies: a monitors-as-memories approach. In: Vanhoof, W., Pientka, B. (eds.) Proceedings of the 19th International Symposium on Principles and Practice of Declarative Programming, pp. 127–138. ACM (2017)
49. Mezzina, C.A., Pérez, J.A.: Reversibility in session-based concurrency: a fresh look. J. Log. Algebr. Methods Program. **90**, 2–30 (2017)
50. Neykova, R., Yoshida, N.: Let it recover: multiparty protocol-induced recovery. In: 26th International Conference on Compiler Construction, pp. 98–108. ACM (2017)
51. Nishida, N., Palacios, A., Vidal, G.: A reversible semantics for Erlang. In: Hermenegildo, M.V., Lopez-Garcia, P. (eds.) LOPSTR 2016. LNCS, vol. 10184, pp. 259–274. Springer, Cham (2017). https://doi.org/10.1007/978-3-319-63139-4_15
52. Perumalla, K.: Introduction to Reversible Computing. CRC Press, Boca Raton (2014)
53. Philippou, A., Psara, K.: Reversible computation in petri nets. In: Kari, J., Ulidowski, I. (eds.) RC 2018. LNCS, vol. 11106, pp. 84–101. Springer, Cham (2018). https://doi.org/10.1007/978-3-319-99498-7_6

54. Philippou, A., Psara, K., Siljak, H.: Controlling reversibility in reversing petri nets with application to wireless communications. In: Thomsen, M.K., Soeken, M. (eds.) RC 2019. LNCS, vol. 11497, pp. 238–245. Springer, Cham (2019). https://doi.org/10.1007/978-3-030-21500-2_15

55. Phillips, I., Ulidowski, I.: Reversing algebraic process calculi. J. Logic Algebraic Program. **73**(1–2), 70–96 (2007)

56. Phillips, I., Ulidowski, I., Yuen, S.: A reversible process calculus and the modelling of the ERK signalling pathway. In: Glück, R., Yokoyama, T. (eds.) RC 2012. LNCS, vol. 7581, pp. 218–232. Springer, Heidelberg (2013). https://doi.org/10.1007/978-3-642-36315-3_18

57. Schordan, M., Jefferson, D., Barnes, P., Oppelstrup, T., Quinlan, D.: Reverse code generation for parallel discrete event simulation. In: Krivine, J., Stefani, J.-B. (eds.) RC 2015. LNCS, vol. 9138, pp. 95–110. Springer, Cham (2015). https://doi.org/10.1007/978-3-319-20860-2_6

58. Schordan, M., Oppelstrup, T., Jefferson, D., Barnes Jr., P.D., Quinlan, D.J.: Automatic generation of reversible C++ code and its performance in a scalable kinetic Monte-Carlo application. In: SIGSIM-PADS 2016 (2016)

59. Schultz, U.P.: Reversible object-oriented programming with region-based memory management. In: Kari, J., Ulidowski, I. (eds.) RC 2018. LNCS, vol. 11106, pp. 322–328. Springer, Cham (2018). https://doi.org/10.1007/978-3-319-99498-7_22

60. Schultz, U.P., Axelsen, H.B.: Elements of a reversible object-oriented language. In: Devitt, S., Lanese, I. (eds.) RC 2016. LNCS, vol. 9720, pp. 153–159. Springer, Cham (2016). https://doi.org/10.1007/978-3-319-40578-0_10

61. Siljak, H.: Reversibility in space, time, and computation: the case of underwater acoustic communications. In: Kari, J., Ulidowski, I. (eds.) RC 2018. LNCS, vol. 11106, pp. 346–352. Springer, Cham (2018). https://doi.org/10.1007/978-3-319-99498-7_25

62. Siljak, H.: Reversible computation in wireless communications. In: Ferreira, C., Lanese, I., Schultz, U., Ulidowski, I. (eds.) Reversible Computation: Theory and Applications. LNCS, vol. 12070. Springer, Heidelberg (2020)

63. Siljak, H., de Rosny, J., Fink, M.: Reversible hardware for acoustic wave time reversal. IEEE Commun. Mag. **58**(1), 55–61 (2020)

64. Siljak, H., Psara, K., Philippou, A.: Distributed antenna selection for massive MIMO using reversing Petri nets. IEEE Wirel. Commun. Lett. **8**(5), 1427–1430 (2019)

65. Siljak, H., Psara, K., Philippou, A.: Reversing Petri nets for resource management in wireless networks (2019, Manuscript in preparation)

66. Tofte, M., Talpin, J.-P.: Region-based memory management. Inf. Comput. **132**(2), 109–176 (1997)

67. Ulidowski, I.: IC1405 - Reversible Computation: extending horizons of computing - Memorandum of Understanding. https://e-services.cost.eu/files/domain_files/ICT/Action_IC1405/mou/IC1405-e.pdf

68. Undo Software: Undodb. Commercial reversible debugger. http://undo-software.com/

69. Vassor, M., Stefani, J.-B.: Checkpoint/Rollback vs causally-consistent reversibility. In: Kari, J., Ulidowski, I. (eds.) RC 2018. LNCS, vol. 11106, pp. 286–303. Springer, Cham (2018). https://doi.org/10.1007/978-3-319-99498-7_20

70. Vulov, G., Hou, C., Vuduc, R.W., Fujimoto, R., Quinlan, D.J., Jefferson, D.R.: The backstroke framework for source level reverse computation applied to parallel discrete event simulation. In: WSC 2011 (2011)

71. Yokoyama, T., Axelsen, H.B., Glück, R.: Reversible flowchart languages and the structured reversible program theorem. In: Aceto, L., Damgård, I., Goldberg, L.A., Halldórsson, M.M., Ingólfsdóttir, A., Walukiewicz, I. (eds.) ICALP 2008. LNCS, vol. 5126, pp. 258–270. Springer, Heidelberg (2008). https://doi.org/10.1007/978-3-540-70583-3_22

72. Yokoyama, T., Axelsen, H.B., Glück, R.: Towards a reversible functional language. In: De Vos, A., Wille, R. (eds.) RC 2011. LNCS, vol. 7165, pp. 14–29. Springer, Heidelberg (2012). https://doi.org/10.1007/978-3-642-29517-1_2

73. Yokoyama, T., Glück, R.: A reversible programming language and its invertible self-interpreter. In: Partial Evaluation and Program Manipulation, Proceedings, pp. 144–153. ACM (2007)

Simulation and Design of Quantum Circuits

Alwin Zulehner and Robert Wille[✉]

Institute for Integrated Circuits, Johannes Kepler University Linz, Linz, Austria
{alwin.zulehner,robert.wille}@jku.at

Abstract. Currently, there is an ongoing "race" to build the first practically useful quantum computer that provides substantial speed-ups for certain problems compared to conventional computers. In addition to the development of such devices, this also requires the development of automated tools and methods that provide assistance in the simulation and design of corresponding applications. Otherwise, a situation might be reached where we have powerful quantum computers but hardly any proper means to actually use them. This work provides an overview of corresponding solutions for the task of quantum circuit simulation, the task of quantum circuit design, as well as corresponding mapping tasks. The covered solutions utilise expertise on efficient data structures and algorithms gained in the design of conventional circuits and systems over the last decades. While the respective descriptions are kept brief and mainly convey the general ideas, references to further readings are provided for a more detailed treatment.

1 Introduction

In quantum computing, so-called quantum bits (i.e., qubits) serve as elementary information unit, which—in contrast to conventional bits—can not only be in one of its two orthogonal basis states (denoted $|0\rangle$ and $|1\rangle$ using Dirac notation), but also in superposition (i.e., a linear combination) of both [1]. Together with further quantum-physical phenomena such as entanglement (the state of a qubit might be influenced by the state of other qubits), this allows that the pure state of a quantum system composed of n qubits may represent a superposition of 2^n basis states and corresponding complex amplitudes—resulting in higher information density and computational power.

Well-known initial representatives of quantum algorithms following this powerful computation paradigm are Grover's search algorithm [2] and Shor's algorithm for integer factorisation in polynomial time [3]—both allowing to significantly outperform conventional machines. Recently, the application area of quantum algorithms has significantly broadened and provides efficient methods in areas like chemistry, solving systems of linear equations, physics simulations, machine learning, and many more [4–6].

These developments are also triggered by the fact that quantum computers are reaching feasibility since "big players" such as *IBM*, *Google*, *Microsoft*, and

I. Ulidowski et al. (Eds.): RC 2020, LNCS 12070, pp. 60–82, 2020.
https://doi.org/10.1007/978-3-030-47361-7_3

Intel as well as specialised startups such as *Rigetti* and *IonQ* have entered this research field and are heavily investing in it [7–11]. In 2017, this led to the first quantum computers that are publicly available through cloud access by IBM. Since then, their machines have been used by more than 100,000 users, who have run more than 6.5 million experiments thus far. Recently, IBM followed with the presentation of their prototype towards a quantum computer for commercial use (a stand-alone quantum computer to be operated outside of their labs)—the *IBM Q System One* presented in January 2019 at CES [12].

Since currently available quantum computers are still limited in the number of qubits, gate fidelity, as well as coherence time, they are classified as *Noisy Intermediate Scale Quantum* (NISQ [5]) devices that will only be able to successfully run some of the quantum algorithms outlined above (due to their limitations). In fact, unveiling the full potential of quantum computing requires—besides further reduction of error rates and improvement of coherence time—error-correcting codes where each logical qubit in a computation is realised by several (up to several hundreds) of physical qubits—eventually resulting in *fault-tolerant* devices that are capable of conducting very deep computations on a large number of qubits and with perfect accuracy [13,14].

In addition to these accomplishments and prospects, also the development of automated tools and methods that provide assistance in the simulation and design of corresponding applications is required. In this regard, the task of quantum circuit simulation, the task of quantum circuit design, as well as corresponding mapping tasks are important. Since modelling (arbitrary) quantum states on conventional machines requires exponential overhead and many design problems are of exponential nature, straightforward solutions for these tasks will not scale to relevant problem sizes. Hence, clever data-structures and algorithms are required that allow for efficient solutions (at least) in certain cases. Otherwise, we are approaching a situation where we might have powerful quantum computers but hardly any proper means to actually use them.

This work provides an overview on solutions which have been developed for these tasks and utilise expertise on efficient data structures and algorithms gained in the design automation community over the last decades for conventional circuits and systems. To this end, the simulation of quantum circuits, their design, as well as technology mapping (compiling) are covered and discussed from a design automation perspective. The reviewed solutions often yield improvements of several orders of magnitude compared to the current state of the art (regarding runtime and corresponding design objectives)—showing the tremendous available potential.

The overview is thereby structured as follows: First, Sect. 2 provides a background on quantum computing. Afterwards, Sect. 3, Sect. 4, and Sect. 5 sketch the developed methods for the considered design tasks, i.e., quantum-circuit simulation, the design of Boolean components occurring in quantum algorithms, as well as mapping quantum circuits to real hardware (including references to further reading for a more detailed treatment). Finally, Sect. 6 concludes the paper.

2   Background on Quantum Computing

Quantum computations operate on *qubits*—two-level quantum systems that can be combined into n-qubit systems. The state of a qubit is given by a linear combination (i.e., a *superposition*) of these basis states $|\varphi\rangle = \alpha_0 \cdot |0\rangle + \alpha_1 \cdot |1\rangle$, where the complex *amplitudes* α_0 and α_1 satisfy $\alpha_0\alpha_0^* + \alpha_1\alpha_1^* = 1$.

The joint state of n qubits (also denoted as the system's *wave function*) is contained in the *tensor product* of n two-dimensional Hilbert spaces—the 2^n-dimensional Hilbert space spanned by the basis $|0\rangle, \ldots, |2^n - 1\rangle$. Hence, a *superposition* of all computational basis states may need up to 2^n complex-valued parameters—appearing as the amplitudes of the unit-norm state vector.

Definition 1. *Consider a quantum system composed of n qubits. Then, all possible states of the system are of the form*

$$|\varphi\rangle = \sum_{x \in \{0,1\}^n} \alpha_x \cdot |x\rangle, \ \text{where} \ \sum_{x \in \{0,1\}^n} \alpha_x\alpha_x^* = 1 \ \text{and} \ \alpha_x \in \mathbb{C}.$$

The state $|\varphi\rangle$ can be also represented by a column vector $\varphi = [\varphi_i]$ with $0 \le i < 2^n$ and $\varphi_i = \alpha_x$, where $nat(x) = i$.

Quantum states cannot be directly observed. To extract (partial) information from quantum states in the form of conventional bits, one performs a *measurement operation*. In contrast to conventional computers, this measurement modifies the quantum state. In the process of measurement, the quantum state non-deterministically collapses to one of these basis states where the probability of each outcome reflects the proximity to the respective basis state. More precisely, measuring a one-qubit state $\alpha_0 \cdot |0\rangle + \alpha_1 \cdot |1\rangle$ (with $\alpha_0\alpha_0^* + \alpha_1\alpha_1^* = 1$) changes the state to $|0\rangle$ or $|1\rangle$ with probabilities $\alpha_0\alpha_0^*$ and $\alpha_1\alpha_1^*$, respectively.

Example 1. *Consider a quantum system composed of $n = 3$ qubits q_0, q_1, and q_2 that assumes the state $|\varphi\rangle = |q_0q_1q_2\rangle = \frac{1}{2} \cdot |010\rangle + \frac{1}{2} \cdot |100\rangle - \frac{1}{\sqrt{2}} \cdot |110\rangle$. Then, the state vector of the system is given by*

$$\varphi = \left[0, 0, \frac{1}{2}, 0, \frac{1}{2}, 0, -\frac{1}{\sqrt{2}}, 0\right]^T.$$

Measuring the system yields basis states $|010\rangle$, $|100\rangle$, and $|110\rangle$ with probabilities $\frac{1}{4}$, $\frac{1}{4}$, and $\frac{1}{2}$, respectively. Measuring only qubit q_0 collapses q_0 into basis state $|0\rangle$ and $|1\rangle$ with probabilities $\frac{1}{4}$ and $\frac{1}{4} + \frac{1}{2} = \frac{3}{4}$, respectively—changing the state of the system either to $|\varphi'\rangle = |010\rangle$ or to $|\varphi''\rangle = \frac{1}{\sqrt{3}} \cdot |100\rangle - \sqrt{\frac{2}{3}} \cdot |110\rangle$.

Aside from measurements, quantum computers apply quantum operations to a fixed set of qubits, altering the joint state of the qubits in a reversible fashion. These operations are described by unitary matrices of size $2^n \times 2^n$. Simple quantum operations (also denoted *gates*) are defined over one or two qubits only. Mathematically speaking, the resulting $2^n \times 2^n$ matrix can then be computed as the Kronecker product of the matrix representing the gate's operation and a large identity matrix.

Commonly used quantum gates for generating a superposition (the Hadamard operation H), inverting a quantum state (X), and applying phase shifts by -1 (Z), are respectively defined as

$$H = \tfrac{1}{\sqrt{2}} \begin{bmatrix} 1 & 1 \\ 1 & -1 \end{bmatrix}, \text{NOT} = X = \begin{bmatrix} 0 & 1 \\ 1 & 0 \end{bmatrix}, Z = \begin{bmatrix} 1 & 0 \\ 0 & -1 \end{bmatrix}.$$

Two-qubit gates can couple pairs of qubits and are represented by 4×4 unitary matrices. By applying arbitrary two-qubit gates to different pairs of qubits, it is possible to effect any 2^n-dimensional unitary, i.e., attain universal quantum computation (each quantum functionality can be realised with those gates). It is common to allow a variety of one-qubit gates but limit two-qubit gates, e.g., to CNOT gates:

$$\text{CNOT} = \begin{bmatrix} 1 & 0 & 0 & 0 \\ 0 & 1 & 0 & 0 \\ 0 & 0 & 0 & 1 \\ 0 & 0 & 1 & 0 \end{bmatrix}.$$

The two-qubit CNOT gate can also be defined by its action $|x\ y\rangle \mapsto |x\ x \oplus y\rangle$, where $\oplus$ represents the *exclusive-or* (XOR) operation, the unmodified qubit x is called *control*, and the other bit is called *target*.

Quantum circuits [1] are used as proper description means for a finite sequence of "small" gates that cumulatively enact some unitary operator U and, given an initial state $|\varphi\rangle$ (which is usually the basis state $|0\ldots0\rangle$), produce a final state vector $|\varphi'\rangle = |U\varphi\rangle$. Hence, a quantum gate does not represent a physical entity (like in the conventional realm), rather an operation that is applied to a set of qubits.

Definition 2. *In quantum circuits, the qubits are vertically aligned in a circuit diagram, and the time axis (read from left to right) is represented by a horizontal line for each qubit. Boxes on the time axis of a qubit (or enclosing several qubits) indicate gates to be applied.[1] Note that measurement also counts as quantum operation in this context. Control qubits are indicated by • and are connected to the controlled operations by a single line.*

Example 2. *Figure 1 shows a quantum circuit. The circuit contains two qubits, q_0 and q_1, which are both initialised with basis state $|0\rangle$. First, a Hadamard operation is applied to qubit q_0, which is represented by a box labelled H. Then, a CNOT operation is conducted, where q_0 is the control qubit (denoted by •) and q_1 is the target qubit (denoted by $\oplus$). Eventually, qubit q_0 is measured as indicated by the meter symbol.*

When two gates are applied on the same qubits in sequence, the resulting operation is represented by the matrix product of gate matrices. When an

---

[1] Note that an X gate may also be denoted by $\oplus$.

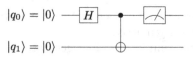

Fig. 1. Quantum circuit.

m-qubit gate A and an n-qubit gate B are applied in parallel (on different qubits), the resulting operation is represented by the *Kronecker product* $A \otimes B$ of two matrices.

Example 3. *Consider again the quantum circuit shown in Fig. 1. The resulting state $|\varphi'\rangle$ (before measurement) is determined by multiplying the respective unitary matrices to the state vector. Since the Hadamard gate shall only affect q_0, the Kronecker product of* H *and the identity matrix I_2 is formed, i.e.,*

$$H \otimes I_2 = \frac{1}{\sqrt{2}} \begin{bmatrix} 1 & 1 \\ 1 & -1 \end{bmatrix} \otimes \begin{bmatrix} 1 & 0 \\ 0 & 1 \end{bmatrix} = \frac{1}{\sqrt{2}} \begin{bmatrix} 1 & 0 & 1 & 0 \\ 0 & 1 & 0 & 1 \\ 1 & 0 & -1 & 0 \\ 0 & 1 & 0 & -1 \end{bmatrix}.$$

Then, $|\varphi'\rangle$ is determined by

$$|\varphi'\rangle = \begin{bmatrix} 1 & 0 & 0 & 0 \\ 0 & 1 & 0 & 0 \\ 0 & 0 & 0 & 1 \\ 0 & 0 & 1 & 0 \end{bmatrix} \cdot \frac{1}{\sqrt{2}} \begin{bmatrix} 1 & 0 & 1 & 0 \\ 0 & 1 & 0 & 1 \\ 1 & 0 & -1 & 0 \\ 0 & 1 & 0 & -1 \end{bmatrix} \cdot \begin{bmatrix} 1 \\ 0 \\ 0 \\ 0 \end{bmatrix} = \frac{1}{\sqrt{2}} \begin{bmatrix} 1 \\ 0 \\ 0 \\ 1 \end{bmatrix}.$$

As can be seen, the two gates entangle the qubits q_0 and q_1—generating a so-called Bell state $|\varphi'\rangle = \frac{1}{\sqrt{2}}(|00\rangle + |11\rangle)$. Measuring qubit q_0 collapses its superposition into one of the two basis states. Since q_0 and q_1 are entangled, q_1 collapses to the same basis state.

3 Quantum-Circuit Simulation

Since physical realisations of quantum computers are limited in their availability, their number of qubits, their gate fidelity, and coherence time, quantum-circuit simulators running on conventional machines are required for many tasks. From a user's perspective, possible applications (or at least their prototypes) for quantum computers are usually first evaluated through simulators that serve as temporary substitute. Moreover, simulation can be adapted to circuit equivalence-checking and other functional verification tasks useful for circuit designers [15–17]. Simulation also plays an important role for designers of quantum systems, e.g., to foster the development of error-correcting codes. Besides that, the urgent need of verifying quantum hardware might be conducted (at least some of the required verification tasks) by comparing runs on these machines to simulation outcome [18,19]. Ultimately, quantum-circuit simulation capabilities provide an estimate on *quantum supremacy* [18] as well as to identify classes of circuits where no quantum speed-up is reachable (i.e., in case these circuits can be simulated efficiently on a conventional machine). In all these scenarios, simulators may give additional insights since, e.g., the precise amplitudes of a quantum state are explicitly determined (while they are not observable in a real quantum computer).

However, quantum-circuit simulation in general constitutes a computationally very complex task since each quantum gate and each quantum state is eventually represented by a unitary matrix or state vector that grows exponentially with the number of qubits. In fact, each quantum operation applied to a quantum state composed of n qubits requires multiplying a $2^n \times 2^n$-dimensional matrix with a 2^n-dimensional vector.[2] This constitutes a serious bottleneck, which prevents the simulation of many quantum applications and, by this, the evaluation of their potential. In fact, the array-like representation of the state vector in current state-of-the-art simulators limits the number of qubits to be simulated to approximately 30 on a modern computer (and to 50 when considering supercomputers with petabytes of distributed memory) [20].

This section presents a complementary simulation approach that aims for overcoming this memory bottleneck (based on [21]). To this end, dedicated *Decision Diagrams* (DDs) are developed, which reduce the memory requirements by representing redundancies in the occurring vectors and matrices by means of shared nodes. This allows gaining significant improvements compared to straightforward realisations (relying on array-like representations) in many cases—often reducing the simulation time from several hours or days to seconds or minutes.[3]

3.1 General Idea

The general idea of the presented complementary approach is to exploit redundancies in the 2^n-dimensional vectors representing quantum states. To this end, decision diagram techniques (similar to those from the conventional realm) are employed. More precisely, a given state vector with entries being complex numbers is decomposed into sub-vectors. To this end, consider a quantum system with qubits $q_0, q_1, \ldots q_{n-1}$, whereby without loss of generality q_0 represents the most significant qubit. Then, the first 2^{n-1} entries of the corresponding state vector represent the amplitudes for the basis states with q_0 set to $|0\rangle$; the other entries represent the amplitudes for states with q_0 set to $|1\rangle$. This decomposition is represented in a decision diagram structure by a node labelled q_0 and two successors leading to nodes representing the sub-vectors. The sub-vectors are

---

[2] Note that different simulation approaches exist that do not compute the complete final state vector, and that it is usually not necessary to represent the exponentially large matrix explicitly. However, this does not decrease the exponential complexity.

[3] Note that previous DD-based simulators (e.g., *QuIDDPro* [22]) did not get established due to their limited applicability (i.e., they provide improvements in rather few cases).

recursively decomposed further until vectors of size 1 (i.e., a complex number) result. This eventually represents the amplitude α_i for the basis state and is given by a terminal node. During these decompositions, equivalent sub-vectors are represented by the same node—allowing for sharing and, hence, a reduction of the memory complexity. An example illustrates the idea.

Example 4. *Consider a quantum system with $n = 3$ qubits situated in a state given by the following vector:*

$$\varphi = \left[0, 0, \frac{1}{2}, 0, \frac{1}{2}, 0, -\frac{1}{\sqrt{2}}, 0\right]^T.$$

Applying the decompositions described above yields a decision diagram as shown in Fig. 2a. The left (right) outgoing edge of each node labelled q_i points to a node representing the sub-vector with all amplitudes for the basis states with q_i set to $|0\rangle$ ($|1\rangle$). Following a path from the root to the terminal node yields the respective entry. For example, following the path highlighted bold in Fig. 2a provides the amplitude for the basis state with $q_0 = |1\rangle$ (right edge), $q_1 = |1\rangle$ (right edge), and $q_2 = |0\rangle$ (left edge), i.e., $-\frac{1}{\sqrt{2}}$ which is exactly the amplitude for basis state $|110\rangle$ (seventh entry in the vector). Since some sub-vectors are equal (e.g., $\left[\frac{1}{2}, 0\right]^T$ represented by the left node labelled q_2), sharing is possible.

However, even more sharing is possible since sub-vectors often differ in a common factor only. This is additionally exploited in the proposed representation by denoting common factors of amplitudes as weights attached to the edges of the decision diagram. Then, the value of an amplitude for a basis state is determined by following the path from the root to the terminal, and additionally multiplying the weights of the edges along this path. Again, an example illustrates the idea.

Example 4 (continued). *As can be seen, the sub-vectors represented by the nodes labelled q_2 (i.e., $\left[\frac{1}{2}, 0\right]^T$ and $\left[-\frac{1}{\sqrt{2}}, 0\right]^T$) differ in a common factor only.*

In the decision diagram shown in Fig. 2b, both sub-trees are merged. This is possible since the corresponding value of the amplitudes is now determined not by the terminals, but the weights on the respective paths. As an example, consider again the path highlighted bold representing the amplitude for the basis state $|110\rangle$. Since this path includes the weights $\frac{1}{2}$, 1, $-\sqrt{2}$, and 1, an amplitude of $\frac{1}{2} \cdot 1 \cdot (-\sqrt{2}) \cdot 1 = -\frac{1}{\sqrt{2}}$ results.

Note that, of course, various possibilities exist to factorise an amplitude. Hence, a normalisation is applied which assumes the left edge to inherit a weight of 1. More precisely, the weights w_l and w_r of the left and right edge are both divided by w_l and this common factor is propagated upwards to the parents of the node. If $w_l = 0$, the node is normalised by propagating w_r upwards to the parents of the node.

The idea used for representing state vectors by means of DDs can be extended to also represent unitary matrices. Here, each DD-node has four successors that

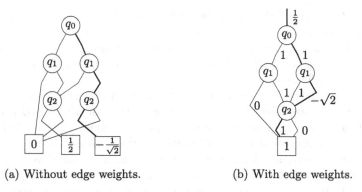

(a) Without edge weights.   (b) With edge weights.

Fig. 2. DD-based representation of state vectors.

represent the four quadrants of the sub-matrix. Having description means for state vectors and unitary matrices (describing the functionality of gates) it is left to provide algorithms for matrix-vector multiplication as well as for measurement. Fortunately, all these operations can be directly employed on the DDs and without the need of explicitly representing the underlying exponentially large entities. For further details we refer to [21].

3.2 Resulting Approaches

Following the general idea outlined above leads to a simulation approach that scales polynomially with the size of the DD representing the state vector. Since the DD often remains rather compact, significant improvements can be observed compared to straightforward Schrödinger-style simulators as well as to previous DD-based simulators in many cases—even though these techniques have been heavily optimised over the last decade and utilise multiple CPU-cores to reduce simulation time (while the proposed approach utilises a single core only). More precisely, the approach proposed in [21] is capable of (1) simulating quantum computations for more qubits than before, (2) in significantly less run-time, and (3) on a regular Desktop machine.

For further details on the basic ideas and required algorithms of the DD-based simulator we refer to [21,23]. Moreover, [21] shows that for many cases, the simulation time can be reduced from several days to just a few seconds or minutes. This initial version of a DD-based simulator did not only lead to a significant improvement compared to the current state of the art, but has also received significant acknowledgement by the community—triggering further optimisations as done for array-based Schrödinger-style simulators for more than a decade.

Using DDs for representing occurring vectors and matrices, the complexity of multiplications depends on the size (i.e, the number of nodes) of the respective operands in DD-based simulation. Together with the fact that the DDs for the usually considered gate matrices are linear in size (with respect to the number of qubits), this implies that it might be beneficial to combine gate operations before applying them to the state vector. In [24], strategies are described for combining operations that allow improving the initial version of the proposed DD-based simulator significantly—up to several orders of magnitude when exploiting application-specific knowledge.

Enormous improvements compared to the state of the art as described above obviously require an efficient implementation of the underlying DD-package—especially for handling the occurring complex numbers. By providing such techniques—in joint consideration of implementation techniques for decision diagrams in the conventional domain developed decades ago—the development of a powerful DD-package for the quantum domain was leveraged in [25]. The evaluation conducted in [25] showed that complex numbers can be handled much more efficiently than in previous implementations and that decision diagrams for established quantum functionality is constructed in significantly less run-time (up to several orders of magnitude). Presumably, this performance boost can be easily passed to DD-based methods for other design automation tasks like synthesis [26,27] or verification [15–17], just by incorporating this new package.

Since handling complex numbers is crucial in DDs for quantum computation (especially when occurring as edge weights), the resulting trade-off between accuracy and compactness has been thoroughly discussed and evaluated in [28]. Since this trade-off requires fine-tuning of parameters on a case-by-case basis and might still yield useless results, an algebraic decision diagram is proposed in [28] to overcome this issue. The proposed algebraic representation guarantees perfect accuracy while remaining compact (all redundancies that are actually present are detected)—with moderate overhead in many cases.

All the endeavours listed above have been implemented in C/C++ and made publicly available at http://iic.jku.at/eda/research/quantum_simulation. Besides that, a stand-alone version of the developed DD-package is available at http://iic.jku.at/eda/research/quantum_dd. Together with the significant improvements gained compared to the state of the art, this did not only result in acknowledgement inside the academic community, but also received interest from big players in the field. More precisely, the developed simulation approach has been acknowledged with a *Google Research Faculty Award* and has recently been officially integrated into IBM's SDK *Qiskit*. This further emphasises the potential of DD-based design methods in the quantum domain—hopefully leading to as powerful DD-based methods as taken for granted in the conventional domain today. Questions on whether hybrid approaches are possible or whether concurrent approaches as well as approximation schemes can be exploited remain open issues for future work. First results towards these questions are provided in [29,30].

4   Design of Boolean Components for Quantum Circuits

Estimating resource requirements of quantum algorithms (i.e., the number of required qubits and run-time on quantum computers), their simulation, or their execution on real hardware requires compiling quantum algorithms containing high-level operations (e.g., modular exponentiation in Shor's algorithm) into quantum circuits composed of elementary gates available on the considered target architecture. Thereby, quantum circuits composed of gates with multiple control qubits (multiple-controlled qubit gates) are usually considered since they (1) describe a rather low-level but still technology independent description of the algorithm, (2) can be directly handled by most simulators, and (3) are usually utilised as input for technology mapping algorithms (which will be covered in the next section).

For the "quantum part" of an algorithm, a decomposition into multiple-controlled qubit gates is usually inherently given by the algorithm, by using common building blocks like a *Quantum Fourier Transform* (QFT [31]), or determined by hand. However, this is different for large Boolean components that are contained in many quantum algorithms, e.g., the modular exponentiation in Shor's algorithm for integer factorisation [3] or a Boolean description of the database that is queried in Grover's algorithm [2].

Even though the functionality of the Boolean components can be described in the conventional domain, corresponding design methods cannot be utilised since the inherent reversibility of quantum computations has to be considered. In fact, determining circuits composed of reversible gates only, requires dedicated *reversible-circuit synthesis* approaches. To manage the complex functionality of Boolean components, they are usually split into several (non-)reversible parts [32]. However, these resulting non-reversible sub-functions have to be *embedded* into reversible ones to ensure the desired unique mapping from inputs to outputs—a task that can either be conducted explicitly or implicitly. This embedding process requires adding several so-called *ancillary qubits*, which shall be kept as small as possible since qubits are a highly limited resource. Besides that, T-count and T-depth of the synthesised reversible circuits serve as cost metric to compare different approaches that yield circuits with an equal (or at least a close-to equal) number of qubits.

This section focuses on the *functional* design flow for synthesising Boolean components (where the reversible function resulting from an explicit embedding step is passed to synthesis algorithm) since it yields circuits with a moderate number of qubits (often the minimum). Investigating this problem from a design automation perspective allows developing efficient methods utilising the decision diagrams introduced in the context of simulation (cf. Sect. 3) [33–35]. However, there is even more (yet) unused potential that allows synthesising cheaper circuits, yields better scalability, and even reduces the number of required qubits below what is currently considered as the minimum (for certain cases)—significantly improving the current state of the art.

4.1   One-Pass Design of Reversible Circuits

Despite using efficient description means like DDs for functional synthesis, the currently established design flow still suffers from the need to conduct embedding and actual synthesis separately—a major drawback that prohibits the exploitation of a huge degree of freedom since embedding is not necessarily conducted in a fashion, which suits the following synthesis step. To overcome this drawback, the work [36,37] introduced a completely new design flow that combines functional synthesis and the embedding to a *one-pass design flow*. This generic flow is not bound to a certain functional synthesis approach and—for the first time—exploits the available degree of freedom to significantly increase scalability and to reduce the costs of the synthesised circuit while keeping the number of required qubits at the minimum.

In the established flow, an individual step is required that embeds the non-reversible function to be synthesised into a reversible one. Thereby, $k = \lceil \log_2 \mu(p_1) \rceil$ further so-called garbage outputs are added (assuming that the most frequent output pattern p_1 occurs $\mu(p_1)$ times) and the additional rows and columns of the truth table are assigned such that a unique mapping from inputs and outputs results [33]. Passing a non-reversible function directly to a functional reversible-circuit synthesis approach will fail, since several input combinations shall be mapped to the same output combination. This can be avoided in two ways:

– Following the *exact* solution guarantees to result in a circuit requiring the minimum number of qubits. The general idea is to add k further variables to the function description (e.g., a DD), but keep all additional entries in the function *don't care*—allowing to exploit the available degree of freedom of their assignment (which does not matter as long as a reversible function results). Having these additional variables allows conducting synthesis (almost) as usual. During synthesis, the *don't cares* are inherently assigned (1) in a way that suits best to the synthesis algorithm, and (2) such that a reversible function results (since only reversible gates are added to the circuit).
– Following the *heuristic* solution does not necessarily result in a circuit requiring the minimum number of qubits, but still bounded. The general idea is to conduct synthesis without embedding. Whenever an error is encountered during synthesis (i.e., synthesis cannot proceed due to the missing embedding step), the function to be synthesised is modified such that the algorithms can continue. Since this obviously results in a circuit different to the intended one, the modifications of the function are stored on so-called buffer-lines (at most one buffer line is required for each variable of the function). After synthesis finishes, these modifications are reverted by a single CNOT gate for each buffer line.
The advantage of the heuristic approach is that no additional variables are added to the function description (as done in the usual functional design flow and the exact one-pass design). Hence, this heuristic approach is even more scalable that the exact solution since the function description remains smaller.

Example 5. *Consider a function $f : \mathbb{B}^n \to \mathbb{B}^m$ with n inputs and m outputs and assume that the most frequent output pattern occurs $\mu(p_1)$ times. Then,* *following the exact solution, the f is enriched by $k = \lceil \log_2 \mu(p_1) \rceil$ further outputs to make all output patterns distinguishable. Hence, the synthesis is conducted on a function with $\max(n, m + k)$ variables—like in the established design flow. However, the additional entries in the truth table remain* don't care *initially and are assigned 0 or 1 during synthesis as suitable.*

Instead, the heuristic solution conducts synthesis directly on f and, hence $\max(n, m)$ variables. The modifications made to f during synthesis require at most $\min(n, m)$ buffer lines—resulting in a quantum circuit with at most $n + m$ qubits.

The evaluations provided in [36] show the advantages of the one-pass design flow (which can be also applied to other functional synthesis approaches) compared to the conventional two-stage design flow. Besides substantial speedups compared to the state-of-the-art design flow, the T-count is reduced by several orders of magnitude in most cases—clearly outperforming the currently established functional design flow for reversible circuits where embedding and synthesis are conducted separately. For further details, we refer to [36].

4.2   Exploiting Coding Techniques

The proposed one-pass design flow can be enriched with the idea of exploiting coding techniques in order to reduce the number of variables that have to be considered during synthesis [38].[4] This idea is based on the fact, that the output patterns in non-reversible functions are not uniformly distributed—leading to a situation where some patterns require many additional outputs while others require only a few. Hence, several garbage outputs are required only for certain output patters. Avoiding this overhead provides significant potential for improving synthesis. In fact, employing a variable-length code allows realising any non-reversible function with a single ancillary qubit only—allowing conducting synthesis on significantly fewer variables than before [39]. The key idea is to represent frequently occurring output patterns (which require more garbage outputs) with a smaller number of variables. Vice versa, less frequently occurring patterns (which require less garbage outputs) are represented with a larger number of variables. In other words, coding techniques are utilised in order to encode the desired function with a variable-length code in which the length of the code word for an output pattern p_i is indirectly proportional to the number $\mu(p_i)$ of times the pattern occurs. An example illustrates that.

Example 6. *Consider the Boolean function shown in Table 1a and its distribution of the output patterns as shown in Table 1b. Following, e.g., the exact one-pass design flow outlined above results in a function with 5 inputs/outputs since the most frequent output pattern $p_1 = 010$ occurs four times and, thus, requires two garbage outputs. However, using a variable-length code as shown in*

---

[4] Note that exploiting coding techniques is also possible in the original design flow composed of an embedding and a synthesis step.

Table 1. Variable-length encoding for one-pass design.

| (a) Orig. function | (b) Output patterns | (c) Encoding | (d) Encoded function |

x_0 x_1 x_2	y_0 y_1 y_2	i	p_i	$\mu(p_i)$	i	p_i	$c(p_i)$	x_0 x_1 x_2	y_0 y_1 y_2
0 0 0	0 1 0	1	010	4	1	010	0 - -	0 0 0	0 - -
0 0 1	0 1 0	2	100	2	2	100	1 0 -	0 0 1	0 - -
0 1 0	1 0 0	3	001	1	3	001	1 1 0	0 1 0	1 0 -
0 1 1	1 0 0	4	011	1	4	011	1 1 1	0 1 1	1 0 -
1 0 0	0 1 1	5	000	0				1 0 0	1 1 1
1 0 1	0 1 0	6	101	0				1 0 1	0 - -
1 1 0	0 1 0	7	110	0				1 1 0	0 - -
1 1 1	0 0 1	8	111	0				1 1 1	1 1 0

Table 1c allows reducing the number of required qubits. There, the most frequent output pattern is encoded by $c(p_1) = 0$. Since this pattern requires two garbage outputs, in total $1+2 = 3$ outputs are required.[5] The second most frequent output pattern $p_2 = 100$ is encoded by $c(p_2) = 10$. Since this pattern occurs only twice, one garbage output is required—again resulting in $2 + 1 = 3$ outputs. The patterns p_3 and p_4 are encoded by $c(p_3) = 110$ and $c(p_4) = 111$, respectively. Here, no garbage outputs are required. The remaining patterns (p_5 to p_8) do not have to be encoded, since they never occur. Overall, this yields an (encoded) reversible function which embeds f as shown in Table 1d and is composed of a total of 3 inputs/outputs only—two qubits fewer than without using coding.

The code is computed by generating a *Pseudo-Huffman* tree: Starting with terminal nodes—one for each output pattern with $\mu(p_i) > 0$ (no code has to be assigned to output patterns that do not occur)—with attached weights representing the number of respectively required garbage outputs (i.e., $\lceil \log_2 \mu(p_i) \rceil$), the *Pseudo-Huffman* tree is then generated by repeatedly combining the two nodes a and b with the smallest attached weights $w(a)$ and $w(b)$ to a new node c with weight $w(c) = \max(w(a), w(b)) + 1$ until a single node results. The weight of such a node $w(c)$ then gives the number of outputs required to represent all combined output patterns uniquely, i.e., one additional variable is required (aside from $\max(w(a), w(b))$) to distinguish between a and b.

Example 7. *Consider the distribution of the output patterns as shown in Table 1b. Determining the Pseudo-Huffman code starts with the nodes v_1, v_2, v_3, and v_4—one for each output pattern p_i with $\mu(p_i) > 0$. These nodes are shown at the bottom of Fig. 3. The weights are drawn inside the respective nodes. The weight of node v_1 is $w_1 = k_1 = 2$, because output pattern $p_1 = 010$ requires two garbage outputs. The weights of the nodes representing p_2, p_3, and p_4 are 1, 0, and 0, respectively. In a first step, the nodes v_3 and v_4 (both have weight 0) are combined. The resulting node v_5 has a weight of $w_5 = \max(0,0) + 1 = 1$. Next, the two nodes with weight 1 (i.e., v_2 and v_5) are combined. The resulting node*

---

[5] The garbage outputs are represented by a dash, since they represent *don't care* values (as long as it is ensured that the resulting function is reversible).

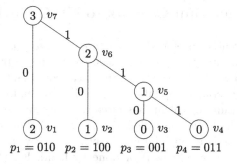

Fig. 3. Huffman tree for the function from Table 1a.

v_6 has a weight of $w_6 = \max(1,1) + 1 = 2$. Finally, the two remaining nodes are combined to a new node v_7 with weight $w_7 = \max(2,2) + 1 = 3$—eventually resulting in the tree shown in Fig. 3.

After generating the Pseudo-Huffman tree, the overall number of variables that are required to realise the encoded function is given by the weight of the root node of the tree. The resulting code is inherently given by the structure of the Pseudo-Huffman tree. In fact, each path from the root node to a leaf node represents a code word, where taking the left (right) edge implies a 0 (1).

Example 7 (continued). *Since the root node has a weight of 3, three variables are required to realise the encoded function (without encoding, $\max(3, 3+2) = 5$ variables would be required). The path from the root node to the leaf node v_2 (which represents output pattern p_2) traverses the right edge of the root node v_7 as well as the left edge of v_6. Consequently, $c(p_2) = 10$ encodes $p_2 = 100$. Since v_2 has weight $w_2 = 1$, one output is used as garbage output in this case. Accordingly, code words for all other output patterns are determined—eventually resulting in the code shown in Table 1c. Dashes again represent don't cares.*

Following this idea, at most $n + 1$ qubits—instead of $\max(n, m + \lceil \log_2 \mu(p_1) \rceil)$—are required to embed any non-reversible function with n inputs. Concerning the design of Boolean components contained in quantum algorithms, the encoded outputs can be handled (1) *locally* where decoders are required for each sub-component that again increase the number of qubits to $\max(n, m + \lceil \log_2 \mu(p_1) \rceil)$, or (2) *globally* where subsequent components that are capable of handling encoded inputs allow remaining at $n + 1$ qubits.

Incorporating the idea of utilising coding techniques into the one-pass design flow introduced above unveils even more potential. In fact, it allows exploiting an even larger degree of freedom since the values of the garbage outputs are basically *don't care* (except the restriction that a reversible function has to be realised)—while still guaranteeing to synthesise a circuit that uses the minimum number of qubits (or even below that minimum if no decoding is required afterwards). This degree of freedom allows for synthesising circuits with significantly smaller T-count [38].

5   Mapping Quantum Circuits to NISQ Devices

In order to use currently developed *Noisy Intermediate-Scale Quantum* (NISQ) devices, the quantum algorithm to be executed has to be properly mapped to these devices such that their underlying physical constraints are satisfied (this is one part of the overall compilation task). To this end, it is assumed that the considered quantum algorithm has already been translated into a quantum circuit composed of multiple-controlled one-qubit gates. For the "quantum part" of the algorithm, this is often inherently given (e.g., by using components for which such translations are known) or done by hand. For the "Boolean part" of the algorithm, a gate-level description is often gained by *reversible circuit synthesis*, as discussed in the previous section.

Then, mapping quantum circuits to NISQ devices requires the consideration of two aspects. First, the occurring gates have to be decomposed into elementary operations provided by the target device—usually a single two-qubit gate as well as a broader variety of one-qubit gates to gain a universal gate set. Second, the *logical* qubits of the quantum circuit have to be mapped to the *physical* qubits of the target device while satisfying the so-called *coupling-constraints* given by the respective device. Since not all physical qubits are coupled directly with each other (due to missing physical connections), two-qubit gates can only be applied to selected pairs of physical qubits. Since it is usually not possible to determine a mapping such that all coupling-constraints are satisfied throughout the whole circuit, the mapping has to change dynamically. This is achieved by inserting additional gates, e.g., realising SWAP operations, in order to "move" the logical qubits to other physical ones.

While there exist several methods to address the first issue, i.e., how to efficiently decompose multiple-controlled one-qubit gates into elementary operations (see [40,41]), there is only few work on how to efficiently satisfy the coupling-constraints of real devices. Although there are similarities with recent work on nearest-neighbour optimisation of quantum circuits as proposed in [42–45], they are not applicable since simplistic architectures with 1-dimensional or 2-dimensional layouts are assumed which have a fixed coupling (all adjacent qubits are coupled) that does not allow modelling all current NISQ devices.

This section covers the mapping of the logical qubit of a quantum circuit to the physical ones of a NISQ device from a design automation perspective. Thereby, *IBM Q devices* are considered as representatives for NISQ devices to discuss the occurring challenges in detail, as well as to describe the proposed solutions. IBM's approach has been chosen, since it provides the first publicly available quantum devices (available since 2017) that can be accessed by everyone (not only academics) through cloud access. Moreover, their coupling-constraints are described more flexibly than those of other companies—allowing to map their coupling-constraints to IBM's model as well.

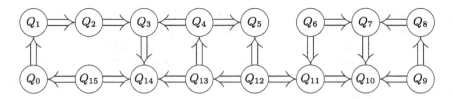

Fig. 4. IBM Q 16 Rueschlikon V1.0.0 (IBM QX3) [46].

5.1 Considered Problem

While one-qubit gates can be applied without limitations in IBM's devices, the physical architecture of the respectively developed quantum computers—usually a linear or rectangular arrays of qubits—limits two-qubit gates to neighbouring qubits that are connected by a superconducting bus resonator. In IBM's devices that use cross-resonance interaction as the basis for CNOT gates, the frequencies of the qubits also determine the direction of the gate (i.e., determining which qubit is the control and which is the target). The possible CNOT gates are captured by so-called coupling maps [46], giving a very flexible description means to specify the *coupling-constraints* of a certain quantum device. Figure 4 shows the coupling map of the IBM QX3 device. Physical qubits are visualised with nodes and a directed edge from physical qubit Q_i to physical qubit Q_j indicates that a CNOT with control qubit Q_i and target qubit Q_j can be applied.

To satisfy the coupling-constraints, one has to map the n logical qubits $q_0, q_1, \ldots, q_{n-1}$ of the decomposed circuit to the $m \geq n$ physical qubits $Q_0, Q_1, \ldots, Q_{m-1}$ of the considered quantum device such that all coupling-constraints given by the corresponding coupling map are satisfied. Unfortunately, it is usually not possible to find a mapping such that the coupling-constraints are satisfied throughout the whole circuit (this is already impossible if the number of other qubits, a logical qubit interacts with, is larger than the maximal degree of the coupling map). More precisely, the following problems—using $CNOT(q_c, q_t)$ to describe a CNOT gate with control qubit q_c and target qubit q_t, and CM to describe the edges of the device's coupling map—may occur:

- A CNOT gate $CNOT(q_c, q_t)$ shall be applied while q_c and q_t are mapped to physical qubits Q_i and Q_j, respectively, and $(Q_i, Q_j) \notin CM$ as well as $(Q_j, Q_i) \notin CM$.
- A CNOT gate $CNOT(q_c, q_t)$ shall be applied while q_c and q_t are mapped to physical qubits Q_i and Q_j, respectively, and $(Q_i, Q_j) \notin CM$ while $(Q_j, Q_i) \in CM$.

To overcome these problems, one strategy is to insert additional gates into the circuit to be mapped. More precisely, to overcome the first issue, one can insert so-called SWAP operations into the circuit that exchange of the states of two physical qubits and, by this, "move" around the logical ones—changing the mapping dynamically.

Example 8. *Figure 5 shows the effect of a SWAP gate as well as its decomposition into elementary gates supported by the IBM Q devices. Assume that the logical qubits q_0 and q_1 are initially mapped to the physical ones Q_0 and Q_1, respectively (indicated by $\rightarrow$). Then, by applying a SWAP gate, the states of Q_0 and Q_1 are exchanged—eventually yielding a mapping where q_0 and q_1 are mapped to Q_1 and Q_0, respectively.*

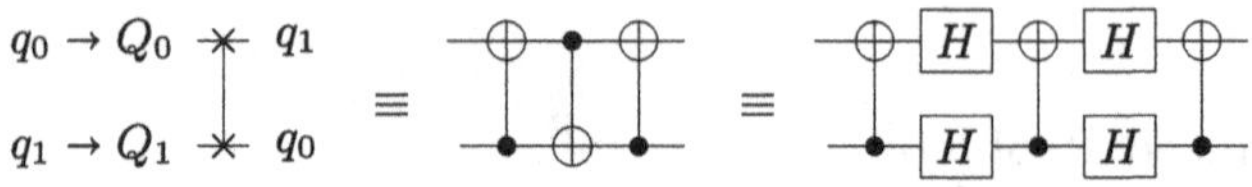

Fig. 5. Decomposition of a SWAP operation.

The second issue may also be solved by inserting SWAP operations. However, it is cheaper (fewer overhead is generated) to insert four Hadamard operations (labelled by H) as they switch the direction of the CNOT gate (i.e., they change the target and the control qubit). This can also be observed in Fig. 5, where H gates switch the direction of the middle CNOT in order to satisfy all coupling-constraints given by the coupling map (assuming that only CNOTs with control qubit Q_1 and target qubit Q_0 are possible).

However, inserting additional gates in order to satisfy the coupling-constraints drastically increases the number of operations—a significant drawback, which affects the fidelity of the quantum circuit since each gate has a certain error rate. Since each SWAP operation is composed of 7 elementary gates (cf. Fig. 5), particularly their number shall be kept as small as possible. Accordingly, this raises the question of how to derive a proper mapping of logical qubits to physical qubits while, at the same time, minimising the number of added SWAP and H operations—an $\mathcal{NP}$-complete problem as recently proven in [47,48].

Example 9. *Consider the quantum circuit composed of 5 CNOT gates shown in Fig. 6a and assume that the logical qubits q_0, q_1, q_2, q_3, q_4, and q_5 are respectively mapped to the physical qubits Q_0, Q_1, Q_2, Q_3, Q_{14}, and Q_{15} of IBM QX3 shown in Fig. 4 on Page 16. The first gate can be directly applied, because the coupling-constraints are satisfied. For the second gate, the direction has to be changed because a CNOT with control qubit Q_0 and target Q_1 is valid, but not vice versa. This can be accomplished by inserting Hadamard gates as shown in Fig. 6b. For the third gate, the mapping has to change. To this end, SWAP operations $SWAP(Q_1, Q_2)$ and $SWAP(Q_2, Q_3)$ are inserted to move logical qubit q_1 to become a neighbour of logical qubit q_4 (see Fig. 6b). Afterwards, q_1 and q_4 are mapped to the physical qubits Q_3 and Q_{14}, respectively, which allows applying the desired CNOT gate. Following this procedure for the remaining qubits eventually results in the circuit shown in Fig. 6b. The mapped circuit is composed of 51 elementary operations and has a depth of 36 when using a naive algorithm—a significant overhead that motivates research on improved approaches.*

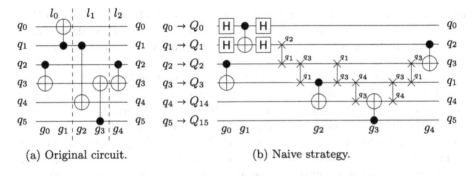

(a) Original circuit.   (b) Naive strategy.

Fig. 6. Mapping of a quantum circuit to IBM QX3.

5.2 Existing Approaches and Results

There exist only very few algorithms that explicitly tackle the mapping problem for IBM Q devices, and, thus, serve as alternative to IBM's own solution provided within its SDK Qiskit [49].[6] To encourage further development in this area, IBM even launched the *IBM Qiskit Developer Challenge* seeking for the best possible solution [50]. This led to the development of several approaches that explicitly consider design automation techniques to tackle the mapping problem.

The work [51] provides—for the first time—an exact approach (using a formal description of the mapping problem that is passed to a powerful reasoning engine) to solve the mapping problem by inserting the minimum number of additional H and SWAP operations. By this, a lower bound on the overhead is provided (when neglecting pre- and post-mapping optimisations), which is required to satisfy the coupling-constraints given by the quantum hardware— allowing to show that IBM's own solution often exceeds the minimal overhead by more than 100 % (even for small instances). However, the exponential nature of the mapping problem (it has been proven to be $\mathcal{NP}$-complete [47]) makes the exact approach applicable for small instances only.

This limitation—together with the fact that IBM's approach generates mapping that are far above the minimum—motivates the development of heuristic approaches. The heuristic methods presented in [52] are heuristic solution that utilises the A* search method to determine proper mappings. This allows reducing the overhead compared to Qiskit by approximately one fourth on average.[7] This difference in quality is mainly because IBM's solution randomly searches for a mapping that satisfies the coupling-constraints—leading to a rather small exploration of the search space so that only rather poor solutions are usually found. In contrast, the proposed approach aims for an optimised solution by exploring more suitable parts of the search space and additionally exploiting

---

[6] Note that IBM's solution randomly searches (guided by heuristics) for mappings of the qubits at a certain point of time.

[7] Note that the proposed approach has additionally been integrated into Qiskit to allow a fair comparison by utilising the same post-mapping optimisations.

information of the circuit. More precisely, a look-ahead scheme is employed that considers gates that are applied in the near future and, thus, allows determining mappings which aim for a global optimum (instead of local optima) with respect to the number of SWAP operations.

Even though this heuristic approach allows outperforming Qiskit's mapping algorithm, it has some scalability issues when used for mapping certain random circuits for validating quantum computers [19], which also served as benchmarks in the *IBM Qiskit Developer Challenge* (a challenge for writing the best quantum-circuit compiler to encourage development). These circuits provide a worst-case scenario that heavily affects the efficiency of the proposed heuristic approach. Therefore, a dedicated approach is proposed in [53], which explicitly considers their structure by using dedicated pre- and post-mapping optimisations. The resulting methodology has been declared as winner of the IBM Qiskit Developer Challenge, since it generated mapped/compiled circuits with at least 10 % lower costs than the other submissions while generating them at least 6 times faster, and is currently being integrated into Qiskit by researchers from IBM. Besides that, all mapping approaches developed in context of this thesis are publicly available at http://iic.jku.at/eda/research/ibm_qx_mapping.

6   Conclusion

This chapter has shown the great potential of bringing knowledge gained from the design automation of conventional circuits and systems into the quantum realm. More precisely, quantum-circuit simulation, the design of Boolean components for quantum algorithms, as well as technology mapping have been considered from a design automation perspective—leading to improvements of several orders of magnitude (with respect to runtime or other design objectives) in many cases. For further information on the developed algorithms we refer to the cited papers. In the future, this development shall continue on a larger scale— eventually providing the foundation for design automation methods that accomplish for quantum computing what the design automation community realised for conventional (electronic) circuits.

Acknowledgments. This work has partially been supported by the European Union through the COST Action IC1405 and the LIT Secure and Correct System Lab funded by the State of Upper Austria.

References

1. Nielsen, M.A., Chuang, I.: Quantum computation and quantum information. AAPT **70**, 558 (2002)
2. Grover, L.K.: A fast quantum mechanical algorithm for database search. In: Symposium on the Theory of Computing, pp. 212–219 (1996)
3. Shor, P.W.: Polynomial-time algorithms for prime factorization and discrete logarithms on a quantum computer. SIAM J. Comput. **26**(5), 1484–1509 (1997)

4. Montanaro, A.: Quantum algorithms: an overview. npj Quantum Inf. **2**, 15023 (2016)
5. Preskill, J.: Quantum computing in the NISQ era and beyond. Quantum **2**, 79 (2018)
6. Coles, P.J., et al.: Quantum algorithm implementations for beginners. arXiv preprint arXiv:1804.03719 (2018)
7. Gambetta, J.M., Chow, J.M., Steffen, M.: Building logical qubits in a superconducting quantum computing system. npj Quantum Inf. **3**(1), 2 (2017)
8. Kelly, J.: A preview of Bristlecone, Google's new quantum processor (2018). https://ai.googleblog.com/2018/03/a-preview-of-bristlecone-googles-new.html
9. Hsu, J.: CES 2018: Intel's 49-qubit chip shoots for quantum supremacy. IEEE Spectrum Tech Talk (2018). https://spectrum.ieee.org/tech-talk/computing/hardware/intels-49qubit-chip-aims-for-quantum-supremacy
10. Sete, E.A., Zeng, W.J., Rigetti, C.T.: A functional architecture for scalable quantum computing. In: International Conference on Rebooting Computing (ICRC), pp. 1–6 (2016)
11. IonQ: IonQ: trapped ion quantum computing. https://ionq.co. Accessed 15 June 2019
12. Nay, C.: IBM unveils world's first integrated quantum computing system for commercial use. https://newsroom.ibm.com/2019-01-08-IBM-Unveils-Worlds-First-Integrated-Quantum-Computing-System-for-Commercial-Use. Accessed 15 June 2019
13. Horsman, C., Fowler, A.G., Devitt, S., Van Meter, R.: Surface code quantum computing by lattice surgery. New J. Phys. **14**(12), 123011 (2012)
14. Gottesman, D.: An introduction to quantum error correction and fault-tolerant quantum computation. In: Quantum Information Science and Its Contributions to Mathematics, Proceedings of Symposia in Applied Mathematics, vol. 68, pp. 13–58 (2010)
15. Yamashita, S., Markov, I.L.: Fast equivalence-checking for quantum circuits. In: International Symposium on Nanoscale Architectures. pp. 23–28. IEEE Press (2010)
16. Niemann, P., Wille, R., Drechsler, R.: Equivalence checking in multi-level quantum systems. In: International Conference of Reversible Computation, pp. 201–215 (2014)
17. Burgholzer, L., Wille, R.: Improved DD-based equivalence checking of quantum circuits. In: Asia and South Pacific Design Automation Conference (ASP-DAC) (2020)
18. Boixo, S., et al.: Characterizing quantum supremacy in near-term devices. Nat. Phys. **14**(6), 595 (2018)
19. Cross, A.W., Bishop, L.S., Sheldon, S., Nation, P.D., Gambetta, J.M.: Validating quantum computers using randomized model circuits. arXiv preprint arXiv:1811.12926 (2018)
20. Smelyanskiy, M., Sawaya, N.P.D., Aspuru-Guzik, A.: qHiPSTER: the quantum high performance software testing environment. arXiv preprint arXiv:1601.07195 (2016)
21. Zulehner, A., Wille, R.: Advanced simulation of quantum computations. IEEE Trans. CAD Integr. Circuits Syst. **38**, 848–859 (2019)
22. Viamontes, G.F., Markov, I.L., Hayes, J.P.: Quantum Circuit Simulation. Springer, Dordrecht (2009). https://doi.org/10.1007/978-90-481-3065-8

23. Niemann, P., Zulehner, A., Wille, R., Drechsler, R.: Efficient construction of QMDDs for irreversible, reversible, and quantum functions. In: Phillips, I., Rahaman, H. (eds.) RC 2017. LNCS, vol. 10301, pp. 214–231. Springer, Cham (2017). https://doi.org/10.1007/978-3-319-59936-6_17

24. Zulehner, A., Wille, R.: Matrix-vector vs. matrix-matrix multiplication: potential in DD-based simulation of quantum computations. In: Design, Automation and Test in Europe, European Design and Automation Association (2019)

25. Zulehner, A., Hillmich, S., Wille, R.: How to efficiently handle complex values? Implementing decision diagrams for quantum computation. In: International Conference on CAD (2019)

26. Niemann, P., Datta, R., Wille, R.: Logic synthesis for quantum state generation. In: International Symposium on Multi-Valued Logic, pp. 247–252. IEEE (2016)

27. Niemann, P., Wille, R., Drechsler, R.: Improved synthesis of Clifford+T quantum functionality. In: Design, Automation and Test in Europe, pp. 597–600 (2018)

28. Zulehner, A., Niemann, P., Drechsler, R., Wille, R.: Accuracy and compactness in decision diagrams for quantum computation. In: Design, Automation and Test in Europe (2019)

29. Hillmich, S., Zulehner, A., Wille, R.: Concurrency in DD-based quantum circuit simulation. In: Asia and South Pacific Design Automation Conference (ASP-DAC) (2020)

30. Zulehner, A., Hillmich, S., Markov, I., Wille, R.: Approximation of Quantum States Using Decision Diagrams. Asia and South Pacific Design Automation Conference (ASP-DAC) (2020)

31. Ekert, A., Jozsa, R.: Quantum computation and Shor's factoring algorithm. Rev. Mod. Phys. **68**(3), 733 (1996)

32. Soeken, M., Roetteler, M., Wiebe, N., De Micheli, G.: LUT-based hierarchical reversible logic synthesis. IEEE Trans. CAD Integr. Circuits Syst. **38**, 848–859 (2018)

33. Zulehner, A., Wille, R.: Make it reversible: efficient embedding of non-reversible functions. In: Design, Automation and Test in Europe, European Design and Automation Association, pp. 458–463 (2017)

34. Soeken, M., Wille, R., Hilken, C., Przigoda, N., Drechsler, R.: Synthesis of reversible circuits with minimal lines for large functions. In: Asia and South Pacific Design Automation Conference, pp. 85–92 (2012)

35. Zulehner, A., Wille, R.: Improving synthesis of reversible circuits: exploiting redundancies in paths and nodes of QMDDs. In: Phillips, I., Rahaman, H. (eds.) RC 2017. LNCS, vol. 10301, pp. 232–247. Springer, Cham (2017). https://doi.org/10.1007/978-3-319-59936-6_18

36. Zulehner, A., Wille, R.: One-pass design of reversible circuits: combining embedding and synthesis for reversible logic. IEEE Trans. CAD Integr. Circuits Syst. **37**(5), 996–1008 (2018)

37. Zulehner, A., Wille, R.: Skipping embedding in the design of reversible circuits. In: International Symposium on Multi-Valued Logic, pp. 173–178. IEEE (2017)

38. Zulehner, A., Wille, R.: Exploiting coding techniques for logic synthesis of reversible circuits. In: Asia and South Pacific Design Automation Conference, pp. 670–675. IEEE Press (2018)

39. Zulehner, A., Niemann, P., Drechsler, R., Wille, R.: One additional qubit is enough: encoded embeddings for Boolean components in quantum circuits. In: International Symposium on Multi-Valued Logic (2019)

40. Amy, M., Maslov, D., Mosca, M., Roetteler, M.: A meet-in-the-middle algorithm for fast synthesis of depth-optimal quantum circuits. IEEE Trans. Comput. Aided Des. Integr. Circuits Syst. **32**(6), 818–830 (2013)
41. Miller, D.M., Wille, R., Sasanian, Z.: Elementary quantum gate realizations for multiple-control Toffoli gates. In: International Symposium on Multi-Valued Logic, pp. 288–293. IEEE (2011)
42. Wille, R., Keszocze, O., Walter, M., Rohrs, P., Chattopadhyay, A., Drechsler, R.: Look-ahead schemes for nearest neighbor optimization of 1D and 2D quantum circuits. In: Asia and South Pacific Design Automation Conference, pp. 292–297 (2016)
43. Shafaei, A., Saeedi, M., Pedram, M.: Optimization of quantum circuits for inter-action distance in linear nearest neighbor architectures. In: Design Automation Conference, pp. 41–46 (2013)
44. Wille, R., Quetschlich, N., Inoue, Y., Yasuda, N., Minato, S.I.: Using πDDs for nearest neighbor optimization of quantum circuits. In: International Conference of Reversible Computation, pp. 181–196 (2016)
45. Zulehner, A., Gasser, S., Wille, R.: Exact global reordering for nearest neighbor quantum circuits using A*. In: Phillips, I., Rahaman, H. (eds.) RC 2017. LNCS, vol. 10301, pp. 185–201. Springer, Cham (2017). https://doi.org/10.1007/978-3-319-59936-6_15
46. IBM Q team: IBM Q 16 Rueschlikon backend specification v1.0.0. https://ibm.biz/qiskit-rueschlikon. Accessed 15 June 2019
47. Botea, A., Kishimoto, A., Marinescu, R.: On the complexity of quantum circuit compilation. In: Symposium on Combinatorial Search (2018)
48. Siraichi, M., Dos Santos, V.F., Collange, S., Pereira, F.M.Q.: Qubit allocation. In: International Symposium on Code Generation and Optimization (CGO), pp. 1–12 (2018)
49. Cross, A.: The IBM Q experience and QISKit open-source quantum computing software. Bull. Am. Phys. Soc. **63**(1) (2018)
50. IBM Q team: QISKit Developer Challenge. https://qx-awards.mybluemix.net/#qiskitDeveloperChallengeAward. Accessed 15 June 2019
51. Wille, R., Burgholzer, L., Zulehner, A.: Mapping quantum circuits to IBM QX architectures using the minimal number of SWAP and H operations. In: Design Automation Conference (2019)
52. Zulehner, A., Paler, A., Wille, R.: An efficient methodology for mapping quantum circuits to the IBM QX architectures. IEEE Trans. CAD Integr. Circuits Syst. **38**, 1226–1236 (2018)
53. Zulehner, A., Wille, R.: Compiling SU(4) quantum circuits to IBM QX architectures. In: Asia and South Pacific Design Automation Conference, pp. 185–190. ACM (2019)

Research on Reversible Functions Having Component Functions with Specified Properties: An Overview

Paweł Kerntopf[1(✉)], Claudio Moraga[2], Krzysztof Podlaski[3], and Radomir Stanković[4]

[1] Institute of Computer Science, Warsaw University of Technology, Warsaw, Poland
pawel.kerntopf@gazeta.pl
[2] Faculty of Computer Science, Technical University of Dortmund, Dortmund, Germany
claudio.moraga@tu-dortmund.de
[3] Faculty of Physics and Applied Informatics, University of Łódź, Łódź, Poland
podlaski@uni.lodz.pl
[4] Department of Computer Science, Faculty of Electronic Engineering, University of Niš, Niš, Serbia
radomir.stankovic@gmail.com

Abstract. In the traditional logic synthesis, different classifications of non-reversible Boolean functions have found many applications. Recently, some attempts to deal with classifications of reversible functions have been published. In this paper, an overview of our results towards constructing a new classification of reversible functions is presented. These results were obtained due to our discussions during two Short Term Scientific Missions (STSMs) as well as during our further research in the framework of COST Action IC1405 "Reversible Computation - Extending Horizons of Computing" and were published in five papers.

Keywords: Reversible functions · Component functions · Classification

1 Introduction

Recent advances in nanotechnology, low-power design, and quantum computing have renewed interest in reversible logic synthesis since they allow for reducing the power dissipation in related circuits and the potential speed-up in quantum computations. More details can be found in [4,25] and references therein.

A reversible function is defined as a bijective mapping $f : A^n \to A^n$, where A is any finite set of elements which can be conveniently identified with non-negative integers $\{0, 1, \ldots, p - 1\}$. In particular, for $p = 2$ and $p = 3$, we speak about binary or Boolean and ternary reversible functions, respectively. Therefore, an n-variable reversible function is actually a permutation on A^n, and can

© The Author(s) 2020
I. Ulidowski et al. (Eds.): RC 2020, LNCS 12070, pp. 83–107, 2020.
https://doi.org/10.1007/978-3-030-47361-7_4

be viewed as a vector of n functions called the *component functions* (CFs), i.e., $F = (f_1, f_2, \ldots, f_n)$. In [27], the term *components* is applied in the similar meaning, meanwhile in the literature on cryptography the term *coordinate functions* is used, see e.g., [3,30]. However, in [30] the term *component function* means a linear combination of *coordinate functions*.

Correspondingly, a reversible circuit is a circuit that realises a reversible function, i.e., performs a bijective mapping of n input signals onto n output signals in a manner specified by the function to be realised.

Recently in [13,14], we discussed the question if it is possible to extend a Boolean function $f : \{0,1\}^n \to \{0,1\}$ into a reversible function $F : \{0,1\}^n \to \{0,1\}^n$, *under the condition that all its component functions have a homogeneous property*. The term homogeneous property means that all component functions express the same particular property Boolean functions might have, e.g. all the component functions belong to the same equivalence class in a particular classification of Boolean functions. The motivation was that if such an embedding of a Boolean function into a reversible function is possible, then new classes of reversible functions can be defined. In [15,17] the same question is explored for ternary functions $F : \{0,1,2\}^n \to \{0,1,2\}^n$ and we have shown that there are significant differences in the theory of binary and ternary reversible functions in the case of linear component functions.

As homogeneous properties, we have chosen typical ones considered in classical logic synthesis: symmetry, affinity, linearity, nonlinearity, self-duality, self-complementarity, monotonicity, unateness (see, e.g. [31]). In papers [13–15,17] the exemplary functions used in proofs of the results were obtained in a constructive manner. In [16] the results on properties of component functions of Boolean reversible functions obtained by the extrapolation approach were demonstrated. An overview of the most relevant of these results in the binary case is presented here. Because of lack of space we have omitted our results on reversible multiple-valued functions. The reader can find them in [15,17].

The presentation is organised in the following way. For the sake of completeness, necessary definitions and basic results from the theory of standard Boolean as well as from reversible Boolean functions are provided in Sect. 2. In Sect. 3, a brief overview of related and background work is presented. Section 4 demonstrates our theoretical results on properties of component functions of reversible functions. Section 5 describes the results of our research on the existence of Boolean reversible functions with all component functions belonging to different equivalence classes while considering well-known and newly constructed reversible functions defined for any number of variables. Section 6 presents our numerical calculations of all equivalence classes of balanced Boolean functions up to $n = 4$ and all reversible functions up to $n = 3$. Finally, Sect. 7 describes our results on the existence of Boolean reversible functions with specified properties of all component functions obtained by extrapolating some properties of reversible functions. The presented research is summarised in Sect. 8.

2   Preliminaries

In this section, the basic definitions and known results are provided for the convenience of the reader. Let us first briefly survey fundamental notions related to standard Boolean functions and reversible Boolean functions.

First we present notation and terminology for fundamental notions. The symbols $+, -, \cdot$ denote ordinary addition, subtraction, and multiplication, respectively. For arbitrary elements x and y in the set $\{0, 1\}$ basic operations in this set (one unary and three binary operations) are defined in the usual way:

Negation $x' = 1 - x$, i.e. if the argument x is 0, then the result is 1, otherwise it is 0;

Product $xy = x \cdot y$, i.e. its value is 1 if and only if both arguments are 1;

Sum $x \vee y = x + y - x \cdot y$, i.e. its value is 0 if and only if both arguments are 0;

EXOR $x \oplus y = x + y (mod 2) = x + y - 2 \cdot x \cdot y$, i.e. its value is 1 if and only if exactly one argument is 1.

In classical logic synthesis, the basic representation of a Boolean function is the Sum-of-Products expression (SOP). In the field of reversible circuit synthesis two other representations are commonly used. Any Boolean function $f : \{0, 1\}^n \rightarrow \{0, 1\}$ can be described using an EXOR-sum of products (ESOP) expression. In ESOPs each variable may appear in both uncomplemented and complemented forms. The Positive Polarity Reed-Muller (PPRM) expression is an ESOP expression which uses only uncomplemented variables. It is a canonical expression and for small functions can be easily generated from a truth table or other representations of the Boolean function.

A Boolean function $f(x_1, x_2, \ldots, x_n)$ depends essentially on its variable x_i if and only if $f(x_1, \ldots, x_{i-1}, 0, x_{i+1}, \ldots, x_n) \neq f(x_1, \ldots, x_{i-1}, 1, x_{i+1}, \ldots, x_n)$.

Definition 1. *A Boolean function depending essentially on all its variables is called* non-degenerate, *otherwise it is called* degenerate.

Example 1. *There are 16 functions of two variables x and y: 0, 1, x, x', y, y', xy, $x'y$, xy', $x'y'$, $x \vee y$, $x' \vee y$, $x \vee y'$, $x' \vee y'$, $x \oplus y = x' \oplus y'$, $x' \oplus y = x \oplus y'$. The first six of them are degenerate: the first two depend essentially on none of the variables, the next four depend essentially on only one of the variables.*   ∎

Let us define an order relation in the set $\{0, 1\}$ in the usual way: $0 < 1$ and a partial order relation in the set $\{0, 1\}^n$: for any two vectors $\mathbf{a} = (a_1, a_2, \ldots, a_n)$, $\mathbf{b} = (b_1, b_2, \ldots, b_n)$ in $\{0, 1\}^n$ $\mathbf{a} \leq \mathbf{b}$ if and only if $a_i \leq b_i$ for $1 \leq i \leq n$.

Definition 2. *A Boolean function f is* monotone increasing *if and only if* $\mathbf{a} \leq \mathbf{b}$ *implies $f(\mathbf{a}) \leq f(\mathbf{b})$ which will simply be called a* monotone *function. By changing the inequalities into inverse ones we obtain a definition of* monotone decreasing *function.*

Example 2. *Both the constant functions 0 and 1 are monotone increasing and monotone decreasing. There are six monotone increasing functions of two variables x and y: 0, 1, x, y, xy, $x \vee y$. Similarly, there are six monotone decreasing functions of two variables x and y: 0, 1, x', y', $x'y'$, $x' \vee y'$.*   ∎

Definition 3. *A Boolean function $f(x_1, x_2, \ldots, x_n)$ is called* unate *(or mixed monotone) if and only if it is a constant or there exists its SOP representation using either uncomplemented or complemented literals for each variable.*

Example 3. *There are 14 unate functions of two variables x and y: only functions $x \oplus y$ and $x' \oplus y$ are not unate.* ∎

Definition 4. *A Boolean function $f(x_1, x_2, \ldots, x_n)$ is called* threshold *(or linearly separable) if and only if there exist real numbers $a_1, a_2, \ldots, a_n$, and b such that $f = 1$ if the sum of all $a_i x_i$, $1 \le i \le n$, is greater than or equal to b, and $f = 0$ otherwise.*

Example 4. *All unate functions of up to three variables are threshold functions. Thus, for two variables there are 14 threshold functions (i.e., all except $x \oplus y$ and $x' \oplus y$), in particular,*

$$\text{when} \quad a_1 = a_2 = 1 \quad \text{and} \quad b = 1.5 \quad \text{then} \quad f = xy,$$
$$\text{when} \quad a_1 = a_2 = 1 \quad \text{and} \quad b = 0.5 \quad \text{then} \quad f = x \vee y,$$
$$\text{when} \quad a_1 = a_2 = -1 \quad \text{and} \quad b = -0.5 \quad \text{then} \quad f = x'y',$$
$$\text{when} \quad a_1 = a_2 = -1 \quad \text{and} \quad b = -1.5 \quad \text{then} \quad f = x' \vee y'.$$

The 4-variable function $f(x_1, x_2, x_3, x_4) = x_1 x_2 \vee x_3 x_4$ is an example of a monotone increasing function which is not a threshold function. ∎

Definition 5. *A Boolean function f on an odd number of arguments is called* majority function *if and only if $f = 1$ when more than half of the arguments are 1.*

Example 5. *The 3-variable majority function $f(x, y, z) = xy \oplus xz \oplus yz$ is a threshold function, where $a_1 = a_2 = a_3 = 1$ and $b = 2$.* ∎

It is well known that the following result holds.

Lemma 1.

(1) Every threshold function is a unate function.
(2) Every majority function is a threshold function.

Definition 6. *A Boolean function f is* linear with respect to a variable x_i *if it can be expressed in the form $f = x_i \oplus g$, where $\oplus$ denotes XOR operation and g is a function independent of x_i (then the variable x_i is called* linear in f*). A function has property LV if it contains at least one linear variable. A function f is called* affine *if and only if each of variable x_i is either linear in f, or f does not depend on x_i, i.e. $f(x_1, x_2, \ldots, x_n) = a_0 \oplus a_1 x_1 \oplus a_2 x_2 \oplus \cdots \oplus a_n x_n$, where $a_0, a_1, a_2, \ldots, a_n \in \{0, 1\}$. If $a_0 = 0$ then it is called* linear. *Any affine function which is not linear can be obtained by negating an appropriate linear function. A Boolean function which is not affine is called* nonlinear.

Example 6. *$f_1(x, y, z) = x \oplus y \oplus yz$ is linear with respect to x as then $g = y \oplus yz$ is independent of x, but f_1 is not linear with respect to y as then $g = x \oplus yz$ is dependent of y. Similarly, $f_2(x, y) = x \oplus y \oplus xy$ is neither linear with respect to x, nor to y.* ∎

Definition 7. *A Boolean function is (totally) symmetric if any permutation of all its variables does not change the function.*

There are 2^{n+1} symmetric Boolean functions.

Definition 8. *If any permutation of a proper subset S of the variables of cardinality at least 2 does not change the Boolean function f, then f is called a* partially symmetric function with respect to S and S is called a partial symmetry of variables of f. *The collection of maximal partial symmetry subsets of variables of f is called* a partial symmetry profile *and is denoted by S_f. The partial symmetry profile of a totally symmetric Boolean function $f(x_1, x_2, \ldots, x_3)$ is equal to $\{\{x_1, x_2, \ldots, x_n\}\}$. Let partial symmetry profiles of Boolean functions $f_1, f_2, \ldots, f_n$ be denoted by $S_1, S_2, \ldots, S_n$, respectively. The intersection of such profiles is the collection of subsets of variables obtained by taking all possibilities of performing intersection operation on an element in S_1, an element in S_2, $\ldots$, and an element in S_n. If the intersection operation on $S_1, S_2, \ldots, S_n$ does not contain an element with at least two variables, then there does not exist a partial symmetry subset of all functions $f_1, f_2, \ldots, f_n$.*

Example 7. *Let $f(u, v, w, x, y, z) = u \oplus vw \oplus xyz$ and $g(u, v, w, x, y, z) = uv \oplus w \oplus xyz$. Then the partial symmetry profile of f is $S_f\{\{v, w\}, \{x, y, z\}\}$, the partial symmetry profile of g is $S_g = \{\{u, v\}, \{x, y, z\}\}$ and the intersection of S_f and S_g is equal to $\{\{v\}, \phi, \{x, y, z\}\}$, i.e. both functions f and g are partially symmetric with respect to $\{\{x, y, z\}\}$ as well as this subset is the only one partial symmetry subset of both functions f and g.* ∎

Definition 9. *A Boolean function $f : \{0, 1\}^n \to \{0, 1\}$ is called balanced if it takes value 1 the same number of times as value 0.*

Example 8. *There are 70 balanced Boolean functions on 3 arguments, including degenerate ones. Only four of them are totally symmetric, namely parity and majority functions and their negations:*

$$\text{parity} \quad x \oplus y \oplus z \quad 1 \oplus x \oplus y \oplus z,$$
$$\text{majority } xy \oplus xz \oplus yz \ 1 \oplus xy \oplus xz \oplus yz.$$

Eight of the balanced functions, including degenerate ones, are partially symmetric with respect to each 2-element subset of variables, for instance, functions

$$x \oplus y, \qquad\qquad 1 \oplus x \oplus y,$$
$$xy \oplus z, \qquad\qquad 1 \oplus xy \oplus z,$$
$$x \oplus y \oplus xy \oplus z, \qquad 1 \oplus x \oplus y \oplus xy \oplus z,$$
$$x \oplus y \oplus xy \oplus xz \oplus yz, 1 \oplus x \oplus y \oplus xy \oplus xz \oplus yz.$$

are partially symmetric with respect to $\{x, y\}$. ∎

Definition 10. *Two Boolean functions are:*

(1) P-equivalent *if they can be converted to each other by the permutation of variables,*

(2) *NP*-equivalent *if they can be converted to each other by the negation and/or permutation of variables,*

(3) *NPN*-equivalent *if they can be converted to each other by negation of variables, permutation of variables and negation of the function.*

Definition 11. *A Boolean function f is* self-complementary *(SC) if f and f' are NP-equivalent.*

Definition 12. *A Boolean function f is* self-dual *(SD) if*

$$f(x_1, x_2, \ldots, x_n) = f'(x_1', x_2', \ldots, x_n').$$

The following results are well-known:

Lemma 2. *(1) All self-complementary functions are balanced,*
(2) All self-dual functions are self-complementary,
(3) All functions having property LV are self-complementary,
(4) If a Boolean function f is linear with respect to a variable x_i then

$$f(x_i = 1) = f'(x_i = 0).$$

In the case of Boolean functions, depending on the operations allowed in a particular classification, the P-equivalent, NP-equivalent, and NPN-equivalent functions are distinguished. In some applications, equivalence classes defined with respect to a restricted set of operations are of a particular interest, as for example, in [5,6]. Here, we are particularly interested in P-equivalent functions when studying the properties of component functions.

Definition 13. *A mapping $F : \{0,1\}^n \to \{0,1\}^n$ is called an $n*n$* reversible *function if it is bijective. Functions which are not reversible are called irreversible. An $n*n$ reversible function F can be considered as a vector of standard Boolean functions called* component functions $f_i : \{0,1\}^n \to \{0,1\}, 1 \leq i \leq n,$ *which are defined at every $x \in \{0,1\}^n$ by $F(x) = (f_1(x), \ldots, f_n(x))$.*

In the truth table of a reversible $n*n$ Boolean function there are n input columns and n output columns. The output rows of such a truth table form a permutation of the input rows. From the bijectivity of reversible functions it follows that all component functions have to be balanced Boolean functions.

By an analogy with the definition of NPN-equivalence classes for standard Boolean functions, the following definition of equivalence classes for Boolean reversible functions can be given.

Definition 14. *Two reversible Boolean functions are* NPNP-equivalent *if they can be transformed to each other by the following operations (including the combinations that do not use all of these operations):*

(1) *Negation of variables,*
(2) *Permutation of variables,*
(3) *Negation of component functions, and*
(4) *Permutation of component functions.*

Each reversible function can be treated as a permutation. This is why we also recall basic notions connected with permutations. Let A be any finite set. A permutation on a set A is a bijective mapping from A to itself. Every permutation can be considered as a collection of disjoint cycles. Here such a collection will be called a cycle structure. We will write a cycle in the form $< a_1, a_2, \ldots, a_k >$, meaning that a_1 is mapped onto $a_2, \ldots, a_k$ is mapped onto a_1. It could be written in different ways, e.g. $< a_2, a_3, \ldots, a_k, a_1 >$. The number of elements in a cycle is called the length of the cycle. A cycle with the length k is called a k-*cycle*. A 2-cycle is also called a *transposition*.

3   Previous Work

The motivation for our studies of reversible functions toward constructing their classifications is borrowed from the classical logic synthesis by referring to an analogy with related problems. For example, in classical logic synthesis, the equivalence of two functions under permutation of the variables is an important problem due to applications in the synthesis of multiplexer-based field-programmable gate arrays [5,6]. The problem is called Boolean matching, and two functions match if they have the same P-representative. The extension to NP-representatives is done in [7,8] in solving the Boolean matching problem in cell-library binding.

Classification of Boolean functions is a classical problem in logic synthesis due to its various applications, with fast prototyping and unification of testing procedures being just two of them [28]. However, a considerably smaller amount of work has been done in the classification of reversible functions. In [18,19] it is presented an approach to enumerate equivalence classes of reversible functions with the equivalence classes defined as follows. Denote by G and H the groups of permutations acting on the inputs and outputs of Boolean reversible functions, respectively. Two functions $f_1(x)$ and $f_2(x)$ are equivalent if for each n-tuple x, there is a $g \in G$ and an $h \in H$ such that $f_1(x) = h(f_2(g(x)))$. It is also provided a list of all NPNP-equivalence classes of 3-variable reversible functions as well as a classification based on properties of the inverses of the representative functions for the equivalence classes considered. The lists consist of triples of balanced Boolean functions specified by ESOPs. Unfortunately, using "prime" for negation led to a number of typographical errors which has been discovered by us recently [13] (see Sect. 6).

A technical report from 1962 by C. S. Lorens [18] and an article by the same author [19] can be viewed as a starting point of subsequent work on an enumeration of equivalence classes of reversible functions by several authors [10,20–23,29]. With the exception of [22], these publications consider the classification of binary reversible functions. These publications were discussed mainly by researchers in combinatorial mathematics and cryptography but hardly used and correspondingly rarely if at all referred within the reversible functions community, the main reason probably being that the term *invertible* instead of *reversible* functions has been used. A classification scheme for reversible functions was the subject of a profound study in [24], however, without a concrete solution proposed.

Recently, certain aspects of the classification problem have been addressed. In [26], the list of all NPNP-equivalence classes for three variable reversible functions from [19] is presented in the context of a study of the complexity of reversible circuits with the representative functions for equivalence classes given in the form of permutations (i.e. without considering individual component functions). The minimal number of nonlinear gates needed in the implementation of reversible functions is used as a classification criterion in [9]. The structure of closed classes of reversible functions is described in [1]. Enumeration of equivalence classes under the action of permutation of the inputs and outputs on the domain and the range is presented in [2].

For the first time in the literature, we solved in [13,14] several problems of the existence of binary reversible functions with all component functions having the same known property (e.g., symmetry, affinity, linearity, nonlinearity, self-duality, self-complementarity, monotonicity, unateness). Solutions of such problems for ternary reversible functions are presented by us in [15]. In [17] we presented results on the existence of ternary/multiple-valued reversible functions with all component functions belonging to different P-equivalence classes. In [16] it is shown how we discovered solutions of some problems by extrapolating properties of previously found reversible functions of 3 and 4 variables.

4   Theoretical Results

This section presents basic theoretical results on properties of component functions of reversible functions. We begin with the following general result:

Theorem 1. *If $f(x_1, x_2, \ldots, x_n) = (f_1, f_2, \ldots, f_n)$ is an $n*n$ reversible (irreversible) Boolean function, then the function obtained from f by any of the following transformations*

- *negation of variables,*
- *permutation of variables,*
- *negation of a component function,*
- *permutation of component functions,*

is also reversible (irreversible).

Proof. It is sufficient to notice that any of the above transformations corresponds to a permutation of rows in the truth table, i.e. preserves the property of bijectivity. $\square$

The following result follows directly from Theorem 1.

Corollary 1. *$n*n$ functions belonging to an NPNP-equivalence class either are all reversible or none of them is reversible.*

There are constraints on using totally and partially symmetric functions as component functions of an $n*n$ reversible function $f(x_1, x_2, \ldots, x_n) = (f_1, f_2, \ldots, f_n)$. Let partial symmetry profiles of the component functions $f_1, f_2, \ldots, f_n$ be denoted by $S_1, S_2, \ldots, S_n$, respectively (see Definition 8).

Theorem 2. *A necessary condition for an $n*n$ function $f(x_1, x_2, \ldots, x_n) = (f_1, f_2, \ldots, f_n)$ to be reversible is as follows: intersection of all profiles $S_1, S_2, \ldots, S_n$, has to be equal to the collection of results each of which has no more than one element.*

Proof. Let us assume that two variables x_i and x_j belong to one subset being an element of the intersection of the profiles $S_1, S_2, \ldots, S_n$, i.e. appear in one subset in all these profiles. It is equivalent to the equation:

$$f(x_1, \ldots, x_{i-1}, 0, x_{i+1}, \ldots, x_{j-1}, 1, x_{j+1}, \ldots, x_n) = f(x_1, \ldots, x_{i-1}, 1, x_{i+1}, \ldots, x_{j-1}, 0,$$
$$x_{j+1}, \ldots, x_n).$$

However, because any reversible function f is a bijective mapping then $f(x_1, \ldots, x_{i-1}, 0, x_{i+1}, \ldots, x_{j-1}, 1, x_{j+1}, \ldots, x_n)$ differs from $f(x_1, \ldots, x_{i-1}, 1, x_{i+1}, \ldots, x_{j-1}, 0, x_{j+1}, \ldots, x_n)$. □

Thus, the following theorem holds.

Theorem 3. *$n*n$ reversible Boolean functions, $n > 1$, with all totally symmetric CFs being non-degenerate do not exist.*

On the other hand, component functions of a reversible function can be totally or partially symmetric if at least two of them are partially symmetric.

Example 9. *It is easy to show that the following function is reversible*

$$f_1 = x_1 \oplus x_2 \oplus x_3, \qquad f_2 = x_1 \oplus x_2, \qquad f_3 = x_1 \oplus x_3,$$

where f_1 is a totally symmetric function and both f_2 and f_3 are partially symmetric functions The simple generalization of the above reversible function to the case of any n can be defined as follows:

$$f_1 = \bigoplus_{i=1}^{n} x_i, \qquad f_k = \bigoplus_{i \neq k} x_i, k \in \{2, \ldots, n\},$$

where the symbol $\oplus$ denotes summing modulo 2. ∎

In some papers, algorithms for synthesis of reversible circuits for (totally) symmetric functions are considered. However, symmetric functions in these papers are first embedded in reversible specifications with additional inputs and/or outputs.

Now let us consider linear and affine CFs. For any n there is only one non-degenerate linear Boolean function:

$$x_1 \oplus x_2 \oplus \cdots \oplus x_n.$$

Hence, by Theorem 1 the following result is true:

Theorem 4. *For $n > 1$ $n*n$ reversible Boolean functions with all linear or affine CFs being non-degenerate do not exist.*

However, reversible Boolean functions having as CFs one of non-degenerate linear (affine) functions and the other functions depending essentially on $k < n$ variables do exist as is shown in Example 9.

Let us consider the following property of monotone Boolean functions.

Lemma 3. *Every monotone Boolean function which is balanced, except projection functions P-equivalent to the identity, cannot be equal to 1 for an assignment with weight 1 (i.e. with only one non-zero entry).*

Proof. Assume that the lemma is not true. Then there exists a balanced monotone Boolean function f, not being a projection function, and an assignment $\mathbf{a} = (a_1, a_2, \ldots, a_n)$ with weight 1 for which $f(\mathbf{a})$ is not equal to zero. Without loss of generality let $\mathbf{a} = (1, 0, \ldots, 0, 0)$, i.e. $x_1 = 1$, $x_i = 0$ for $2 \leq i \leq n$. Because f is monotone so $f(\mathbf{b}) = 1$ for all assignments $\mathbf{b} = (b_1, b_2, \ldots, b_n)$ with $b_1 = 1$. The number of such assignments is equal to 2^{n-1}. As the number of all binary assignments is 2^n hence the number of assignments $\mathbf{c}$ not compatible with assignments $\mathbf{b}$, i.e. having $c_1 = 0$, is equal to $2^n - 2^{n-1} = 2^{n-1}$. A balanced Boolean function takes values 0 and 1 the same number of times so $f = 0$ for all those assignments with $c_1 = 0$. Thus,

$$f(\mathbf{a}) = 0 \quad \text{for all binary assignments} \quad \mathbf{a} = (0, a_2, \ldots, a_{n-1}, a_n),$$
$$f(\mathbf{a}) = 1 \quad \text{for all binary assignments} \quad \mathbf{a} = (1, a_2, \ldots, a_{n-1}, a_n),$$

i.e., f is a projection function what is in contradiction with the initial assumption. □

Theorem 5. *An $n*n$ reversible Boolean function, $n \geq 3$, with all component functions being non-degenerate monotone does not exist.*

Proof. Lemma 3 states that for any monotone balanced Boolean function F and any input assignment $\mathbf{a}$ with weight 1

$$F(\mathbf{a}) = 0.$$

Thus, for any $n*n$ reversible Boolean function G, $n \geq 3$, with all CFs being monotone and any input assignment $\mathbf{a}$ with weight 1

$$G(0, 0, \ldots, 0, 0, 1) = G(0, 0, \ldots, 0, 1, 0) = (0, 0, \ldots, 0, 0, 0),$$

what contradicts the reversibility constraint as G takes value $(0, 0, \ldots, 0, 0, 0)$ more than once. Thus, any $n*n$ Boolean function, $n \geq 3$, with all component functions being monotone, is not reversible.

By Definition 3, Definition 4, Lemma 1, Theorem 1 and Theorem 5 the following result holds. □

Corollary 2. *An $n*n$ reversible Boolean function, $n \geq 3$, with all component functions being non-degenerate and threshold, does not exist.*

5   Results Based on Newly Constructed Functions

Let us first introduce simple notions related to Positive Polarity Reed-Muller expressions for Boolean functions. The number of literals in a term will be called its rank. Denote by $T_{i,j}$ the exclusive-or sum of all terms having a rank not smaller than i and not greater than j ($T_{i,i}$ will denote all terms with rank i).

In [13] we introduced the following $n*n$ reversible function, for arbitrary n, which will be called Negation with Preservation of Constants (in short NPC$n*n$):

Definition 15. *The reversible function $NPCn*n(x_1, x_2, \ldots, x_n)$, $n \geq 3$, is defined in such a manner that its component functions $NPCn$ are defined as follows:*

$$
\begin{aligned}
f_1 &= x_1 \oplus x_2 \oplus x_3 \oplus \cdots \oplus x_{n-2} \oplus x_{n-1} & \oplus T_{2,n-1}, \\
f_2 &= x_1 \oplus x_2 \oplus x_3 \oplus \cdots \oplus x_{n-2} \oplus & x_n \oplus T_{2,n-1}, \\
&\cdots\cdots\cdots\cdots\cdots\cdots\cdots\cdots\cdots\cdots\cdots\cdots\cdots\cdots\cdots\cdots \\
f_{n-1} &= x_1 \quad\;\; \oplus x_3 \oplus \cdots \oplus x_{n-2} \oplus x_{n-1} \oplus x_n \oplus T_{2,n-1}, \\
f_n &= \quad\;\; x_2 \oplus x_3 \oplus \cdots \oplus x_{n-2} \oplus x_{n-1} \oplus x_n \oplus T_{2,n-1},
\end{aligned}
$$

i.e., in each of the above equations exactly one variable is missing, namely in the ith equation variable x_{n-i+1} is missing.

The formulas in Definition 15 can be transformed taking into account that

1. $x_1 \oplus x_2 \oplus x_3 \oplus \cdots \oplus x_{n-2} \oplus x_{n-1} \oplus x_n \oplus T_{2,n} = T_{1,n} =$
$$= x_1 \vee x_2 \vee x_3 \vee \cdots \vee x_{n-1} \vee x_n,$$

(this transformation can be easily proved by induction starting from the well-known formula for $n = 2 : x_1 \vee x_2 = x_1 \oplus x_2 \oplus x_1 x_2$),

2. $f_i = f_i \oplus x_{n-i+1} \oplus x_{n-i+1} \oplus x_1 x_2 \ldots x_n \oplus x_1 x_2 \ldots x_n = T_{1,n} \oplus x_{n-i+1} \oplus x_1 x_2 \ldots x_n$
$= (x_1 \vee x_2 \vee x_3 \vee \cdots \vee x_{n-1} \vee x_n) \oplus x_{n-i+1} \oplus x_1 x_2 \ldots x_n,$

where we applied the following three obvious formulas:

$$f_i = f_i \oplus 0, \qquad x_{n-i+1} \oplus x_{n-i+1} = 0, \qquad x_1 x_2 \ldots x_n \oplus x_1 x_2 \ldots x_n = 0,$$

and the transformation used in case 1:

$f_i \oplus x_{n-i+1} \oplus x_1 x_2 \ldots x_n = x_1 \oplus x_2 \oplus x_3 \oplus \cdots \oplus x_{n-2} \oplus x_{n-1} \oplus x_n \oplus T_{2,n-1} \oplus x_1, x_2 \ldots x_n$
$= x_1 \oplus x_2 \oplus x_3 \oplus \cdots \oplus x_{n-2} \oplus x_{x-1} \oplus x_n \oplus T_{2,n} = T_{1,n}.$

Using the above formulas we will show by example how the values of the function f_i can be calculated. Without loss of generality we will show this for f_1:

Step 1. Calculate $f_1^{(1)} = x_1 \vee x_2 \vee x_3 \vee \cdots \vee x_{n-1} \vee x_n$ (see Table 1).

Step 2. Calculate $f_1^{(2)} = (x_1 \vee x_2 \vee x_3 \vee \cdots \vee x_{n-1} \vee x_n) \oplus x_1$ (by negating the lower half of the truth table obtained in Step 1).

Step 3. Calculate $f_1 = (x_1 \vee x_2 \vee x_3 \vee \cdots \vee x_{n-1} \vee x_n) \oplus x_1 \oplus x_1 x_2 \ldots x_n$ (by negating the output value in the last row of the truth table obtained in Step 2). These steps are performed for $n = 3$ in Table 1.

Thus, f_1 has the well-known property of preserving constants:

$$f_1(0,0,0) = 0 \quad \text{and} \quad f_1(1,1,1) = 1,$$

as well as is negating the input x_1 for all other vectors of input values. Similarly (see Table 2), the reversible function NPC3*3 is preserving constants:

$$\text{NPC3*3}(0,0,0) = (0,0,0) \quad \text{and} \quad \text{NPC3*3}(1,1,1) = (1,1,1),$$

as well as negating all the other input vectors. This is why we gave this reversible function the name Negation with Preservation of Constants.

Table 1. Establishing values of the 3-variable function f_1 in three steps

$x_1 x_2 x_3$	$f_1^{(1)}$	$f_1^{(2)}$	f_1
0 0 0	0	0	0
0 0 1	1	1	1
0 1 0	1	1	1
0 1 1	1	1	1
1 0 0	1	0	0
1 0 1	1	0	0
1 1 0	1	0	0
1 1 1	1	0	1

By analogy with the above example it is easy to show that the following two results hold for any n:

Lemma 4. *Each function NPCn*n is reversible.*

Lemma 5. *Each component function of NPCn*n can be obtained from the Boolean function NPCn as a result of a permutation of its variables.*

Table 2. Truth table for the function NPC3∗3

$x_1 x_2 x_3$	$f_1 f_2 f_3$
0 0 0	0 0 0
0 0 1	1 1 0
0 1 0	1 0 1
0 1 1	1 0 0
1 0 0	0 1 1
1 0 1	0 1 0
1 1 0	0 0 1
1 1 1	1 1 1

Theorem 6. *All component functions of NPCn∗n, $n \geq 3$, are (1) nonlinear, (2) self-dual, (3) self-complementary, (4) P-equivalent, and (5) unate.*

Proof. (1) The function NPCn is nonlinear because its PPRM contains terms of rank 2 for any $n > 2$.

(2) Without loss of generality we write $\text{NPC}n(x_1, x_2, \ldots, x_n) = (x_1 \lor x_2 \lor \cdots \lor x_n) \oplus x_1 \oplus x_1 x_2 \ldots x_n$ On the other hand, by De Morgan's laws the following two formulas hold:

$$(x_1' \lor x_2' \lor \cdots \lor x_n') = (x_1 x_2 \ldots x_n)' = 1 \oplus x_1 x_2 \ldots x_n,$$
$$x_1' x_2' \ldots x_n' = (x_1 \lor x_2 \lor \cdots \lor x_n)' = 1 \oplus (x_1 \lor x_2 \lor \cdots \lor x_n).$$

Thus,

$$(\text{NPC}n)'(x_1', x_2', \ldots, x_n') = 1 \oplus [(x_1' \lor x_2' \lor \cdots \lor x_n') \oplus x_1' \oplus x_1' x_2' \ldots x_n']$$
$$= 1 \oplus [(x_1 x_2 \ldots x_n)' \oplus x_1' \oplus (x_1 \lor x_2 \lor \cdots \lor x_n)']$$
$$= 1 \oplus [1 \oplus x_1 x_2 \ldots x_n \oplus 1 \oplus x_1 \oplus 1 \oplus (x_1 \lor x_2 \lor \cdots \lor x_n)]$$
$$= (x_1 \lor x_2 \lor \cdots \lor x_n) \oplus x_1 \oplus x_1 x_2 \ldots x_n$$
$$= \text{NPC}n(x_1, x_2, \ldots, x_n).$$

and by Definition 12 any NPCn is self-dual.

(3) From Lemma 2 it follows that it is self-complementary.

(4) P-equivalence follows from Lemma 5.

(5) Once again, without loss of generality we can write

$$\text{NPC}n(x_1, x_2, \ldots, x_n) = [(x_1 \lor x_2 \lor \cdots \lor x_n) \oplus x_1] \oplus x_1 x_2 \ldots x_n,$$

and transform it using well-known formulas $a \oplus b = ab' + a'b, aa' = 0$, $a = a \lor ab$, and De Morgan's laws:

$$\text{NPC}n(x_1, x_2, \ldots, x_n) = [(x_1 \lor x_2 \lor \cdots \lor x_n)x_1' \lor (x_1 \lor x_2 \lor \cdots \lor x_n)'x_1] \oplus x_1 x_2 \ldots x_n$$
$$= [x_1' x_2 \lor x_1' x_3 \lor \cdots \lor x_1' x_n \lor (x_1' x_2' \ldots x_n')x_1] \oplus x_1 x_2 \ldots x_n$$
$$= (x_1' x_2 \lor x_1' x_3 \lor \cdots \lor x_1' x_n)(x_1 x_2 \ldots x_n)' \lor (x_1' x_2 \lor x_1' x_3 \lor \cdots \lor x_1' x_n)'(x_1 x_2 \ldots x_n)$$
$$= x_1' x_2 \lor x_1' x_3 \lor \cdots \lor x_1' x_n \lor x_2 \ldots x_n.$$

Thus, in the reduced SOP for NPCn the variable x_1 appears only as complemented and all the other variables are uncomplemented, i.e. NPCn is unate. □

Corollary 3. *For any $n \geq 3$ there exist reversible functions having all component functions being:*

(1) nonlinear,
(2) self-dual,
(3) self-complementary,
(4) P-equivalent,
(5) unate.

6   Computational Results

By running simple programs on a laptop we have obtained the computational results described in this section. The configuration of the laptop we used was standard: i7 processor and 4 GB of RAM. Each of the computational tasks took less than one hour. First we calculated in an exhaustive manner all NPN-equivalence classes of balanced Boolean functions of 1, 2, 3 and 4 variables. The results for $n = 1, 2, 3$ are shown in Table 3 and for $n = 4$ in Table 4 together with sizes and functional properties of all these classes. These results were published for the first time in [13]. Each row gives one equivalence class identified by its representative expressed in the form of PPRM expressions. For our purpose considering each component function separately is a more convenient form than permutation which is shorter but in which component functions are not shown explicitly. For each class, the table shows the number of variables (n), the name of the class (Class), the size of the equivalence class (Size), a *Representative* of the class, and the classical *Properties* the class possesses (the meanings of abbreviations L, LV, NL, SC and SD were introduced in Sect. 2). Equivalence classes are sorted first by the size of the number of terms in PPRM expression and in case of a tie by the sizes of the consecutive terms in the expression (the terms of the same size are given in the lexicographic order). To decrease the width of Tables 4 and 5 we used names a, b, c and d to denote variables (instead of x_1, x_2, x_3, x_4 which we use in the rest of the paper).

We have checked that only for the following 18 out of 58 classes of balanced Boolean functions up to 4 variables (B1.1-B4.52) it is *impossible* to find four functions belonging to the same class which would constitute a 4-variable reversible function: B2.1, B3.2, B4.2, B4.3, B4.4, B4.7 (this class includes only 2 functions), B4.13, B4.15, B4.27, B4.28, B.4.31, B4.33, B4.34, B4.35, B4.38, B4.42, B4.48, B4.51.

We used this result for extrapolation of some properties for a larger number of variables. We also expect that several interesting conjectures can be formulated on the basis of the above results.

We have also calculated all NPNP-equivalence classes of 3-variable reversible functions (see Table 5 organised under the same assumptions as Tables 3 and 4).

Table 3. NPN-equivalence classes of n-variable balanced Boolean functions for $n \leq 3$

Class	Size	Representative	Properties				
			L	LV	NL	SC	SD
$B1.1$	8	a	+	+		+	+
$B2.1$	12	$a \oplus b$	+	+		+	
$B3.1$	96	$a \oplus bc$		+	+	+	
$B3.2$	8	$a \oplus b \oplus c$	+	+		+	+
$B3.3$	96	$a \oplus ab \oplus bc$			+	+	
$B3.4$	32	$ab \oplus ac \oplus bc$			+	+	+

For the synthesis of reversible functions, NPNP-equivalence classes are interesting because permutations of component functions do not change values of cost functions of optimal reversible circuits implementing them. It is because a permutation of component functions leads to permutation of lines in the circuit which does not change the cost of the circuit.

As mentioned in Sect. 3 such a table was published in [19] but we were able to find (probably typographic) errors in it. One type of these errors consists in non-reversibility of two classes' representatives. To show precisely where the errors are located let us point that Lorens' Table VI is split into three parts based on properties of the inverses of the classes' representatives:

(A) 21 functions having their inverses identical to the function (called self-inverse functions),
(B) 3 classes of functions having their inverses in the same NPNP-equivalence class,
(C) 28 classes of functions having their inverses in a different NPNP-equivalence class.

It is easy to check that the following two classes' representatives from the Lorens' table are not reversible:

$f_1 = x_1' \oplus x_2 x_3, f_2 = x_2 \oplus x_1 x_3', f_3 = x_3 \oplus x_1' x_2$ (Part A, row 16),
$f_1 = x_1 x_2 \oplus x_2 x_3 \oplus x_3 x_1, f_2 = x_1 \oplus x_2 x_3', f_3 = x_3 \oplus x_2 x_1'$ (Part C, column 1, row 13).

It seems that the correct expressions were supposed to be as follows:

$f_1 = x_1' \oplus x_2 x_3, f_2 = x_2 \oplus x_1 x_3', f_3 = x_3 \oplus x_1' x_2'$ (adding a "prime" to the last literal),
$f_1 = x_1 x_2 \oplus x_2 x_3 \oplus x_3 x_1, f_2 = x_1 \oplus x_2' x_3, f_3 = x_3 \oplus x_2 x_1'$ (swapping the "prime" in the 2nd term in f_2).

The last two functions are reversible and belong to our classes R28 and R31, respectively, which are not covered by the other representatives in Table VI in [19].

In Lorens' Table VI we have also found two pairs of representatives that belong to the same class:

Table 4. NPN-equivalence classes of n-variable balanced Boolean functions for $n = 4$

Class	Size	Representative	L	LV	NL	SC	SD
$B4.1$	64	$a \oplus bcd$		+	+	+	
$B4.2$	48	$a \oplus b \oplus cd$		+	+	+	
$B4.3$	192	$a \oplus b \oplus acd$		+	+	+	
$B4.4$	96	$a \oplus bc \oplus bd$		+	+	+	
$B4.5$	768	$a \oplus bc \oplus abd$			+		
$B4.6$	192	$a \oplus abc \oplus bcd$			+	+	
$B4.7$	2	$a \oplus b \oplus c \oplus d$	+	+		+	
$B4.8$	192	$a \oplus b \oplus c \oplus abd$		+	+	+	
$B4.9$	96	$a \oplus b \oplus ac \oplus cd$		+	+	+	
$B4.10$	384	$a \oplus b \oplus cd \oplus abc$			+		
$B4.11$	384	$a \oplus b \oplus abc \oplus acd$			+	+	
$B4.12$	96	$a \oplus ab \oplus bc \oplus bd$			+	+	
$B4.13$	32	$a \oplus bc \oplus bd \oplus cd$		+	+	+	
$B4.14$	384	$a \oplus bc \oplus abc \oplus abd$			+	+	
$B1.15$	64	$a \oplus b \oplus c \oplus d \oplus abc$		+	+	+	
$B4.16$	192	$a \oplus b \oplus c \oplus abc \oplus abd$			+	+	
$B4.17$	32	$a \oplus b \oplus ac \oplus ad \oplus cd$		+	+	+	+
$B4.18$	384	$a \oplus b \oplus ab \oplus ac \oplus bcd$			+	+	
$B4.19$	384	$a \oplus b \oplus ac \oplus ad \oplus bcd$			+		
$B4.20$	384	$a \oplus b \oplus ac \oplus acd \oplus bcd$			+		
$B4.21$	384	$a \oplus b \oplus ac \oplus abd \oplus bcd$			+		
$B4.22$	384	$a \oplus b \oplus abc \oplus acd \oplus bcd$			+		
$B4.23$	48	$a \oplus ab \oplus ac \oplus bd \oplus cd$			+	+	+
$B4.24$	384	$a \oplus ab \oplus bc \oplus bd \oplus acd$			+		
$B4.25$	384	$a \oplus ab \oplus bc \oplus abd \oplus acd$			+		
$B4.26$	192	$a \oplus ab \oplus cd \oplus abc \oplus acd$			+	+	
$B4.27$	384	$a \oplus bc \oplus bd \oplus abd \oplus acd$			+	+	
$B4.28$	192	$a \oplus bc \oplus bd \oplus acd \oplus bcd$			+		
$B4.29$	192	$a \oplus ab \oplus abc \oplus abd \oplus bcd$			+	+	
$B4.30$	384	$a \oplus bc \oplus abc \oplus abd \oplus acd$			+		
$B4.31$	48	$ab \oplus ac \oplus ad \oplus bc \oplus bd$			+	+	
$B4.32$	384	$a \oplus b \oplus c \oplus ab \oplus ad \oplus bcd$			+	+	
$B4.33$	192	$a \oplus b \oplus c \oplus ad \oplus abc \oplus bcd$			+		
$B4.34$	384	$a \oplus b \oplus c \oplus ad \oplus abd \oplus bcd$			+	+	
$B4.35$	24	$a \oplus b \oplus ab \oplus ac \oplus bd \oplus cd$			+	+	
$B4.36$	384	$a \oplus b \oplus ac \oplus cd \oplus abc \oplus abd$			+	+	
$B4.37$	192	$a \oplus b \oplus ac \oplus cd \oplus abd \oplus acd$			+	+	
$B4.38$	192	$a \oplus b \oplus ab \oplus abc \oplus abd \oplus acd$			+	+	
$B4.39$	768	$a \oplus b \oplus ac \oplus abd \oplus acd \oplus bcd$			+		
$B4.40$	96	$a \oplus b \oplus abc \oplus abd \oplus acd \oplus bcd$			+		
$B4.41$	96	$a \oplus ab \oplus ac \oplus bc \oplus bd \oplus cd$			+	+	
$B4.42$	192	$a \oplus ab \oplus bc \oplus bd \oplus acd \oplus bcd$			+		
$B4.43$	384	$a \oplus ab \oplus bc \oplus cd \oplus abd \oplus acd$			+	+	
$B4.44$	384	$a \oplus ab \oplus cd \oplus abc \oplus abd \oplus acd$			+		
$B4.45$	384	$a \oplus bc \oplus bd \oplus abc \oplus acd \oplus bcd$			+	+	
$B4.46$	64	$a \oplus b \oplus c \oplus ad \oplus abd \oplus acd \oplus bcd$			+	+	
$B4.47$	384	$a \oplus b \oplus ac \oplus cd \oplus abc \oplus abd \oplus acd$			+	+	
$B4.48$	192	$a \oplus b \oplus ab \oplus abc \oplus abd \oplus acd \oplus bcd$			+		
$B4.49$	384	$a \oplus b \oplus ac \oplus abc \oplus abd \oplus acd \oplus bcd$			+	+	
$B4.50$	64	$a \oplus ab \oplus cd \oplus abc \oplus abd \oplus acd \oplus bcd$			+	+	+
$B4.51$	64	$a \oplus b \oplus c \oplus d \oplus ab \oplus abc \oplus abd \oplus acd$			+	+	
$B4.52$	64	$a \oplus b \oplus c \oplus ab \oplus cd \oplus abc \oplus abd \oplus acd \oplus bcd$			+	+	+

Table 5. Representatives of NPNP-equivalence classes of reversible Boolean functions for $n = 3$

Class	Size	$f_1(a, b, c)$	$f_2(a, b, c)$	$f_3(a, b, c)$	BF classes
R1	48	a	b	c	1.1 1.1 1.1
R2	288	a	b	$a \oplus c$	1.1 1.1 2.1
R3	576	a	b	$c \oplus ab$	1.1 1.1 3.1
R4	144	a	b	$a \oplus b \oplus c$	1.1 1.1 3.2
R5	144	a	$a \oplus b$	$a \oplus c$	1.1 2.1 2.1
R6	288	a	$a \oplus b$	$b \oplus c$	1.1 2.1 2.1
R7	1152	a	$a \oplus b$	$c \oplus ab$	1.1 2.1 3.1
R8	288	a	$a \oplus b$	$a \oplus b \oplus c$	1.1 2.1 3.2
R9	576	a	$b \oplus c$	$b \oplus ab \oplus ac$	1.1 2.1 3.3
R10	1152	a	$b \oplus ac$	$b \oplus c \oplus ab$	1.1 3.1 3.1
R11	576	a	$b \oplus ac$	$b \oplus c \oplus ac$	1.1 3.1 3.1
R12	2304	a	$b \oplus ac$	$c \oplus ab \oplus ac$	1.1 3.1 3.3
R13	576	a	$b \oplus ac$	$a \oplus b \oplus c \oplus ac$	1.1 3.2 3.1
R14	576	a	$a \oplus b \oplus c$	$b \oplus ab \oplus ac$	1.1 3.2 3.3
R15	288	a	$b \oplus ab \oplus ac$	$c \oplus ab \oplus ac$	1.1 3.3 3.3
R16	288	a	$b \oplus ab \oplus ac$	$a \oplus c \oplus ab \oplus ac$	1.1 3.3 3.3
R17	144	$a \oplus b$	$a \oplus c$	$a \oplus b \oplus c$	2.1 2.1 3.2
R18	576	$a \oplus b$	$a \oplus c$	$ab \oplus ac \oplus bc$	2.1 2.1 3.4
R19	576	$a \oplus b$	$c \oplus ab$	$a \oplus c \oplus ab$	2.1 3.1 3.1
R20	1152	$a \oplus b$	$c \oplus ab$	$a \oplus ac \oplus bc$	2.1 3.1 3.3
R21	1152	$a \oplus b$	$c \oplus ab$	$a \oplus c \oplus ab \oplus ac \oplus bc$	2.1 3.1 3.4
R22	576	$a \oplus b$	$a \oplus b \oplus c$	$a \oplus ac \oplus bc$	2.1 3.2 3.3
R23	288	$a \oplus b$	$a \oplus ac \oplus bc$	$a \oplus c \oplus ac \oplus bc$	2.1 3.3 3.3
R24	288	$a \oplus b$	$a \oplus ac \oplus bc$	$b \oplus c \oplus ac \oplus bc$	2.1 3.3 3.3
R25	1152	$a \oplus b$	$a \oplus ac \oplus bc$	$a \oplus c \oplus ab \oplus ac \oplus bc$	2.1 3.3 3.4
R26	576	$a \oplus b$	$ab \oplus ac \oplus bc$	$a \oplus c \oplus ab \oplus ac \oplus bc$	2.1 3.4 3.4
R27	2304	$a \oplus bc$	$a \oplus b \oplus ac$	$c \oplus ab \oplus ac$	3.1 3.1 3.3
R28	384	$a \oplus bc$	$a \oplus b \oplus ac$	$a \oplus b \oplus c \oplus ab$	3.1 3.1 3.1
R29	1152	$a \oplus bc$	$a \oplus b \oplus ac$	$a \oplus b \oplus c \oplus ac$	3.1 3.1 3.1
R30	1152	$a \oplus bc$	$a \oplus b \oplus ac$	$b \oplus c \oplus ac \oplus bc$	3.1 3.1 3.3
R31	1152	$a \oplus bc$	$a \oplus b \oplus ac$	$a \oplus c \oplus ab \oplus ac \oplus bc$	3.1 3.1 3.4
R32	576	$a \oplus bc$	$a \oplus b \oplus bc$	$a \oplus c \oplus bc$	3.1 3.1 3.1
R33	1152	$a \oplus bc$	$a \oplus b \oplus bc$	$c \oplus ab \oplus bc$	3.1 3.1 3.3
R34	576	$a \oplus bc$	$b \oplus ab \oplus ac$	$c \oplus ab \oplus ac$	3.1 3.3 3.3
R35	2304	$a \oplus bc$	$b \oplus ab \oplus ac$	$c \oplus ab \oplus bc$	3.1 3.3 3.3
R36	576	$a \oplus bc$	$b \oplus ab \oplus ac$	$a \oplus b \oplus c \oplus bc$	3.1 3.3 3.1
R37	1152	$a \oplus bc$	$b \oplus ab \oplus ac$	$a \oplus c \oplus ab \oplus ac$	3.1 3.3 3.3
R38	1152	$a \oplus bc$	$b \oplus ac \oplus bc$	$b \oplus c \oplus ab \oplus bc$	3.1 3.3 3.3
R39	1152	$a \oplus bc$	$b \oplus ac \oplus bc$	$b \oplus c \oplus ac \oplus bc$	3.1 3.3 3.3
R40	2304	$a \oplus bc$	$b \oplus ac \oplus bc$	$a \oplus c \oplus ab \oplus ac \oplus bc$	3.1 3.3 3.4
R41	576	$a \oplus bc$	$a \oplus b \oplus c \oplus bc$	$a \oplus b \oplus ab \oplus ac \oplus bc$	3.1 3.1 3.4
R42	576	$a \oplus bc$	$a \oplus b \oplus ab \oplus ac \oplus bc$	$a \oplus c \oplus ab \oplus ac \oplus bc$	3.1 3.4 3.4
R43	1152	$a \oplus b \oplus c$	$a \oplus ab \oplus bc$	$b \oplus ac \oplus bc$	3.2 3.3 3.3
R44	288	$a \oplus b \oplus c$	$a \oplus ab \oplus bc$	$c \oplus ab \oplus bc$	3.2 3.3 3.3
R45	288	$a \oplus b \oplus c$	$a \oplus ab \oplus bc$	$a \oplus b \oplus ab \oplus bc$	3.2 3.3 3.3
R46	384	$a \oplus ab \oplus bc$	$b \oplus ac \oplus bc$	$c \oplus ab \oplus ac$	3.3 3.3 3.3
R47	1152	$a \oplus ab \oplus bc$	$b \oplus ac \oplus bc$	$a \oplus c \oplus ac \oplus bc$	3.3 3.3 3.3
R48	1152	$a \oplus ab \oplus bc$	$b \oplus ac \oplus bc$	$b \oplus c \oplus ab \oplus ac \oplus bc$	3.3 3.3 3.4
R49	576	$a \oplus ab \oplus bc$	$c \oplus ab \oplus bc$	$a \oplus b \oplus ab \oplus bc$	3.3 3.3 3.3
R50	576	$a \oplus ab \oplus bc$	$c \oplus ab \oplus bc$	$a \oplus b \oplus ab \oplus ac \oplus bc$	3.3 3.3 3.4
R51	576	$a \oplus ab \oplus bc$	$a \oplus b \oplus ab \oplus ac \oplus bc$	$b \oplus c \oplus ab \oplus ac \oplus bc$	3.3 3.4 3.4
R52	192	$ab \oplus ac \oplus bc$	$a \oplus b \oplus ab \oplus ac \oplus bc$	$a \oplus c \oplus ab \oplus ac \oplus bc$	3.4 3.4 3.4

- one pair is in Part A, rows 13 and 14 (both representatives belong to our class R40),
- the other pair: Part C, column 1, row 10, and Part C, column 2, row 11 (both representatives belong to our class R45).

Thus, 4 out of 52 NPNP-equivalence classes of 3∗3 reversible functions are not represented in Lorens' Table VI.

In Table 4, in comparison with [19], we added sizes of the classes and information showing to which NPN-equivalence class of balanced functions each of the component functions belongs. The latter information was useful in our extrapolation of some properties of reversible functions [16] (for an example see Sect. 7).

7 Extrapolation Based on Cycle Structures

In [11,12] it has been demonstrated that it is possible to extrapolate some properties of reversible functions by considering their cycle structures. This is why we tried to exploit the same approach to discover infinite sequences of reversible functions with all their component functions being non-degenerate and belonging to different P-classes. We established that there are 26 NPNP-classes of 3-variable functions (R27-R52) that possess all component functions depending essentially on all three variables. Among them, there is only one class that consists of reversible functions all whose component functions belong to different NPN-classes. Below the PPRM expressions for a member of this class are shown:

NPNP-class R40

$$A = a \oplus c \oplus ab \oplus ac \oplus bc,$$
$$B = b \oplus ab \oplus ac,$$
$$C = c \oplus ab.$$

The above PPRM expressions show some regular features. However, our experience is so that extrapolation of such features of PPRMs is very difficult because: (1) usually a component function is obtained which is not balanced, (2) even if all PPRMs correspond to balanced functions then their collection does not constitute a reversible function. Therefore we have decided to apply extrapolation based on cycle structures. By considering the appropriate mappings $\{0,1\}^3 \to \{0,1\}^3$ it is easy to establish that the earlier defined member of the NPNP-class R40 has the following cycle structure:

$$< 000 > < 010 > < 011 > < 100 > < 001, 101, 111, 110 > .$$

Let us note that binary n-tuples in the unique cycle having more than one element form a regular pattern:

$$001,$$
$$101,$$
$$111,$$
$$110.$$

Namely, it is easy to note that

- the first and the second n-tuples differ only in the 1st bit position,
- the second and the third n-tuples differ only in the 2nd bit position,
- the third and the fourth n-tuples differ only in the 3rd bit position.

Thus, we observe here a certain periodicity which can be easily extrapolated leading to the desired infinite sequence of reversible functions as will be seen later. In this case, extrapolating was quite simple. Let us introduce additional notions.

Definition 16. *A set of variable assignments over $\{0,1\}$ with specified numbers of p 0s and r 1s is called a block and denoted by $b_{p,r}$.*

Example 10. *The set of all eight variable assignments for 3-variable Boolean functions can be partitioned into the following four blocks:*

$$b_{3,0} = \{000\}, \quad b_{2,1} = \{001, 010, 100\}, \quad b_{1,2} = \{011, 101, 110\}, \quad b_{0,3} = \{111\}.$$
∎

Definition 17. *For any Boolean function f let $B^0(f)$ and $B^1(f)$ denote the sets of blocks including all variable assignments for which f is equal 0 and 1, respectively.*

Example 11. *Let us consider the following Boolean projection functions:*

$$f(x_1, x_2, x_3) = x_1, \quad g(x_1, x_2, x_3) = x_2, \quad h(x_1, x_2, x_3) = x_3.$$

Then,

$$B^0(f) = \{\{000\}, \{001, 010\}, \{011\}\}, \quad B^1(f) = \{\{100\}, \{101, 110\}, \{111\}\},$$
$$B^0(g) = \{\{000\}, \{001, 100\}, \{101\}\}, \quad B^1(g) = \{\{010\}, \{011, 110\}, \{111\}\},$$
$$B^0(h) = \{\{000\}, \{010, 100\}, \{110\}\}, \quad B^1(h) = \{\{001\}, \{011, 101\}, \{111\}\}.$$

Notice that for each 3-variable Boolean reversible function k the union of $B^0(k)$ and $B^1(k)$ is equal to the set of all 8 Boolean variable assignments. For each of the component functions of an arbitrary reversible function cardinalities of unions of their B^i sets are the same. ∎

Example 12. *Let us consider a 3-variable Boolean reversible function* $F(x_1, x_2, x_3) = (f_1, f_2, f_3)$ *defined in such a manner that the only non-identical mappings of variable assignments in* F *are as follows*

$$001 \rightarrow 101,$$
$$101 \rightarrow 111,$$
$$111 \rightarrow 110,$$
$$110 \rightarrow 001.$$

When we consider the reversible function F *as a permutation of output assignments it is a single cycle of four elements:*

$$< 001, 101, 111, 110 > .$$

Notice that in the above mappings

- *in the 1st row the leftmost bit is being negated,*
- *in the 2nd row the second bit is being negated*
- *in the 3rd row the third bit is being negated*
- *in the 4th row all bits are being negated.*

This observation will be generalised later to functions of any number of variables.

Now let us note what changes have been done in the sets B_i, $0 \leq i \leq 1$, *for functions* f_1, f_2, *and* f_3, *in comparison with the sets for the function in Example 11 (the assignments moved to another block are shown bolded and underlined):*

$$B^0(f_1) = \{\{000\}, \{010\}, \{011, \mathbf{\underline{110}}\}\}, \qquad B^1(f_1) = \{\{\mathbf{\underline{001}}, 100\}, \{101\}, \{111\}\},$$
$$B^0(f_2) = \{\{000\}, \{001, 100\}, \{\mathbf{\underline{110}}\}\}, \qquad B^1(f_2) = \{\{010\}, \{011, \mathbf{\underline{101}}\}, \{111\}\},$$
$$B^0(f_3) = \{\{000\}, \{010, 100\}, \{\mathbf{\underline{111}}\}\}, \qquad B^1(f_3) = \{\{001\}, \{011, 101\}, \{\mathbf{\underline{110}}\}\}.$$

Let us summarise the above observations.

The values of the function f_1 *differ from the values of the projection function* x_1 *only for the assignments* 001 *and* 110. *Namely, we can notice that*

$$\begin{array}{ll} f(0,0,1) = 0 & f_1(0,0,1) = 1, \\ f(1,1,0) = 1 & f_1(1,1,0) = 0. \end{array}$$

As a result, the function f_1 *can be obtained from the projection function* x_1 *by swapping its values for variable assignments* 001 *and* 110.

Values of each of the other two component functions, f_2 *and* f_3, *also differ from the values of the corresponding projection functions only for two assignments.*

Swaps for f_2 in comparison with the projection function x_2 are as follows:

$$g(1,0,1) = 0 \qquad\qquad f_2(1,0,1) = 1,$$
$$g(1,1,0) = 1 \qquad\qquad f_2(1,1,0) = 0.$$

Swaps for f_3 in comparison with the projection function x_3 are as follows:

$$h(1,1,1) = 1 \qquad\qquad f_3(1,1,1) = 0,$$
$$h(1,1,0) = 0 \qquad\qquad f_3(1,1,0) = 1.$$

Let us show that component functions f_1 and f_2 belong to different P-equivalence classes. Assume that f_1 and f_2 belong to the same P-equivalence class. Then, since any permutation over the variable set $\{x_1, x_2, x_3\}$ does not change the assignment 111 there should be $f_1(1,1,1) = f_2(1,1,1)$, however, $f_1(1,1,1) = 0$ and $f_2(1,1,1) = 1$. It is in contradiction with our assumption that f_1 and f_2 belong to the same P-equivalence class. Thus, f_1 and f_2 belong to different P-equivalence classes.

In a similar manner it can be shown that the other two pairs of component functions of F, (f_1, f_3) and (f_2, f_3), belong to different P-equivalence classes.

Let us show that component functions f_1 and f_3 belong to different P-equivalence classes. Assume that f_1 and f_3 belong to the same P-equivalence class. Then, since any permutation over variable set $\{x_1, x_2, x_3\}$ does not change the assignment 111 there should be $f_1(1,1,1) = f_3(1,1,1)$, however $f_1(1,1,1) = 0$ and $f_3(1,1,1) = 1$. It is in contradiction with our assumption that f_1 and f_3 belong to the same P-equivalence class. Thus, f_1 and f_3 belong to different P-equivalence classes.

Let us show that component functions f_2 and f_3 belong to different P-equivalence classes. Assume that f_2 and f_3 belong to the same P-equivalence class. Then, let us consider the permutation of variables consisting in swapping variables x_2 and x_3. Then there should be $f_2(1,0,0) = f_3(1,0,0)$, however $f_2(1,0,0) = 0$ and $f_3(1,0,0) = 1$. It is in contradiction with our assumption that f_2 and f_3 belong to the same P-equivalence class. Thus, f_2 and f_3 belong to different P-equivalence classes. ∎

Now the presented above methodology of proving that two component functions of F belong to different P-equivalence classes will be extended to Boolean reversible functions of any number of variables. To prove that Boolean reversible functions with all component functions belonging to different P-equivalence classes exist for any number of variables $n \geq 3$, we will define the following infinite sequence of reversible functions:

Definition 18. *The reversible Boolean function $H^n(x_1, x_2, \ldots, x_n) = (f_1, f_2, \ldots, f_n)$, $n \geq 3$, is defined in such a manner that the only non-identical mappings of variable assignments in H^n are as follows:*

$$a_1\, a_2\, \ldots\, a_{n-1}\, a_n\ \rightarrow\ a_1'\, a_2\, \ldots\, a_{n-1}\, a_n,$$
$$a_1'\, a_2\, \ldots\, a_{n-1}\, a_n\ \rightarrow\ a_1'\, a_2'\, \ldots\, a_{n-1}\, a_n,$$
$$\ldots\ldots\ldots\ldots\ldots\ldots\ldots\ldots\ldots\ldots\ldots\ldots\ldots$$
$$a_1'\, a_2'\, \ldots\, a_{n-1}'\, a_n\ \rightarrow\ a_1'\, a_2'\, \ldots\, a_{n-1}'\, a_n',$$
$$a_1'\, a_2'\, \ldots\, a_{n-1}'\, a_n'\ \rightarrow\ a_1\, a_2\, \ldots\, a_{n-1}\, a_n,$$

where the starting variable assignment is as follows:

$$a_1 a_2 a_3 \ldots a_{n-1} a_n = 000 \ldots 01.$$

Notice that in the ith row of the mappings in Definition 18, $1 \leq i \leq n$, the ith bit is being negated, and in the last mapping, all bits are being negated.

When we consider the function H^n as a permutation of variable assignments it is a cycle of $n + 1$ elements:

$$< a_1, a_2, \ldots, a_{n-1}, a_n,$$
$$a_1', a_2, \ldots, a_{n-1}, a_n,$$
$$a_1', a_2', \ldots, a_{n-1}, a_n,$$
$$\ldots\ldots\ldots\ldots\ldots\ldots\ldots$$
$$a_1', a_2', \ldots, a_{n-1}', a_n,$$
$$a_1', a_2', \ldots, a_{n-1}', a_n' > .$$

Theorem 7. *Each $n*n$ function H^n is reversible for any $n \geq 3$, where H^n is formulated in Definition 18.*

Proof. Because non-identical mappings of variable assignments in H^n form a cycle, this function is bijective for any $n \geq 3$. Hence, it is reversible.   □

In a manner similar to Example 12 we proved in [16] that the following result holds.

Theorem 8. *Any two component functions of the Boolean reversible function H^n belong to different P-equivalence classes for $n \geq 3$.*

It is obvious that by Theorem 8 the following result holds:

Corollary 4. *For any $n \geq 3$ there exist binary reversible functions having all component functions that belong to different P-equivalence classes.*

8   Conclusions and Future Work

The chapter presents our results on properties of component functions of Boolean reversible functions. The solved problems were described briefly in Sects. 4, 5, 6 and 7. They can be summarised as follows:

(A) For any $n \geq 3$ there does not exist a Boolean reversible function with all component functions being non-degenerate and

- totally symmetric,
- linear/affine,
- monotone,
- majority,
- threshold.

(B) For any $n \geq 3$ there exists a Boolean reversible function with all component functions being nondegenerate and

- nonlinear,
- self-complementary,
- self-dual,
- unate.
- P-equivalent.

(C) For any $n \geq 3$ there exists a Boolean reversible function with all component functions being non-degenerate and belonging to different P-equivalence classes.

Our work has not been finished. We plan to continue efforts for constructing a classification of reversible Boolean functions which would be useful in the synthesis of reversible circuits.

Acknowledgements. The authors acknowledge partial support of COST Action IC1405 on "Reversible Computation - Extending Horizons of Computing". They are grateful to Philipp Niemann, one of the reviewers, for many comprehensive remarks.

References

1. Aaronson, S., Grier, D., Schaeffer, L.: The classification of reversible bit operations. Preprint arXiv:1504.05155 [quant-ph] (2015)
2. Carić, M., Živković, M.: On the number of equivalence classes of invertible Boolean functions under action of permutation of variables on domain and range. Publications de l'Institut Mathématique **100**(114), 95–99 (2016)
3. Carlet, C.: Vectorial Boolean functions for cryptography. In: Crama, Y., Hammer, P. (eds.) Boolean Models and Methods in Mathematics, Computer Science, and Engineering, pp. 398–472. Cambridge University Press, Cambridge (2010)
4. De Vos, A.: Reversible Computing: Fundamentals, Quantum Computing, and Applications. Wiley-VCH Verlag, Weinheim (2010)
5. Debnath, D., Sasao, T.: Fast Boolean matching under variable permutation using representative. In: Proceedings of the Asia and South Pacific Design Automation Conference, pp. 359–362 (1999)
6. Debnath, D., Sasao, T.: Efficient computation of canonical form for Boolean matching in large libraries. In: Proceedings of the Asia and South Pacific Design Automation Conference, pp. 591–596 (2004)
7. Debnath, D., Sasao, T.: Fast Boolean matching under permutation by efficient computation of canonical form. IEICE Trans. Fundam. Electron. Commun. Comput. Sci. **E87-A**(12), 3134–3140 (2004)
8. Debnath, D., Sasao, T.: Efficient computation of canonical form under variable permutation and negation for Boolean matching in large libraries. IEICE Trans. Fundam. Electron. Commun. Comput. Sci. **E89-A**(12), 3443–3450 (2006)

9. Draper, T.G.: Nonlinear complexity of Boolean permutations. Ph.D. thesis, Department of Mathematics, University of Maryland, College Park, Maryland, USA (2009)
10. Harrison, M.A.: The number of classes of invertible Boolean functions. J. ACM **10**, 25–28 (1963)
11. Jegier, J., Kerntopf, P.: Progress towards constructing sequences of benchmarks for quantum Boolean circuits synthesis. In: Proceedings of the 14th IEEE International Conference on Nanotechnology, pp. 250–255 (2014)
12. Jegier, J., Kerntopf, P., Szyprowski, M.: An approach to constructing reversible multi-qubit benchmarks with provably minimal implementations. In: Proceedings of the 13th IEEE International Conference on Nanotechnology, pp. 99–104 (2013)
13. Kerntopf, P., Moraga, C., Podlaski, K., Stanković, R.: Towards classification of reversible functions. In: Steinbach, B. (ed.) Proceedings of the 12th International Workshop on Boolean Problems, pp. 21–28 (2018)
14. Kerntopf, P., Moraga, C., Podlaski, K., Stanković, R.: Towards classification of reversible functions with homogeneous component functions. In: Steinbach, B. (ed.) Further Improvements in the Boolean Domain, pp. 386–406. Cambridge Scholars Publishing, Newcastle upon Tyne (2018)
15. Kerntopf, P., Podlaski, K., Moraga, C., Stanković, R.: Study of reversible ternary functions with homogeneous component functions. In: Proceedings of the 47th IEEE International Conference on Multiple-Valued Logic, pp. 191–196 (2017)
16. Kerntopf, P., Podlaski, K., Moraga, C., Stanković, R.: New results on reversible Boolean functions having component functions with specified properties. In: Drechsler, R., Soeken, M. (eds.) Advanced Boolean Techniques, pp. 217–236. Springer, Cham (2020). https://doi.org/10.1007/978-3-030-20323-8_10
17. Kerntopf, P., Stanković, R., Podlaski, K., Moraga, C.: Ternary/MV reversible functions with component functions from different equivalence classes. In: Proceedings of the 48th IEEE International Conference on Multiple-Valued Logic, pp. 109–114 (2018)
18. Lorens, C.S.: Invertible Boolean functions. Tech. rep. 21, Space-General Corp., El Monte, CA, Research Memorandum (1962)
19. Lorens, C.S.: Invertible Boolean functions. IEEE Trans. Electron. Comput. **EC–13**(5), 529–541 (1964)
20. Primenko, E.A.: Invertible Boolean functions and fundamental groups of transformations of algebras of Boolean functions. Avtomatika & Vychislitelnaya Tekhnika **3**, 17–21 (1976)
21. Primenko, E.A.: On the number of types of invertible Boolean functions. Avtomatika & Vychislitelnaya Tekhnika **6**, 12–14 (1977)
22. Primenko, E.A.: On the number of types of invertible transformations in multivalued logic. Kibernetika **5**, 27–29 (1977)
23. Primenko, E.A.: Equivalence classes of invertible Boolean functions. Kibernetika **6**, 1–5 (1984)
24. Rice, J.E.: Considerations for determining a classification scheme for reversible Boolean functions. Tech. rep. TR-CSJR2-2007, Department of Mathematics and Computer Science, University of Lethbridge, Lethbridge, Alberta, Canada (2007)
25. Saeedi, M., Markov, I.L.: Synthesis and optimization of reversible circuits: a survey. ACM Comput. Surv. **45**(2), 21:1–21:34 (2013)
26. Soeken, M., Abdessaied, N., De Micheli, G.: Enumeration of reversible functions and its application to circuit complexity. In: Devitt, S., Lanese, I. (eds.) RC 2016. LNCS, vol. 9720, pp. 255–270. Springer, Cham (2016). https://doi.org/10.1007/978-3-319-40578-0_19

27. Soeken, M., Wille, R., Keszocze, O., Miller, D.M., Drechsler, R.: Embedding of large Boolean functions for reversible logic. ACM J. Emerg. Technol. Comput. Syst. **12**(4), 41:1–41:26 (2015)
28. Stanković, R.S., Astola, J.T., Steinbach, B.: Former and recent work in classification of switching functions. In: Steinbach, B. (ed.) Proceedings of the 8th International Workshop on Boolean Problems, pp. 115–126 (2008)
29. Strazdins, I.E.: On the number of types of invertible binary networks. Avtomatika & Vychislitelnaya Tekhnika **1**, 30–34 (1974)
30. Tokareva, N.: Bent Functions, Results and Applications to Cryptography. Academic Press, London (2015)
31. Tsai, C.C., Marek-Sadowska, M.: Boolean functions classification via fixed polarity Reed-Muller forms. IEEE Trans. Comput. **46**(2), 173–186 (1997)

A Case Study for Reversible Computing: Reversible Debugging of Concurrent Programs

James Hoey[1], Ivan Lanese[2], Naoki Nishida[3], Irek Ulidowski[1],
and Germán Vidal[4(✉)]

[1] School of Informatics, University of Leicester, Leicester, UK
{jbh11/iu3}@leicester.ac.uk
[2] Focus Team, University of Bologna/Inria, Bologna, Italy
ivan.lanese@gmail.com
[3] Graduate School of Informatics, Nagoya University, Nagoya, Japan
nishida@i.nagoya-u.ac.jp
[4] MiST, VRAIN, Universitat Politècnica de València, Valencia, Spain
gvidal@dsic.upv.es

Abstract. Reversible computing allows one to run programs not only in
the usual forward direction, but also backward. A main application area
for reversible computing is debugging, where one can use reversibility
to go backward from a visible misbehaviour towards the bug causing
it. While reversible debugging of sequential systems is well understood,
reversible debugging of concurrent and distributed systems is less settled.
We present here two approaches for debugging concurrent programs, one
based on *backtracking*, which undoes actions in reverse order of execution,
and one based on *causal consistency*, which allows one to undo any action
provided that its consequences, if any, are undone beforehand. The first
approach tackles an imperative language with shared memory, while the
second one considers a core of the functional message-passing language
Erlang. Both the approaches are based on solid formal foundations.

1 Introduction

Reversible computing has been attracting interest due to its applications in fields
as different as, e.g., hardware design [12], computational biology [4], quantum
computing [2], discrete simulation [6] and robotics [31].

One of the oldest and more explored application areas for reversible computing is *program debugging*. This can be explained by looking, on the one hand, to

This work has been partially supported by COST Action IC1405 on Reversible Computation - Extending Horizons of Computing. The second author has been partially
supported by the French National Research Agency (ANR), project DCore n. ANR-
18-CE25-0007. The third author has been partially supported by JSPS KAKENHI
Grant Number JP17H01722. The last author has been partially supported by the EU
(FEDER) and the *Spanish MICINN/AEI* under grant TIN2016-76843-C4-1-R and by
the *Generalitat Valenciana* under grant Prometeo/2019/098 (DeepTrust).

I. Ulidowski et al. (Eds.): RC 2020, LNCS 12070, pp. 108–127, 2020.
https://doi.org/10.1007/978-3-030-47361-7_5

the relevance of the problem, and, on the other hand, to how naturally reversible computing fits in the picture. Concerning the former, finding and fixing bugs inside software has always been a main activity in the software development life cycle. Indeed, according to a 2014 study [47], the cost of debugging amounts to $312 billions annually. Another recent study [3] estimates that the time spent in debugging is 49.9% of the total programming time. Concerning how naturally reversible computing fits in this context, consider that debugging means finding a bug, i.e., some wrong line of code, causing some visible misbehaviour, i.e., a wrong effect of a program, such as a wrong message printed on the screen. In general, the execution of the wrong line precedes the wrong visible effect. For instance, a wrong assignment to a variable may imply a misbehaviour later on, when the value of the variable is printed on the screen. Usually, the programmer has a very precise idea about which line of code makes the misbehaviour visible, but a non trivial debugging activity may be needed to find the bug. Indeed, debugging practice requires to put a breakpoint before the line of code where the programmer thinks the bug is, and use step-by-step execution from there to find the wrong line of code. However, the guess of the location of the bug is frequently wrong, causing the breakpoint to occur too late (after the bug) and a new execution with an updated guess is often needed. Reversible debugging practice is more direct: first, run the program and stop when the visible misbehaviour is reached; then, execute backwards (possibly step-by-step) looking for the causes of the misbehaviour until the bug is found.

With these premises, it is no surprise that reversible debugging has been deeply explored, as shown for instance by the survey in [11]. Indeed, many debuggers provide features for reversible execution, including popular open source debuggers such as GDB [8] as well as tools from big corporations such as Microsoft, the case of WinDbg [34].

However, the problem is far less settled for concurrent and distributed programs. We remark that nowadays most of the software is concurrent, either since the platform is distributed, the case of Internet or the Cloud, or to overcome the advent of the power wall [46]. Finding bugs in concurrent and distributed software is more difficult than in sequential software [33], since faults may appear or disappear according to the speed of the different processes and of the network communications. The bugs generating these faults, called Heisenbugs, are thus particularly challenging because they are rather difficult to reproduce. Two approaches to reversible debugging of concurrent systems have been proposed. Using *backtracking*,[1] actions are undone in reverse order of execution, while using *causal-consistent reversibility* [25] actions can be undone in any order, provided that the consequences of a given action, if any, are undone beforehand. Note that, by exploring a computation back and forth using either backtracking or causal-consistent reversibility one is guaranteed that Heisenbugs that occurred in the computation will not disappear.

---

[1] Backtracking sometimes refer to the exploration of a set of possibilities: this is not the case here, since backward execution is (almost) deterministic.

This paper will present two lines of research on debugging for concurrent systems developed within the European COST Action IC1405 on "Reversible Computation - Extending Horizons of Computing" [23]. They share the use of state saving to enable backward computation (this is called a Landauer embedding [24], and it is needed to tackle languages which are irreversible) and a formal approach aiming at supporting debugging tools with a theory guaranteeing the desired properties. The first line of research [20–22] (Sect. 3) supports backtracking (apart from some non relevant actions) for a concurrent imperative language with shared memory, while the second line of research [28–30,36] (Sect. 4) supports causal-consistent reversibility for a core subset of the functional message-passing language Erlang. We will showcase both the approaches on the same airline booking example (Sect. 2), coded in the two languages. Related work is discussed in Sect. 5 and final remarks are presented in Sect. 6.

2   Airline Booking Example

In this section we will introduce an example program that contains a bug, and discuss a specific execution leading to a corresponding misbehaviour. This example will be used as running example throughout the paper. We will show this example in the two programming languages needed for the two approaches mentioned above. We begin by introducing each of these languages.

2.1   Imperative Concurrent Language

Our first language is much like any while language, consisting of assignments, conditional statements and while loops. Support has also been added for block statements containing the declaration of local variables and/or procedures, as well as procedure call statements. Further to this, *removal statements* are introduced to "clean up" at the end of a block, where any variables or procedures declared within the block are removed. Our language also contains unique names given to each conditional, loop, block, procedure declaration and call statement, named *construct identifiers* (represented as i1.0, w1.0, b1.0, etc.), and sequences of block names in which a given statement resides named *paths* (represented as pa). Both of these are used to handle variable scope, allowing one to distinguish different variables with the same name. The final addition to our language is *interleaving parallel composition*. A parallel statement, written P par Q allows the execution of the programs P and Q to interleave. All statements except blocks contain a stack A that is used to store identifiers (see below). The syntax of our language follows, where ε represents an empty program. Note that ε is the neutral element of sequential and parallel composition. We write (pa,A)? to denote the fact that (pa,A) is optional. We also write In, Wn, Bn, Cn to range, respectively, over identifiers for conditionals, while loops, blocks and call statements. Also, n refers to the name of a procedure.

```
P ::= ε | S | P; P | P par P
S ::= skip (pa,A)? | X = E (pa,A) | if In B then P else Q end (pa,A)
    | while Wn B do P end (pa,A) | begin Bn BB end | call Cn n (pa,A)
BB ::= DV; DP; P; RP; RV
```

DV ::= ε | var X = v (pa,A); DV   DP ::= ε | proc Pn n is P end (pa,A); DP

RV ::= ε | remove X = v (pa,A); RV   RP ::= ε | remove Pn n is P end (pa,A); RP

Operational Semantics. Our approach (see [20] for a detailed explanation) to reversing programs starts by producing two versions of the original program. The first one, named the *annotated version*, performs forward execution and saves any information that would be lost in a normal computation but is needed for inversion (named *reversal information* and saved into our auxiliary store δ). Identifiers are assigned to statements as we execute them, capturing the interleaving order needed for correct inversion. The second one, named the *inverted version*, executes forwards but simulates reversal using the reversal information as well as the identifiers to follow backtracking order. We comment here that we use 'inversion' to refer to both the process of producing the program code of the inverted version (program inverter [1]), and to the process of executing the inverted version of a program. A reverse execution computes all parallel statements as in a forward execution, but it uses identifiers to determine which statement to invert next (instead of nondeterministically deciding). For programs containing many nested parallel statements, the overhead of determining the correct interleaving order increases, though we still deem this as reasonable [19]. Note that using a nondeterministic interleaving for the reverse execution is not possible, since it is not guaranteed to behave correctly (e.g., requiring information from the auxiliary store that is not there may cause an execution to be stuck). However, a small number of execution steps, including closing a block and removing a skip, do not use an identifier and can therefore be interleaved nondeterministically during an inverse execution. Forward and reverse execution are each defined in terms of a non-standard, small step operational semantics. Our semantics perform both the expected execution (forward and reverse respectively) and all necessary saving/using of the reversal information. Consider the example rule [D1a] for assignments, which is a reversibilisation of the traditional irreversible semantics of an assignment statement [51].

$$[\text{D1a}] \quad \frac{\texttt{m = next()} \quad (\texttt{e pa} \mid \delta,\sigma,\gamma,\square) \hookrightarrow_a^* (\texttt{v} \mid \delta,\sigma,\gamma,\square) \quad evalV(\gamma,\texttt{pa},\texttt{X}) = 1}{(\texttt{X = e (pa,A)} \mid \delta,\sigma,\gamma,\square) \xrightarrow{m} (\texttt{skip m:A} \mid \delta[(\texttt{m},\sigma(1)) \rightharpoonup \texttt{X}], \sigma[1 \mapsto \texttt{v}], \gamma, \square)}$$

As shown here, this rule consists of the evaluation of the expression e to the value v, evaluation of the variable X to a memory location 1 and finally the assigning of the value v to the memory location 1 as expected. Alongside this, the rule also pushes the old value of the variable (the current value held at the memory location, namely $\sigma(1)$) onto the stack for this variable name within δ ($\delta[(\texttt{m},\sigma(1)) \rightharpoonup \texttt{X}]$, where $\rightharpoonup$ denotes a push operation). This old value is saved alongside the next available identifier m, returned via the function next() and used within the rule to record interleaving order (represented using the labelled

$$program ::= fun_1 \ \ldots \ fun_n$$

$$fun ::= a_1(p_{11}, \ \ldots, \ p_{1n_1}) \text{ when } g_1 \to e_1;$$

$$\ldots$$

$$a_m(p_{m1}, \ldots, p_{mn_m}) \text{ when } g_m \to e_n \ .$$

$$e \ni expr ::= X \mid literal \mid [e_1|e_2] \mid \{e_1, \ldots, e_n\} \mid a(e_1, \ldots, e_n) \mid p = e \mid e_1, e_2$$

$$\mid \ \text{receive } c_1; \ldots; c_n \text{ end} \mid \text{spawn}(mod, a, [e_1, \ldots, e_n]) \mid e_1 \ ! \ e_2 \mid \text{self}()$$

$$c \ni clause ::= p \text{ when } g \to e \qquad p \ni pat ::= X \mid literal \mid [p_1|p_2] \mid \{p_1, \ldots, p_n\}$$

Fig. 1. Language syntax rules

arrow $\xrightarrow{m}$). This identifier m is also inserted into the stack A corresponding to this specific assignment statement, represented as m:A.

Now consider the rule [D1r] from our inverse semantics for reversing assignments (that executed forwards via [D1a]).

$$[D1r] \quad \frac{A = m:A' \quad m = \text{previous}() \quad \delta(X) = (m,v):X' \quad evalV(\gamma,\text{pa},X) = 1}{(X = e \ (\text{pa},A) \mid \delta, \sigma, \square) \xrightarrow{m} (\text{skip } A' \mid \delta[X/X'], \sigma[1 \mapsto v], \square)}$$

This rule first ensures this is the next statement to invert using the identifier m, which must match the last used identifier (previous()) and be present in both the statements stack (A = m:A') and the auxiliary store alongside the old value ($\delta(X) = (m,v):X'$). Provided this is satisfied, this rule then removes all occurrences of m, and assigns the old value v retrieved from δ to the corresponding memory location. Note that e appears exactly as in the original version but it is not evaluated, and that the functions next() and previous() both update the next and previous identifiers respectively as a side effect.

2.2 Erlang

Our second approach deals with a relevant fragment of the functional and concurrent language Erlang. We show in Fig. 1 the syntax of its main constructs, focusing on the ones needed in our running example. We drop from the syntax some declarations related to module management, which are orthogonal to our purpose in this paper.

A program is a sequence of function definitions, where each function has a name (an *atom*, denoted by a) and is defined by a number of equations of the form $a_i(p_{i1}, \ \ldots, \ p_{in_i})$ when $g_i \ \to \ e_i$, where $p_{i1}, \ \ldots, \ p_{in_i}$ are *patterns* (i.e., terms built from variables and data constructors), g_i is a *guard* (typically an arithmetic or relational expression only involving built-in functions), and e_i is an arbitrary expression. As is common, the variables in $p_{i1}, \ \ldots, \ p_{in_i}$ are the only variables that may occur free in g_i and e_i. The body of a function is an *expression*, which can include variables, literals (i.e., atoms, integers, floating point numbers, the empty list [ ], etc.), lists (using Prolog-like notation, i.e., $[e_1|e_2]$ is a list with head e_1 and tail e_2), tuples (denoted by $\{e_1, \ldots, e_n\}$),[2]

---

[2] The only data constructors in Erlang (besides literals) are the predefined functions for lists and tuples.

function applications (we do not consider higher order functions in this paper for simplicity), pattern matching, sequences (denoted by comma), receive expressions, spawn (for creating new processes), "!" (for sending a message), and self. Note that some of these functions are actually built-ins in Erlang.

In contrast to expressions, *patterns* are built from variables, literals, lists, and tuples. Patterns can only contain fresh variables. In turn, *values* are built from literals, lists, and tuples (i.e., values are ground patterns). In Erlang, variables start with an uppercase letter.

Let us now informally introduce the semantics of Erlang constructions. In the following, *substitutions* are denoted by Greek letters σ, θ, etc. A substitution σ denotes a mapping from variables to expressions, where $\mathcal{D}om(\sigma)$ is its domain. Substitution application $\sigma(e)$ is also denoted by $e\sigma$.

Given the pattern matching $p = e$, we first evaluate e to a value, say v; then, we check whether v matches p, i.e., there exists a substitution σ for the variables of p with $v = p\sigma$ (otherwise, an exception is raised). Then, the expression reduces to v, and variables are bound according to σ. Roughly speaking, a sequence $(p = e_1, e_2)$ is equivalent to the expression let $p = e_1$ in e_2 in most functional programming languages.

A similar pattern matching operation is performed during a function application $a(e_1, \ldots, e_n)$. First, one evaluates $e_1, \ldots, e_n$ to values, say $v_1, \ldots, v_n$. Then, we scan the left-hand sides of the equations defining the function a until we find one that matches $a(v_1, \ldots, v_n)$. Let $a(p_1, \ldots, p_n)$ when $g \to e$ be such equation, with $a(v_1, \ldots, v_n) = a(p_1, \ldots, p_n)\sigma$. Here, we should also check that the guard, $g\sigma$, reduces to true. In this case, execution proceeds with the evaluation of the function's body, $e\sigma$.

Let us now consider the concurrent features of our language. In Erlang, a running system can be seen as a pool of processes that can only interact through message sending and receiving (i.e., there is no shared memory). Received messages are stored in the queues of processes until they are consumed; namely, each process has one associated local (FIFO) queue. A process is uniquely identified by its *pid* (process identifier). Message sending is asynchronous, while receive instructions block the execution of a process until an appropriate message reaches its local queue (see below).

We consider the following functions with side-effects: self, "!", spawn, and receive. The expression self() returns the pid of a process, while p ! v evaluates to v and, as a side-effect, sends message v to the process with pid p, which will be eventually stored in p's local queue. New processes are spawned with a call of the form spawn($mod, a, [v_1, \ldots, v_n]$), where mod is the name of the module declaring function a, and the new process begins with the evaluation of the function application $a(v_1, \ldots, v_n)$. The expression spawn($mod, a, [v_1, \ldots, v_n]$) returns the (fresh) pid assigned to the new process.

Finally, an expression "receive p_1 when $g_1 \to e_1; \ldots; p_n$ when $g_n \to e_n$ end" should find the *first* message v in the process' queue (if any) such that v matches some pattern p_i (with substitution σ) and the instantiation of the corresponding guard $g_i\sigma$ reduces to true. Then, the receive expression evaluates to $e_i\sigma$, with the side effect of deleting the message v from the process' queue. If there is no matching message in the current queue, the process *suspends* until a matching message arrives.

2.3   Airline Code

We are now ready to describe the example. Consider a model of an airline booking system, where multiple agents sell tickets for the same flight. In order to keep the example concise, we consider only two agents selling tickets in parallel, with three seats initially available. The code of the example is shown in Listing 1.1, written in the concurrent imperative programming language described in Sect. 2.1.

The code contains two while loops operating in parallel (lines 10–16 and 18–24), where each loop models the operation of a single agent. Let us consider the first loop. For each iteration, the agent checks whether any seat remains (line 11). As long as the number of currently available seats is greater than zero, the agent is free to sell a ticket via the procedure named `sell` (called at line 12). Once the number of available tickets has reached zero, each agent will then close, terminating its loop.

As previously mentioned, this program can show a misbehaviour under certain execution paths. Recall the simplified setting of three initially available seats. Consider an execution that begins with each agent selling a single ticket (allocating one seat) via one full iteration of each while loop (the interleaving among the two iterations is not relevant). At this point, both agents remain open (since `agent1 = 1` and `agent2 = 1`), and the current number of seats is 1. Now assume that the execution continues with the following interleaving. The condition of each while loop is checked, both of which will evaluate to true as each agent is open. Next, the execution of each loop body begins with the evaluation of the guard of each conditional statement. They will both evaluate to true, as there is at least one seat available. At this point, each agent is committed to selling one more ticket, even if only one seat is available. The rest of the execution can then be finished under any interleaving. The important thing to note here is that the final number of free seats is -1. This is an obvious misbehaviour, as the two agents allocated four tickets when only three seats were available. This misbehaviour occurs since the programmer assumed that the checking for an available seat and its allocation were atomic, but there is no mechanism enforcing this.

Listing 1.2 shows the same example coded in Erlang. A call to the initial function, `main`, spawns two processes (the *agents*) that start with the execution of function calls `agent(1,Main)` and `agent(2,Main)`, respectively. Here, `Main` is a variable with the *pid* of the main process, which is obtained via a call to the predefined function `self`.

Then, at line 8, the main process calls to function `seats` with argument 3 (the initial number of available seats). From this point on, the main process behaves as a *server* that executes a potentially infinite loop that waits for requests and replies to them. Here, the *state* of the process is given by the argument Num which

```
1  seats = 3;
2  begin b0.0
3    var agent1 = 1;
4    var agent2 = 1;
5    proc p0.0 sell is
6      seats = seats - 1;
7    end;
8
9    par {
10     while w0.0 (agent1 == 1) do
11       if i0.0 (seats > 0) then
12         call c0.0 sell;
13       else
14         agent1 = 0;
15       end;
16     end;
17   } {
18     while w1.0 (agent2 == 1) do
19       if i1.0 (seats > 0) then
20         call c1.0 sell;
21       else
22         agent2 = 0;
23       end;
24     end;
25   }
26   remove proc p0.0 sell end;
27   remove var agent2 = 1;
28   remove var agent1 = 1;
29 end
```

Listing 1.1. Airline booking example in a concurrent imperative language. All paths and identifier stacks are omitted as these are inserted automatically.

represents the current number of available seats. The server accepts two kinds of messages: {numOfSeats,Pid}, a request to know the current number of available seats, and {sell,Pid}, to decrease the number of available seats (analogously to the procedure sell in Listing 1.1). In the first case, the number of available seats is sent back to the agent that performed the request (Pid ! Num); in the second case, the number of the booked seat is sent.[3] The behaviour of the agents (lines 17–23) is simple. An agent first sends a request to know the number of available seats, Pid ! {numOfSeats,self()}, where self() is required for the main process to be able to send a reply back to the sender. Then, the agent suspends its execution waiting for an answer {seats,Num}: if Num is greater than zero, the agent sends a new message to sell a seat (Pid ! {sell,self()}) and

---

[3] We note that the number of the booked seat, Num, is not used by function **agent** in our example, but might be used in a more realistic program. We keep this value anyway since it will ease the understanding of the trace in Sect. 4.

```
1   -module(airline).
2   -export([main/0,agent/2]).
3   8
4   main() ->
5       Main = self(),
6       spawn(?MODULE, agent, [1,Main]),
7       spawn(?MODULE, agent, [2,Main]),
8       seats(3).
9
10  seats(Num) ->
11      receive
12          {numOfSeats,Pid} -> Pid ! {seats,Num}, seats(Num);
13          {sell,Pid} -> io:format("Seat sold!~n"),
14                        Pid ! {booked,Num},seats(Num-1)
15      end.
16
17  agent(NAg,Pid) ->
18      Pid ! {numOfSeats,self()},
19      receive
20          {seats,Num} when Num > 0 -> Pid ! {sell,self()},
21                    receive {booked,_} -> agent(NAg,Pid) end;
22          _ -> io:format("Agent~p done!~n",[NAg])
23      end.
```

Listing 1.2. Airline booking example, in Erlang.

receives the confirmation ({booked,_});[4] otherwise, it terminates the execution with the message "AgentN done!", where N is either 1 or 2.

3   Backtracking in a Concurrent Imperative Language

In this section we describe a state-saving approach to reversibility in the concurrent imperative programming language described in Sect. 2.1. We begin by discussing our approach and its use within the debugging of the airline example (see Sect. 2.3), along with our simulation tool [20,21].

As described in more detail in [21], we have produced a simulator implementing the operational semantics of our approach. This simulator is capable of parsing a program, automatically inserting removal statements, construct identifiers and paths, and simulating both forward and reverse execution. Each execution can be either end-to-end, or step-by-step.

We first execute the forward version of our airline example completely. This execution produces the annotated version in Fig. 2a, where the identifier stack for each statement has been populated capturing an interleaving order that experiences the bug as outlined in Sect. 2.3. The inverted version of the airline example is shown in Fig. 2b, where the overall statement order has been inverted. Note that some annotations are omitted to keep this source code concise (e.g., no paths

---

[4] Anonymous variables are denoted by an underscore "_".

```
1   seats = 3 [0];                           1   //Expect seats=0, not seats=-1
2   begin b0.0                               2   begin b0.0
3     var agent1 = 1 [1];                    3     var agent1 = 1 [40];
4     var agent2 = 1 [2];                    4     var agent2 = 1 [39];
5     proc p0.0 sell is                      5     proc p0.0 sell is
6       seats = seats - 1 [7,13,22,23];      6       seats = seats - 1 [7,13,22,23];
7     end [3];                               7     end [38];
8                                            8
9     par {                                  9     par {
10      while w0.0 (agent1 == 1) do          10      while w0.0 (agent1 == 1) do
11        if i0.0 (seats > 0) then           11        if i0.0 (seats > 0) then
12          call c0.0 sell [6,8,20,24];      12          call c0.0 sell [6,8,20,24];
13        else                               13        else
14          agent1 = 0 [31];                 14          agent1 = 0 [31];
15        end [5,9,18,26,30,32];             15        end [5,9,18,26,30,32];
16      end [4,17,29,33];                    16      end [4,17,29,33];
17    } {                                    17    } {
18      while w1.0 (agent2 == 1) do          18      while w1.0 (agent2 == 1) do
19        if i1.0 (seats > 0) then           19        if i1.0 (seats > 0) then
20          call c1.0 sell [12,14,21,25];    20          call c1.0 sell [12,14,21,25];
21        else                               21        else
22          agent2 = 0 [35];                 22          agent2 = 0 [35];
23        end [11,15,19,27,34,36];           23        end [11,15,19,27,34,36];
24      end [10,16,28,37];                   24      end [10,16,28,37];
25    }                                      25    }
26    remove proc p0.0 sell end [38];        26    remove proc p0.0 sell end [3];
27    remove var agent2 = 1 [39];            27    remove var agent2 = 1 [2];
28    remove var agent1 = 1 [40];            28    remove var agent1 = 1 [1];
29  end                                      29  end
30  //Finishes with seats = -1               30  seats = 3 [0];
```

   (a) Annotated program (executed)   (b) Inverted program (not yet executed)

Fig. 2. Final annotated and inverted versions of the airline example, with paths omitted

are shown). We start the debugging process at the beginning of the execution of
the inverted version (line 1 of Fig. 2b). Recall that all expressions or conditions
are not evaluated or used during an inverse execution. Using the final program
state showing the misbehaviour (produced via the annotated execution with
seats = -1), the simulator begins by opening the block and re-declaring both
local variables and the procedure, using identifiers 40–38. From here, the execution continues with the parallel statement. The final iteration of each while loop
is reversed (simulating the inversion of the closing of each agent) using identifiers
37–28. Now the penultimate iteration of each while loop must be inverted. The
consecutive identifiers 27 and 26 are then used to ensure that each of the conditional statements (lines 11 and 19) are opened, using two true values retrieved
from the reversal information saved.

The execution then continues using identifiers 25–20, where each loop almost
completes the current iteration, reversing the last time each of them allocated a

```
Simulator: Rev-Ex> display loops
|--Displaying the current while loop environment
------------------------------------------------------------
currently executing a parallel statement
Loop Name      | Program
------------------------------------------------------------
w0.0           | while w0.0 (agent1Open == 1) do
               |   if i0.2 (numOfSeats > 0) then
               |     call c0.2 sellTicket(b0.0;) [6, 8]
               |   else
               |     agent1Open = 0 (b0.0;) []
               |   fi (b0.0;) [5, 9, 18] <--------
               | elihw (b0.0;) [4, 17]
------------------------------------------------------------
------------------------------------------------------------
w1.0           | while w1.0 (agent2Open == 1) do
               |   if i1.2 (numOfSeats > 0) then
               |     call c1.2 sellTicket(b0.0;) [12, 14]
               |   else
               |     agent2Open = 0 (b0.0;) []
               |   fi (b0.0;) [11, 15, 19] <--------
               | elihw (b0.0;) [10, 16]
------------------------------------------------------------
------------------------------------------------------------
```

Fig. 3. Stopping position of the inverse execution (containing paths automatically inserted by the simulator)

seat. This produces the state where seats = 1, and where the next available step is to close either of the inverse conditional statements. Though the identifiers ensure we must start by closing the conditional with identifier 19, the fact that both can be closed implies that both are open at the same time. This current position within the inverse execution is shown in Fig. 3, where the command 'display loops' outputs all current while loops (agents) with arrows indicating the next statement to be executed. It is clear from our semantics (see [20]) that the closing of an inverted conditional is the reverse of opening its forward version. Since the two conditionals have been opened using consecutive identifiers, one can see that each committed to selling a ticket. Given that the current state has seats = 1, this execution commits to selling two tickets when only one remains. It is therefore clear that this is an atomicity violation, since interleaving of other actions is allowed between the checking for at least one free seat and the allocation of it. We have therefore shown how the simulator implementing our approach to reversibility can be used during the debugging process of an example bug.

4   Causal-Consistent Reversibility in Erlang

In this section we will discuss how to apply causal-consistent reversible debugging to the airline booking example in Sect. 2.3. Our approach to reversible debugging is based on the following principles [29, 30]:

- First, we consider a *reduction* semantics for the language (a subset of Core Erlang [5], which is an intermediate step in Erlang compilation). Our semantics includes two transition relations, one for expressions (which is mostly a call-by-value semantics for a functional language) and one for *systems*, i.e., collections of processes, possibly interacting through message passing. An advantage of this modular design is that only the transition relation for systems needs to be modified in order to produce a reversible semantics.
- Then, we instrument the standard semantics in different ways. On the one hand, we instrument it to produce a *log* of the computation; namely, by recording all actions involving the sending and receiving of messages, as well as the spawning of new processes (see [30] for more details). On the other hand, one can instrument the semantics so that the configurations now carry enough information to undo any execution step, i.e., a typical Landauer embedding. Producing then a *backward* semantics that proceeds in the opposite direction is not difficult. Here, the configurations may include both a *log*—to drive forward executions—and a *history*—to drive backward executions.
- It is worthwhile to note that forward computations need not follow exactly the same steps as in the recorded computation (indeed the log does not record the total order of steps). However, it is guaranteed that the admissible computations are *causally equivalent* to the recorded one; namely, they differ only for swaps of concurrent actions. Analogously, backward computations need not be the exact inverse of the considered forward computation, but ensuring that backward steps are *causal-consistent* suffices. This degree of freedom is essential to allow the user to focus on the process and/or actions of interest during debugging, rather than inspecting the complete execution (which is often impractical).
- Finally, we define another layer on top of the reversible semantics in order to *drive* it following a number of *requests* from the user, e.g., rolling back up to the point where a given process was spawned, going forward up to the point where a message is sent, etc. This layer essentially implements a stack of requests that follows the causal dependencies of the reversible semantics.

In the following, we consider the causal-consistent reversible debugger CauDEr [27, 28] which follows the principles listed above.

CauDEr first translates the airline example into Core Erlang [5]. Then one can execute the program, either using a built-in scheduler, or using the log of an actual execution [30].

Here, if we compile the program in the standard environment and execute the call main(), we get the following output:

```
Seat sold!
Seat sold!
Seat sold!
Seat sold!
Agent1 done!
Agent2 done!
```

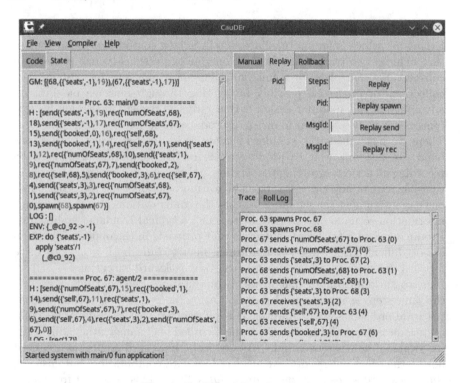

Fig. 4. CauDEr debugging session

which is clearly incorrect since we only had three seats available.

By using the logger and, then, loading both the program and the log into CauDEr (as described in [30]), we can replay the entire execution and explore the sequence of concurrent actions. Figure 4 shows the final state (on the left) and the sequence of concurrent actions (on the right), where process 63 is the main process, and processes 67 and 68 are the agents.

Now, we can look at the sequence of concurrent actions, where messages are labelled with a unique identifier, added by CauDEr, which is shown in brackets to the right of the corresponding line:

```
Proc. 63 spawns Proc. 67
Proc. 63 spawns Proc. 68
Proc. 67 sends {'numOfSeats',67} to Proc. 63 (0)

... 19 lines ...

Proc. 63 receives {'numOfSeats',68} (10)
Proc. 63 sends {'seats',1} to Proc. 68 (12)
Proc. 67 receives {'seats',1} (9)
Proc. 67 sends {'sell',67} to Proc. 63 (11)
Proc. 63 receives {'sell',67} (11)
```

```
Proc. 63 sends {'booked',1} to Proc. 67 (14)
Proc. 68 receives {'seats',1} (12)
Proc. 68 sends {'sell',68} to Proc. 63 (13)
Proc. 63 receives {'sell',68} (13)
Proc. 63 sends {'booked',0} to Proc. 68 (16)
Proc. 67 receives {'booked',1} (14)
Proc. 67 sends {'numOfSeats',67} to Proc. 63 (15)
Proc. 63 receives {'numOfSeats',67} (15)
Proc. 63 sends {'seats',-1} to Proc. 67 (17)
Proc. 68 receives {'booked',0} (16)
Proc. 68 sends {'numOfSeats',68} to Proc. 63 (18)
Proc. 63 receives {'numOfSeats',68} (18)
Proc. 63 sends {'seats',-1} to Proc. 68 (19)
```

One can see that seat number 0 (which does not exist!) has been booked by process 68, and the notification has been provided via message number 16.

A good state to explore is the one where message number 16 has been sent. Here a main feature of causal-consistent reversible debugging comes handy: the possibility of going to the state just before a relevant action has been performed, by undoing it, including all and only its consequences. This is called a causal-consistent rollback. CauDEr provides causal-consistent rollbacks for various actions, including send actions. Thus, the programmer can invoke a Roll send command with message identifier 16 as a parameter.

In this way, one discovers that the message has been sent by process 63 (as expected, since process 63 is the main process). By exploring its state one understands that, from the point of view of process 63, sending message 16 is correct, since it is the only possible answer to a sell message. The bug should be thus before.

From the program code, the programmer knows that whether seat Num is available or not is checked by a message of the form {numOfSeats,Pid}, which is answered with a message of the form {seats,Num}, where Num is the number of available seats.

Looking again at the concurrency actions, the programmer can see that process number 68 was indeed notified of the availability of a seat by message number 12.

We can use again Roll send, now with parameter 12, to check whether this send is correct or not. We discover that indeed the send is correct since, when the message is sent, there is one available seat. However, here, another window comes handy: the Roll log window that shows which actions (causally dependent on the one undone) have been undone during a rollback, which shows:

```
Roll send from Proc. 63 of {'booked',1} to Proc. 67 (14)
Roll send from Proc. 67 of {'numOfSeats',67} to Proc. 63 (15)
Roll send from Proc. 63 of {'seats',1} to Proc. 68 (12)
Roll send from Proc. 68 of {'sell',68} to Proc. 63 (13)
```

By checking it the programmer sees that also the interactions between process 67 and process 63 booking seat 1 are undone. Hence the problem is that, in between the check for availability and the booking, another process may interact with `main`, stealing the seat; thus, the error is an atomicity violation.

Of course, given the simplicity of the system, one could have spotted the bug directly by looking at the code or at the full sequence of message exchanges, but the technique above is quite driven by the visible misbehaviour, hence it will better scale to larger systems (e.g., with more seats and agents, or with additional functionalities).

We remark that, while the presentation above concentrates on the debugger and its practical use, this line of research also deeply considered its theoretical underpinning, as briefly summarised at the beginning of the section. Thanks to this, relevant properties have been proved, e.g., that if a misbehaviour occurs in a computation then the same misbehaviour will occur also in each replay [30].

5   Related Work

Reversible computation in general, and reversible debugging in particular, have been deeply explored in the literature.

A line of research considers naturally reversible languages, that is languages where only reversible programs can be written. Such approaches include the imperative languages Janus [49,50], R-CORE [17] and R-WHILE [16], and the object-oriented languages Joule [43] and ROOPL [18]. These approaches require dedicated languages, and cannot be applied to mainstream languages like Erlang or a classic imperative language, as we do in this paper.

The backtracking approach has been applied, e.g., in the Reverse C Compiler (RCC) defined by Perumalla et al. [6,37]. It supports the entire programming language C, but lacks a proof of correctness, which is instead provided by our approaches. The Backstroke framework [48] is a further example, supporting the vast majority of the programming language C++. This framework has been used to provide reverse execution in the field of Parallel Discrete Event Simulation (PDES) [13], as described in more recent works by Schordan et al. [40–42]. Similar approaches have been used for debugging, e.g., based on program instrumentation techniques [7]. Identifiers and keys are used to control execution in the work by Phillips and Ulidowski [38,39]. Another related work is omniscient debugging, where each assignment and method call is stored in an execution history, which can be used to restore any desired program state. An example of such a debugger written for Java was proposed by Lewis [32].

Causal-consistent reversibility has been mainly studied in the area of foundational process calculi such as CCS [10] and its variants [35,38], π-calculus [9], and higher-order π-calculus [26] and coordination languages such as Klaim [15]. The application to debugging has been first proposed in [14] in the context of the toy functional language μOz. A related approach is Actoverse [44], for Akka-based applications. It provides many relevant features complementary to ours, such as a partial-order graphical representation of message exchanges. On the other side, Actoverse allows one to explore only some states of the computation, such as the ones corresponding to message sending and receiving. We also mention Causeway [45], which however is not a full-fledged debugger, but just a post-mortem traces analyser.

6 Conclusion

We presented two approaches to reversible debugging of concurrent systems, we will now briefly compare them. Beyond the language they consider, the main difference between the two approaches is in the order in which execution steps can be reversed. The backtracking approach undoes them in reverse order of execution. This means that there is no need to track dependencies, and the user of the debugger can easily anticipate which steps will be undone by looking at identifiers. The causal-consistent approach instead allows independent steps of an execution to be reversed in any order, hence tracking dependencies between steps is crucial. This offers the benefit that only the steps strictly needed to reach the desired point of an execution need to be reversed, and steps which happened in between but were actually independent are disregarded.

Debugging is a relevant application area for reversible computation, but reversible debugging for concurrent and distributed systems is still in its infancy. While different techniques have been put forward, they are not yet able to deal with real, complex systems. A first reason is that they do not tackle mainstream languages (Erlang could be considered mainstream, but only part of the language is currently covered). When this first step will be completed, then runtime overhead and size of the logs will become relevant problems, as they are now in the setting of sequential reversible debugging.

References

1. Abramov, S., Glück, R.: Principles of inverse computation and the universal resolving algorithm. In: Mogensen, T.Æ., Schmidt, D.A., Sudborough, I.H. (eds.) The Essence of Computation. LNCS, vol. 2566, pp. 269–295. Springer, Heidelberg (2002). https://doi.org/10.1007/3-540-36377-7_13
2. Altenkirch, T., Grattage, J.: A functional quantum programming language. In: Proceedings of the 20th IEEE Symposium on Logic in Computer Science (LICS 2005), pp. 249–258. IEEE Computer Society (2005). https://doi.org/10.1109/LICS.2005.1
3. Britton, T., Jeng, L., Carver, G., Cheak, P., Katzenellenbogen, T.: Reversible debugging software - quantify the time and cost saved using reversible debuggers (2012). http://www.roguewave.com
4. Cardelli, L., Laneve, C.: Reversible structures. In: Fages, F. (ed.) Proceedings of the 9th International Conference on Computational Methods in Systems Biology (CMSB 2011), pp. 131–140. ACM (2011). https://doi.org/10.1145/2037509.2037529
5. Carlsson, R., et al.: Core Erlang 1.0.3. language specification (2004). https://www.it.uu.se/research/group/hipe/cerl/doc/core_erlang-1.0.3.pdf

6. Carothers, C.D., Perumalla, K.S., Fujimoto, R.: Efficient optimistic parallel simulations using reverse computation. ACM Trans. Model. Comput. Simul. **9**(3), 224–253 (1999)
7. Chen, S., Fuchs, W.K., Chung, J.: Reversible debugging using program instrumentation. IEEE Trans. Softw. Eng. **27**(8), 715–727 (2001). https://doi.org/10.1109/32.940726
8. Conrod, J.: Tutorial: reverse debugging with GDB 7 (2009). http://jayconrod.com/posts/28/tutorial-reverse-debugging-with-gdb-7
9. Cristescu, I., Krivine, J., Varacca, D.: A compositional semantics for the reversible π-calculus. In: Proceedings of the 28th Annual ACM/IEEE Symposium on Logic in Computer Science (LICS 2013), pp. 388–397. IEEE Computer Society (2013). https://doi.org/10.1109/LICS.2013.45
10. Danos, V., Krivine, J.: Reversible communicating systems. In: Gardner, P., Yoshida, N. (eds.) CONCUR 2004. LNCS, vol. 3170, pp. 292–307. Springer, Heidelberg (2004). https://doi.org/10.1007/978-3-540-28644-8_19
11. Engblom, J.: A review of reverse debugging. In: Morawiec, A., Hinderscheit, J. (eds.) Proceedings of the 2012 System, Software, SoC and Silicon Debug Conference (S4D), pp. 28–33. IEEE (2012)
12. Frank, M.P.: Introduction to reversible computing: motivation, progress, and challenges. In: Bagherzadeh, N., Valero, M., Ramírez, A. (eds.) Proceedings of the Second Conference on Computing Frontiers, pp. 385–390. ACM (2005). https://doi.org/10.1145/1062261.1062324
13. Fujimoto, R.: Parallel discrete event simulation. Commun. ACM **33**(10), 30–53 (1990). https://doi.org/10.1145/84537.84545
14. Giachino, E., Lanese, I., Mezzina, C.A.: Causal-consistent reversible debugging. In: Gnesi, S., Rensink, A. (eds.) FASE 2014. LNCS, vol. 8411, pp. 370–384. Springer, Heidelberg (2014). https://doi.org/10.1007/978-3-642-54804-8_26
15. Giachino, E., Lanese, I., Mezzina, C.A., Tiezzi, F.: Causal-consistent rollback in a tuple-based language. J. Log. Algebraic Meth. Program. **88**, 99–120 (2017)
16. Glück, R., Yokoyama, T.: A linear-time self-interpreter of a reversible imperative language. Comput. Softw. **33**(3), 108–128 (2016)
17. Glück, R., Yokoyama, T.: A minimalist's reversible while language. IEICE Trans. **100-D**(5), 1026–1034 (2017)
18. Haulund, T.: Design and implementation of a reversible object-oriented programming language. Master's thesis, Faculty of Science, University of Copenhagen (2017). https://arxiv.org/abs/1707.07845
19. Hoey, J.: Reversing an imperative concurrent programming language. Ph.D. thesis, University of Leicester (2020)
20. Hoey, J., Ulidowski, I., Yuen, S.: Reversing imperative parallel programs with blocks and procedures. In: 2018 Proceedings of Express/SOS (2018)
21. Hoey, J., Ulidowski, I.: Reversible imperative parallel programs and debugging. In: Thomsen, M.K., Soeken, M. (eds.) RC 2019. LNCS, vol. 11497, pp. 108–127. Springer, Cham (2019). https://doi.org/10.1007/978-3-030-21500-2_7
22. Hoey, J., Ulidowski, I., Yuen, S.: Reversing parallel programs with blocks and procedures. In: Pérez, J.A., Tini, S. (eds.) Proceedings of the Combined 25th International Workshop on Expressiveness in Concurrency and 15th Workshop on Structural Operational Semantics (EXPRESS/SOS 2018), EPTCS, vol. 276, pp. 69–86 (2018). https://doi.org/10.4204/EPTCS.276.7
23. European COST actions IC1405 on "reversible computation - extending horizons of computing". http://www.revcomp.eu/

24. Landauer, R.: Irreversibility and heat generated in the computing process. IBM J. Res. Dev. **5**, 183–191 (1961)
25. Lanese, I., Mezzina, C.A., Tiezzi, F.: Causal-consistent reversibility. Bull. EATCS **114**, 121–139 (2014)
26. Lanese, I., Mezzina, C.A., Stefani, J.B.: Reversibility in the higher-order π-calculus. Theor. Comput. Sci. **625**, 25–84 (2016)
27. Lanese, I., Nishida, N., Palacios, A., Vidal, G.: CauDEr. https://github.com/mistupv/cauder
28. Lanese, I., Nishida, N., Palacios, A., Vidal, G.: CauDEr: a causal-consistent reversible debugger for Erlang. In: Gallagher, J.P., Sulzmann, M. (eds.) FLOPS 2018. LNCS, vol. 10818, pp. 247–263. Springer, Cham (2018). https://doi.org/10.1007/978-3-319-90686-7_16
29. Lanese, I., Nishida, N., Palacios, A., Vidal, G.: A theory of reversibility for Erlang. J. Log. Algebraic Meth. Program. **100**, 71–97 (2018)
30. Lanese, I., Palacios, A., Vidal, G.: Causal-consistent replay debugging for message passing programs. In: Pérez, J.A., Yoshida, N. (eds.) FORTE 2019. LNCS, vol. 11535, pp. 167–184. Springer, Cham (2019). https://doi.org/10.1007/978-3-030-21759-4_10
31. Laursen, J.S., Schultz, U.P., Ellekilde, L.: Automatic error recovery in robot assembly operations using reverse execution. In: Proceedings of the 2015 IEEE/RSJ International Conference on Intelligent Robots and Systems (IROS 2015), pp. 1785–1792. IEEE (2015). https://doi.org/10.1109/IROS.2015.7353609
32. Lewis, B.: Debugging backwards in time. In: Ronsse, M., Bosschere, K.D. (eds.) Proceedings of the Fifth International Workshop on Automated Debugging (AADEBUG 2003), pp. 225–235 (2003). https://arxiv.org/abs/cs/0310016
33. Lu, S., Park, S., Seo, E., Zhou, Y.: Learning from mistakes: a comprehensive study on real world concurrency bug characteristics. In: Eggers, S.J., Larus, J.R. (eds.) Proceedings of the 13th International Conference on Architectural Support for Programming Languages and Operating Systems (ASPLOS 2008), pp. 329–339. ACM (2008). https://doi.org/10.1145/1346281.1346323
34. McNellis, J., Mola, J., Sykes, K.: Time travel debugging: root causing bugs in commercial scale software. CppCon talk (2017). https://www.youtube.com/watch?v=l1YJTg_A914
35. Mezzina, C.A.: On reversibility and broadcast. In: Kari, J., Ulidowski, I. (eds.) RC 2018. LNCS, vol. 11106, pp. 67–83. Springer, Cham (2018). https://doi.org/10.1007/978-3-319-99498-7_5
36. Nishida, N., Palacios, A., Vidal, G.: A reversible semantics for Erlang. In: Hermenegildo, M.V., Lopez-Garcia, P. (eds.) LOPSTR 2016. LNCS, vol. 10184, pp. 259–274. Springer, Cham (2017). https://doi.org/10.1007/978-3-319-63139-4_15
37. Perumalla, K.: Introduction to Reversible Computing. CRC Press, Boca Raton (2014)
38. Phillips, I., Ulidowski, I.: Reversing algebraic process calculi. J. Log. Algebraic Program. **73**(1–2), 70–96 (2007)
39. Phillips, I., Ulidowski, I., Yuen, S.: A reversible process calculus and the modelling of the ERK signalling pathway. In: Glück, R., Yokoyama, T. (eds.) RC 2012. LNCS, vol. 7581, pp. 218–232. Springer, Heidelberg (2013). https://doi.org/10.1007/978-3-642-36315-3_18
40. Schordan, M., Jefferson, D., Barnes, P., Oppelstrup, T., Quinlan, D.: Reverse code generation for parallel discrete event simulation. In: Krivine, J., Stefani, J.-B. (eds.) RC 2015. LNCS, vol. 9138, pp. 95–110. Springer, Cham (2015). https://doi.org/10.1007/978-3-319-20860-2_6

41. Schordan, M., Oppelstrup, T., Jefferson, D.R., Barnes Jr., P.D.: Generation of reversible C++ code for optimistic parallel discrete event simulation. New Gener. Comput. **36**(3), 257–280 (2018). https://doi.org/10.1007/s00354-018-0038-2

42. Schordan, M., Oppelstrup, T., Jefferson, D.R., Barnes Jr, P.D., Quinlan, D.J.: Automatic generation of reversible C++ code and its performance in a scalable kinetic Monte-Carlo application. In: Fujimoto, R., Unger, B.W., Carothers, C.D. (eds.) Proceedings of the 2016 Annual ACM Conference on SIGSIM Principles of Advanced Simulation (SIGSIM-PADS 2016), pp. 111–122. ACM (2016). https://doi.org/10.1145/2901378.2901394

43. Schultz, U.P., Axelsen, H.B.: Elements of a reversible object-oriented language. In: Devitt, S., Lanese, I. (eds.) RC 2016. LNCS, vol. 9720, pp. 153–159. Springer, Cham (2016). https://doi.org/10.1007/978-3-319-40578-0_10

44. Shibanai, K., Watanabe, T.: Actoverse: a reversible debugger for actors. In: Proceedings of the 7th ACM SIGPLAN International Workshop on Programming Based on Actors, Agents, and Decentralized Control (AGERE 2017), pp. 50–57. ACM (2017). https://doi.org/10.1145/3141834.3141840

45. Stanley, T., Close, T., Miller, M.S.: Causeway: a message-oriented distributed debugger. Technical report, HP Labs tech report HPL-2009-78 (2009). http://www.hpl.hp.com/techreports/2009/HPL-2009-78.html

46. Sutter, H.: The free lunch is over: a fundamental turn toward concurrency in software. Dr. Dobb's J. **30**(3), 202–210 (2005)

47. Undo Software: Increasing software development productivity with reversible debugging (2014). http://undo-software.com/wp-content/uploads/2014/10/Increasing-software-development-productivity-with-reversible-debugging.pdf

48. Vulov, G., Hou, C., Vuduc, R.W., Fujimoto, R., Quinlan, D.J., Jefferson, D.R.: The backstroke framework for source level reverse computation applied to parallel discrete event simulation. In: Jain, S., Creasey Jr, R.R.., Himmelspach, J., White, K.P., Fu, M.C. (eds.) Proceedings of the Winter Simulation Conference (WSC 2011), pp. 2965–2979. IEEE (2011). https://doi.org/10.1109/WSC.2011.6147998

49. Yokoyama, T., Glück, R.: A reversible programming language and its invertible self-interpreter. In: Ramalingam, G., Visser, E. (eds.) Proceedings of the 2007 ACM SIGPLAN Workshop on Partial Evaluation and Semantics-Based Program Manipulation (PEPM 2007), pp. 144–153. ACM (2007)

50. Yokoyama, T., Axelsen, H.B., Glück, R.: Principles of a reversible programming language. In: Ramírez, A., Bilardi, G., Gschwind, M. (eds.) Proceedings of the 5th Conference on Computing Frontiers, pp. 43–54. ACM (2008). https://doi.org/10.1145/1366230.1366239

51. Yokoyama, T., Axelsen, H.B., Glück, R.: Fundamentals of reversible flowchart languages. Theor. Comput. Sci. **611**, 87–115 (2016). https://doi.org/10.1016/j.tcs.2015.07.046

Towards Choreographic-Based Monitoring

Adrian Francalanza[1], Claudio Antares Mezzina[2(✉)], and Emilio Tuosto[3,4]

[1] University of Malta, Msida, Malta
[2] Dipartimento di Scienze Pure e Applicate, Università di Urbino, Urbino, Italy
claudio.mezzina@uniurb.it
[3] Gran Sasso Science Institute, L'Aquila, Italy
[4] University of Leicester, Leicester, UK

Abstract. Distributed programs are hard to get right because they are required to be open, scalable, long-running, and dependable. In particular, the recent approaches to distributed software based on (micro-) services, where different services are developed independently by disparate teams, exacerbate the problem. Services are meant to be composed together and run in open contexts where unpredictable behaviours can emerge. This makes it necessary to adopt suitable strategies for monitoring the execution and incorporate recovery and adaptation mechanisms so to make distributed programs more flexible and robust. The typical approach that is currently adopted is to embed such mechanisms within the program logic. This makes it hard to extract, compare and debug. We propose an approach that employs formal abstractions for specifying failure recovery and adaptation strategies. Although implementation agnostic, these abstractions would be amenable to algorithmic synthesis of code, monitoring, and tests. We consider message-passing programs (a la Erlang, Go, or MPI) that are gaining momentum both in academia and in industry. We first propose a model which abstracts away from three aspects: the definition of formal behavioural models encompassing failures; the specification of the relevant properties of adaptation and recovery strategy; and the automatic generation of monitoring, recovery, and adaptation logic in target languages of interest. To show the efficacy of our model, we give an instance of it by introducing *reversible choreographies* to express the normal forward behaviour of the system and the condition under which adaptation has to take place. Then we show how it is possible to derive Erlang code directly from the global specification.

1 Introduction

Distributed applications are notoriously complex and guaranteeing their correctness, robustness, and resilience is particularly challenging. These reliability

Research partly supported by the EU H2020 RISE programme under the Marie Skłodowska-Curie grant agreement No 778233 and by COST Action IC1405 on Reversible Computation - Extending Horizons of Computing. The second author has been partially supported by the French National Research Agency (ANR), project DCore n. ANR-18-CE25-0007.

I. Ulidowski et al. (Eds.): RC 2020, LNCS 12070, pp. 128–150, 2020.
https://doi.org/10.1007/978-3-030-47361-7_6

requirements cannot be tackled without considering the problems that are not generally encountered when developing *non*-distributed software. In particular, the execution and behaviour of distributed applications is characterised by a number of factors, a few of which we discuss below:

- Firstly, communication over networks is subject to *failures* (hardware or software) and to *security* concerns: nodes may crash or undergo management operations, links may fail or be temporarily unavailable, access policies may modify the connectivity of the system.
- Secondly, *openness*—a key requirement of distributed applications— introduces other types of failures. A paradigmatic example are (micro-) service architectures where distributed components dynamically bind and execute together. In this context, failures in the communication infrastructures are possibly aggravated by those due to services' unavailability, their (behavioural) incompatibility, or to unexpected interactions emerging from unforeseen compositions.
- Also, distributed components may belong to different administrative domains; this may introduce unexpected changes to the interaction patterns that may not necessarily emerge at design time. In addition, unforeseen behaviour may emerge because components may evolve independently (e.g., the upgrade of a service may hinder the communication with partner services).
- Another element of concern is that it is hard to determine the causes of errors, which in turn complicates efforts to rectify and/or mitigate the damage via recovery procedures. Since the boundary of an application are quite "fluid", it becomes infeasible to track and confine errors whenever they emerge. These errors are also hard to reproduce for debugging purposes, and some of them may even constitute instances of Heisenbugs [27].

For the above reasons (and others), developers have to harness their software with mechanisms that ensure (some degree of) dependability. For instance, the use of monitors capable of detecting failures and triggering automated counter-measures can avoid catastrophic crashes in distributed settings [24]. The typical mechanisms to foster reliability are redundancy (typically to tackle hardware failures) and exception handling for software reliability. It has been observed (see e.g., [42]) that the use of exception handling mechanisms naturally leads to defensive approaches in software development. For instance, network communications in languages such as Java require to extensively cast code in try-catch blocks in order to deal with possible exceptions due to communications. This muddles the main program logic with auxiliary logic related to error handling. Defensive programming, besides being inelegant, is not appealing; in fact, it requires developers to entangle the application-specific software with the one related to recovery procedures.

We advocate the use of choreographies to specify, analyse, and implement reliable strategies for recovery and monitoring of distributed message-passing applications. We strive towards a setup that teases apart the main program logic from the coordination of error detection, correction and recovery. The rest of the paper motivates our approach: Sect. 2 further introduces our motivations,

Sect. 3 presents our (abstract) model by posing some research challenges, while Sects. 4 to 6 provide and instance of such model. We draw some conclusions in Sect. 7.

Disclaimer. This paper gathers the results obtained in [13,23] with the intent to present them as a whole. In particular, the model presented in Sect. 3 is taken from [13], while Sects. 4 to 6 are adapted from [23]. These results were obtained during the COST Action IC1405 within the case study "Reversible Choreographies via Monitoring in Erlang" of the Working Group 4 on case studies. We thank Carla Ferreira and Ulrik Pagh Schultz for having wisely led such working group.

2 Motivation

We are interested in *message-passing* frameworks, *i.e.,* models, systems, and languages where distributed components coordinate by exchanging messages. One archetypal model of the message-passing paradigm is the *actor model* [5] popularised by industry-strength language implementations such as those found in Akka (for both Scala and Java) [46], Elixir [44], and Erlang [15]. In particular, one effective approach to fault-tolerance is the model adopted by Erlang.

Rather than trying to achieve absolute error freedom, Erlang's approach concedes that failures are hard to rule out completely in the setting of open distributed systems. Accordingly, Erlang-based program development takes into account the possibility of computation going wrong. However, instead of resorting to the usual defensive programming, it adopts the so-called "let it fail" principle. In place of intertwining the software realising the application logic with logic for handling errors and faults, Erlang proposes a supervisory model whereby components (*i.e.,* actors) are monitored within a hierarchy of independently-executing *supervisors* (which can be monitor for other supervisors themselves). When an error occurs within a particular component, it is quarantined by letting that component fail (in isolation); the absence of global shared memory of the actor model facilitates this isolation. Its supervisor is then notified about this failure, creating a traceable event that is useful for debugging. More importantly to our cause, this mechanism also allows the supervisor to take *remedial action* in response to the reported failure. For instance, the failing component may be restarted by the supervisor. Alternatively, other components that may have been contaminated by the error could also be terminated by the supervisor. Occasionally supervisors themselves fail in response to a supervised component failing, thus percolating the error to a higher level in the supervision hierarchy.

Erlang's model is an instance of a programming paradigm commonly termed as Monitor Oriented Programming (MOP) [16,35]. It neatly separates the application logic from the recovery policy by encapsulating the logic pertaining to the recovery policy within the supervision structure encasing the application. Despite this clear advantage, the solution is not without its shortcomings. For instance, the Erlang supervision mechanism is still inherently tied to the constructs of the host language and it is hard to transfer to other technologies.

Despite it being localised within supervisor code, manual effort is normally still required to disentangle it from the context where it is defined in order to be understood in isolation. Also, the manual construction of logic associated with recovery is itself prone to errors.

We advocate for a recovery mechanism that sits at a higher level of abstraction than the bare metal of the programming language where it is deployed. In particular, we envisage the three challenges outlined below:

1. The explicit identification and design of recovery policies in a technology agnostic manner. This will facilitate the comprehension and understanding of recovery policies and allow for better separation of concerns during program development.
2. The automated code synthesis from high-level policy descriptions. There exist only a handful of methods for recovery policy specification and these have limited support for the automatic generation of monitors that implement those policies.
3. The evaluation of recovery policies. We require automated techniques that allow us to ascertain the validity of recovery policies with respect to notions of recovery correctness. We are also unaware of many frameworks that permit policies to be compared with one another and thus determine whether one recovery policy is better than (or equivalent to) another one.

To the best of our knowledge, there is a lack of support to take up the first challenge. For instance, Erlang folklore's to recovery policies simply prescribes the "one-for-one" or the "one-for-all" strategies. Recently, Neykova and Yoshida have shown how better strategies are sometimes possible [40]. We note that the approach followed in [40] is based on simple yet effective choreographic models.

The second challenge somehow depends on the support one provides for the design and implementation of recovery strategies. A basic requirement of (good) abstract software models is that an artefact has a clear relationship with the other artefacts that it interacts with, possibly at different levels of abstraction. This constitutes the essence of model-driven design. The preservation of these clearly defined interaction-points (across different abstraction levels) is crucial for sound software refinement. Such a translation from one abstraction level to a more concrete one forms the basis for an actual "compilation" from one model to the other. In cases where such relations have a clear semantics, they can be exploited to verify properties of the design (and the implementation) as well as to transform models (semi-)automatically. In our case, we would expect runtime monitors to be derived from their abstract models, to ease the development process and allow developers to focus on the application logic (such as in [6,11]).

Finally, the right abstraction level should provide the foundations necessary to develop formal techniques to analyse and compare recovery policies as outlined in our third challenge. The right abstraction level would also permit us to tractably apply these techniques to specific policy instances; these may either have been developed specifically for the policy formalism considered by the technique or obtained via reverse-engineering methods from a technology-specific application. Possible examples that may be used as starting points for such an investigation are [20], where various pre-orders for monitor descriptions are developed, and [21] where intrinsic monitor correctness criteria such as consistent detections are studied.

3   The Model

We advocate that the development of recovery logic is *orthogonal* to the application logic, and this separation of concerns could induce separate development efforts which are, to a certain degree, independent from one another. Similar to the case for the application logic, we envisage global and local points of view for the recovery logic whereby the latter is attained by projecting the global strategy. Our approach is schematically described in Fig. 1. The left-most part of the diagram illustrates the top-down approach of choreographies of the application logic described in Sect. 4.1. We propose to develop a similar approach for the recovery logic as depicted in the right-most part of Fig. 1, where the triangular shape for monitors evokes that monitors are possibly arranged in a complex structure (as e.g., the *hierarchy* of Erlang supervisors). In fact, we envisage that a local strategy could correspond to a subsystem of monitors as in the case of [6,10] (unlike the choreographies for the application logic, where each local view typically yields one component).

Fig. 1. A global-local approach to adaptation strategies incorporating the three research challenges identified in Sect. 2

Models to Express Global and Local Strategies. Choreographic models should be equipped with features allowing us to design and analyse the recovery logic of systems. This requires, on the one hand, the identification of suitable linguistic mechanisms for expressing global/local strategies and, on the other hand, to define principles of monitors programming by looking at state-of-the-art techniques. For example, the (global) recovery logic should allow us to specify *recovery* points where parties can roll-back if some kind of error is met or *compensations* to activate when anomalous configurations are reached.

A challenge here is the definition of projection operations that enable featuring recovery mechanisms. A first step in this direction is a recent proposal of Mezzina and Tuosto [39] who extend the global graphs reviewed in Sect. 4.1 with *reversibility guards* to recover the system when it reaches undesired configurations. A promising research direction in this respect is to extend the language of reversibility guards with the patterns featured by adaptEr [10–12] and then define projection operations to automatically obtain adaptEr monitors.

Properties of Recovery Logic. We should understand general properties of interest of recovery as well as specific ones. One general property could be the fact that the strategy guides the application toward a *safe* state (*i.e.* stability envelope [35]) when errors occur. For example, the recovery strategy could guarantee *causal consistency*, namely that a safe state is one that the execution could have reached, possibly following a different interleaving of concurrent actions. Recovery strategies may be subject to resource requirements that need to be taken into consideration and/or adhered to. One such example would be the minimisation of the number of components that have to be re-started when a recovery procedure is administered, whereby the restarted components are causally related to the error detected. The work discussed in [10,11] provides another example of resource requirements for recovery strategies: in an asynchronous monitoring setting, component synchronisations are considered to be expensive operations and, as a result, the monitors are expected to use the least number of component synchronisations for the adaptation actions to be administered correctly.

Also, as typical for choreographies, we should unveil the conditions under which a recovery strategy is realisable in a distributed settings. In other words, not all globally-specified recovery policies are necessarily implementable in a choreographed distributed setting; we therefore seek to establish *well-formedness* criteria that allow us to determine when a global recovery policy can be projected (and thus implemented) in a decentralised setup.

Compliance. In the case of recovery strategies, it is unclear when monitors are deemed to be compliant with their local strategy. A central aspect that we should tackle is that of understanding what it actually means for monitors and local strategy to be compliant, and subsequently to give a suitable compliance definition that captures this understanding. One possible approach to address this problem is to emulate and extend what was done for the application logic where several notions of behavioural compliance have been studied (e.g. [8,14]).

Another potential avenue worth considering is the work on monitorability [2,22] and enforceability [4,43] that relates the behaviour of the monitor to that specified by the correctness property of interest; the work in [25] investigates these issues for a target actor calculus that is deeply inspired by the Erlang model. In such cases we would need to extend the concept of monitorability and enforceability to adaptability with respect to the local strategy derived from the global specification.

Once we identify and formalise our notions of compliance, we should study their decidability properties, and investigate approaches to check compliance such as type-checking or behavioural equivalence checking (*e.g.*, via testing pre-orders or bisimulations [3,20]).

Seamless Integration. A key driving principle of our proposed approach is that the recovery logic should be orthogonal to the application logic. This separation of concerns allows the traditional designers to focus on the application logic and just declare the error conditions to be managed by the recovery logic. The dedicated designers of the recovery logic would then use those error conditions and the structure of the choreography of the application logic to specify a recovery strategy. Finally, the application and recovery logic should be integrated via appropriate code instrumentation mechanisms to cater for reliability. The driving principle we will follow is that of minimising the entanglement between the respective models of the application logic and those of the recovery logic. This principled approach with clearly delineated separation of concerns should also manifest itself at the code level of the systems produced, that will, in turn, improve the maintainability of the resulting systems.

4   An Instance

We propose a line of research that aims to combine the run-time monitoring and local adaptation of distributed components with the top-down decomposition approach brought about by choreographic development. Our manifesto may thus be distilled as:

**Local Runtime Adaptation   +   Static Choreography Specifications
=   Choreographed MOP**

Our work stems from two existing bodies of work. On the one hand, our investigation is grounded on the Erlang monitoring framework developed and implemented in [10,11], which showed that these concepts are realisable. On the other hand, the end point of what we want to achieve is driven by the design of a choreographic model for distributed computation with global views and local projections of [34], reviewed in Sect. 4.1.

4.1   Global and Local Specifications

A key reason that makes choreographies appealing for the modelling, design, and analysis of distributed applications is that they do not envisage centralisation points. Roughly, in a choreographic model one describes how a few distributed components interact in order to coordinate with each other. There is a range of possible interpretations for choreographies [7]; a widely accepted informal description is the one suggested by W3C's [30]:

> [...] a contract containing a global definition of the common ordering conditions and constraints under which messages are exchanged, is produced that describes, from a **global viewpoint** [...] observable behaviour [...]. Each party can then use the **global definition** to build and test solutions that conform to it. The global specification is in turn realised by combination of the resulting **local systems** [...]

According to this description, a **global** and a **local** view are related as in the left-most diagram in Fig. 1 which evokes the following software development methodology. First, an architect designs the global specification and then uses the global specification to derive, via a 'projection' operation, a local specification for the distributed components. Programmers can then use the local specifications to check that the implementation of their components are compliant with the local specification. The keystones of this process are (i) that the global specification can be used to guarantee good behaviour of the system abstracting away from low level details (typically assuming synchronous communications), (ii) that projection operation can usually be automatised so to (iii) produce local specifications at a lower level of abstraction (where communication are asynchronous) while preserving the behaviour of the global specification.

We remark that the relations among views and systems of choreographies are richer than those discussed here. For instance, local views can also be compiled into template code of components and the projection operation may have an "inverse" (cf. [34]). Those aspects are not in scope here.

We choose two specific formalisms for global and local specifications. More precisely, we adapt to our needs the *global graphs* of [34] for global specifications and Erlang actors to express local views of choreographies.

Global Specifications. Global graphs, originally proposed in [18] and recently generalised in [28,45], are a convenient specification language for global views of message-passing systems. They yield both a formal framework and a simple visual representation that we review here, adapting notation and definition from [45].

Hereafter we fix two disjoint sets $\mathcal{P}$ and $\mathcal{M}$; the former is a finite set of *participants* (ranged over by A, B, etc.) and $\mathcal{M}$ is the set of *messages* (ranged over by m, x, etc.). To exchange messages and coordinate with each other, participants use asynchronous point-to-point communication via *channels* following the *actor model* [5,29]. We remark that global graphs abstract away from data; the messages specified in interactions of global graphs have to be thought of as data types rather than values.

The syntax of global graphs is defined by the grammar

$$G ::= A{\rightarrow}B : m \quad | \quad G;G' \quad | \quad G\,|\,G' \quad | \quad G{+}G' \quad | \quad *G@A$$

A global graph can be a simple interaction $A{\rightarrow}B : m$ (for which we require $A \neq B$), the sequential composition $G;G'$ of G and G', the parallel composition (for which the participants of G and of G' are disjoint), a nondeterministic choice $G{+}G'$ between G and G', or the iteration $*G@A$ of G. The syntax captures the structure of a visual language of distributed workflows illustrated in Fig. 2. Each global graphs G can be represented as a rooted diagram with a single source node and a single sink node respectively represented as ○ and ◎. Other nodes are drawn as ● and a dotted edge from/to a ●-node singles out the source/sink nodes the edge connects to. For instance, in the diagram for the sequential composition, the top-most edge identifies the sink node of G and the other edge identifies the

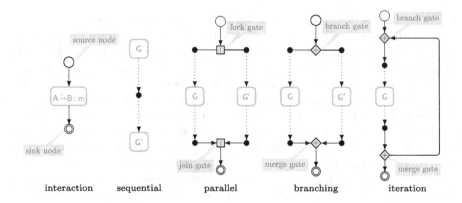

Fig. 2. A visual notation for global graphs

source node of G′; intuitively, ● is the node of the sequential composition of G and G′ obtained by "coalescing" the sink of G with the source of G′. In our diagrams, branches and forks are marked respectively by ◇ and □ nodes; also, to each branch/fork nodes corresponds a "closing" gate merge/join gate.

Example 1. Consider a protocol where iteratively participant C sends a newReq message to a logging service L. In parallel, a C's partner, A, makes either requests of either type req_1 or type req_2 to a service B, which, in turn, replies via two different types of responses, namely res_1 and res_2. Once a request is served, B also sends a report to A, which logs this activity on L. This protocol can be modelled with the graph $G = *(G_1 \mid G_1′);G_2;G_3@A$ where

$$G_1 = C{\to}L: \text{newReq} \qquad\qquad G_1′ = A{\to}B: req_1;B{\to}A: res_1$$
$$G_2 = L{\to}C: \text{ack} \mid B{\to}A: \text{rep} \qquad\qquad +$$
$$G_3 = A{\to}L: \text{log} \qquad\qquad A{\to}B: req_2;B{\to}A: res_2$$

The decision to leave or repeat the loop is non-deterministically taken by one of the participants (in this case A) which then communicates to all the others what to do. This will become clearer in Sect. 6. The diagram in Fig. 3 is the visual counterpart of G.   ◇

The (forward) semantics of global graphs can be defined in terms of partial orders of communication events [28,45]. We do not present this semantics here (the reader is referred to [28,45]) for space limitations; instead, we give only a brief and informal account through a "token game" similar to the one of Petri nets based on Fig. 3. The token game would start from the source node and flow down along the edges in the diagram as described by the test in Fig. 3.

For the semantics of global graphs to be defined, *well-branchedness* [28,45] is a key requirement. This is a simple condition guaranteeing that *all* the participants involved in a distributed choice follow a same branch. Well-branchedness requires that each branch in a global graph (*i*) has a unique *active* participant (that is a

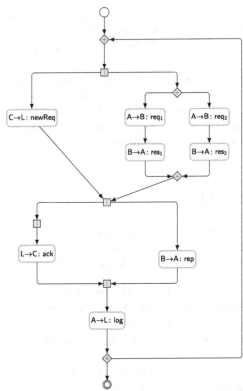

The topmost ◈ gate is the entry point of a loop which simply lets the token to flow. At the first ⊡ gate, the token is duplicated, forking the computations along the two threads. In the leftmost thread, the token enables the interaction C→L: newReq; this allows the output event from C (which then waits for the ack message from L) and later the input event of L. The token on the leftmost thread then enables the last interaction L→C: ack. Observe that, after the input of message ack, C can start the next iteration while the other threads may still be completing the current iteration. Concurrently, the token flowing on the rightmost thread reaches another branch gate ◈ which non-deterministically routes the token either on the left or on the right branch. On both branches A and B execute a request-response type of protocol similarly to what C and L run on the leftmost thread. When the token flows through the merge gate at the end of the choice, it enable a last interaction from B to A (which allows B to go the next iteration) and subsequently, the last logging interaction between A and L. Finally, also A and L can repeat the loop.

Note that the body of an iteration is executed at least once.

Fig. 3. The diagram of a global graph and its semantics

unique participant taking the decision on which branch to follow) and (ii) that any other participant is *passive*, namely that it is either able to ascertain which branch was selected from the messages it receives or it does not play any role in the branching.

Example 2. In the branch of Example 1, A is the active participant while the others are passive; in fact, C and L are not involved in the choice, while B can determine that the left or the right branch was selected depending on which type of request it receives.   ◇

Local Specifications. We adopt systems of CFSMs [9] as our model of local specifications. A CFSM is a finite-state automaton where transitions represent input or output events from/to other machines. Each machine in the system corresponds to an actor which can send or receive messages to/from other machines. Communications take place on unbound FIFO buffers: for each pair of machines, say A and B, there is a buffer from A to B and one from B to A. Basically, when a machine A is in a state q with a transition to a state q' whose label is an output of message m to B, then m is put in the buffer from A to B and A moves to state q'. Similarly, when B is in a state q with a transition to a state q' whose label is an input of m from B and the m is on the top of the buffer from A to B then B pops m from the buffer and moves to state q'.

Noteworthy, the model of CFSMs is very close to the actor model and CFSMs can be projected from global graphs automatically. Moreover, when the global graph, say G, is *well-formed* then the behaviour of the projected machines faithfully refines the semantics of G [28]. In this paper, we will directly synthesise Erlang code from the global specification, that is we will use Erlang actors to model our local specifications.

5   Global Graphs for Reversibility

We propose a variant of global graphs, dubbed *reversibility-enabling (global) graphs* (REGs for short) that generalises the branching construct to cater for reversibility. We will use REGs to render the recovery model in Sect. 3.

Example 3. Recall the global graph in Example 1. A possible reversion guard for B could specify that the port required to respond A needs to be available at the time of communication, or that the size of the communication buffer for this port does not exceed a given threshold. At runtime, both conditions may prohibit the respective participants from completing the execution of the specified protocol. By reversing the choice taken (*i.e.* A making requests of either type req_1 or of type req_2), the participants involved can make alternative choices.   ◇

The syntax of REGs uses *control points*[1] to univocally identify positions where choices have to be made on how to continue the protocol. Syntactically, control points are written as $_i$G, where i is a strictly positive integer.

Definition 1 (Reversibility-enabling global graphs). *The set $\mathcal{G}$ of reversibility-enabling global graphs (REGs) consists of the terms G derived by the following grammar:*

$$G ::= A \rightarrow B : m \quad | \quad G;G' \quad | \quad {}_i.(G \,|\, G') \quad |$$
$$\qquad {}_i.\big(G_1 \text{ unless } \phi_1 + G_2 \text{ unless } \phi_2\big)\, | \qquad\qquad (1)$$

$$\qquad {}_i.\big(*G@A\big) \qquad\qquad\qquad (2)$$

that satisfy the following conditions:

- *in ${}_i.(*G@A)$, A is the active participant of G and*
- *for any two control points i and j occurring in different positions of a REG it must be the case that the indices are distinct, $i \neq j$.*

---

[1] Control points can be automatically generated; for simplicity, we explicitly put them in the syntax of REGs.

In (1), the formulas ϕ_h (for $h \in \{1,2\}$) are reversion guards expressed in terms of boolean expressions.

In Definition 1, the participant A in (2) decides whether to repeat the body G or exit an iteration. Hereafter, we consider equivalent REGs that differ only in the indices of control points (the indices of control points are, in fact, irrelevant as long as they are unique) and may omit control points when immaterial, e.g. writing G $_{\text{unless}}$ ϕ + G′ $_{\text{unless}}$ ϕ' instead of i.$\big($G $_{\text{unless}}$ ϕ + G′ $_{\text{unless}}$ $\phi'\big)$.

The new branching construct (1) extends the usual branching construct of choreographies to control reversible computations. The semantics of this constructs is rendered by the encoding in Sect. 6 which realises the following intended behaviour. The execution of i.$\big($G$_1$ $_{\text{unless}}$ ϕ_1 + G$_2$ $_{\text{unless}}$ $\phi_2\big)$ requires first to non-deterministically choose $h \in \{1,2\}$ and execute the REG G$_h$. At the end of the execution of G$_h$ then its guard ϕ_h is checked. It the guard is false, then the execution exits the branch and continues executing normally. It the guard is true we may have two sub-cases depending whether the other branch has been already reversed or not. In the first case, then the execution is forced to proceed normally (e.g., there is no alternatives to try), in the second case then the execution of G$_h$ is reversed and the other branch is executed.

Note that, by keeping track of all reversed branches and fully executing the last branch when all the others have been reversed, we can easily generalise to a branching construct i.$\big($G$_1$ $_{\text{unless}}$ ϕ_1 + $\cdots$ + G$_h$ $_{\text{unless}}$ $\phi_h\big)$ with $h \geq 2$; for simplicity we just consider $h = 2$ here.

Definition 1 parameterises REGs on the notion of reversion guard. However, our study required us to address crucial design choice on how reversion guards are rendered in a language like Erlang (without a global state). Roughly, reversion guards can be thought of as propositions predicating on the state of the forward execution. A key requirement for a proper projection, however, is that the evaluation of such guards must be "distributable", *i.e.* we want revision guards to be "projectable" from the global view to the components realising the behaviour of the participants. To meet this requirements, we use *local guards*, *i.e.* boolean expression that predicate on the state of a specific participant and assume that a revision guard is a *conjunction of the local guards at each partici-pant*. More concretely, we exploit Erlang's support [1] for accessing the status of a process implementing a participant via system functions such as `process_info` or `system_info`, which return a dictionary with miscellaneous information about a process or a physical node respectively.

Example 4. Consider the following concrete examples of revision guards:

```
queue_len(Threshold, State) ->
    Info = from_list(State),
    {_,Len} = find(message_queue_len, State),
    (Len > Threshold).
message_exists(Filter, State) ->
    Info = from_list(State),
    {_,messages} = find(message_queue_len,State),
    Filter(messages).
```

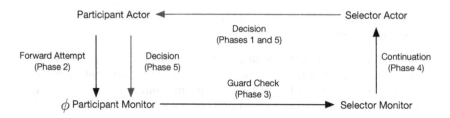

Fig. 4. The instrumentation architecture connecting participant actors, coordinating (selector) actors and their respective monitor actors

Predicate `queue_len` checks if the size of the mailbox is above a threshold, whereas `message_exists` checks for the presence of a message matching some pattern in a mailbox. Other examples of reversion guards are conditions on PIDs and port identifiers, heap size, or the status of processes (e.g., waiting, running, runnable, suspended).   ◇

Our reversible semantics still requires well-branchedness: a REG, say G, is well-branched when the global graph obtained by removing reversion guards from G is well-branched (as defined in Sect. 4). This guarantees communication soundness in presence of reverse executions.

6   From REGs to Erlang

This section shows how we map REGs into Erlang programs. This mapping corresponds to the definition of *projection* from the global view provided by REGs into Erlang implementations of their local view. Our encoding embraces the principles advocated in [13] and reviewed in Sect. 3: we strive for a solution yielding a high degree of decoupling between forward and reverse executions. Unsurprisingly, the most challenging aspect concerns how branches are projected. This is done by realising a coordination mechanism which interleaves forward and reversed behaviour, as described in Sect. 5. In the following, we first describe the architecture of our solution. We then show how forward and reversed executions are rendered in it.

6.1   Architecture

The abstract architecture of our proposal is given in Fig. 4. Each participant of a REG is mapped to a *pair* of Erlang actors, the *participant actor* and the *participant monitor* which liaise with one another in order to realise reversible distributed choices. The execution of a distributed choice is supported by another pair of (dynamically generated) actors, the *selector actor* which liaises with its corresponding *selector monitor*. The basic idea is that participant and selector actors are in charge of executing the forward logic part of the choice while their respective monitors deal with the reversibility logic.

A key structural invariant of the architecture is that monitors can interact only with their corresponding participant or with the monitors of the selectors currently in execution, as depicted in Fig. 4. This organisation is meant to represent the information and control flow of our solution. The coordination protocol required to resolve a distributed choice specified in a REG is made of the following phases:

1. **Inception**: The selector actor (started at a branching point) decides which branch to execute and communicates its decision to the participants involved.
2. **Forward attempt**: Participant actors execute the selected branch accordingly and report their local state at the end of the branch to their participant monitor.
3. **Guards checking**: Participant monitors check their reversion guard and communicate the outcome to the selector monitor.
4. **Continuation**: The selector monitor aggregates the individual outcome of all participant monitors and reports the aggregated result to the selector actor.
5. **Decision**: Based on suggestion forwarded by the selector monitor, the selector actor decides whether to continue forward or reverse the execution and communicates the decision to all participants, which in turn propagate it to their participant monitor.

These phases roughly correspond to the arrows in Fig. 4.

6.2 Branching Actors and Monitors

We now describe the behaviour of actors and monitors in a choice, with the help of their automata-like representation in Fig. 5. The coordination protocol that we describe here resembles a 2-phase commit protocol where participants report the outcome of local computations to a coordinator that then decides how to continue the execution.

When participant actors (start to) reach a branching point, the inception phase begins. The actor corresponding to the (unique) active participant of the choice spawns the selector actor and waits from the selector message telling which branch to take in the choice; all other participant actors just wait for the selector's decision. The act of spawning the selector arrow by the active participant is represented in Fig. 5 via the gray arrow and the cloud in the automaton of the participant actor. Subsequently, all the actor participants involved in a branch will wait from the selector to instruct them with the branch (either left or right) to take—these are the yellow arrows in the automaton of Fig. 5. Upon the receipt of such a message, participant actors first forward this message to their monitor and then enter the second phase executing the branch—represented by the cloud in the automaton. Unless the chosen branch diverges, the third phase starts when participant actors finish the branch (possibly at different times) and they signal to their monitor that they are ready to exit the choice. This is signalled by the exit message which also carries the local state of execution (described in Sect. 5). At this point, participant actors take part only in

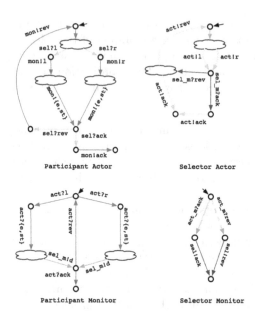

- The syntax of labels is of the form id!msg or id?msg indicating respectively the act of sending (!) or receiving (?) the message msg to or from the actor id.
- Messages e, st, r, and l stand respectively for exit, state, right and left.
- Transitions of different automata are coloured to help the reader understanding the flow of the communication: outputs or inputs of actors match when the corresponding transitions in the automata have the same colour.
- The fat arrow in the selector monitor represents that an input action is expected from all participant monitors involved into a branch; likewise, the fat arrow in the selector actor represent that the outputs will be done for all participant actors. The fat dashed arrow in the selector monitor indicates that an input action is expected from all the participant monitors and that at least one of them is a **rev** message.

Fig. 5. Automata-like description of actors and monitors for the projection of branches

the last phase: they receive from the selector either an ack message (confirming that the choice has been resolved) or a rev message to reverse the execution. In either case, they propagate the message to their monitor and either "commit" the branch or return to the state that waits for the message dictating the next branch to take. Participant actors behave uniformly but for the active one, which has the additional task of spawning the selector at the very beginning (for non-active participants the grey transition is an internal step not affecting communications).

Each participant monitor waits for the message carrying the local state that its participant actor sends at the end of the second phase in the exit message. The state is used to check whether the reversion guard of the branch, say ϕ, holds or not. If ϕ holds for the local state of the participant actor, then the participant monitor sends the selector monitor a request to *reverse* the branch (message **rev**). Otherwise the monitor sends a message to commit the choice (message **exit**). In Fig. 5 this is represented by the label sel_m!d, where d stands for decision and sel_m binds to the unique identifier of the selection monitor implemented as an actor. After this, the monitor waits from its participant actor for the **rev** or the **ack** message sent in the last phase: if **rev** is received the monitor returns to its initial state and leaves the branch otherwise.

The selector actor spawned in the inception phase starts by spawning a selector monitor and then deciding which branch to take initially—represented in Fig. 5 by the grey transition and the cloud in the automaton of the selector. After communicating its decision to all participant actors, the selector waits for the request of its monitor and starts phase five of Sect. 6.1 by deciding whether to reverse the branch or not. The decision process is as follows: if the selector receives an **ack** message then the branch is committed and the selector monitor terminates. Otherwise, the selector participants receive a **rev** message to reverse the branch. If there are branches that have not been taken yet, then the last executed branch is marked as "tried", a branch that has not been attempted yet is selected, and a **rev** message is sent to all participant actors. Otherwise, the decision to commit the branch is taken and the **ack** message is sent to all participant actors. In the former case, the selector returns to its initial state, and terminates otherwise.

The selector monitor participates to the fourth phase. It first gathers all the outcomes from the guard-checking phase from *all* the participant monitors involved into the choice. Recall that a **rev** message is received from any participant monitor whose revision guard becomes true, while an **ack** message is received from any participant monitor whose revision guard does not hold. Then, the selector monitor computes an outcome to be sent to the selector actor: if all received messages are **ack** then an **ack** message is sent to the selector actor, otherwise the monitor sends a **rev** message to the selector actor. In both cases, the selector monitor terminates; a new selector monitor is spawned by the selector actor if the branch is actually reversed.

Iteration is a simplification of a distributed choice: we just generate a selector for an iteration but not its monitor. The reason for not having a monitor for the iterator selector is due to the fact that there is no reversible semantics to be implemented for the iteration. This does not imply that within the body of an iteration a reversible step can not be taken (e.g. there can be an inner choice), but just that iterations are not points at which the computation can be reversed. The selector (instantiated by the active participant of the iteration, similarly to choices) just decides whether to iterate or exit the loop. A participant actor within a loop, after completing an iteration, awaits the decision from the selector actor and continues accordingly.

6.3 Compiling to Erlang

The code generated for the projections from REGs to Erlang is discussed below. We focus on the compiled code for the branches constructs, since the compilation of the other constructs is standard and therefore omitted. Our discussion uses auxiliary functions for which the code is not reported.

```
1   act_A_cp() ->
2     %Pid = list_to_atom("sel_act_"
3     %++ integer_to_list(cp)),
4     %register("Pid,
5     %           spawn(sel_act, [cp])),
6     receive
7       {cp,left} ->
8         mon_A ! {cp, left}
9         %CODE OF LEFT BRANCH
10      ;
11      {cp,right} ->
12        mon_A ! {cp, right}
13        %CODE OF RIGHT BRANCH
14    end,
15    mon_A!{cp, exit, process_info(self())},
16    receive
17      {cp,ack} -> mon_A ! {cp, ack};
18      {cp,rev} ->
19        mon_A ! {cp, rev},
20        act_A_cp()
21    end.

22  mon_A_cp() ->
23    receive
24      {cp, left} ->
25        %CODE FOR LEFT BRANCH MONITOR%
26        receive{cp, exit, Info} ->
27          G = check_guard(Left_guard, Info)
28        end;
29      {cp, right} ->
30        %CODE FOR RIGHT BRANCH MONITOR%
31        receive{cp, exit, Info} ->
32          G = check_guard(Right_guard, Info)
33        end
34    end,
35    Sel_m = get_selector_monitor(cp),
36    case G of
37      true -> Sel_m ! {cp, rev};
38      _    -> Sel_m ! {cp, ack}
39    end,
40    receive
41      {cp, rev} -> mon_A_cp();

42      {cp, ack} -> ok
43  end.

44  sel_act(Attempt,CP) ->
45    Pid = list_to_atom("sel_mon_"
46          ++ integer_to_list(CP)),
47    register(Pid,
48          spawn(sel_mon, [CP, self()])),
49    Sel =
50      case Attempt of
51        [] -> getBranch();
52        [left] -> right;
53        [right] -> left;
54        _ -> throw("panic....") %this case never happens
55      end,
56    P = participants(CP),
57    foreach(fun(X) -> X!{CP, Sel} end, P),
58    receive {CP,Outcome} ->
59      Decision =
60        case {Outcome,Attempt} of
61          {ack,_} -> ack;
62          {rev,[]} -> rev;
63          {_,_} -> ack
64        end
65    end,
66    foreach(fun(X) -> X!{CP, Decision} end, P),
67      case Decision of
68        rev -> sel_act(Attempt ++ [Sel], CP);
69        _    -> end_branch
70    end.

71  sel_mon(CP, SelPid)->
72    MP = participants(CP),
73    MsgList = lists:map(fun(_) ->
74      receive {CP,M} -> M end end, MP),
75    Msg =
76      case lists:member(rev, MsgList) of
77        true -> rev;
78        _    -> ack
79      end,
80    SelPid ! {CP, Msg}.
```

The code for the participant actor (lines 1–21) is parametrised with respect to cp, the value of the control point[2] univocally identifying the point of branch in the REG. The commented lines 2–5 are generated only for the code of the active participant which spawns the selector actor of the branch CP. Note that the process is registered under a unique name sel_act_cp (which is an atom). This snippet is actually a template which would be filled up with the code generated for the participant communications respectively on the left and on the right branches (*i.e.* the commented lines 9 and 13).

The Erlang process spawned by a participant actor implementing the selector actor executes the function on lines 44–70. This function takes two parameters: the Attempt representing the branches chosen so far and the control point CP identifying the choice. The former parameter is a list of atoms left and right; note that the empty list is passed initially when the process is spawned and that (in our case) the size of this list should never exceed 1. As discussed above, the selector chooses a branch (lines 49–55) and communicates its decision to the participants of the branch (lines 56–57, where participants is computed at compile time, from the global graph script, and returns the participants of a branch given its control point). Finally, the selector enters the fourth phase of Sect. 6.1, waiting for the message from its monitor, and decides accordingly how to continue the execution of the choreographed choice.

---

[2] Note that the value cp is statically determined by the compiler.

As in the case of the participant actor, the snippet of the participant monitor (lines 22–43) does not make explicit the code for the monitoring of the left and right branches (commented lines 25 and 30). The auxiliary function check_guard returns the evaluation of the guard for the state provided by the participant (lines 26–28 and 31–33). The function get_selector_monitor retrieves the PID of the selector monitor from the control point value CP.

The selector monitor, spawned by the selector process, is registered with the name sel_mon_cp (lines 45–48) where cp is the second actual CP when invoking sel_act. Note that the invocation to get_selector_monitor on line 35 returns the atom sel_mon_cp. The snippet for the selector monitor uses the auxiliary function participants returning the list of participant actors involved in the branch cp. The outcome Msg is computed on lines 73–79 and sent to the selector on line 80. The selector monitor awaits a message from all the participant monitors involved in the branch (lines 73–74), and then it decides the message to communicate to the selector actor. If at least one of the messages received is rev, then the final message is rev, otherwise the final message is ack.

7   Conclusions

We have presented a methodology to automate the process of adding recovery strategies to message passing systems specified via a global protocol. In particular, our model abstracts from (1) the definition of formal behavioural models encompassing failures, (2) the specification of the relevant properties of adaptation and recovery strategy, (3) the automatic generation of monitoring, recovery, and adaptation logic in target languages of interest.

In line with the principles advocated by our model, we then have presented a minimally-intrusive extension to global graph choreographies [28] for expressing reversible computation. We showed how these descriptions could be realised into executable actor-based Erlang programs that compartmentalise the reversion logic as Erlang monitors, minimally tainting the application logic.

Related Work. The closest work to ours is [19, 33, 40]. In [33] a reversible semantics for a subset of Erlang is given. The goal of [33] is a debugger based on a fully reversible semantics. To achieve this, they modify the Erlang semantics in order to keep track of the computational history and build an ad-hoc interpreter for it. Our goal is different since we focus on *controlled reversibility* [31]. Our framework automates the derivation of rollback points (namely the exact point at which the execution has to revert) from the recovery logic. Also, the use of monitors avoids any changes to Erlang's run-time support. Choreographies are used in [40] to devise an algorithm that optimises Erlang's recovery policies. More precisely, global views specify dependencies from which a global recovery tables are derived. Such tables tell which are the safe rollback points. The framework then exploits the supervision mechanism of Erlang to pair participants with a monitor. In case of failure, the monitor restarts the actor to a consistent rollback point. One could combine our approach with the recovery mechanism of [40] so as to generalise our reversible semantics to harness fault tolerance. This is not a trivial task, because the fault-tolerance mechanism of [40] needs to follow a specific protocol, making it unclear whether participants can be automatically derived. In [19] actors are extended with checkpoints primitives, which the programmer has to specify in order to rollback the execution. In order to reach globally-consistent checkpoints severe conditions have to be met. Thanks to the correctness-by-design principle induced by global views, our approach automatically deals with checkpoints, relieving this burden from the programmer.

Other works [37,38,41] have investigated the use of monitors to steer reversibility in concurrent systems. In [41] a monitored reversible process algebra is presented where each agent is paired with a monitor. But, unlike our approach, the monitor tells the agent what to do both in the forward and in the reverse way. In [37,38] the authors investigate the use of monitors to steer reversibility in message oriented systems. Here monitors are used as *memories* storing information about the forward execution of the monitored participants, and this information is then used to reconstruct previous states. As in our approach, in [38] participants and their monitors are derived from a global specification as well. We diverge from [37,38] in several aspects. Firstly, our monitors do not store any information about the forward computation. Secondly, all the monitors coordinate amongst each other to decide whether to revert a particular computation or not. The coordination mechanism of our monitors is automatically derived. Moreover in our approach reversibility is triggered at run-time when certain conditions (specified at design-time in the recovery logic) are met.

Conclusions. We have presented a method to automatically derive reversible computation as Erlang actors. A key aspect of our approach is the ability to express, from a global point of view, *when* a reverse distributed computation has to take place and not *how*. Starting from a global specification of the system, branches can be decorated with conditions that at run-time will enable the coordinated undoing of a certain branch. Another novelty of our approach is the use of monitors to enact reversibility. We leave as future work the measurement of the overhead of our approach on the normal forward semantics of the actors, in terms of messages and memory consumption. Another research direction is to integrate our recovery logic with existing monitoring frameworks for Erlang. In [10,11], Cassar *et al.* developed the monitoring tool adaptEr[3] for synthesising adaptation monitors for actor systems developed in Erlang. Specifications in adaptEr are defined using a version of Safe Hennessy Milner Logic with recursion (sHML) that is extended with data binding, if statements for inspecting data, adaptations and synchronisation actions. We will investigate the idea of extending this logic with reversibility capabilities, and then to synthesise monitors directly from this logic formulae.

---

[3] The tool adaptEr is open-source and downloadable from https://bitbucket.org/casian/adapter.

Several works have shown that reversible debuggers can be built on top of reversible semantics [17,26,32]. In line with these works, our ultimate goal would also be to build a (reversible) debugger for Erlang systems. One idea could be to integrate our automatic synthesis of reversible code with commercial systems which are able to monitor and aggregate several information (events) of a message passing system. One of such candidate is WombatAOM[4]. Such an integration will allow our reversion guards to predicate on real runtime information. On a different topic, REGs could also be used to enhance *Continuous Integrations* [36] scenarios, by proposing a formalism to express workflows imbued with reversible behaviour to support automatic tests generation and flakiness detection.

References

1. Erlang run-time system application, reference manual version 9.2 (2017)
2. Aceto, L., Achilleos, A., Francalanza, A., Ingólfsdóttir, A., Lehtinen, K.: Adventures in monitorability: from branching to linear time and back again. Proc. ACM Program. Lang. **3**(POPL), 52:1–52:29 (2019)
3. Aceto, L., Achilleos, A., Francalanza, A., Ingólfsdóttir, A., Lehtinen, K.: Testing equivalence vs. runtime monitoring. In: Boreale, M., Corradini, F., Loreti, M., Pugliese, R. (eds.) Models, Languages, and Tools for Concurrent and Distributed Programming. LNCS, vol. 11665, pp. 28–44. Springer, Cham (2019). https://doi.org/10.1007/978-3-030-21485-2_4
4. Aceto, L., Cassar, I., Francalanza, A., Ingólfsdóttir, A.: On runtime enforcement via suppressions. In: 29th International Conference on Concurrency Theory, CONCUR 2018, Beijing, China, 4–7 September 2018. LIPIcs, vol. 118, pp. 34:1–34:17. Schloss Dagstuhl - Leibniz-Zentrum fuer Informatik (2018)
5. Agha, G.A.: ACTORS - A Model of Concurrent Computation in Distributed Systems. MIT Press Series in Artificial Intelligence. MIT Press, Cambridge (1990)
6. Attard, D.P., Francalanza, A.: A monitoring tool for a branching-time logic. In: Falcone, Y., Sánchez, C. (eds.) RV 2016. LNCS, vol. 10012, pp. 473–481. Springer, Cham (2016). https://doi.org/10.1007/978-3-319-46982-9_31
7. Basile, D., Degano, P., Ferrari, G.-L., Tuosto, E.: Relating two automata-based models of orchestration and choreography. JLAMP **85**(3), 425–446 (2016)
8. Bernardi, G., Hennessy, M.: Mutually testing processes. LMCS **11**(2), 1–23 (2015)
9. Brand, D., Zafiropulo, P.: On communicating finite-state machines. J. ACM **30**(2), 323–342 (1983)
10. Cassar, I., Francalanza, A.: Runtime adaptation for actor systems. In: Bartocci, E., Majumdar, R. (eds.) RV 2015. LNCS, vol. 9333, pp. 38–54. Springer, Cham (2015). https://doi.org/10.1007/978-3-319-23820-3_3
11. Cassar, I., Francalanza, A.: On implementing a monitor-oriented programming framework for actor systems. In: Ábrahám, E., Huisman, M. (eds.) IFM 2016. LNCS, vol. 9681, pp. 176–192. Springer, Cham (2016). https://doi.org/10.1007/978-3-319-33693-0_12
12. Cassar, I., Francalanza, A., Attard, D.P., Aceto, L., Ingólfsdóttir, A.: A suite of monitoring tools for Erlang. In: Reger, G., Havelund, K. (eds.) RV-CuBES 2017. An

---

[4] https://www.erlang-solutions.com/products/wombatoam.html.

International Workshop on Competitions, Usability, Benchmarks, Evaluation, and Standardisation for Runtime Verification Tools. Kalpa Publications in Computing, vol. 3, pp. 41–47. EasyChair (2017)

13. Cassar, I., Francalanza, A., Mezzina, C.A., Tuosto, E.: Reliability and fault-tolerance by choreographic design. In: PrePost@iFM. EPTCS, vol. 254 (2017)

14. Castagna, G., Gesbert, N., Padovani, L.: A theory of contracts for web services. ACM Trans. Program. Lang. Syst. **31**(5), 1–61 (2009)

15. Cesarini, F., Thompson, S.: Erlang behaviours: programming with process design patterns. In: Horváth, Z., Plasmeijer, R., Zsók, V. (eds.) CEFP 2009. LNCS, vol. 6299, pp. 19–41. Springer, Heidelberg (2010). https://doi.org/10.1007/978-3-642-17685-2_2

16. Chen, F., Jin, D., Meredith, P., Roşu, G.: Monitoring oriented programming - a project overview. In: Proceedings of the Fourth International Conference on Intelligent Computing and Information Systems (ICICIS 2009), pp. 72–77. ACM (2009)

17. de Vries, F., Pérez, J.A.: Reversible session-based concurrency in Haskell. In: Pałka, M., Myreen, M. (eds.) TFP 2018. LNCS, vol. 11457, pp. 20–45. Springer, Cham (2019). https://doi.org/10.1007/978-3-030-18506-0_2

18. Deniélou, P.-M., Yoshida, N.: Multiparty session types meet communicating automata. In: Seidl, H. (ed.) ESOP 2012. LNCS, vol. 7211, pp. 194–213. Springer, Heidelberg (2012). https://doi.org/10.1007/978-3-642-28869-2_10

19. Field, J., Varela, C.A.: Transactors: a programming model for maintaining globally consistent distributed state in unreliable environments. In: POPL 2005. ACM (2005)

20. Francalanza, A.: A theory of monitors - (extended abstract). In: Jacobs, B., Löding, C. (eds.) FoSSaCS 2016. LNCS, vol. 9634, pp. 145–161. Springer, Heidelberg (2016). https://doi.org/10.1007/978-3-662-49630-5_9

21. Francalanza, A.: Consistently-detecting monitors. In: 28th International Conference on Concurrency Theory, CONCUR 2017, 5–8 September 2017. LIPIcs, vol. 85, pp. 8:1–8:19. Schloss Dagstuhl - Leibniz-Zentrum fuer Informatik (2017)

22. Francalanza, A., Aceto, L., Ingolfsdottir, A.: Monitorability for the Hennessy-Milner logic with recursion. Formal Methods Syst. Des. **51**, 1–30 (2017). https://doi.org/10.1007/s10703-017-0273-z

23. Francalanza, A., Mezzina, C.A., Tuosto, E.: Reversible choreographies via monitoring in Erlang. In: Bonomi, S., Rivière, E. (eds.) DAIS 2018. LNCS, vol. 10853, pp. 75–92. Springer, Cham (2018). https://doi.org/10.1007/978-3-319-93767-0_6

24. Francalanza, A., Pérez, J.A., Sánchez, C.: Runtime verification for decentralised and distributed systems. In: Bartocci, E., Falcone, Y. (eds.) Lectures on Runtime Verification. LNCS, vol. 10457, pp. 176–210. Springer, Cham (2018). https://doi.org/10.1007/978-3-319-75632-5_6

25. Francalanza, A., Seychell, A.: Synthesising correct concurrent runtime monitors. Formal Methods Syst. Des. (FMSD) **46**(3), 226–261 (2015). https://doi.org/10.1007/s10703-014-0217-9

26. Giachino, E., Lanese, I., Mezzina, C.A.: Causal-consistent reversible debugging. In: Gnesi, S., Rensink, A. (eds.) FASE 2014. LNCS, vol. 8411, pp. 370–384. Springer, Heidelberg (2014). https://doi.org/10.1007/978-3-642-54804-8_26

27. Gray, J.: Why do computers stop and what can be done about it? In: SRDS. IEEE (1986)

28. Guanciale, R., Tuosto, E.: An abstract semantics of the global view of choreographies. In: ICE 2016, Heraklion, Greece, pp. 67–82 (2016)

29. Hewitt, C., Bishop, P., Steiger, R.: A universal modular ACTOR formalism for artificial intelligence. In: IJCAI. Morgan Kaufmann Publishers Inc. (1973)

30. Kavantzas, N., Burdett, D., Ritzinger, G., Fletcher, T., Lafon, Y.: Web services choreography description language version 1.0 (2004). http://www.w3.org/TR/2004/WD-ws-cdl-10-20041217

31. Lanese, I., Mezzina, C.A., Stefani, J.-B.: Controlled reversibility and compensations. In: Glück, R., Yokoyama, T. (eds.) RC 2012. LNCS, vol. 7581, pp. 233–240. Springer, Heidelberg (2013). https://doi.org/10.1007/978-3-642-36315-3_19

32. Lanese, I., Nishida, N., Palacios, A., Vidal, G.: CauDEr: a causal-consistent reversible debugger for Erlang. In: Gallagher, J.P., Sulzmann, M. (eds.) FLOPS 2018. LNCS, vol. 10818, pp. 247–263. Springer, Cham (2018). https://doi.org/10.1007/978-3-319-90686-7_16

33. Lanese, I., Nishida, N., Palacios, A., Vidal, G.: A theory of reversibility for Erlang. J. Log. Algebraic Methods Program. **100**, 71–97 (2018)

34. Lange, J., Tuosto, E., Yoshida, N.: From communicating machines to graphical choreographies. In: POPL, pp. 221–232 (2015)

35. Meredith, P.O., Jin, D., Griffith, D., Chen, F., Roşu, G.: An overview of the MOP runtime verification framework. Int. J. Softw. Tech. Technol. Transf. **14**, 249–289 (2011)

36. Meyer, M.: Continuous integration and its tools. IEEE Softw. **31**(3), 14–16 (2014)

37. Mezzina, C.A., Pérez, J.A.: Causally consistent reversible choreographies: a monitors-as-memories approach. In: PPDP (2017)

38. Mezzina, C.A., Pérez, J.A.: Reversibility in session-based concurrency: a fresh look. J. Log. Algebr. Meth. Program. **90**, 2–30 (2017)

39. Mezzina, C.A., Tuosto, E.: Choreographies for automatic recovery. CoRR, abs/1705.09525 (2017)

40. Neykova, R., Yoshida, N.: Let it recover: multiparty protocol-induced recovery. In: CC. ACM (2017)

41. Phillips, I., Ulidowski, I., Yuen, S.: A reversible process calculus and the modelling of the ERK signalling pathway. In: Glück, R., Yokoyama, T. (eds.) RC 2012. LNCS, vol. 7581, pp. 218–232. Springer, Heidelberg (2013). https://doi.org/10.1007/978-3-642-36315-3_18

42. Rook, P.: Software Reliability Handbook. Elsevier Science Inc., New York (1990)

43. Schneider, F.B.: Enforceable security policies. ACM Trans. Inf. Syst. Secur. **3**(1), 30–50 (2000)

44. Thomas, D.: Programming Elixir: Functional, Concurrent, Pragmatic, Fun, 1st edn. Pragmatic Bookshelf (2014)

45. Tuosto, E., Guanciale, R.: Semantics of global view of choreographies. J. Log. Algebr. Meth. Program. **95**, 17–40 (2018)

46. Wyatt, D.: Akka Concurrency. Artima Incorporation, USA (2013)

Reversibility in Chemical Reactions

Stefan Kuhn[1]($^{\boxtimes}$) (iD), Bogdan Aman[2,3] (iD), Gabriel Ciobanu[2,3] (iD),
Anna Philippou[4] (iD), Kyriaki Psara[4] (iD), and Irek Ulidowski[5] (iD)

[1] School of Computer Science and Informatics, De Montfort University, Leicester, UK
`stefan.kuhn@dmu.ac.uk`
[2] Romanian Academy, Institute of Computer Science, Iaşi, Romania
[3] Faculty of Computer Science, A.I. Cuza University, Iaşi, Romania
`{bogdan.aman,gabriel}@info.uaic.ro`
[4] Department of Computer Science, University of Cyprus, Nicosia, Cyprus
`{annap,kpsara01}@cs.ucy.ac.cy`
[5] School of Informatics, University of Leicester, Leicester, UK
`irek.ulidowski@leicester.ac.uk`

Abstract. In this chapter we give an overview of techniques for the modelling and reasoning about reversibility of systems, including out-of-causal-order reversibility, as it appears in chemical reactions. We consider the autoprotolysis of water reaction, and model it with the Calculus of Covalent Bonding, the Bonding Calculus, and Reversing Petri Nets. This exercise demonstrates that the formalisms, developed for expressing advanced forms of reversibility, are able to model autoprotolysis of water very accurately. Characteristics and expressiveness of the three formalisms are discussed and illustrated.

Keywords: Reversible computation · Reaction modelling · Calculus of Covalent Bonding · Bonding Calculus · Reversing Petri Nets

1 Introduction

Biological reactions, pathways, and reaction networks have been extensively studied in the literature using various techniques, including process calculi and Petri nets. Initial research was mainly focused on reaction rates by the modelling and simulating networks of reactions, in order to analyse or even predict the common paths through the network. Reversibility was not considered explicitly. Later on reversibility started to be taken into account, since it plays a crucial rôle in many processes, typically by going back to a previous state in the system. Two common types of reversibility are backtracking and causally-consistent reversibility [8,19,25]. Backtracking executes exactly the inverse order of the forward execution, and causally-consistent reversibility allows undoing effects before causes, but not necessarily in the exact inverse order. Beyond backtracking and

The authors acknowledge partial support of COST Action IC1405 on Reversible Computation - Extending Horizons of Computing.

I. Ulidowski et al. (Eds.): RC 2020, LNCS 12070, pp. 151–176, 2020.
https://doi.org/10.1007/978-3-030-47361-7_7

causally-consistent reversibility, there is a more general form of reversibility, known as out-of-causal-order reversibility [28], which makes it possible to get to states which cannot be reached by forward reactions alone. Such sequences of forward and reverse reaction steps are important as they lead to new chemical structures and new reactions, which would not be possible without out-of-causal-order reversibility [28]. A typical example is a catalytic reaction: a catalyst C enables compounds A and B to combine, a combination that would not normally happen or be very unlikely without the presence of C. Initially, catalyst C binds with B resulting in a compound BC. Then A combines with BC creating ABC. Finally, with its job done, C breaks away from ABC, leaving A and B bonded. This sequence of reactions can be written as follows:

$$A + B + C \rightarrow A + BC \rightarrow ABC \rightarrow AB + C$$

This is a typical example of out-of-causal order reversibility since the bond between B and C is undone before its effect, namely the bond from A to B (which is not undone at all). The modelling of such reactions is the focus of this chapter. For further motivation, formal definitions and more illustrating examples of the various types of reversibility we refer the reader to [8,19,25,28].

1.1 Contribution

This chapter presents and compares three formalisms, the Calculus of Covalent Bonding (CCB) [15,16], the Bonding Calculus [1], and Reversing Petri Nets [23], that have been developed during COST Action IC1405. These models are variations of existing formalisms and set out to study reversible computation by allowing systems to reverse at any time leading to previously visited states or even new states without the need of additional forward actions. The contribution of this chapter is a comparative overview of the three formalisms, a discussion of their expressiveness, and a demonstration of their use on a common case study, namely the autoprotolysis of water reaction.

Our case study was selected to be non-trivial, of manageable size, and to allow us to exhibit the crucial features of the formalisms. It is a chemical reaction that involves small molecules, so it is different from biological reactions that involve proteins and other macromolecules. New modelling techniques may be needed in order to capture fully reversible behaviour of biological systems, however, in this chapter we concentrate on chemical reactions, a domain that offers interesting examples of out-of-causal-order reversibility.

The discussed formalisms enable us to model the intermediate steps of chemical reactions where some bonds are only "helping" to achieve the overall aim of the reaction: specifically, they are only formed to be broken before the end of the reactions. Thus, the allowed level of detail makes a more accurate depiction of the reversibility possible, and allows a more thorough understanding of the underlying reaction mechanisms compared to higher-level models.

1.2   Related Work

Process calculi, originally designed for the modelling of sequential and concurrent computation, have been applied to biochemical and biological systems. The main instances are the π-calculus [34], BioAmbients [33], the stochastic π-calculus [30], beta binders [31] and bioPEPA [6]. Another way to model biochemical reactions is with rule-based formalisms such as BIOCHAM [10], the κ-calculus [7], and the BioNetGen Language (BNGL) [9]. The formalisms κ and BNGL can be used to model interactions between proteins, while this is not possible in BIOCHAM. BNGL allows the use of molecule sites having the same name, which is not allowed in the κ-calculus.

Most of the formalisms mentioned above do not explicitly represent reversibility. If an action is the reverse of another action performed before, there is no explicit knowledge of that in the model. Reversibility was added explicitly to process calculi in RCCS [8], CCSK [25], and reversible π [17,18]. CCSK and RCCS are based on the Calculus of Communicating Systems (CCS) [21]. They extend CCS by keeping track of past actions and enabling an undo of those. So a reverse action is the reverse execution of a forward action. These calculi support backtracking and causally-consistent reversibility. Out-of-causal-order reversibility was first addressed in CCSK extended with controller processes [28], and in the context of reversible event structures [26,27,37]. CCB [16] allows all types of reversibility in the context of chemical reactions and in other settings.

Petri nets (PNs) [35] are another formalism that has been widely used to model and reason about a wide range of applications featuring concurrency and distribution. They are a graphical language associated with a rich mathematical theory and supported by a variety of tools. Their use in systems biology dates back to [12,32]. Since then, they have been employed for the modelling, analysis, and simulation of biochemical reactions in metabolic pathways, gene expression, signal transduction, and neural processes [2,4,5]. Indeed, PNs seem to be a natural framework for representing biochemical systems as they constitute a set of interdependent transitions/reactions which consume and produce resources, and are represented graphically in a similar fashion to the systems in question. Several specialised Petri net classes, such as qualitative, stochastic, continuous, or hybrid Petri nets and their coloured counterparts, have been used to describe different biochemical systems [13,20,22,29,38].

Even though classical PNs and their extensions have been extensively used to model biochemical systems, they cannot directly model reversibility. Specifically, when modelling reversible reactions in these formalisms it is required to employ mechanisms involving two distinct transitions, one for the forward and one for the reverse version of a reaction. This may result in expanded models and less natural and/or less accurate models of reversible behaviour. It is also in contrast to the notion of reversible computation, where the intention is not to return to a state via arbitrary execution but to reverse the effect of already executed transitions. For this reason, the formalism of reversing Petri nets [23] has been proposed to allow systems to reverse already executed transitions leading to previously visited states or even new ones without the need of additional forward actions.

Reversing Petri nets have also been extended with a mechanism for controlling transition reversal by associating transitions with conditions [24].

1.3 Paper Organisation

In the next section, we introduce the autoprotolysis of water reaction, which will be modelled using our three formalisms. This is followed by a section introducing the formalisms, their syntax and, informally, their operational semantics. We also give three models of the autoprotolysis of water using the formalisms. In Sect. 4, we compare the formalisms and the models of our example reaction, and we also briefly discuss software support for the three formalisms. Finally, Sect. 5 concludes the paper.

2 Autoprotolysis of Water

We consider a chemical reaction that transfers a hydrogen atom between two water molecules. This reaction is known as the *autoprotolysis of water* and is shown in Fig. 1. There, O indicates an oxygen atom and H a hydrogen atom. The lines indicate bonds. Positive and negative charges on atoms are shown by $\oplus$ and $\ominus$ respectively. The meaning of the curved arrows and the dots will be explained in the next paragraphs. The reaction is reversible and it takes place at a relatively low rate, making pure water slightly conductive. We have chosen this reaction as our example reaction, since it is non-trivial but manageable, and has some interesting aspects to be represented.

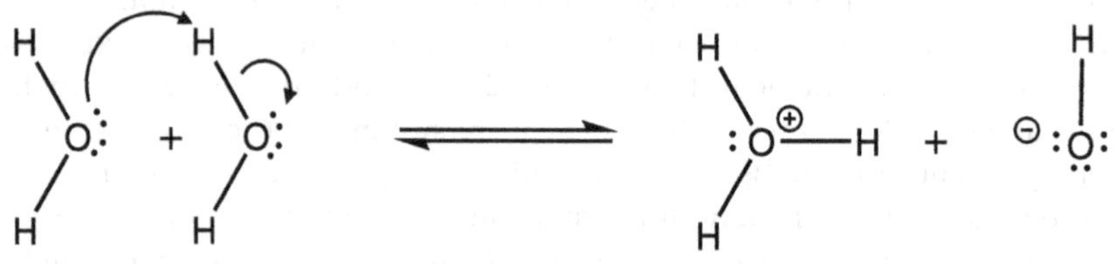

Fig. 1. Autoprotolysis of water.

To model the reaction we need to understand why it takes place and what causes it. The main reason is that the oxygen in the water molecule is *nucleophilic*, meaning it has the tendency to bond to another atomic nucleus, which would serve as an *electrophile*. This is because oxygen has a high electronegativity, therefore it attracts electrons and has an abundance of electrons around it. The electrons around the atomic nucleus are arranged on electron shells, where only those in the outer shell participate in bonding. Oxygen has four electrons in its outer shell, which are not involved in the initial bonding with hydrogen atoms. These electrons form two *lone pairs* of two electrons each, which can form new bonds (lone pairs are shown in Fig. 1 by pairs of dots). All this makes oxygen nucleophilic: it tends to connect to other atomic nuclei by forming bonds from its lone pairs. Since oxygen attracts electrons, the hydrogen atoms in water have a positive partial charge and oxygen has a negative partial charge.

The reaction starts when an oxygen in one water molecule is attracted by a hydrogen in another water molecule due to their opposite charges. This results in a *hydrogen bond*. This bond is formed out of the electrons of one of the lone pairs of the oxygen. The large curved arrow in Fig. 1 indicates the movements of the electrons. Since a hydrogen atom cannot have more than one bond, the creation of a new bond is compensated by breaking the existing hydrogen-oxygen bond (indicated by the small curved arrow). When this happens, the two electrons, which formed the original hydrogen-oxygen bond, remain with the oxygen. Since a hydrogen contains one electron and one proton, it is only the proton that is transferred, so the process can be called a proton transfer as well as a hydrogen transfer. The forming of the new bond and the breaking of the old bond are *concerted*, meaning that they happen together without a stable intermediate configuration. As a result we have reached the state where one oxygen atom has three bonds to hydrogen atoms and is positively charged, represented on the right side of the reaction in Fig. 1. This molecule is called *hydronium* and is written as H_3O^+. The other oxygen atom bonds to only one hydrogen and is negatively charged, having an electron in surplus. This molecule is called a *hydroxide* and is written as OH^-.

Note that the reaction is reversible: the oxygen that lost a hydrogen can pull back one of the hydrogens from the other molecule, the H_3O^+ molecule. This is the case since the negatively charged oxygen is a strong nucleophile and the hydrogens in the H_3O^+ molecule are all positively charged. Thus, any of the hydrogens can be removed, making both oxygens formally uncharged, and restoring the two water molecules. In Fig. 1 the curved arrows are given for the reaction going from left to right. Since the reaction is reversible (indicated by the double arrow) there are corresponding electron movements when going from right to left. These are not given in line with usual conventions, but can be inferred.

In this simple reaction, the forward and the reverse step consist of two steps each. The breaking of the old and the forming of the new bond occur simultaneously. This means that there is no strict causality of actions, since none of them can be called the cause of the overall reaction. Furthermore, the reverse step can be done with a different atom to the one used during the forward step because each of the molecules are in a sense identical and in practice there does not exist a single "reverse" path corresponding to a forward one.

It should be noted that there are two types of bonding modelled here. Firstly, we have the initial bonds where two atoms contribute an electron each. Secondly, the *dative* or *coordinate bonds* are formed where both electrons come from one atom (an oxygen in this case). Both are *covalent bonds*, and once formed they cannot be distinguished. Specifically, in the oxygen with three bonds all bonds are the same and no distinction can be made. If one of the bonds is broken by a deprotonation (as in the autoprotolysis of water) the two electrons are left behind and they form a lone pair. If the broken bond was not previously formed as a dative bond, the electrons changed their "rôle". This explains why any proton can be transferred in the reverse reaction and not just the one that was involved in the forward path.

3   Formalisms for Reversible Chemical Reactions

3.1   Calculus of Covalent Bonding

In this subsection we introduce the Calculus of Covalent Bonding (CCB) [16], concentrating on the new general prefixing operator $(s; b).P$ which, together with a generalised composition operator, produces pairs of *concerted* actions. Then we present a CCB model of the autoprotolysis of water.

Definition of CCB. We recall the definition of CCB, presenting only the main ideas. More details can be found in [15, 16]. First, we introduce some preliminary notions and notations.

Let $\mathcal{A}$ be the set of (forward) action labels, ranged over by a, b, c, d, e, f. We partition $\mathcal{A}$ into the set of *strong actions*, written as $\mathcal{SA}$, and the set of *weak actions*, written as $\mathcal{WA}$. Reverse (or past) action labels are members of $\underline{\mathcal{A}}$, with typical members $\underline{a}, \underline{b}, \underline{c}, \underline{d}, \underline{e}, \underline{f}$, and represent undoing of actions. The set $\mathcal{P}(\mathcal{A} \cup \underline{\mathcal{A}})$ is ranged over by L.

Let $\mathcal{K}$ be an infinite set of *communication keys* (or *keys* for short) [25], ranged over by k, l, m, n. The Cartesian product $\mathcal{A} \times \mathcal{K}$, denoted by $\mathcal{AK}$, represents past actions, which are written as $a[k]$ for $a \in \mathcal{A}$ and $k \in \mathcal{K}$. Correspondingly, we have the set $\underline{\mathcal{AK}}$ that represents undoing of past actions. We use α, β to identify actions which are either from $\mathcal{A}$ or $\mathcal{AK}$. It would be useful to consider sequences of actions or past actions, namely the elements of $(\mathcal{A} \cup \mathcal{AK})^*$, which are ranged over by s, s' and sequences of purely past actions, namely the elements of $\mathcal{AK}^*$, which are ranged over by t, t'. The empty sequence is denoted by ϵ. We use the notation "α, s" and "s, s'" to denote a concatenation of elements, which can be strings or single actions.

We shall also use two sets of auxiliary action labels, namely the set $(\mathcal{A}) = \{(a) \mid a \in \mathcal{A}\}$, and its product with the set of keys, namely $(\mathcal{A})\mathcal{K}$. These labels will be used in the auxiliary rules when defining the semantics of CCB. They denote the execution of a weak action, which makes it possible in the SOS rules to force breaking of a bond for those actions only.

The syntax of CCB is given below where P is a process term:

$$P ::= S \mid S \stackrel{def}{=} P \mid (s; b).P \mid P|Q \mid P \backslash L$$

The set of process identifiers (constants) $\mathcal{PI}$ contains typical elements S and T. Each process identifier S has a defining equation $S \stackrel{def}{=} P$ where P contains only forward actions (and no past actions). There is also a special identifier **0**, denoting the deadlocked process, which has no defining equation. For restrictions $L \subseteq \mathcal{A}$ holds.

We have a general prefixing operator $(s; b).P$, where s is a non-empty sequence of actions or past actions. This operator extends the prefixing operator in [28]. The action b is a weak action and it can be omitted, in which case the prefixing is written as $(s).P$ and is called the *simple prefix*. The simple prefix (which is still a sequence) is the prefixing operator in [28]. Exactly one of the actions in s in $(s).P$ may be a weak action from $\mathcal{WA}$. A weak action in s is only allowed for the simple prefix, in the $(s; b)$ operator b is the only allowed weak action. If s is a sequence that contains a single action, then the action is a strong action and the operator is the prefixing operator of CCS [21]. We omit trailing **0**s so, for example, $(s).\mathbf{0}$ is written as (s). The new feature of the operator $(s; b).P$ is the execution of the weak action b, which can happen only after all the actions in s have taken place. Performing b then forces undoing one of the past actions in s (by the concert rule in Fig. 4). If a $(s; b)$ operator is followed by another sequence of actions, where all actions in s have already taken place, then there is a non-deterministic choice of either doing b or progressing to the next sequence of actions (see act1 and act2).

$P \mid Q$ represents two systems P and Q which can perform actions or reverse actions on their own, or which can interact with each other according to a communication function γ. As in the calculus ACP [11], the communication function is a partial function $\gamma : \mathcal{A} \times \mathcal{A} \rightarrow \mathcal{A}$ which is commutative and associative. The function γ is used in the operational semantics to define when two processes can interact. Processes P and Q in $P \mid Q$ can also perform a pair of concerted actions, which is the new feature of our calculus. We also have the ACP-like restriction operator $\backslash L$, where L is a set of labels. It prevents actions from taking place and, due to the synchronisation algebra used, it also blocks communication. If $\gamma(a, b) = c$ then $a.P$ and $b.Q$ cannot communicate in $(a.P \mid b.Q) \backslash c$.

The set Proc of *process terms* is ranged over by P, Q and R. In the setting of CCB these terms are simply called *processes*. We define the semantics of our calculus using SOS rules (Figs. 2, 3, 4) and rewrite rules (Fig. 5).

We use some predicates and functions, which are formally defined in [16]. Informally, a process P is standard, written $\mathsf{std}(P)$, if it contains no past actions (hence no keys). A key n is fresh in Q, written $\mathsf{fsh}[n](Q)$, if Q contains no past action with the key n. Function k returns the keys in a sequence of actions, whereas keys returns the keys in a process, and fn gives the actions of a process which could be executed.

The forward and reverse SOS rules for CCB are given in Figs. 2 and 3. Figure 4 contains the SOS rules that define the new concerted actions transitions. The rule concert defines when a pair of concerted actions takes place. This enables the linking of forming and breaking of bonds, and therefore a degree of control over the reversing of actions. The modelling in the next section will give examples of the application. Note that the concert rule uses *lookahead* [36]. Lookahead is a property of SOS rules, where a variable appears both on the right hand side and

S. Kuhn et al.

$$\text{act1} \quad \frac{\text{std}(P) \quad \text{fsh}[k](s,s')}{(s,a,s';b).P \xrightarrow{a[k]} (s,a[k],s';b).P}$$

$$\text{act2} \quad \frac{P \xrightarrow{a[k]} P' \quad \text{fsh}[k](t)}{(t;b).P \xrightarrow{a[k]} (t;b).P'}$$

$$\text{par} \quad \frac{P \xrightarrow{a[k]} P' \quad \text{fsh}[k](Q)}{P \mid Q \xrightarrow{a[k]} P' \mid Q}$$

$$\text{com} \quad \frac{P \xrightarrow{a[k]} P' \quad Q \xrightarrow{d[k]} Q'}{P \mid Q \xrightarrow{c[k]} P' \mid Q'} \ (*)$$

$$\text{res} \quad \frac{P \xrightarrow{a[k]} P'}{P \backslash L \xrightarrow{a[k]} P' \backslash L} \ a \notin L$$

$$\text{con} \quad \frac{P \xrightarrow{a[k]} P'}{S \xrightarrow{a[k]} P'} \ S \overset{\text{def}}{=} P$$

Fig. 2. Forward SOS rules for CCB. The condition (*) is $\gamma(a,d) = c$, and $b \in \mathcal{WA}$. Recall that s is a sequence of actions and past actions and t is a sequence of purely past actions.

$$\text{rev act1} \quad \frac{\text{std}(P)}{(s,a[k],s';b).P \xrightarrow{a[k]} (s,a,s';b).P}$$

$$\text{rev act2} \quad \frac{P \xrightarrow{a[k]} P'}{(t;b).P \xrightarrow{a[k]} (t;b).P'}$$

$$\text{rev par} \quad \frac{P \xrightarrow{a[k]} P' \quad \text{fsh}[k](Q)}{P \mid Q \xrightarrow{a[k]} P' \mid Q}$$

$$\text{rev com} \quad \frac{P \xrightarrow{a[k]} P' \quad Q \xrightarrow{d[k]} Q'}{P \mid Q \xrightarrow{c[k]} P' \mid Q'} \ (*)$$

$$\text{rev res} \quad \frac{P \xrightarrow{a[k]} P'}{P \backslash L \xrightarrow{a[k]} P' \backslash L} \ a \notin L$$

$$\text{rev con} \quad \frac{P \xrightarrow{a[k]} P'}{P \xrightarrow{a[k]} S} \ S \overset{\text{def}}{=} P'$$

Fig. 3. Reverse SOS rules for CCB. The condition (*) is $\gamma(a,d) = c$, and $b \in \mathcal{WA}$.

on the left hand side of a transition in the premises. for example P' and Q' in concert. The rule concert par requires that k is fresh in Q, correspondingly as in par. Moreover, we need to ensure that when we reverse h with the key l in P we do not leave out any actions with the key l in Q which make up a multiaction communication with the key l. Hence, we also include the premise $\text{fsh}[l](Q)$ in concert par. The rule concert act requires, correspondingly as act, that k is fresh in t. Our operational semantics guarantees that if a standard process evolves to $(t;b).P$, for some P, and P reverses an action with the key l, then l is fresh in t. Hence, we do not include $\text{fsh}[l](t)$ in the premises of concert act. Overall, the transitions in Figs. 2, 3 and 4 are labelled with $a[k] \in \mathcal{AK}$, or with $\underline{c}[l] \in \underline{\mathcal{AK}}$, or with concerted actions $(a[k], \underline{c}[l])$.

Next, we recall the main new rewrite rules for a reduction relation for CCB in Fig. 5. All the rules can be found in [15,16] but here we only give rules for *promotion* of actions. These are prom, move-r, and move-l which promote weak bonds (here b) to strong bonds (here a). The rule prom applies to the full version of our prefix operator (with the; construct), and move-r and move-l apply only to the simple prefix. These three rules are here to model what happens in chemical systems: a bond on a weak action is temporary and as soon as there is a strong action that can accommodate that bond (as the result of concerted

$$\text{aux1} \; \frac{\text{std}(P) \quad \text{fsh}[k](t)}{(t;b).P \xrightarrow{(b)[k]} (t;b[k]).P} \qquad \text{aux2} \; \frac{P \xrightarrow{(b)[k]} P' \quad \text{fsh}[k](t)}{(t;b').P \xrightarrow{(b)[k]} (t;b').P'}$$

$$\text{concert} \; \frac{P \xrightarrow{(b)[k]} P' \quad P' \xrightarrow{a[l]} P'' \quad Q \xrightarrow{\alpha[k]} Q' \quad Q' \xrightarrow{d[l]} Q''}{P \mid Q \xrightarrow{\{e[k], \underline{f}[l]\}} P'' \mid Q''}(*)$$

$$\text{concert act} \; \frac{P \xrightarrow{\{a[k], \underline{h}[l]\}} P' \quad \text{fsh}[k](t)}{(t;b).P \xrightarrow{\{a[k], \underline{h}[l]\}} (t;b).P'}$$

$$\text{concert par} \; \frac{P \xrightarrow{\{a[k], \underline{h}[l]\}} P' \quad \text{fsh}[k](Q) \quad \text{fsh}[l](Q)}{P \mid Q \xrightarrow{\{a[k], \underline{h}[l]\}} P' \mid Q}$$

$$\text{concert res} \; \frac{P \xrightarrow{\{a[k], \underline{h}[l]\}} P'}{P \backslash L \xrightarrow{\{a[k], \underline{h}[l]\}} P' \backslash L}(**)$$

Fig. 4. SOS rules for concerted actions in CCB. The condition (*) is 1. $\alpha = c \vee \alpha = (c)$ and $\exists c \in \mathcal{A} | \gamma(b, c) = e$, and 2. $\gamma(a, d) = f$. The condition (**) is $a, \underline{h} \notin L \cup (L)$. Recall that $t \in \mathcal{AK}^*$, and $b \in \mathcal{WA}$.

$$\text{prom} : \quad (s, a, s'; b[k]).P \Rightarrow (s, a[k], s'; b).P \qquad \text{if } a \in \mathcal{SA}, b \in \mathcal{WA}$$

$$\text{move-r} : (s, a, s', b[k], s'').P \Rightarrow (s, a[k], s', b, s'').P \quad \text{if } a \in \mathcal{SA}, b \in \mathcal{WA}$$

$$\text{move-l} : (s, b[k], s', a, s'').P \Rightarrow (s, b, s', a[k], s'').P \quad \text{if } a \in \mathcal{SA}, b \in \mathcal{WA}$$

Fig. 5. New reduction rules for CCB. Sequences s, s', s'' are members of $(\mathcal{A} \cup \mathcal{AK})^*$.

actions) the bond establishes itself on the strong action thus releasing the weak action. In order to align the use of these three rules to what happens in chemical reactions, we insist that they are used as soon as they becomes applicable, a formal definition is given in [15,16].

We shall call henceforth the transitions derived by the forward SOS rules the *forward transitions* and, the transitions derived by the reverse SOS rules the *reverse transitions*. Correspondingly, there are the *concerted (action)* transitions.

The Autoprotolysis of Water in CCB. When modelling the autoprotolysis of water in CCB, we shall model the hydrogen and oxygen atoms as processes H and O as follows, where h, o are actions representing the bonding capabilities of the atoms and n, p representing negative and positive charges, respectively. H' and O' are process constants, and p and n are weak actions.

$$H \overset{def}{=} (h; p).H' \quad O \overset{def}{=} (o, o, n).O'$$

The synchronisation function γ is as follows:

$$\gamma(h, o) = ho \qquad \gamma(n, p) = np \qquad \gamma(n, h) = nh$$

Each water molecule is a structure consisting of two hydrogen atoms and one oxygen atom which are bonded appropriately. We shall use subscripts to distinguish the individual copies of atoms and actions; for example H_1 is a specific copy of hydrogen defined by $(h_1; p).H_1'$, similarly for O_1 defined as $(o_1, o_2, n).O_1'$. The atoms are composed with the parallel composition operator "$|$" using the communication keys (which are natural numbers) to combine actions into bonds. So a water molecule is modelled by the following process, where the key 1 shows that h_1 of H_1 has bonded with o_1 of O_1 (correspondingly for key 2). The restriction $\setminus \{h_1, h_2, o_1, o_2\}$ ensures that these actions cannot happen on their own, but only together with their partners, forming a bond.

$$((h_1[1]; p).H_1' \mid (h_2[2]; p).H_2' \mid (o_1[1], o_2[2], n).O_1') \setminus \{h_1, h_2, o_1, o_2\}$$

The system of two water molecules in Fig. 1 is represented by the parallel composition of two water processes, where the restriction $\setminus \{n, p\}$ represses actions n, p from taking place separately by forcing them to combine into bonds (according to γ).

$$(((h_1[1]; p).H_1' \mid (h_2[2]; p).H_2' \mid (o_1[1], o_2[2], n).O_1') \setminus \{h_1, h_2, o_1, o_2\} \mid$$
$$((h_3[3]; p).H_3' \mid (h_4[4]; p).H_4' \mid (o_3[3], o_4[4], n).O_2') \setminus \{h_3, h_4, o_3, o_4\}) \setminus \{n, p\}$$

Following a general principle in process calculi in the style of CCB we can move the restrictions to the outside. The rule used can be written as $(P \mid Q) \setminus L = P \setminus L \mid Q$ if the actions of L are not used in Q. Applying this gives us a water molecule modelled as follows:

$$((h_1[1]; p).H_1' \mid (h_2[2]; p).H_2' \mid (o_1[1], o_2[2], n).O_1') \mid (h_3[3]; p).H_3' \mid$$
$$(h_4[4]; p).H_4' \mid (o_3[3], o_4[4], n).O_2')) \setminus \{h_1, h_2, o_1, o_2\} \setminus \{h_3, h_4, o_3, o_4\} \setminus \{n, p\}$$

Note the $\underline{h_i}$, $\underline{o_j}$, and $\underline{n}$ are not restricted: this allows us to break bonds via concerted actions involving these actions. We will see an example of this shortly. We now leave out the restrictions to improve readability.

Actions n in O_1 and p in H_3 combine (we use the new key 5), representing a transfer of a proton from one atom of oxygen (O_2 in our model) to another one (O_1 in our model). As a hydrogen atom consists of a proton and an electron, and the electron stays in such a transfer, it can either be called a proton transfer or the transfer of a (positively charged) hydrogen atom. We perform the transfer of H_3 from O_2 to O_1. The creation of the bond with key 5 from O_1 to H_3 forces a break of the bond with key 3 (between h_3 and o_3) due to the property of the operator $(s; b).P$ discussed earlier. These two reactions happen almost simultaneously so we represent them as a pair of *concerted actions*.

$$(h_1[1]; p).H_1' \mid (h_2[2]; p).H_2' \mid (o_1[1], o_2[2], n).O_1' \mid (h_3[3]; p).H_3'$$
$$\mid (h_4[4]; p).H_4' \mid (o_3[3], o_4[4], n).O_2')$$
$$\xrightarrow{\{np[5], \underline{h_3 o_3}[3]\}}$$
$$((h_1[1]; p).H_1' \mid (h_2[2]; p).H_2' \mid (o_1[1], o_2[2], n[5]).O_1' \mid (\boldsymbol{h_3}; p[5]).H_3'$$
$$\mid (h_4[4]; p).H_4' \mid (\boldsymbol{o_3}, o_4[4], n).O_2'$$

We have now arrived at the state on the right hand side in Fig. 1. There are weak bonds between n and p (denoted by key 5) and *strong* bonds between h_i and o_j for all appropriate i, j. Since H_3 is weakly bonded to O_1 and its strong capability h_3 has become available, the bond 5 gets promoted to the stronger bond, releasing the capability p of H_3. We represent this change as a rewrite and we obtain the following process:

$$((h_1[1]; p).H_1' \mid (h_2[2]; p).H_2' \mid (o_1[1], o_2[2], n[\mathbf{5}]).O_1' \mid (\mathbf{h_3}; p[\mathbf{5}]).H_3'$$
$$\mid (h_4[4]; p).H_4' \mid (o_3, o_4[4], n).O_2'$$
$$\Rightarrow$$
$$((h_1[1]; p).H_1' \mid (h_2[2]; p).H_2' \mid (o_1[1], o_2[2], n[\mathbf{5}]).O_1') \mid (h_3[\mathbf{5}]; p).H_3')$$
$$\mid (h_4[4]; p).H_4' \mid (o_3, o_4[4], n).O_2'$$

Note that we wrote h_3, o_3 and the key 5, the actions and keys affected by the promotion, in bold font to improve readability. We shall do correspondingly below.

Oxygen O_1 is still blocked, which represents it being fully bonded (and positively charged). Oxygen O_2 has a free n capability and can remove any of the hydrogens from O_1. As a result the process can reverse to its original state.

We show this by again transferring H_3. We then execute promotion again:

$$(((h_1[1]; p).H_1' \mid (h_2[2]; p).H_2' \mid (o_1[1], o_2[2], n[\mathbf{5}]).O_1') \mid (h_3[\mathbf{5}]; p).H_3')$$
$$\mid (h_4[4]; p).H_4' \mid (o_3, o_4[4], n).O_2'$$
$$\xrightarrow{\{np[3], \underline{nh_3}[5]\}}$$
$$(((h_1[1]; p).H_1' \mid (h_2[2]; p).H_2' \mid (o_1[1], o_2[2], \mathbf{n}).O_1') \mid (\mathbf{h_3}; \mathbf{p[3]}).H_3')$$
$$\mid (h_4[4]; p).H_4' \mid (o_3, o_4[4], \mathbf{n[3]}).O_2'$$
$$\Rightarrow$$
$$(((h_1[1]; p).H_1' \mid (h_2[2]; p).H_2' \mid (o_1[1], o_2[2], \mathbf{n}).O_1') \mid (\mathbf{h_3[3]}; \mathbf{p}).H_3')$$
$$\mid (h_4[4]; p).H_4' \mid (\mathbf{o_3[3]}, o_4[4], \mathbf{n}).O_2'$$

This corresponds to the original process. Putting back restrictions we obtain

$$((h_1[1]; p).H_1' \mid (h_2[2]; p).H_2' \mid (o_1[1], o_2[2], n).O_1' \mid (h_3[3]; p).H_3'$$
$$\mid (h_4[4]; p).H_4' \mid (o_3[3], o_4[4], n).O_2') \setminus \{h_1, h_2, o_1, o_2\} \setminus \{h_3, h_4, o_3, o_4\} \setminus \{n, p\}$$

and then if we apply the movement of restrictions in reverse we get

$$(((h_1[1]; p).H_1' \mid (h_2[2]; p).H_2' \mid (o_1[1], o_2[2], n).O_1') \setminus \{h_1, h_2, o_1, o_2\} \mid$$
$$((h_3[3]; p).H_3' \mid (h_4[4]; p).H_4' \mid (o_3[3], o_4[4], n).O_2') \setminus \{h_3, h_4, o_3, o_4\}) \setminus \{n, p\}$$

3.2   Bonding Calculus

In this subsection we recall briefly the Bonding Calculus [1], and illustrate its expressiveness by modelling the autoprotolysis of water.

Definition of the Bonding Calculus. The abstraction "processes as interactions" from process calculi is used in the Bonding Calculus, but processes are not able to communicate values in order to interact. Just like in the BNGL [9], the Bonding Calculus allows the use of molecule sites having the same name, while this is not possible in the κ-calculus. While the κ-calculus describes molecules as a set of sites and uses rules to manipulate these sites between two or more molecules, in the Bonding Calculus a molecule is described by the sequence of operations it can perform on its sites (including also non-deterministic choices), regardless of the form of the other molecules. This allows to use the compositionality of the process calculus.

The syntax of the Bonding Calculus syntax is presented in Fig. 6. Let us consider the set $\mathbb{N}$ of natural numbers, the set $\mathcal{N} = \{x, x^+, x^-, \dots\}$ of bond names, the set $\mathcal{M} = \{a, b, \dots\}$ of molecules and the set $\mathcal{P} = \{P, Q, \dots\}$ of processes. A multiset over $\mathcal{N}$ is defined as a partial function $N : \mathcal{N} \to \mathbb{N}$. In the Bonding Calculus each molecule has a unique name, and the bond x between two molecules a and b is denoted by $\{a -^x b\}$.

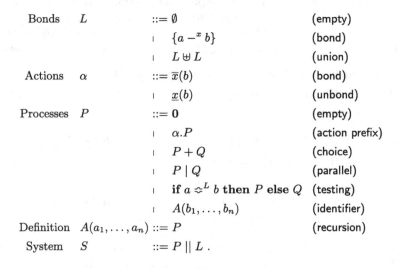

Fig. 6. Syntax of the Bonding Calculus

A bond prefix $\overline{x}(b)$ is used to indicate the availability of a molecule with name b to create a new bond with name x, while an unbond prefix $\underline{x}(b)$ indicates the availability of b to destroy an existing bond x. Creating or breaking a bond leads to an update of the global bond memory L. As several similar bonds can exist between the same molecules, L is actually a multiset of bonds.

The process $\mathbf{0}$ denotes inactivity. The availability to perform an action α, and then to continue the execution as process P is denoted by the process $\alpha.P$. The process $P + Q$ offers a choice between the processes P and Q, while the process $P \mid Q$ allows the execution of processes P and Q in parallel, with possible interactions between them by using appropriate actions.

As we work with bonds, we use the function $\approx: \mathcal{M} \times \mathbb{N}^{\mathcal{N}} \times \mathcal{M} \to Bool$ to check whether between two molecules there exist certain bonds. For example, $a \approx^N b$ checks for the existence of all bonds in N between the molecules a and b; it returns true when such bonds exist, and false otherwise. When we consider $N = \emptyset$, then $a \approx^\emptyset b$ checks if at least a bond exists between the two molecules. When $b = \varepsilon$, then $a \approx^N \varepsilon$ checks if a has all of bonds from N, regardless of the molecules he has them with. The Boolean result $a \approx^N b$ used in the testing process is defined formally as:

$$a \approx^N b = \begin{cases} (\biguplus_{x \in N} \{a -^x b\}) \in L & N \neq \emptyset \text{ and } a \neq b \neq \varepsilon \\[2ex] (\biguplus_{x \in \mathcal{N}} \{a -^x b\}) \cap L \neq \emptyset & N = \emptyset \text{ and } a \neq b \neq \varepsilon \\[2ex] \bigwedge_{x \in N} (|L|_{a,x} = |N|_x) & N \neq \emptyset \text{ and } a \neq \varepsilon \text{ and } b = \varepsilon \\[2ex] undefined & otherwise, \end{cases}$$

where $|L|_{a,x}$ is the number of bonds containing the molecule a and bond name x that appear in the multiset L, while $|N|_x$ is the number of occurrences of x in N.

Depending on the truth value of $a \approx^N b$, the process **if** $a \approx^N b$ **then** P **else** Q executes either P or Q. An identifier $A(b_1, \ldots, b_n)$ is used to provide recursion by creating new instances of processes defined as $A(a_1, \ldots, a_n) = P$, where $a_i \neq a_j$ for all $i \neq j \in \{1, \ldots, n\}$; the new process is defined as $A(b_1, \ldots, b_n) = P\{b_1/a_1, \ldots, b_n/a_n\}$, where $\{b_i/a_i\}$ denotes the replacement of variable a_i by value b_i. A system S is given as a composition of a process P and the multiset of bonds L, written as $P \parallel L$.

The structural congruence relation $\equiv$ is the least congruence such that $(\mathcal{P}, +, \mathbf{0})$ and $(\mathcal{P}, |, \mathbf{0})$ are commutative monoids and the unfolding law $A(b_1, \ldots, b_n) \equiv P\{b_1/a_1, \ldots, b_n/a_n\}$ holds whenever $A(a_1, \ldots, a_n) = P$.

The calculus presented in [1] was intended to model the creation and breaking of covalent bonds. In order to be able to model both covalent and hydrogen bonds, we apply a minor update to the operational semantics in [1] because we need two instances of the rules used to create and to break bonds. The only difference between the two instances of the same rule is given by the names of the bonds appearing in the interacting processes, and by the fact that a bond cannot be created using the names x^+ and x^- if other bonds exist between the same molecules; more details about this restriction are given in the example below.

The operational semantics of the Bonding Calculus is given in Fig. 7. The rules (CREATE1) and (CREATE2) describe the creation of a new bond $\{a -^x b\}$, while the rules (REMOVE1) and (REMOVE2) describe the breaking of a bond $\{a -^x b\}$. If there exist two bonds $\{a -^x b\}$ in L, then any of these bonds is broken. The rule (PAR) is used to compose processes in parallel, while the rules (TRUE) and (FALSE) choose one of the branches of the testing process based on the result of the checking. The rule (IDE) describes the recursion, while the (STRUCT) rule indicates the fact that we reason up to the structural congruence.

$$\text{(CREATE1)}\ \frac{P = \overline{x}(b).P' + P'' \quad Q = \overline{x}(a).Q' + Q''}{(P \mid Q) \mid\mid L \to (P' \mid Q') \mid\mid L \uplus \{a -^{x} b\}}$$

$$\text{(CREATE2)}\ \frac{P = \overline{x^{+}}(b).P' + P'' \quad Q = \overline{x^{-}}(a).Q' + Q'' \quad a \mathrel{\diamond}^{\emptyset} b\ is\ false\ w.r.t.\ L}{(P \mid Q) \mid\mid L \to (P' \mid Q') \mid\mid L \uplus \{a -^{x} b\}}$$

$$\text{(REMOVE1)}\ \frac{P = \underline{x}(b).P' + P'' \quad Q = \underline{x}(a).Q' + Q'' \quad a \mathrel{\diamond}^{x} b\ is\ true\ w.r.t.\ L}{(P \mid Q) \mid\mid L \to (P' \mid Q') \mid\mid L \backslash \{a -^{x} b\}}$$

$$\text{(REMOVE2)}\ \frac{P = \underline{x^{+}}(b).P' + P'' \quad Q = \underline{x^{-}}(a).Q' + Q'' \quad a \mathrel{\diamond}^{N} b\ is\ true\ w.r.t.\ L}{(P \mid Q) \mid\mid L \to (P' \mid Q') \mid\mid L \backslash \{a -^{x} b\}}$$

$$\text{(PAR)}\ \frac{P \mid\mid L \to P' \mid\mid L}{(P \mid Q) \mid\mid L \to (P' \mid Q) \mid\mid L}$$

$$\text{(TRUE)}\ \frac{a \mathrel{\diamond}^{N} b\ is\ true\ w.r.t.\ L}{(\textbf{if}\ a \mathrel{\diamond}^{N} b\ \textbf{then}\ P\ \textbf{else}\ Q) \mid\mid L \to P \mid\mid L}$$

$$\text{(FALSE)}\ \frac{a \mathrel{\diamond}^{N} b\ is\ false\ w.r.t.\ L}{(\textbf{if}\ a \mathrel{\diamond}^{N} b\ \textbf{then}\ P\ \textbf{else}\ Q) \mid\mid L \to Q \mid\mid L}$$

$$\text{(IDE)}\ \frac{P\{b_1/a_1, \ldots, b_n/a_n\} \to P'}{A(b_1, \ldots, b_n) \to P'} \quad \text{if}\ A(a_1, \ldots, a_n) = P$$

$$\text{(STRUCT)}\ \frac{S_1 \to S_1' \quad S_1 \equiv S_2 \quad S_2 \to S_2'}{S_1' \to S_2'}$$

Fig. 7. Operational Semantics of the Bonding Calculus.

The Autoprotolysis of Water in the Bonding Calculus. We use two types of bond names, namely c and h, to stand for the covalent and hydrogen bonds, respectively. Using our calculus, the system composed of two molecules of water is described by:

$$\begin{aligned} &MolOxy_2(O_1) \mid MolHy_1(H_1) \mid MolHy_1(H_2)\\ &\mid MolOxy_2(O_2) \mid MolHy_1(H_3) \mid MolHy_1(H_4)\\ &\mid\mid \{O_1 -^{c} H_1, O_1 -^{c} H_2, O_2 -^{c} H_3, O_2 -^{c} H_4\} \end{aligned}$$

where the molecules are those of hydrogen and oxygen that are described below:

$$\begin{aligned} &MolHy_0(H_i) = \overline{c}(H_i).MolHy_1(H_i)\\ &MolHy_1(H_i) = \underline{c}(H_i).MolHy_0(H_i) + \overline{h^{+}}(H_i).MolHy_2(H_i);\\ &MolHy_2(H_i) = \underline{c}(H_i).\overline{c}(H_i).\underline{h^{+}}(H_i).MolHy_1(H_i).\\ &MolOxy_0(O_i) = \overline{c}(O_i).MolOxy_1(O_i);\\ &MolOxy_1(O_i) = \underline{c}(O_i).MolOxy_0(O_i) + \overline{c}(O_i).MolOxy_2(O_i);\\ &MolOxy_2(O_i) = \underline{c}(O_i).MolOxy_1(O_i) + \overline{h^{-}}(O_i).MolOxy_3(O_i).\\ &MolOxy_3(O_i) = \underline{h^{-}}(O_i).MolOxy_2(O_i). \end{aligned}$$

Each molecule of water is a structure consisting of one molecule of oxygen and two molecules of hydrogen which are properly bonded. For example, the process $MolOxy_2(O_1) \mid MolHy_1(H_1) \mid MolHy(H_2)$ together with the bonds $\{O_1 -^c H_1, O_1 -^c H_2\}$ model one molecule of water. We use unique names for the molecules given as O_i (for oxygen) and H_i (for hydrogen), while the processes having the names $MolHy_i$ and $MolOxy_i$ identify processes modelling hydrogen and oxygen molecules with i bonds, respectively. For example, the process $MolOxy_1(O_i)$ can either create or break bonds, and this is why we use the operator $+$ to describe such a (non-deterministic) choice.

Now we present the steps of one of the possible sequences of reactions modelling the autoprotolysis of water. The system of two molecules of water can be rewritten as follows (where we extend the definitions for the processes that will interact in the next step, and bold the actions to be executed):

$$\underline{c}(O_1).MolOxy_1(O_1) + \overline{h^-}(\mathbf{O_1}).MolOxy_3(O_1) \mid MolHy_1(H_1) \mid MolHy_1(H_2)$$
$$\mid MolOxy_2(O_2) \mid MolHy_1(H_3) \mid \underline{c}(H_4).MolHy_0(H_4) + \overline{h^+}(\mathbf{H_4}).MolHy_2(H_4)$$
$$\parallel \{O_1 -^c H_1, O_1 -^c H_2, O_2 -^c H_3, O_2 -^c H_4\}$$

This leads to the next system, where we again bold the processes to be executed:

$$MolOxy_3(O_1) \mid MolHy_1(H_1) \mid MolHy_1(H_2)$$
$$\mid \underline{c}(\mathbf{O_2}).MolOxy_1(O_2) + \overline{h^-}(O_2).MolOxy_3(O_1) \mid MolHy_1(H_3)$$
$$\mid \underline{c}(\mathbf{H_4}).\overline{c}(H_4).\underline{h^+}(\mathbf{H_4}).MolHy_1(H_4)$$
$$\parallel \{O_1 -^c H_1, O_1 -^c H_2, O_1 -^h H_4, O_2 -^c H_3, O_2 -^c H_4\}$$

The creation of the hydrogen bond forces the break of the other bond in which the hydrogen molecule H_4 is involved. This leads to the following system containing the H_3O and HO molecules:

$$MolOxy_3(O_1) \mid MolHy_1(H_1) \mid MolHy_1(H_2)$$
$$\mid \underline{c}(O_2).MolOxy_0(O_2) + \overline{c}(\mathbf{O_2}).MolOxy_2(O_2)$$
$$\mid MolHy_1(H_3) \mid \overline{c}(\mathbf{H_4}).\underline{h^+}(H_4).MolHy_1(H_4)$$
$$\parallel \{O_1 -^c H_1, O_1 -^c H_2, O_1 -^h H_4, O_2 -^c H_3\}$$

Since some bonds are weaker, the system is evolving to:

$$\underline{h^-}(\mathbf{O_1}).MolOxy_2(O_1) \mid MolHy_1(H_1) \mid MolHy_1(H_2)$$
$$\mid MolOxy_2(O_2) \mid MolHy_1(H_3) \mid \underline{h^+}(\mathbf{H_4}).MolHy_1(H_4)$$
$$\parallel \{O_1 -^c H_1, O_1 -^c H_2, O_1 -^h H_4, O_2 -^c H_3, O_2 -^c H_4\}$$

followed by the breaking of the hydrogen bond $O_1 -^h H_4$:

$$MolOxy_2(O_1) \mid MolHy_1(H_1) \mid MolHy_1(H_2)$$
$$\mid MolOxy_2(O_2) \mid MolHy_1(H_3) \mid MolHy_1(H_4)$$
$$\parallel \{O_1 -^c H_1, O_1 -^c H_2, O_2 -^c H_3, O_2 -^c H_4\}$$

The obtained system contains again two water molecules of water.

3.3   Reversing Petri Nets

In this subsection we present Reversing Petri Nets [23] (RPNs, pronounced as 'reversing Petri nets'), an extension of Petri nets developed for the modelling reversing computations, and we employ the formalism to model the autoprotolysis of water.

Definition of RPNs. We consider an extension of reversing Petri nets suitable for describing chemical reactions by allowing multiple tokens of the same type as well as the possibility for transitions to break bonds. Thus, a transition may simultaneously create and/or destroy bonds, and its reversal results in the opposite effect. Formally, a Reversing Petri net is defined as follows:

Definition 1. A *reversing Petri net* (RPN) is a tuple (P, T, A, A_V, B, F) where:

1. P is a finite set of *places* and T is a finite set of *transitions*.
2. A is a finite set of *base* or *token types* ranged over by $a, b, \ldots$. $\overline{A} = \{\overline{a} \mid a \in A\}$ contains a "negative" version for each token type. We assume that for any token type a there may exist a finite number of *token instances*. We write $a_1, \ldots$, for instances of type a and A_I for the set of all token instances.
3. A_V is a finite set of *token variables*. We write $type(v)$ for the type of variable v and assume that $type(v) \in A$ for all $v \in A_V$.
4. $B \subseteq A \times A$ is a finite set of undirected *bond* types ranged over by $\beta, \gamma, \ldots$. We use the notation $a-b$ for a bond $(a, b) \in B$. $\overline{B} = \{\overline{\beta} \mid \beta \in B\}$ contains a "negative" version for each bond type. $B_I \subseteq A_I \times A_I$ is a finite set of *bond instances*, where we write β_i for elements of B.
5. $F : (P \times T \cup T \times P) \rightarrow \mathcal{P}(A_V \cup (A_V \times A_V) \cup \overline{A} \cup \overline{B})$ is a set of directed labelled *arcs*.

A reversing Petri net is built on the basis of a set of *tokens* or *bases*. These are organised in a set of token types A, where each token type is associated with a set of token instances. Token instances correspond to the basic entities that occur in a system and they may occur as stand-alone elements but as computation proceeds they may also merge together to form *bond instances*. Places and transitions have the standard meaning and are connected via directed arcs, which are labelled by a set of elements from $A_V \cup (A_V \times A_V) \cup \overline{A} \cup \overline{B}$. Intuitively, these labels express the requirements for a transition to fire when placed on arcs incoming the transition, and the effects of the transition when placed on the outgoing arcs. Graphically, a RPN is portrayed as a directed bipartite graph where token instances are indicated by •, places by circles, transitions by boxes, and bond instances by lines between token instances.

Before we recall the semantics of RPNs we need to introduce some notation. Note that in what follows we omit the discussion of negative tokens and negative bonds as they are not relevant to our case study. We write $\circ t = \{x \in P \mid F(x, t) \neq \emptyset\}$ and $t\circ = \{x \in P \mid F(t, x) \neq \emptyset\}$ for the incoming and outgoing places of transition t, respectively. Furthermore, we write $\mathsf{pre}(t) = \bigcup_{x \in P} F(x, t)$

for the union of all labels on the incoming arcs of transition t, and $\mathsf{post}(t) = \bigcup_{x \in P} F(t, x)$ for the union of all labels on the outgoing arcs of transition t.

Definition 2. A reversing Petri net is *well-formed*, if for all $t \in T$:

1. $A_V \cap \mathsf{pre}(t) = A_V \cap \mathsf{post}(t)$,
2. $F(t, x) \cap F(t, y) \cap A_V = \emptyset$ for all $x, y \in P$, $x \neq y$.

Thus, a reversing Petri net is well-formed if (1) whenever a variable exists in the incoming arcs of a transition then it also exists on the outgoing arcs, which implies that transitions do not erase tokens, and (2) tokens/bonds cannot be cloned into more than one outgoing places.

As with standard Petri nets the association of token/bond instances to places is called a *marking* such that $M : P \rightarrow 2^{A_I \cup B_I}$, where we assume that if $(u, v) \in M(x)$ then $u, v \in M(x)$. In addition, we employ the notion of a *history*, which assigns a memory to each transition $H : T \rightarrow \mathbb{N}$. Intuitively, a history of $H(t) = 0$ for some $t \in T$ captures that the transition has not taken place, or every execution of it has been reversed, and a history of $H(t) = k, k > 0$, captures that the transition had k forward executions that have not been reversed. Note that $H(t) > 1$ may arise due to the consecutive execution of the transition with different token instances. A pair of a marking and a history, $\langle M, H \rangle$, describes a *state* of a RPN with $\langle M_0, H_0 \rangle$ the initial state, where $H_0(t) = 0$ for all $t \in T$.

Finally, we define $\mathsf{con}(a_i, C)$, where $a_i \in A_I$ and $C \subseteq 2^{A_I \cup B_I}$, to be the token instances connected to a_i as well as the bonds creating these connections according to set C.

Forward Execution. During the forward execution of a transition in a RPN, a set of tokens and bonds, as specified by the incoming arcs of the transition, are selected and moved to the outgoing places of the transition, as specified by the transition's outgoing arcs, possibly forming or destructing bonds, as necessary. Due to the presence of multiple instances of the same token type, it is possible that different token instances are selected during the transition's execution.

A transition is forward-enabled in a state $\langle M, H \rangle$ of a reversing Petri net if there exists a selection of token instances available at the incoming places of the transition matching the requirements on the transitions incoming arcs. Formally:

Definition 3. Given a RPN (P, T, A, A_V, B, F), a state $\langle M, H \rangle$, and a transition t, we say that t is *forward-enabled* in $\langle M, H \rangle$ if there exists a surjective function $U : \mathsf{pre}(t) \cap A_V \rightarrow A_I$ such that:

1. for all $v \in \mathsf{pre}(t)$, if $type(v) = a$ then $type(U(v)) = a$
2. for all $a \in F(x, t)$, then $U(a) \in M(x)$ and for all $(a, b) \in F(x, t)$, then $(U(a), U(b)) \in M(x)$,
3. for all $(a, b) \in \mathsf{post}(t) - \mathsf{pre}(t)$ then $(U(a), U(b)) \notin M(x)$ for all $x \in \circ t$.

Thus, t is enabled in state $\langle M, H \rangle$ if (1) there is a type-respecting assignment of token instances to the variables on the incoming edges, with (2) the token instances originating from the appropriate input places of the transition and connected with bonds as required by the variable bonds occurring on the incoming edges, and (3) if a bond occurs in the outgoing edges of the transition but not the incoming ones, then the selected instances associated with the bond's variables should not be bonded together in the incoming places of the transition (thus transitions do not recreate bonds). We refer to U as a forward enabling assignment.

To execute a transition t according to an enabling assignment U, the selected token instances, along with their connected components, are relocated to the outgoing places of the transition as specified by the outgoing arcs, with bonds created and destructed accordingly. Furthermore, the history of the executed transition is increased by one.

Definition 4. Given a RPN (P, T, A, A_V, B, F), a state $\langle M, H \rangle$, and an enabling assignment U, we write $\langle M, H \rangle \xrightarrow{t}_S \langle M', H' \rangle$ where for all $x \in P$:

$$M'(x) = M(x) - \bigcup_{a \in f(x,t)} \text{con}(U(a), M(x)) \cup \bigcup_{a \in f(t,x), U(a) \in M(y)} \text{con}(U(a), S)$$

where $S = (M(y) - \{(U(a), U(b)) \mid (a, b) \in F(y, t)\}) \cup \{(U(a), U(b)) \mid (a, b) \in F(t, x)\}$

$$\text{and} \quad H'(t') = \begin{cases} H(t') + 1, & \text{if } t' = t \\ H(t'), & \text{otherwise} \end{cases}$$

Reversing Execution. We now move on to reversing transitions. A transition can be reversed in a certain state if it has been previously executed and there exist token instances in its output places that match the requirements on its outgoing arcs. Specifically, we define the notion of reverse enabledness as follows:

Definition 5. Consider a RPN (P, T, A, A_V, B, F), a state $\langle M, H \rangle$, and a transition t. We say that t is *reverse-enabled* in $\langle M, H \rangle$ if (1) $H(t) \neq 0$, and (2) there exists a surjective function $W : \text{post}(t) \cap A_V \to A_I$ such that:

1. for all $v \in \text{post}(t)$, if $type(v) = a$ then $type(W(v)) = a$,
2. for all $a \in F(t, x)$, then $W(a) \in M(x)$ and for all $(a, b) \in F(t, x)$, then $(W(a), W(b)) \in M(x)$,
3. for all $(a, b) \in \text{pre}(t) - \text{post}(t)$ then $(W(a), W(b)) \notin M(x)$ for all $x \in \circ t$.

Thus, a transition t is reverse-enabled in $\langle M, H \rangle$ if (1) the transition has been executed and (2) there exists a type-respecting assignment of token instances, from the instances in the out-places of the transition, to the variables on the outgoing edges of the transition, and where the instances are connected with bonds as required by the transition's outgoing edges. Also we do not recreate existing bonds when going backwards. We refer to W as a reversal enabling assignment. To implement the reversal of a transition t according to a reversal enabling assignment W, the selected instances are relocated from the outgoing places of the transition to the incoming places, as specified by the incoming arcs of the transition, with bonds created and destructed accordingly.

Definition 6. Given a RPN (P, T, A, A_V, B, F), a state $\langle M, H \rangle$, and a transition t reverse-enabled in $\langle M, H \rangle$ with W a reversal enabling assignment, we write $\langle M, H \rangle \xrightarrow{t} \langle M', H' \rangle$ where for all x:

$$M'(x) = M(x) - \bigcup_{a \in f(t,x)} \mathrm{con}(W(a), M(x)) \cup \bigcup_{a \in f(x,t), W(a) \in M(y)} \mathrm{con}(W(a), S)$$

where $S = (M(y) - \{(W(a), W(b)) \mid (a,b) \in F(t,y)\}) \cup \{(W(a), W(b)) \mid (a,b) \in F(x,t)\}$

$$\text{and} \quad H'(t') = \begin{cases} H(t') - 1, & \text{if } t' = t \\ H(t'), & \text{otherwise} \end{cases}$$

The Autoprotolysis of Water in RPNs. Figure 8 shows the graphical representation of the forming of a water molecule as a RPN. In this model, we assume two token types, H for hydrogen and O for oxygen. They are instantiated via four token instances of H (H_1, H_2, H_3, and H_4) and two token instances of O, (O_1 and O_2). The net consists of five places and three transitions and the edges between them are associated with token variables and bonds, where we assume that $type(o) = type(o_1) = type(o_2) = O$ and $type(h) = type(h_1) = type(h_2) = type(h_3) = type(h_4) = H$. Looking at the transitions, transition t_1 models the formation of a bond between a hydrogen token and an oxygen token. Precisely, the transition stipulates a selection of two such molecules with the use of variables o and h on the incoming arcs of the transition which are bonded together, as described in the outgoing arc of the transition. Subsequently, transition t_2 completes the formation of a water molecule by selecting an oxygen token from place x and a hydrogen token from place v and forming a bond between them, placing the resulting component at place y. Note that the selected oxygen instance in this transition will be connected to a hydrogen token via a bond created by transition t_1; this bond is preserved and the component resulting from the creation of the new $o - h$ bond will be transferred to place y. Finally, transition t_3 models the autoprotolysis reaction: assuming the existence of two distinct oxygen instances, as required by the variables o_1 and o_2 on the incoming arc of the transition, connected with hydrogen instances as specified in $F(y, t_3)$, the transition breaks the bond $o_2 - h_3$ and forms the bond $o_1 - h_3$. As such, assuming the existence of two water molecules at place y, the transition will form a hydronium (H_3^+O) and a hydroxin (OH^-) molecule in place z of the net. The reversibility semantics of RPNs ensures that reversing the transition t_3 will result in the re-creation of two water molecules placed at y, while the use of variables allows the formation of water molecules consisting of different bonds between the hydrogen and oxygen instances.

The first net in Fig. 9 shows the system after the execution of transition t_1 with enabling assignment $U(h) = H_1$, $U(o) = O_1$. Note that the term [1] written over transition t_1 captures that at this point $H(t_1) = 1$ since the

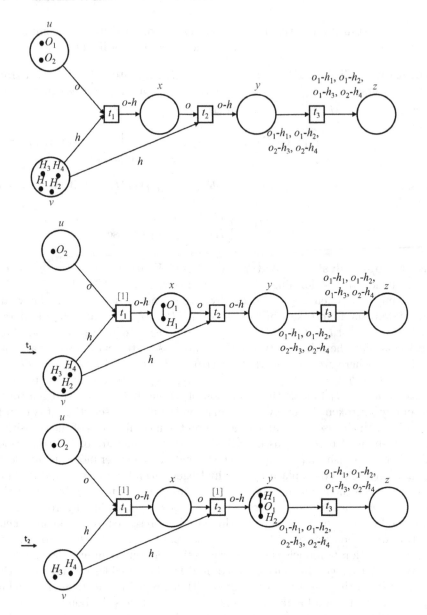

Fig. 8. RPN model of the formation of a water molecule.

transition has been executed once. This notation is generally used for histories in the graphical representation with occasional missing histories corresponding to histories equal to 0. Subsequently, we have the model after execution of transition t_2 with enabling assignment $U(h) = H_2$, $U(o) = O_1$, creating the bond $O_1 - H_2$, thus forming the first water molecule. A second

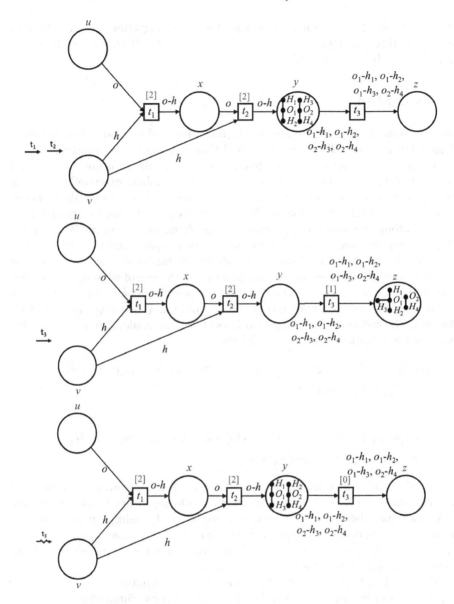

Fig. 9. RPN model of the execution of the autoprotolysis of water.

execution of transitions t_1 and t_2 results in the second molecule of water in the system, placed again at place y, as shown in the third net in the figure. At this state, transition t_3 is forward-enabled and, with enabling assignment $U(o_1) = O_1, U(o_2) = O_2, U(h_1) = H_1, U(h_2) = H_2, U(h_3) = H_3, U(h_4) = H_4$, we have the creation of the hydronium and hydroxide depicted at place z in the fourth net of the figure. At this stage, transition t_3 is now reverse-enabled and the last net in the figure illustrates the state resulting after reversing t_3 with reversal enabling assignment $W(o_1) = O_1, W(o_2) = O_2, W(h_1) = H_1, W(h_2) = H_3, W(h_3) = H_2, W(h_4) = H_4$.

4   Evaluation

We have presented three formalisms which can be used to model chemical reactions. CCB is a reversible version of ACP that employs communication keys to record executed actions. Its main feature is a mechanism to link forming and breaking of bonds, which gives rise to a type of explicit reversibility we call "locally controlled reversibility". We have modelled a simple covalent chemical reaction in CCB. A similar modelling approach can be used to model more complex atoms and reactions, for example, involving carbon atoms [16]. Finally, CCB can also be used to model reactions beyond simple chemical reactions [14]. In CCB, we can actually distinguish different instances of the same atom or molecule, and of identical actions in a process via the use of subscripts. As mentioned above, the reverse reaction in the autoprotolysis of water can work by transferring any of the hydrogens of the hydronium. When reversing the reaction in CCB, instead of the transition in Sect. 3.1, we could also have done this (writing the transition and the rewrite together):

$$((((h_1[1];p).H_1' \mid (h_2[2];p).H_2' \mid (o_1[1],o_2[2],n[5]).O_1') \mid (h_3[5];p).H_3')$$
$$\mid (h_4[4];p).H_4' \mid (o_3,o_4[4],n).O_2'$$
$$\underrightarrow{\{np[3],\underline{nh_1[1]}\}} \Rightarrow$$
$$((((\boldsymbol{h_1}[\boldsymbol{3}];p).H_1' \mid (h_2[2];p).H_2' \mid (\boldsymbol{o_1}[\boldsymbol{5}],o_2[2],\boldsymbol{n}).O_1') \mid (h_3[5];p).H_3')$$
$$\mid (h_4[4];p).H_4' \mid (\boldsymbol{o_3}[\boldsymbol{3}],o_4[4],\boldsymbol{n}).O_2'$$

The result is different from that in Sect. 3.1, but identical from a chemical point of view, since the hydrogens are all identical. On the other hand a technique called isotopic labelling can be used to trace atoms by using different isotopes of, in this case hydrogen, confirming that the different options happen in reality. In CCB, we can trace the atoms as well as show which results are identical from a chemical point of view (see Section 6.5 of [16]).

The Bonding Calculus is suitable for modelling in a natural way the autoprotolysis of water by using only bond and unbond actions. Simulations by using a software platform can describe the dynamics of the bonding systems, and so it is possible to test the validity of some underlying assumptions. Also, we can verify various properties of the bonding compounds described by using the calculus.

Reversing Petri Nets are Petri net structures that assume tokens to be distinct and persistent. During the execution of transitions individual tokens can be bonded/unbonded with each other, and the creation/destruction of these bonds is considered to be the effect of a transition, whereas their destruction/creation is the effect of the transition's reversal. Reversing Petri Nets are a natural choice to model and analyse biochemical reaction systems, such as the autoprotolysis of water, which by nature has multi-party interactions, is inherently concurrent, and features reversible behaviour. In particular, the feature of token multiplicity and the use of variables allows to non-deterministically select different combinations of atoms of a particular element when creating molecules. Also the ability of transitions to break bonds allows to model concerted actions where, for example, a transition simultaneously destroys a water molecule and creates a hydronium whose reversal results in the opposite effect. Moreover, the collective token interpretation adopted in the framework, treating all tokens of the same type as equivalent, allows the reaction to reverse into two different water molecules than the original ones, i.e. using different instances of the atoms (as is possible in CCB). Note that the presented model abstracts away the positive/negative charge of the atoms and captures the existence of electrons by the enabledness of transitions. A model at a lower level of abstraction would be possible by introducing tokens to represent the electrons bonded to the associated atom tokens to illustrate the relevant charges.

The three formalisms presented can model our example fairly well but, as expected, there are some differences. In order to evaluate each formalism, we consider as first criterion if all chemically valid interactions between the compounds of the reaction can be represented well in our formalisms. CCB shows the linked forming and breaking of bonds. RPNs can also express these concerted actions, since a transition enables the simultaneous creation and destruction of bonds. In the Bonding Calculus, this link is not expressed. Each of the formalisms can perform the forward reaction using any of the hydrogens involved. CCB and RPNs can perform the reverse reaction by transferring arbitrary hydrogens, whereas the Bonding Calculus in the reverse reaction permits only the transfer of exactly those hydrogens that were used in the forward reaction. All models presented use subscripts and enable the tracking of atoms.

The other criterion for assessing the suitability of our formalisms for the modelling of chemical reactions is to ask if they enable in the produced model any transitions that actually do not occur in reality. Each formalism does not permit a H_3O^+ molecule to be formed directly. CCB allows one reaction which is not realistic: If there are many water molecules and therefore several hydroxide and water molecules at the same time, it is possible that the remaining hydrogen is transferred from the hydroxide to a water. In reality, this is not possible since the hydroxide is strongly negatively charged and no hydrogen bond can form. Due to the nondeterministic behaviour of processes written with the '+' operator, such as those for hydrogen and oxygen in Subsect. 3.2, the Bonding Calculus also presents the same problem. However, this is not the case for RPNs since, on the one hand, a transition's conditions make restrictions on the types of molecules that will participate in a transition firing or its reversal and, on the other hand, places impose a form of locality for molecules. For instance, in the autoprotolysis example, each place is the location of specific types of molecules, e.g., transition t_3 modelling the autoprotolysis reaction is only applied on water molecules and its reversal only on pairs of a hydronium and a hydroxide molecule, as required.

There are a number of software tools that can aid simulation and analysis for our formalisms. Regarding the Bonding Calculus, we can simulate various bonding descriptions by using an existing software platform called UPPAAL (as shown in [1]). For CCB, there is a simulation tool presented in [14]. It allows a much closer form of representation of chemical notation than that possible with a typical programming language. Reversing Petri nets have been shown to be closely related to Coloured Petri Nets, as a subset of the former model has been encoded into the latter [3]. Thus, an algorithmic translation can be implemented that transforms RPNs to CPNs in an automated manner using the transformation techniques discussed in [3]. This allows RPNs to exploit tools such as CPNTools that support traditional models of Petri nets.

5   Conclusion

We have presented the Calculus of Covalent Bonding, the Bonding Calculus, and Reversing Petri Nets as models of chemical reactions and reversible processes in general. We have shown that they can all model the out-of-causal-order reversibility present in such reactions. We have also noted that the two process calculi allow few reactions which do not happen in reality. This is due to the modelling that abstracts away from some chemical properties of atoms and molecules such as, for example, spacial arrangement and distance between molecules. In future work, we plan to develop these formalisms further and apply them to the modelling and reasoning about reversible biochemical reactions and processes.

References

1. Aman, B., Ciobanu, G.: Bonding calculus. Nat. Comput. **17**(4), 823–832 (2018). https://doi.org/10.1007/s11047-018-9709-7
2. Baldan, P., Cocco, N., Marin, A., Simeoni, M.: Petri nets for modelling metabolic pathways: a survey. Nat. Comput. **9**(4), 955–989 (2010)
3. Barylska, K., Gogolińska, A., Mikulski, Ł., Philippou, A., Piątkowski, M., Psara, K.: Reversing computations modelled by coloured Petri nets. In: Proceedings of ATAED 2018. CEUR Workshop Proceedings, vol. 2115, pp. 91–111 (2018)
4. Blätke, M.A., Heiner, M., Marwan, W.: Petri nets in systems biology. Technical report, Otto-von-Guericke University Magdeburg (2011)
5. Chaouiya, C.: Petri net modelling of biological networks. Brief. Bioinform. **8**(4), 210–219 (2007)
6. Ciocchetta, F., Hillston, J.: Bio-PEPA: a framework for the modelling and analysis of biological systems. Theoret. Comput. Sci. **410**(33–34), 3065–3084 (2009)
7. Danos, V., Feret, J., Fontana, W., Harmer, R., Krivine, J.: Rule-based modelling of cellular signalling. In: Caires, L., Vasconcelos, V.T. (eds.) CONCUR 2007. LNCS, vol. 4703, pp. 17–41. Springer, Heidelberg (2007). https://doi.org/10.1007/978-3-540-74407-8_3
8. Danos, V., Krivine, J.: Reversible communicating systems. In: Gardner, P., Yoshida, N. (eds.) CONCUR 2004. LNCS, vol. 3170, pp. 292–307. Springer, Heidelberg (2004). https://doi.org/10.1007/978-3-540-28644-8_19

9. Faeder, J.R., Blinov, M.L., Hlavacek, W.S.: Rule-based modeling of biochemical systems with BioNetGen. Methods Mol. Biol. **500**, 113–167 (2009)
10. Fages, F., Soliman, S., Chabrier-Rivier, N.: Modelling and querying interaction networks in the biochemical abstract machine BIOCHAM. J. Biol. Phys. Chem. **4**, 64–73 (2004)
11. Fokkink, W.: Introduction to Process Algebra. Springer, Heidelberg (2000). https://doi.org/10.1007/978-3-662-04293-9
12. Hofestädt, R.: A Petri net application of metabolic processes. J. Syst. Anal. Model. Simul. **16**, 113–122 (1994)
13. Hofestädt, R., Thelen, S.: Quantitative modeling of biochemical networks. Silico Biol. **1**(1), 39–53 (1998)
14. Kuhn, S.: Simulation of base excision repair in the calculus of covalent bonding. In: Kari, J., Ulidowski, I. (eds.) RC 2018. LNCS, vol. 11106, pp. 123–129. Springer, Cham (2018). https://doi.org/10.1007/978-3-319-99498-7_8
15. Kuhn, S., Ulidowski, I.: A calculus for local reversibility. In: Devitt, S., Lanese, I. (eds.) RC 2016. LNCS, vol. 9720, pp. 20–35. Springer, Cham (2016). https://doi.org/10.1007/978-3-319-40578-0_2
16. Kuhn, S., Ulidowski, I.: Local reversibility in a calculus of covalent bonding. Sci. Comput. Program. **151**(Supplement C), 18–47 (2018)
17. Lanese, I., Mezzina, C.A., Schmitt, A., Stefani, J.-B.: Controlling reversibility in higher-order Pi. In: Katoen, J.-P., König, B. (eds.) CONCUR 2011. LNCS, vol. 6901, pp. 297–311. Springer, Heidelberg (2011). https://doi.org/10.1007/978-3-642-23217-6_20
18. Lanese, I., Mezzina, C.A., Stefani, J.-B.: Controlled reversibility and compensations. In: Glück, R., Yokoyama, T. (eds.) RC 2012. LNCS, vol. 7581, pp. 233–240. Springer, Heidelberg (2013). https://doi.org/10.1007/978-3-642-36315-3_19
19. Lanese, I., Mezzina, C.A., Stefani, J.-B.: Reversing higher-order Pi. In: Gastin, P., Laroussinie, F. (eds.) CONCUR 2010. LNCS, vol. 6269, pp. 478–493. Springer, Heidelberg (2010). https://doi.org/10.1007/978-3-642-15375-4_33
20. Matsuno, H., Nagasaki, M., Miyano, S.: Hybrid Petri net based modeling for biological pathway simulation. Nat. Comput. **10**(3), 1099–1120 (2011)
21. Milner, R. (ed.): A Calculus of Communicating Systems. LNCS, vol. 92. Springer, Heidelberg (1980). https://doi.org/10.1007/3-540-10235-3
22. Peleg, M., Rubin, D.L., Altman, R.B.: Using Petri net tools to study properties and dynamics of biological systems. J. Am. Med. Inform. Assoc. **12**(2), 181–199 (2005)
23. Philippou, A., Psara, K.: Reversible computation in Petri nets. In: Kari, J., Ulidowski, I. (eds.) RC 2018. LNCS, vol. 11106, pp. 84–101. Springer, Cham (2018). https://doi.org/10.1007/978-3-319-99498-7_6
24. Philippou, A., Psara, K., Siljak, H.: Controlling reversibility in reversing Petri nets with application to wireless communications. In: Thomsen, M.K., Soeken, M. (eds.) RC 2019. LNCS, vol. 11497, pp. 238–245. Springer, Cham (2019). https://doi.org/10.1007/978-3-030-21500-2_15
25. Phillips, I., Ulidowski, I.: Reversing algebraic process calculi. J. Logic Algebraic Program. **73**(1–2), 70–96 (2007)
26. Phillips, I., Ulidowski, I.: Reversibility and asymmetric conflict in event structures. In: D'Argenio, P.R., Melgratti, H. (eds.) CONCUR 2013. LNCS, vol. 8052, pp. 303–318. Springer, Heidelberg (2013). https://doi.org/10.1007/978-3-642-40184-8_22
27. Phillips, I., Ulidowski, I., Yuen, S.: Modelling of bonding with processes and events. In: Dueck, G.W., Miller, D.M. (eds.) RC 2013. LNCS, vol. 7948, pp. 141–154. Springer, Heidelberg (2013). https://doi.org/10.1007/978-3-642-38986-3_12

28. Phillips, I., Ulidowski, I., Yuen, S.: A reversible process calculus and the modelling of the ERK signalling pathway. In: Glück, R., Yokoyama, T. (eds.) RC 2012. LNCS, vol. 7581, pp. 218–232. Springer, Heidelberg (2013). https://doi.org/10.1007/978-3-642-36315-3_18
29. Popova-Zeugmann, L., Heiner, M., Koch, I.: Time Petri nets for modelling and analysis of biochemical networks. Fundam. Informaticae **67**(1–3), 149–162 (2005)
30. Priami, C.: Stochastic π-calculus. Comput. J. **38**(7), 578–589 (1995)
31. Priami, C., Quaglia, P.: Beta binders for biological interactions. In: Danos, V., Schachter, V. (eds.) CMSB 2004. LNCS, vol. 3082, pp. 20–33. Springer, Heidelberg (2005). https://doi.org/10.1007/978-3-540-25974-9_3
32. Reddy, V.N., Mavrovouniotis, M.L., Liebman, M.N.: Petri net representations in metabolic pathways. In: Proceedings of the 1st International Conference on Intelligent Systems for Molecular Biology, pp. 328–336. AAAI (1993)
33. Regev, A., Panina, E.M., Silverman, W., Cardelli, L., Shapiro, E.: BioAmbients: an abstraction for biological compartments. Theoret. Comput. Sci. **325**(1), 141–167 (2004)
34. Regev, A., Shapiro, E.: The π-calculus as an abstraction for biomolecular systems. In: Ciobanu, G., Rozenberg, G. (eds.) Modelling in Molecular Biology, pp. 219–266. Springer, Heidelberg (2004). https://doi.org/10.1007/978-3-642-18734-6_11
35. Reisig, W.: Understanding Petri Nets - Modeling Techniques, Analysis Methods, Case Studies. Springer, Heidelberg (2013). https://doi.org/10.1007/978-3-642-33278-4
36. Ulidowski, I.: Equivalences on observable processes. In: Proceedings of the 7th Annual IEEE Symposium on Logic in Computer Science, pp. 148–159. IEEE (1992)
37. Ulidowski, I., Phillips, I., Yuen, S.: Reversing event structures. New Gener. Comput. **36**(3), 281–306 (2018)
38. Voss, K., Heiner, M., Koch, I.: Steady state analysis of metabolic pathways using Petri nets. Silico Biol. **3**(3), 367–387 (2003)

Reversible Control of Robots

Ulrik Pagh Schultz[✉][ID]

SDU UAS, MMMI, University of Southern Denmark, Odense, Denmark
ups@mmmi.sdu.dk

Abstract. Programming industrial robots is challenging due to the difficulty of precisely specifying general yet robust operations. As the complexity of these operations increases, so does the likelihood of errors. Certain classes of errors during industrial robot operations can however be addressed using reverse execution, allowing the robot to temporarily back out of an erroneous situation, after which the operation can be automatically retried. Moreover reverse execution permits automatically deriving programs that physically reverse the operations of an industrial robot. This can be useful in industrial assembly, where a disassembly program can be automatically derived from the assembly program.

In this case study we investigate robotic assembly from the point of view of reversibility, investigating to what extent program inversion of a robotic assembly sequence for a given product can be considered to derive a robotic disassembly sequence for this same product, and investigating to what extent changing the execution direction at runtime (i.e., backtracking and retrying) using program inversion can be used as an automatic error handling procedure. The programming model used to reversibly control industrial robots is based on an abstract semantics-based model, extended with various features required for reversible control of industrial robots in real-world scenarios, and implemented as a domain-specific programming language.

1 Introduction

Robots normally have one or more degrees of freedom controlled by a computational process; using reversible computing to control the robot potentially gives rise to new reverse behaviours. For example, major industrial robot manufacturers such as ABB and KUKA offer limited forms of ad-hoc reverse execution for interactive programming and debugging, but due to limitations in the underlying execution models, their programming models are incapable of reversing complex actions such as steps of an industrial assembly process [5,6]. We attribute the ad-hoc limitations to the lack of an underlying reversible model. The first investigation of fully reversible robot behaviours was for self-reconfigurable robots [10]. The useful application of reversibility to this type of robot is however only observed for self-reconfiguration operations, significantly limiting the notion of

The author acknowledges partial support of COST Action IC1405 on Reversible Computation - Extending Horizons of Computing.

I. Ulidowski et al. (Eds.): RC 2020, LNCS 12070, pp. 177–186, 2020.
https://doi.org/10.1007/978-3-030-47361-7_8

reversibility and real-world interaction that can be studied using this type of robot. To better understand the underlying relation between reversible computation and physical reversibility, we in this case study investigate reversible control of industrial robots.

Programming industrial robots is challenging due to the difficulty of precisely specifying general yet robust operations. As the complexity of these operations increases, so does the likelihood of errors. Certain classes of errors during industrial robot operations can however be addressed using reverse execution, allowing the robot to temporarily back out of an erroneous situation, after which the operation can be automatically retried. Specifically, this approach has been shown to be useful for automatic error recovery for small-sized batch production of assembly operations [11]. Moreover, reversibility can in this case be used to automatically derive a disassembly sequence from a given assembly sequence, or vice versa. These results were demonstrated using an initial design and implementation of a reversible domain-specific language (DSL) for specifying such assembly sequences [5,11]. The area however remains largely unexplored, both from a theoretical and practical point of view. There is for example a large design space for different programming language approaches, both in terms of the generality of the language and the means by which reversibility is achieved. At a more fundamental level, the notion of reversible control of a reversible physical system remains largely unexplored. From a practical point of view, only the specific case of assembly operations has been investigated, and only using a specific set of industrial use cases. There has been no attempt at integration into an existing robotics platform, although we observe that many existing platforms offer limited notions of reversibility for using during programming and debugging.

The result of this case study is significant progress in the area of reversibility for industrial robots [4]. Key developments include an improved understanding of the interaction between reversible computing and real-world systems that only are partially reversible, as well as a substantial experimental evaluation of the use of reversible languages to control industrial robots performing assembly and disassembly in the context of small-batch production. Overall this work experimentally demonstrates the use of reversible computing to improve system reliability.

2   Related Work

Reversibility has previously been investigated for self-reconfigurable robots. Self-reconfigurable, modular robots are distributed robotic devices that can autonomously change their physical shape [13]. Self-reconfiguration from one shape to another is typically achieved through a specific sequence of actuation operations distributed across the modules of the robot. Automatically reversing the sequence of operations can bring the robot back to its initial shape, as has been experimentally demonstrated using the DynaRole reversible language [10]. DynaRole however only allows simple sequences of operations to be reversed, which is suitable for reversing self-reconfiguration sequences, but lacks the generality needed to implement more complex behaviours. Initial ideas on generalising the DynaRole language to support a wider range of modular robot control scenarios retain the possibility of reversing distributed sequences [8,9], but have neither been formalised nor experimentally demonstrated.

Large-scale modular robotic systems can be considered as intensive parallel systems [7]. Reversibility for intensive parallel systems was studied by Agrigoroaiei and Ciobanu [1]. Here, the process of reversing is presented as a form of duality (a notion from category theory). A related approach presenting reversibility for the bio-inspired formalism of membrane systems is given by the same authors [2].

Partial reversibility has been studied for reversible programming languages [12] using logging of program state to handle irreversible operations. This approach would in our case correspond to recording the motions of the robot and replaying them in reverse, which is applicable to any operation but does not normally serve to reverse actions in the real world. Rather, our approach relies on the programmer explicitly writing reverse code that, through a different sequence of operations, brings the system back to a previous state. This approach can be compared to causal-consistent reversibility [3] in the sense that the observable events (i.e., the state of the system the robot is working on) is reversed in a consistent way; unlike causal-consistent reversibility we however require the programmer to manually implement the basic reverse operations using the notion of indirect reversibility.

3   Reversible Assembly Tasks

We investigate robotic assembly tasks from the point of view of reversibility, investigating to what extent program inversion of a robotic assembly sequence for a given product can be considered to derive a robotic disassembly sequence for this same product, and investigating to what extent changing the execution direction at runtime (i.e., backtracking and retrying) using program inversion can be used as an automatic error handling procedure [4].

3.1   Robotics, Assembly, and Reversibility

Robotic assembly and disassembly is done in terms of sequences of operations such as precise placement of objects, insertions with tight fits, screwing operations and so forth. All are challenged by uncertainties from sensors, robot kinematics and part tolerances; not all are reversible, some are not even repeatable. Our approach has been tested with a standard robotic platform based on a Universal Robots UR5, shown in Fig. 1 together with the two industrial assembly cases used to evaluate the approach [4].

Fig. 1. The experimental platform and two assembly test cases (from [4]).

3.2 Reversibility

Many physical phenomena and actions are in principle reversible, although this reversibility may depend on the abstraction level at which they are observed. For example, an industrial robot that pushes an object to a new position could easily move this object back to its original position, but cannot simply do this by reversing its movements as pulling requires gripping the object first. Moreover, some operations, such as cutting, should in general be considered nonreversible. A study of 13 real-world industrial cases showed roughly 76% of the operations to be reversible [4], but many of the operations require the robot to perform different physical actions to reverse a given action. Based on this observation, we can divide the reversible operations into two categories: *directly reversible* and *indirectly reversible* operations. Operations which can be reversed through program inversion are considered directly reversible. Indirectly reversible operations on the other hand can be reversed, but require a different sequence of instructions.

3.3 Repeatability

Unlike Janus-style reversible computing, where programs can be said to be time-invertible [14], with robotics physical changes made to the environment from the execution influences the repeatability of operations. Operations that can be done again and again can be referred to as *fully repeatable*. Other actions can only be done a limited number of times, e.g., due to wear and tear, and are said to be *partially-repeatable*. Last, *nonrepeatable* operations are those that cannot be retried.

3.4 Reversibility and Repeatability

Considering reversibility and repeatability together leads to a classification of robotic assembly operations [4]. Operations that are fully repeatable and directly reversible can be automatically managed using a program inversion approach, whereas indirectly reversible operations require explicit reverse code to be provided by a programmer, partially repeatable operations limit how many times a program can be reversed, and certain operations are fundamentally irreversible and thus mark points across which the program cannot be reversed.

4 Programming Model

The programming model developed in our case study is based on an abstract semantics-based model [11] extended with various features required for reversible control of industrial robots in real-world scenarios [4].

4.1 Basic Model

A robot assembly task is programmed as a sequential flow of operations. It is sequential since in practice assembly tasks tend to be a simple sequence of operations (except for error handling, but we aim to automatically handle errors using reverse execution). Reversibility is relevant due to the presence of random behaviour of the physical operations: reversing and re-executing an operation may produce a different results. Each operation represents high-level assembly case logic and is a sequence of instructions. *Instructions* are either reversible, providing a two-way reversible forward/backward mapping of hardware instructions, or non-reversible, providing a single-directional mapping. Instructions are implemented using traditional nonreversible programming. Taking inspiration from Janus [14], it is possible to both call and uncall operations, the latter causing the operation to be interpreted in reverse.

The programming model used to represent robot assembly tasks is built on the following principles. (1) Instructions always map the robot system from a known state to a known state, but may have different semantics for forward and reverse. (2) Indirect reversibility is achieved by modelling instruction sequences that are different for forwards and reverse execution using the principle of over-ridden reverse flow, where users can write different code for forwards and backwards execution. (3) Instructions can be marked as nonreversible. A directed graph is used to model the underlying reversible assembly sequence. In this graph each node corresponds to a primitive instruction which is executable on the physical platform. Furthermore, each node contains pointers to the next forward instruction and the next reverse instruction (if any). Overall the graph is evaluated through forward/backwards interpretation and each instruction is evaluated using instruction inversion in the sense that different semantics are applied for forward and backwards execution.

```
operation attach_nut_bolt {
  state begin_nut_bolt (...tool pos...) bolt:(...pos...) nut:(...pos...)
  moveto (...pos above table...)
  pickup (nut, fixed_gripper, (...pos of nut...))
  moveto (...)
  ...
}
operation apply_and_turn_nut { ...commands... }
reverse { ...commands that undo apply_and_turn_nut... }
```

Fig. 2. Sample RASQ program, vector constants are omitted for clarity (adapted from [11]).

4.2   Implementation

The basic model provides the foundation for programming realistic assembly cases [4]. The principle of indirect reversibility is in practice instantiated in many different ways, such as movement or error detection instructions that only activate in one execution direction. Error handling is implemented in the interpreter: when an error is detected during forwards execution the direction is immediately reversed for a number of steps, after which forwards execution is again resumed. The same model is applied for execution in reverse, and even applies recursively, i.e., if an error is detected during reverse execution triggered due to an error. Each instruction carries specific information describing how to handle switching of execution direction, specifically whether the instruction should be repeated in reverse or not when switching direction due to the instruction failing. A simple error handling strategy that changes execution direction for a random number of steps and that ensures termination by bounding the total number of steps was observed to work well in practice.

4.3   Language

The idea of reversible control of industrial robots was initially presented using a high-level programming language [11]. An example is shown in Fig. 2. The program declares two operations, attach_nut_bolt and apply_and_turn_nut. The operation attach_nut_bolt only specifies a single (forwards) body for both forwards and reverse execution, so reverse execution will inversely evaluate the forwards body in reverse order. The first statement is a state assertion, named begin_nut_bolt, specifying the spatial positioning of the tool and the respective positions of the bolt and nut objects. The next statement of the program is a move, which moves the robot to the given position (again, the position is given as a constant, not shown). After the move follows a pick up instruction that causes the pickup operation associated with the name fixed_gripper and the object nut to be evaluated. Last follows the declaration of the second operation apply_and_turn_nut, which is not shown in detail, but has both a forwards and a reverse body, so forwards execution evaluates the forwards body in forwards

```
operation("screwdriver_activate").
  io(screwdriver, Switch::on).
  wait(0.3).
  wait(screwingFinished).
  reverseWith("screwing_finished_backwards");
  io(screwdriver, Switch::off).
  io(screwdriverBackwards, Switch::off);
```

Fig. 3. Sample SCP-RASQ program (adapted from [4]).

order, and reverse execution evaluates the reverse body in forwards order (i.e., in the order written in the program).

In practice it turned out to be more useful to rely on an internal DSL implemented in C++, using a model-driven approach that serialises the program to an XML structure that can subsequently be instantiated as the graph structure used by the reversible interpreter. This internal DSL, named SCP-RASQ for "Simple C++ RASQ", is exemplified in Fig. 3. This program declares an operation that performs IO operations to communicate with the screwdriver, and shows how indirect reversibility can be programmed in-place using the reverseWith declaration.

5   Results

This section will give an overview of the experimental results demonstrated in earlier work on several industrial use cases [4].

5.1   Methodology

Error recovery using reverse execution was tested using two industrial assembly tasks use-cases; the physical robot platform and the assembled products are shown in Fig. 1. An SCP-RASQ program was created for each of the use cases. Both cases include a final step where the finished product is discarded into a box. This step was not performed when running the programs backwards, as it is a nonreversible task since our current setup cannot bin-pick the part out again.

5.2   Experiment 1: Reversing the Programs

Both use-cases were used to test the principle of reversible assembly. Forward execution performs assembly while reverse execution performs disassembly. For each case the program is executed forward to assemble an object. Afterwards the finished objects is then manually placed back into the system, and the program is then executed backwards to disassemble the object. This was done a total of three times for each case, with no errors.

In our test programs directly reversible operations made up 45% of all operations. Moreover, directly reversible operations such as the "pick screwdriver" were used in both their forward and backwards form in the same program using the call and uncall functionality. Both use-cases could be made almost entirely reversible using either directly or indirectly reversible operations through the execution model and the programming language. We believe that if the reversibility concept was to be integrated more deeply into the design of assembly processes and external equipment such as feeders, an even greater degree of directly reversible instructions could be achieved.

5.3   Experiment 2: Assembling 100 Objects

By assembling a large number of objects the use of reverse execution as an effective error correction tool was demonstrated. The workcell was set to assemble 100 objects of each type consecutively and without pause. During these 200 assemblies a total of 22 errors occurred, of which 18, corresponding to 82%, were automatically resolved and corrected using reverse execution. Errors that were automatically corrected include failed peg-in-hole operations (fixed by backtracking and trying again), dropping a tube (fixed by reversing until a new tube was picked from the feeder), failed to grasp a screw, and screwing failing due to misalignment. Errors that could not be automatically corrected include airtubing from the gripper getting stuck on the platform, causing the gripper to misalign, and a screw being inserted at a skewed angle causing a bracket to misalign, which could not be corrected as the system had no means of detecting the bracket misalignment.

This experiment shows that reverse execution is capable of solving a wide variety of errors and that the exact method for solving each kind of error need not always be the same, as backtracking was done randomly at different lengths and sometimes resulted in different solutions to the same problem. Moreover we see that the backtracking system is promising in handling errors related to small uncertainties in the assembly tasks, but that errors resulting in larger and mechanical failures still need to be addressed either in the design phase or by some other error handling mechanism. Last, the experiments also show that while reverse execution can be used for solving a wide variety of errors, it also places strong demands on the error detection system.

6   Conclusion

From a society point of view, industrial robots are key to maintaining production in Europe, and reversible computation has the potential to increase robustness for specific kinds of operations such as small-batch assembly, and moreover facilitate the programming of such operations. In this case study we have introduced a programming model which enables robot assembly programs to be executed in reverse. We have experimentally demonstrated that temporarily switching the direction of program execution can be an efficient error recovery mechanism. Moreover, we have shown that additional benefits arise from supporting reversibility in our robotic assembly language, namely increased code reuse and automatically derived disassembly sequences.

This case study has resulted in an improved understanding of the interaction between reversible computing and real-world systems that only are partially reversible, as well as a substantial experimental evaluation of the use of reversible programming languages to control industrial robots performing assembly and disassembly in the context of small-batch production. Overall this case study has experimentally demonstrated the use of reversible computing to improve system reliability.

Acknowledgements. Thanks to Gabriel Ciobanu for help in describing the related work on reversibility of massively parallel systems.

References

1. Agrigoroaiei, O., Ciobanu, G.: Dual P systems. In: Corne, D.W., Frisco, P., Păun, G., Rozenberg, G., Salomaa, A. (eds.) WMC 2008. LNCS, vol. 5391, pp. 95–107. Springer, Heidelberg (2009). https://doi.org/10.1007/978-3-540-95885-7_7

2. Agrigoroaiei, O., Ciobanu, G.: Reversing computation in membrane systems. J. Logic Algebraic Program. **79**(3), 278–288 (2010)

3. Lanese, I., Mezzina, C.A., Tiezzi, F.: Causal-consistent reversibility. Bull. EATCS **114** (2014)

4. Laursen, J., Ellekilde, L., Schultz, U.: Modelling reversible execution of robotic assembly. Robotica **36**(5), 625–654 (2018)

5. Laursen, J.S., Schultz, U.P., Ellekilde, L.P.: Automatic error recovery in robot assembly operations using reverse execution. In: Evers, C., Sheaffer, J., Tourbabin, V., Naylor, P.A., Romanoni, A., Matteucci, M. (eds.) International Conference on Intelligent Robots and Systems (IROS 2015). IEEE/RSJ (2015)

6. Mühe, H., Angerer, A., Hoffmann, A., Reif, W.: On reverse-engineering the KUKA robot language. In: Schultz, U.P., Stinckwich, S., Ziane, M. (eds.) Proceedings of the First International Workshop on Domain-Specific Languages for Robotic Systems (DSLRob 2010) (2010). arXiv:1009.5004 [cs.RO]

7. Păun, G.: Membrane Computing. An Introduction. Springer, Heidelberg (2002). https://doi.org/10.1007/978-3-642-56196-2

8. Schultz, U.P.: Using scheme to control simulated modular robots. In: Danvy, O. (ed.) Proceedings of the 2012 Annual Workshop on Scheme and Functional Programming, pp. 90–95. ACM (2012)

9. Schultz, U.P.: Towards a general-purpose, reversible language for controlling self-reconfigurable robots. In: Glück, R., Yokoyama, T. (eds.) RC 2012. LNCS, vol. 7581, pp. 97–111. Springer, Heidelberg (2013). https://doi.org/10.1007/978-3-642-36315-3_8

10. Schultz, U., Bordignon, M., Støy, K.: Robust and reversible execution of self-reconfiguration sequences. Robotica **29**, 35–57 (2011)

11. Schultz, U.P., Laursen, J.S., Ellekilde, L.-P., Axelsen, H.B.: Towards a domain-specific language for reversible assembly sequences. In: Krivine, J., Stefani, J.-B. (eds.) RC 2015. LNCS, vol. 9138, pp. 111–126. Springer, Cham (2015). https://doi.org/10.1007/978-3-319-20860-2_7

12. Tyagi, N., Lynch, J., Demaine, E.D.: Toward an energy efficient language and compiler for (partially) reversible algorithms. In: Devitt, S., Lanese, I. (eds.) RC 2016. LNCS, vol. 9720, pp. 121–136. Springer, Cham (2016). https://doi.org/10.1007/978-3-319-40578-0_8
13. Yim, M., et al.: Modular self-reconfigurable robot systems [grand challenges of robotics]. IEEE Robot. Autom. Mag. **14**(1), 43–52 (2007)
14. Yokoyama, T., Axelsen, H.B., Glück, R.: Principles of a reversible programming language. In: Proceedings of the 5th Conference on Computing Frontiers (CF 2008), pp. 43–54. ACM (2008)

Reversible Languages and Incremental State Saving in Optimistic Parallel Discrete Event Simulation

Markus Schordan[1]([⊠]), Tomas Oppelstrup[1], Michael Kirkedal Thomsen[2], and Robert Glück[2]

[1] Lawrence Livermore National Laboratory, Livermore, USA
{schordan1,oppelstrup2}@llnl.gov
[2] University of Copenhagen, Copenhagen, Denmark
m.kirkedal@di.ku.dk, glueck@acm.org

Abstract. Optimistic parallel discrete event simulation (PDES) requires to do a distributed rollback if conflicts are detected during a simulation due to the massively parallel optimistic execution approach. When a rollback of a simulation is performed each node that is determined to be in a wrong state must be restored to one of its previous states. This can be achieved through reverse computation or by restoring a previous checkpoint. In this paper we investigate and compare both approaches, reverse computation and a variant of checkpointing, incremental state saving (also called incremental checkpointing), to restore a previous program state as part of an optimistic parallel discrete event simulation. We present a benchmark model that is specifically designed for evaluating the performance of approaches to reversibility in PDES. Our benchmarking model has mathematical properties that allow to tune the amount of arithmetic operations relative to the amount of memory operations. These tuning opportunities are the basis for our systematic performance evaluation.

1 Introduction

Discrete event simulation (DES) is a simulation paradigm suitable for systems whose states are modeled as changing *discontinuously* and *irregularly* at discrete moments of simulation time. State changes occur at simulation times that are calculated dynamically rather than determined statically as typical in time-stepped simulations. Most irregular systems whose behavior is not describable by continuous equations and do not happen to be suitable for simple time-stepped models are candidates for DES. Efficient *parallel* discrete event simulation (PDES) is much more complicated than the sequential version. There are two broad approaches to resolving the PDES synchronization issue, called *conservative* and *optimistic* [1]. Recently Omelchenko and Karimabadi have developed an asynchronous flux-conserving DES technique for physical simulations [2]. Their preemptive event processing approach to parallel synchronization complements

© The Author(s) 2020
I. Ulidowski et al. (Eds.): RC 2020, LNCS 12070, pp. 187–207, 2020.
https://doi.org/10.1007/978-3-030-47361-7_9

standard optimistic and conservative strategies for PDES. In this paper we will discuss optimistic PDES, which requires reversibility, in more detail.

In particular, we will focus on PDES using the Time Warp optimistic synchronization method [3]. The optimistic classification of Time Warp implies that it employs speculative execution to enable parallelism. In order to allow roll-backs needed to resolve incorrect speculation, the original formulation of Time Warp utilized checkpointing of the entire system state. This can be very wasteful, so in recent years reverse computation has become a key concept in optimistic parallel discrete event simulation [4,5], as it allows one to reduce the overhead in the forward execution in comparison to checkpointing and, thus, improve the performance. Fundamentally, there are two ways to achieve reversibility: (1) incremental state saving and (2) reverse execution. *Incremental state saving* (also called incremental checkpointing in [5]) is a well-established approach, which has the advantage that only a few language constructs need to be augmented to establish reversibility of an arbitrary piece of code. However, it (often) results in a high runtime overhead as any checkpointing is a memory-heavy method. *Reverse execution* is based on the idea that for many programs there exists an inverse program that can uncompute all results of the (forward) computed program. The inverse program can be achieved either through implementation of reverse code from a given forward code, or by implementing the program in a reversible programming language that offers the capability to automatically generate the inverse program: the imperative reversible language Janus [6] has such functionality.[1]

In this paper we systematically evaluate the generation of forward and reverse C++ code from Janus code (Sect. 4) as well as automatically generated code based on incremental state saving (Sect. 5). We also discuss the differences in methodology, whether a model code is written in a "destructive" language such as C/C++ or in the reversible language Janus, and its applications when implementing (and debugging) a model for PDES.

For this purpose and in order to validate the simulator and also check correctness of generated code, we have developed a new discrete event benchmark model that can be scaled in various dimensions. For execution of our model codes we use the ROSS general purpose discrete event simulator. Our new discrete event benchmark model is similar to the classic PHOLD benchmark model, but includes some extra state variables and computations that aid in detecting simulation errors. In our new model each event involves non-commutative matrix algebra, and the matrix that results from the simulation of the model serves as a checksum or hash of the simulation, and is sensitive to the order of events. The size of this matrix can be controlled by the user, as can the number of bits in its elements. This new benchmark is particularly useful for debugging simulations that are computed with the Time Warp Algorithm as its mathematical properties allow for checking of various assertions.

In our new model we can also tune the amount of arithmetic operations relative to the amount of memory modifying operations. This enables a systematic

---

[1] Online Janus interpreter at https://topps.diku.dk/pirc/?id=janus.

comparison of hand-written reverse code with multiple approaches of automatically generated reverse code and code instrumented for incremental state saving.

In our performance evaluation we use several different versions of the model code: (1) the original forward code with hand written reverse code, (2) Backstroke instrumented code to perform incremental state saving [7], and (3) Janus generated code for forward/reverse functions.

The forward/reverse code generated from Janus is particularly interesting because it allows to get forward code with no memory overhead and in some cases no runtime overhead, whereas for instrumented code one can only try to reduce the runtime and memory overhead in the forward code.

To the best of our knowledge this is the very first runtime comparison of the two approaches to reversible computation: generating reverse code and incremental state saving. In the optimistic PDES setting incremental state saving is suitable because optimistic PDES follows the Forward-Reverse-Commit (FRC) paradigm. In that paradigm, after an event has been executed in the forward direction, it can either be reversed (e.g. in the case it was incorrect to run it forward in the first place), or committed (when it has been proved that it was a correct event). When an event is committed its associated data is no longer needed, which allows to dispose recorded traces with every commit. In this paper we also investigate whether the combination of both the reversible language and incremental checkpointing approaches can be beneficial.

After giving a brief overview of PDES in Sect. 2, we describe our benchmark model and its properties in Sect. 3. In Sect. 4 we describe the reversible language Janus and how we generated forward/reverse function from Janus code. In Sect. 5 we briefly describe what source code transformations are applied to code to support incremental state saving with the Forward-Reverse-Commit paradigm. In Sect. 6 we describe the discrete event simulator that we use for optimistic parallel discrete event simulation and some adaptations that we implemented to better support the Forward-Reverse-Commit paradigm. The performance evaluation results are presented in Sect. 7. In Sect. 8 we discuss previous work that is related to our evaluated approaches and in Sect. 9 we discuss conclusions from the observed performance results.

2   Optimistic Parallel Discrete Event Simulation (PDES)

In this section we give a brief overview of PDES. A more detailed overview can be found in our previous work [7]. The general approach is to divide the simulation and its state into semi-independent units called LPs (logical processes) that can execute concurrently and communicate asynchronously, each maintaining its own state. A simulated event generally triggers a state change in one LP and affects only that LP's state. Any event may schedule other events to happen in the future of the current LP's simulation time. Events scheduled for other LPs must be transmitted to them as event messages with a timestamp indicating the simulation time when the event happens. Arriving event messages get enqueued in the event queues of the receiving LPs in increasing time stamp order. The LP has to allocate enough memory to store these queues.

Every LP must execute all of its events in strictly non-decreasing timestamp order irrespective of the order in which events may arrive or what timestamps they may carry. This poses a synchronization problem.

In contrast to optimistic PDES, conservative synchronization in conservative PDES uses conventional process blocking primitives along with extra knowledge about the simulation model (called *lookahead* information) to prevent the execution from ever getting into a situation in which an event message arrives at an LP with a timestamp in its past. Conservative synchronization is limited to models with static communication graphs.

Optimistic synchronization, by contrast, employs speculative execution to allow dynamic communication graphs and exposure of more parallelism. As a result, there is the danger of a *causality violation* when an LP that is behind in simulation time, e.g. at t_1, sends an event message with a (future) timestamp $t_2 > t_1$ that arrives at a receiver that has already simulated to time $t_3 > t_2$ due to its optimistic execution. In that case the receiver has already simulated past the simulation time when it *should* have executed the event at t_2, but it would be incorrect to execute events out of order because this may produce different results. Whenever that occurs, the simulator needs to roll back the LP from t_3 to the state it was in at time t_2, cancel all event messages the LP had sent after t_2, execute the arriving event, and then re-execute forward from time t_2 to t_3 and beyond. All event executions are therefore *speculative* or *provisional*, and are subject to rollback if the simulator detects a local causality conflict.

Each LP computes its local virtual time (LVT) based on the time stamps of event messages it receives. Because of rollbacks the LVT can also be reset to an earlier point in time. The global virtual time (GVT) is defined to be the minimum of all of the LVTs. Several algorithms exist to compute an estimate of the GVT during the simulation. Any events with time stamps older than GVT can be *committed* because it is guaranteed that they never need to be reversed. For more detail see [3,5]. That events are committed once they are older than GVT, allows to delete all information that may have been stored to enable reversibility. This commit operation is the same that we also use for incremental state saving, described in Sect. 5, to dispose recorded execution traces of memory modifying operations.

3   PDES Model Benchmark

In order to validate the simulator and also check the correctness of automatically generated code suitable for reversible computation, we have developed a new discrete event benchmark model. It is similar to the classic PHOLD benchmark model, but includes some extra state variables and computations which aid in detecting simulation errors. The state of each LP contains two square matrices: an accumulation matrix A, and a transformation matrix T, each of size $n \times n$, where n is an integer constant chosen by the user. Each event message contains the transformation matrix of the sender, and upon execution of an event the receiving LP multiplies its accumulation matrix to the right with the received transformation matrix. When an event is executed the receiving LP schedules a new event for a randomly selected LP at an exponentially distributed time delay.

At the end of the simulation, the matrices of all LP's are multiplied together, in LP ID (rank) order. The resulting matrix is the output of the simulation. Since matrix multiplication is in general non-commutative, the output depends on the individual events being executed in the correct order. The output serves as a check sum or hash of the simulation, and its size can be controlled by choosing the matrix size and the number of bits in the matrix elements.

The kernel of the event execution is a matrix multiplication, which (in the conventional implementation that we use) takes $O(n^3)$ arithmetic operations for $n \times n$ matrices. Reverse computation involves calculating a matrix inverse (or solving a matrix equation $A' = A \times T$ for A), which also requires $O(n^3)$ arithmetic operations. Each event or event message contains an $n \times n$ matrix and requires n^2 words of storage, and the same amount of data to be transmitted if communicated over a network. For bench-marking studies we can tune the ratio of arithmetic operations to memory/communication needs. This ratio is $O(n)$ for $n \times n$ matrices. We want to emphasize that this model is perfectly reversible, in the sense that no extra state besides the event itself is needed to undo the forward event: We simply invert the matrix in the event message and multiply the accumulation matrix to the right with this inverse.

We let the matrix elements be of a standard unsigned integral data type (e.g. 8, 16, 32, or 64 bits). For each of these types, the standard computer multiplication, addition, and subtraction perform arithmetic in an associated finite integer ring; Z_{2^k} where k is the number of bits in the data type, e.g. $k \in \{8, 16, 32, 64\}$. In these finite rings, all odd numbers have an inverse, and so half of the numbers in each ring can be used as denominators in division.

In this chapter we are interested in comparing different approaches to generate reversal of events to support roll-back. One of these approaches is reverse computation. In order for reverse computation to be applicable, events execution need to be reversible. To guarantee that, we select the transformation matrices to be non-singular over the integer ring of their elements. To simplify the expression of reversible multiplication, we additionally pick the transformation matrices so that Gaussian elimination can be completed successfully without pivoting.

3.1   Ring Inverses and Non-singular Matrices

The C++ language provides us with addition, subtraction, and multiplication in the relevant integer rings. We also need a division, which can be implemented as multiplication with the inverse. In order to find a ring inverse, we can use Euclid's extended algorithm. To be specific, we use the following implementation:

The function in Listing 1.1 returns the inverse of b if b is invertible in Z_{2^k}, otherwise it returns zero. We have the relation $b \equiv 1 \mod 2 \Rightarrow b * \mathrm{intinv}(b) = b$.

```
myuint intinv(myuint b) {
  // Find inverse in integer ring of Z_{2^k}, where k is
  // the number of bits in the myuint data type. It is
  // expected that myuint is an unsigned integer type.
  myuint t0 = 0,t = 1,q,r;
  myuint a = 0; // Want initial a to be 2^k, which can not be
                // represented, so we use the lower order bits,
                // i.e. a = 0.

  if(b <= 1) return b;

  q = (~a) / b; // Surrogate for 2^k div b, where 'div'
                // is standard integer division (/). Unless
                // b is a power of 2, 2^k div b = = (2^k-1) div b.

  if(b*q+b = = 0) return 0; // Catches when b is power of 2.

  r = a - q*b;
  while(r > 0) {
    const myuint temp = t0 -q*t;
    t0 = t;
    t = temp;
    a = b;
    b = r;
    q = a/b;
    r = a - q*b;
  }
  if(b = = 1) return t;
  else return 0;
}
```

Listing 1.1. Computation of inverse in Z_{2^k}.

One might initially worry that it can be hard to find non-singular matrices over Z_{2^k}. It turns out that a significant fraction of such matrices where the elements are picked from a uniformly random distribution are non-singular. We can determine this as follows. First, a matrix is non-singular if and only if Gaussian elimination with row pivoting can be completed successfully. We note that since we work with a finite set of numbers (ring), there is no need to worry about stability – all calculations are exact and there are no round-off errors. Let M be an $n \times n$ matrix with elements independently selected uniformly from Z_{2^k}, where $k > 0$ is an integer. To perform Gaussian elimination on a M we first need to find a pivot element p in the first row. Any invertible element will do. The probability that we find one is $1 - \left(\frac{1}{2}\right)^n$. Assume p is in column j. Now swap column j and column 1. For all rows r and for all columns c in M, set $M'_{rc} = M_{rc} - M_{r1}p^{-1}M_{1c}$. Gaussian elimination proceeds by recursively performing elimination of the submatrix S of M' resulting from removing its first row and first column. For $r > 1$ and $c > 1$, the parity (oddness) of M'_{rc} is swapped if $M_{r1}M_{1c}$ is odd, and unchanged otherwise. The parity of M_{rc} is uniformly random, and the parity of $M_{r1}M_{1c}$ is independent of M_{rc}. Therefore the parity of M'_{rc} is also uniformly random, since an independent flip does not change the distribution. By induction, the probability of finding a pivot element in S is $1 - \left(\frac{1}{2}\right)^{n-1}$, and carrying out the recursion to the end, yields the probability of M being non-singular to be

$$\prod_{i=1}^{n} \left(1 - \left(\frac{1}{2}\right)^{n}\right) \approx 0.288788\ldots.$$

This means that a little bit over one quarter of all uniformly random matrices over Z_{2^k} are non-singular. Therefore we can find suitable ones relatively efficiently by trial and error. Further, in order to create matrices for which we can do Gaussian elimination without pivoting, we pick a non-singular matrix T, and then permute the columns in the schedule dictated by the pivot columns given by computing Gaussian elimination with row pivoting on (a copy of) T.

4 Forward/Backward Code from Reversible Programs

The defining property of reversible programming languages is their forward and backward determinism, that is, in each computation state not only the successor state is uniquely defined, but also the predecessor state [8]. The computation is information preserving. In contrast, mainstream (irreversible) programming languages, such as C, are forward, but not backward deterministic.

In a reversible imperative programming language, such as Janus, every assignment statement is non-destructive, that is a *reversible update*, such as x -= e, where variable x may not occur in expression e on the right side (e.g., x -= x is not backward deterministic). In case of an assignment to an array element, for example a[i,j] -= a[k,l], a runtime check ensures that i ≠ k or j ≠ l.

All control-flow statements, such as conditionals and loops, are equipped with assertions, in one way or another, to ensure their backward determinism. The variant of Janus used for the programs in this paper has a two-way deterministic loop **iterate** i = e1 **to** e2; s; **end**, where neither the index variable i nor the variables occurring in expressions e1 and e2, defining the start- and end-values of i, may be modified in the body statement s, which is executed once per iteration. Hence, the number of iterations is known before and after the loop.

An advantage of reversible programming languages is that their programs do not require instrumentation to restore a previous computation state from the current state, which is usually necessary in irreversible languages. Backward determinism opens new opportunities for program development because a procedure p cannot only be called by a usual **call** p, but its inverse semantics can be invoked by an **uncall** p. Forward and backward execution of a procedure are equally efficient, thus is makes no difference which direction is implemented in a program, which therefore is usually the one that is easier to write. We will make use of this possibility to reuse code by uncalling a procedure.

```
procedure crout(int LDU[][], int n)
  iterate int j = 0 to n-1
    iterate int i = j to n-1
      iterate int k = 0 to j-1
        LDU[i][j] -= LDU[i][k] * LDU[k][j]
      end
    end
    iterate int i = j+1 to n-1
      iterate int k = 0 to j-1
        LDU[j][i] -= LDU[j][k] * LDU[k][i]
      end
      uncall mult(LDU[j][i], LDU[j][j])
    end
  end
```

Listing 1.2. Janus implementation of the Crout matrix decomposition.

Translation from Janus to C++. Reversible programs can be translated to a mainstream (irreversible) programming language, which in this paper is C++. Usually, this requires the implementation of additional runtime checks in the target program to preserve the semantics of the source program. Assuming that the source program is correct and only applied to values for which it is well defined, the runtime checks in the target program can be turned off. The translation of Janus into C++ which we use for the benchmarks is straightforward, e.g., **iterate** is translated into a **for**-loop, and no further optimizations are performed by the Janus-to-C++ translator.

Only the translation of an **uncall** p requires an unconventional step in the translator, namely first the *program inversion* of procedure p into its inverse procedure p-inv, both p and p-inv written in Janus, followed by the translation of p-inv into the target language and the replacement of every **uncall** p by the functionally equivalent **call** p-inv. The target program then contains the C++ implementation of p and its inverse p-inv. Program inversion is straightforward in a reversible language (cf. [6]), e.g., a reversible assignment x -= e is inverted to x += e and a statement sequence is inverted to the reversed sequence of its inverted statements.

As a non-trivial example, Listing 1.2 shows the Janus implementation of the Crout algorithm for LDU matrix decomposition. The translation from Janus into C++ for the forward code is straightforward, and a **uncall** mult in Janus becomes a call to mult-inv in C++. To illustrate the generated inverted code, its C++ translation can be found in Listing 1.3. The iteration is translated into nested for-loops and the reversible assignment in Janus requires only a minor adaptation to the C++ syntax. In the C++ listing the mult(a,b) is effectively a standard integer product $a := a \times b$ with appropriate assertions that it can be inverted, i.e. the inverse of b exists. mult-inv uses intinv from Listing 1.1 to compute the ring inverse.

```
template<typename myuint>
void crout_inv(myuint *LDU, int &n) {
   for (int j = n - 1 ; j != 0 + 0 - 1 ; j += 0 - 1) {
      for (int i = n - 1 ; i != j + 1 + 0 - 1 ; i += 0 - 1) {
      mult(LDU[j*n+i], LDU[j*n+j]);
      for (int k = j - 1 ; k != 0 + 0 - 1 ; k += 0 - 1) {
            LDU[j*n+i] += LDU[j*n+k] * LDU[k*n+i];
         }
      }
      for (int i = n - 1 ; i != j + 0 - 1 ; i += 0 - 1) {
         for (int k = j - 1 ; k != 0 + 0 - 1 ; k += 0 - 1) {
            LDU[i*n+j] += LDU[i*n+k] * LDU[k*n+j];
         }
      }
   }
}
```

Listing 1.3. Reverse code of C++ translation of Listing 1.2.

```
procedure matrix_mult(int A[][], int B[][], int n)
   call crout(B, n)    // In-place LDU decomposition of B
   call multLD(A, B, n) // A := A*LD in place
   call multU(A, B, n)  // A := A*U in place
   uncall crout(B, n)  // Revert LDU decomposition to recover B
```

Listing 1.4. Janus implementation of matrix multiplication.

Matrix Multiplication in Janus. A conventional matrix-matrix multiplication needs temporary storage, and the individual steps are not reversible. Since a reversible language requires each operation to be reversible we need a different approach. One approach is to use LU or LDU decomposition, which can be performed in place, and is step-wise reversible. Multiplication with the resulting triangular matrices can also be done in-place and step-wise reversible. In the approach here, to compute $A := A \times B$, we perform the Crout algorithm for LDU decomposition, $B = L \times D \times U$ in place, then the sequence $A := A \times L$, $A := A \times D$, $A := A \times U$. Finally we reverse the LDU decomposition in place, to recover the original input B. For a Janus implementation of the in-place matrix multiplication, see Listing 1.4. The code for multiplication with triangular matrices is shown in Listing 1.5. This approach needs no temporary storage and is step-wise reversible. The price for this reversibility and in-place operation is more arithmetic operations than a standard matrix product by a factor of about 5/3 (for sufficiently large n, say $n > 10$). In the full implementation, we used a local temporary variable to reduce the number of calls to the ring-inverse function for speed optimization, since it is much more costly than a multiplication or addition. This does not change any of the reversibility features.

```
procedure multLD(int A[][], int LDU[][], int n)
  iterate int i = 0 to n-1
    iterate int j = 0 to n-1
      call mult(A[j][i], LDU[i][i])
      iterate int k = i+1 to n-1
        A[j][i] += LDU[k][i] * A[j][k]
      end
    end
  end

procedure multU(int A[][], int LDU[][], int n)
  iterate int i = n-1 by -1 to 0
    iterate int j = 0 to n-1
      iterate int k = 0 to i-1
        A[j][i] += LDU[k][i] * A[j][k]
      end
    end
  end
```

Listing 1.5. Janus implementation of in-place multiplication with triangular matrices. multLD(A,LDU) computes $A := A*(LD)$ and multU(A,LDU) computes $A := A \times U$.

5   Automatic Generation of Reversible Code for the Forward-Reverse-Commit Paradigm

In the forward-reverse-commit (FRC) paradigm [5] the original code is transformed such that during its forward execution it stores all information required to reverse all effects of the forward execution and restore the previous state of the program, or commit (possibly deferred) operations at a later point in time. Hence, we add the history of the computation to each saved state, which is usually called a Landauer's embedding. In both reverse and commit functions the additional information stored in the forward code is eventually disposed. Before that the reverse function uses the stored data to undo all memory modifying operations, in the commit function performs the deferred memory deallocation.

We generate transformed forward code to implement incremental state saving. The idea is to only store information about what changes in the program state because of a state transition, not the entire state. This approach is also briefly described in [5] for the programming language C (called "incremental check pointing" by the author). After performing a forward execution of the transformed program followed by a corresponding reverse operation, the program is restored to its original state, i.e. the exact same state as the original program was before performing any operation. Therefore, the execution of a forward function and a reverse operation is equivalent to executing no code (i.e. a no-op).

After performing a forward execution of the transformed program followed by a commit operation, the program is in the exact same state as executing the original program. Therefore, the execution of a forward function and its corresponding commit operation performs the same changes to the program state as the execution of the original function.

This transformation can also be considered to turn the program into a transactional program, where each execution step can be reversed (undone) or committed after which it cannot be reversed since all information necessary to reverse it is disposed by the commit operation. This is an important aspect when performing long running discrete event simulations: the forward-commit pairs ensures that no additional memory is consumed after a commit has been performed. As we shall see, the optimistic parallel discrete event simulation ensures that such a point in time at which all events can be committed up to a certain point in the past, can always be computed during the simulation.

In [9] we have shown how this approach can be extended to address C++ without templates. In [10] we have applied this approach to all of C++98, including templates and in [7] we have shown that this approach is general enough to be applied to C++11 standard containers and algorithms.

Our approach to generating reversible forward code introduces one additional function call, an instrumentation, for each memory modifying operation. Memory modifying operations are destructive assignments and memory allocation and deallocation. We only instrument operations of built-in types. For user-defined types either the existing user-provided assignment operator is instrumented (like any other code), or we generate a reversible default assignment operator if it is not user-provided. This is sufficient to cover all forms of memory modifying operations – of built-in types as well as user-defined types – because our runtime library that is linked with the instrumented code performs all necessary book-keeping at run-time. In particular, it also contains C++11 compile-time predicates. Those predicates check whether a provided type is a built-in type or a user-defined type and handle assignments of user-defined types (e.g. entire structs) as fall-through cases because they are handled component-wise by the respective overloaded assignment operator (which is either user-provided and automatically instrumented or generated). For a formal definition of the semantics of the instrumentations we refer the reader to [7].

We have implemented our approach in a tool called *Backstroke*[2] as source-to-source transformation based on the compiler infrastructure ROSE[3]. The Backstroke compiler for generating reversible programs from C++ was released to the public in March 2017 (version 2.1.0). This was the first public release of Backstroke V2 using incremental state saving.

---

[2] https://github.com/LLNL/backstroke.

[3] https://www.rosecompiler.org.

```
template<typename myuint>
void matmul(int n,myuint A[],myuint B[],myuint AB[]) {
  for(int i = 0; i<n; i++) {
    for(int j = 0; j<n; j++) {
      myuint s = 0;
      for(int k = 0; k<n; k++) {
        s =  s + A[i*n+k]*B[k*n+j];
      }
      AB[i*n+j] = s;
    }
  }
}
```

Listing 1.6. Original C++ Matrix Multiplication Code Fragment from the Benchmark.

```
template<typename myuint>
void matmul(int n,myuint A[],myuint B[],myuint AB[]) {
  for(int i = 0; i<n; i++)
    for(int j = 0; j<n; j++) {
      myuint s = 0;
      for(int k = 0; k<n; k++) {
        (xpdes::avpushT(s)) = s +A[i*n+k]*B[k*n+j];
      }
      (xpdes::avpushT(AB[i*n+j])) = s;

    }
}
```

Listing 1.7. Backstroke Generated Reversible C++ Forward Code (non-optimized).

5.1   Backstroke Instrumented Code

Three variants of the matrix multiplication are shown: (1) the original C++ code in Listing 1.6 for the matrix multiplication, (2) the non-optimized Backstroke generated code in Listing 1.7, and (3) the optimized Backstroke generated code in Listing 1.8. Backstroke's optimization detects local variables and ensures that direct accesses to local variables are not instrumented because those never need to be restored since memory for local variables is reserved on the runtime stack. Backstroke instrumented code records memory modifications only for heap allocated data since only this data persists across event function calls. In the presence of pointers the accesses to memory locations on the stack may be instrumented, but a runtime check in the Backstroke library ensures that only heap allocated data is stored.

This runtime check is always performed in the xpdes::avpush function because due to pointer aliasing, in general it is not known at compile time where

```
template<typename myuint>
void matmul(int n,myuint A[],myuint B[],myuint AB[]) {
  for(int i = 0; i<n; i++) {
    for(int j = 0; j<n; j++) {
      myuint s = 0;
      for(int k = 0; k<n; k++) {
        s =  s + A[i*n+k]*B[k*n+j];
      }
      (xpdes::avpushT(AB[i*n+j])) = s;
    }
  }
}
```

Listing 1.8. Backstroke Generated Reversible C++ Forward Code (automatically optimized).

the data that a pointer is referring to may be allocated. This check is performed based on the memory addresses of the argument passed to avpush and the stack boundaries determined as part of the initialization of the Backstroke runtime library.

In the presented model only C++ assignments are instrumented because no memory allocation happens in the event functions. The memory for the matrices is allocated in the initialization of the simulation, i.e. in the initialization function for each LP.

The avpush function passes a reference to the memory section denoted by the respective expression as argument and stores a pair of the address (of the denoted memory location) and the value at that address in a queue in the Backstroke runtime library. It returns the very same address such that the code can execute as usual and perform the write access. Consequently, avpush always stores the old value before the assignment happens. When a previous state needs to be restored, the reverse function simply iterates over all those address-value pairs stored by the avpush function and restores the memory locations at those addresses to the stored value. The avpush functions are strictly typed, and restoration follows in exact reverse order, which is important in case a memory location is written more than once or any forms of aliasing occur. For more details on the instrumentation functions we refer the reader to [7].

The difference of the non-optimized version to the optimized version is that the instrumentation in the innermost loop is not necessary because it is a write to a local variable s. In Listing 1.8 the innermost loop is not instrumented and therefore the number of instrumentations is only executed n^2 times where n is the size of the quadratic matrices. Without this optimization the Backstroke generated code would always be slower than the Janus generated code as we will discuss in more detail in Sect. 7. In general, accesses to memory which only holds temporary data, not defining the state of an LP, need not be instrumented.

The more precise a static analysis is that determines this property, the more instrumentations to temporary memory locations can be avoided.

Backstroke also offers program annotations (through pragmas) for users to manually minimize the number of instrumentations and interface functions to turn on/off the recording of data at runtime. For example, with this feature one can add conditions in loops to only record data in the very first iteration, but not in subsequent iterations that write to the same memory location. Alternatively, one can unroll a loop and only instrument the first (unrolled) iteration and exclude the remaining loop from instrumentation. Thus, with Backstroke one can also manually optimize the recording of data.

6   ROSS Simulator

For execution of our model codes we use the ROSS general purpose discrete event simulator, developed at RPI by C. Carothers et al. [11]. ROSS has been developed for more than a decade. It has the capability of running simulations both sequentially and in parallel using either the YAWNS conservative or Time Warp optimistic mechanism. Time Warp is an optimistic approach, where each processor employs speculative execution to process any event messages it is aware of. Causality conflicts, such as when a previously unknown message which should already have been processed is received, are handled through local roll back. During roll back the effects of messages that were processed in error are undone.

In order to use Time Warp in a ROSS model, a reverse event function must be provided, which is responsible for undoing the state changes that the forward event function incurred for the same event.

6.1   Adaptations of the ROSS Simulator for the FRC Paradigm

For our evaluation we are using the same ROSS implementation as in [7]. This version offers a commit method. Whenever an event is committed (during fossil collection) a commit function is called for the corresponding LP with the event as an argument. This is a time when non-reversible functions such as file I/O can be called safely. In particular, this is very useful for Backstroke, since commit time is the earliest known moment at which the state saved by the Backstroke instrumented forward code can be released, and memory deallocated by the forward event can be returned to the system. In addition to the commit methods, we extended ROSS to support a C++ class for the simulation time data structure, as opposed to the default double data type for representing time. This allows the sender to encode additional bits in the message timestamp to help with tie breaking of events.

7   Evaluation

We have evaluated the performance of three different implementations for the forward and reverse code of the matrix mode: Original code with hand written

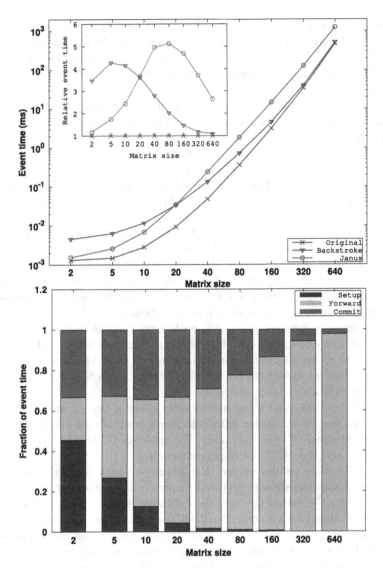

Fig. 1. *Top:* Performance of original, Backstroke, and Janus versions of the matrix model code. The graph shows the execution time per event for the three approaches. The inset shows execution time relative to the original code. *Bottom:* The time for the event function for the Backstroke code separated into event setup time, forward event time, and commit time costs.

reverse code, forward code implemented in Janus with reverse code generated by the Janus compiler, and forward code instrumented by Backstroke. For these performance evaluations we used the Backstroke code with local variable optimization.

First we focus on forward event code, which consists of three phases: event setup, forward computation, and commit. It is only the Backstroke instrumented code that has any significant work to perform in the setup and commit phases. We ran the matrix model sequentially using 8000 LP's and running up to 20 time units.

Figure 1 shows the matrix model performance as a function of matrix size for the four different reverse code approaches. The upper panel shows total event execution time, while the lower panel shows the relative cost of the three event execution phases for the Backstroke instrumented code.

The standard procedure, which we employ in the original code, for multiplying two $n \times n$ matrices performs n^3 multiplications and additions, and thus in general the execution time for an event should scale as $O(n^3)$ for sufficiently large n.

The Janus code must perform an LU factorization before carrying out the multiplications, and undo the factorization after the multiplication is complete. The total number of operations is about $\frac{5}{3}$ times as many as for the standard procedure. We can thus expect the Janus code to be almost twice as slow as the original code for large matrices. For very small matrices the number of operations of the Janus implementation is similar to the original code.

The Backstroke instrumented code with local variable optimization instruments $2n^2$ memory operations (n^2 for the matrix multiplication, and another n^2 for copying the result into the destination memory). Since there are $O(n^3)$ arithmetic operations, we expect the Backstroke instrumented code to incur negligible overhead for sufficiently large matrices.

We performed the runs using matrix sizes ranging from 2 to 640. The simulations were run on an cluster with Infiniband interconnect and 2.6GHz Intel Xeon E5-2670 cpus, 16 cores per node. We used the GNU g++ compiler with version 4.9.3, and the "-O3" optimization switches.

In the evaluation results we see that Janus performs best for small matrix sizes, whereas the Backstroke generated incremental state saving code performs better the larger the matrix size becomes, with a cross-over point at the size of a matrix size of 20 and for a matrix size of 640 the performance becomes almost the same as the non-instrumented version of the original forward code. The reason is that the Backstroke generated code only instruments those memory modifications that actually change the state of the simulation, i.e. elements in the matrix, whereas the computation of the intermediate results is not instrumented. This optimization is straightforward because this corresponds to not instrumenting accesses to local (stack-allocated) variables. Since optimistic PDES follows the forward-reverse-commit paradigm the trace only grows to a certain size, until the commit function is invoked by the simulator. The simulator guarantees that this happens in reasonable time intervals. The non-monotonic performance behavior for small matrices in Backstroke, and for intermediate size matrices in Janus (see inset in Fig. 1), is likely due to simulator and timing overhead, and cache effects, respectively.

The advantage of Janus generated forward/reverse code is that it does not need to store any additional data since the Janus implementation of the forward code is reversible. Saving memory is useful particularly in Time Warp simulations, since the amount of memory available dictates how much speculation can be performed. A challenge to implementing an algorithm in Janus is that it requires to writing assertions at the end of constructs that enable reverse execution to take the right execution path (i.e. reverse conditionals). In addition, reversibility may require algorithms that use inherently more operations than the most efficient ones available in traditional non-reversible computing.

8 Related Work

Jefferson started the subject of rollback-based synchronization in 1984 [3]. The paper discusses rollback implemented by restoring a snapshot of an old state, but today we are interested in using reverse computation and/or incremental state saving for that purpose. Also, that paper is written as if discrete event simulation is one of several applications of virtual time, but in fact it was then and is now the primary application. Although the term "virtual time" is used, you can safely read it as "simulation time".

In 1999 Carothers et al. published the first paper [4], that suggests using reverse computation instead of snapshot restoration as the mechanism for rollback, but it does not contemplate using a reversible language. It is written in terms of very simple and conventional programming constructs (C-like rather than C++ -like) and instrumenting the forward code to store near minimal trace information to allow rollback of side effects by reverse computation.

Barnes et al. demonstrated in 2013 [12], how important reverse computation can be in a practical application area. The fastest and most parallel discrete event simulation benchmark ever executed was done at LLNL on one of the world's largest supercomputers using reverse computation as its rollback method for synchronization. The reverse code was hand-generated, and methodologically we know that this is unsustainable. For practical applications we need a way of automatically generating reverse code from forward code, and this is what we address with the work presented in this paper - to have a tool available, Backstroke (version 2), for generating reverse code that can be applied to the full C++ language.

Kalyan Perumalla and Alfred Park discuss the use of Reverse Computation for scalable fault tolerant computations [13]. The paper is limited in a number of ways, but they make a fundamental point, which is that Reverse Computation can be used to recover from faults by mechanisms that are much faster than check pointing mechanisms.

In [14] Justin LaPre et al. discuss reverse code generation for PDES. The presented method is similar to one of our previous approaches in the work on Backstroke [15] as it takes control flow into account and generates code for computing additional information required to reconstruct the execution path that had been taken in the forward code. The approach we evaluate in this paper is different as it does not need to take control flow information into account. Our initial discussion of incremental state saving was presented in [9], but was limited to C++ without templates. In this paper we evaluate a model that is implemented using C++ templates as well. The automatic optimization that we evaluate was also not present in [9].

An example for an optimistic PDES simulation with an automatically generated code using incremental state saving running thousands of LPs was published for a Kinetic Monte-Carlo model in [10]. In this crystal grain simulation, a piece of solid is modeled as a grid of unit elements. Each unit element represents a microscopic piece of material, big enough to be able to exhibit a well defined crystal orientation, but much smaller than typical grain sizes. These unit elements are commonly called spins, since the nature of grain evolution resembles evolution of magnetic domains. In the experiment the biggest model was run with a size of 768×768 spins divided into a grid of $96 \times 96 = 9216$ LPs with a slow-down factor in comparison to the hand-written reverse code of 4.7 to 4.3. In a new experiment presented in [7], the model was run at a much bigger scale with 1536×1536 spins in 256×256 logical processes (LPs) and implemented using C++ Standard containers and algorithms and user-defined types. After the transformation by Backstroke the model was run for 2 time units, or a total of 47633718 events on LLNL's IBM BlueGene/Q supercomputer with 16 cores per node, using up to 8192 cores. This version showed a penalty of 2.7. to 2.9 in comparison to the hand-written reverse code.

In [16] an autonomic system is presented that can utilize both an incremental and a full checkpointing mode. At run time both code variants are available and the system switches between the two variants, trying to select the more efficient checkpointing version. With our approach to incremental checkpointing we aim to reduce the number of instrumentations based on static analysis and offer a directive to the user for enabling or disabling the recording of data at runtime, allowing to also manually optimize instrumented code.

In [17] an instrumentation technique is applied to relocatable object files. Specifically, it operates on the Executable and Linkable Format (ELF). It uses the tool Hijacker [18] to instrument the binary code to generate a cache of disassembly information. This allows to avoid disassembly of instructions at run time. In contrast to our approach, the reverse instructions are built on-the-fly at runtime, and using pre-compiled tables of instructions. Similar to our approach there is also an overhead for each instrumentation. The information that it extracts from instructions, the target address and the size of a memory write, is similar to our address-value pairs. Recently progress has been made also in utilizing hardware transactional memory for further optimizing single node performance [19].

9   Conclusion

We have presented a new benchmark model for evaluating approaches to optimistic parallel discrete event simulation. We evaluated the performance of using

Janus generated forward/reverse code and incremental state saving (also called incremental checkpointing). The benchmark model has as its core operation a matrix multiplication.

From the results for our presented benchmark model we can conclude that depending on the matrix size either the Janus generated code or the Backstroke generated code performs best. Therefore, an implementation could include both codes and call the respective implementation dependent on the matrix size. If memory consumption becomes a limiting factor, the Janus implementation could be favored over the Backstroke implementation as well, since the Janus code does not store any additional data.

It also could be interesting to further explore how the Janus translator can be optimized and how this impacts the native C++ compiler. The Janus translator used in the benchmarks is non-optimizing, which means it implements every Janus statements in the target program, even when irreversible alternatives provide a faster implementation and some statements may be redundant in C++. Depending on the architecture, locality can be exploited to improve the runtime behavior, e.g., when translating summation `iterate ... A[i,j]+=e end` the use of a temporary variable in conventional assignments is an option: `s=A[i,j]; for ... s+=e end; A[i,j]=s;`. Some optimizations are performed by the native C++ compiler, others are better done by the Janus translator. Also, Janus may be extended with translator hints that allow a programmer to mark compute-uncompute pairs, which makes it easier to determine redundant statements.

Acknowledgments. This work was performed under the auspices of the U.S. Department of Energy by Lawrence Livermore National Laboratory under Contract DE-AC52-07NA27344 and was supported by the LLNL-LDRD Program under Project No. 19-ERD-026. IM release number LLNL-BOOK-780059. The authors acknowledge the partial support of EU COST Action IC1405 on Reversible Computation—Extending Horizons of Computing.

References

1. Fujimoto, R.M.: Parallel and Distribution Simulation Systems, 1st edn. Wiley, New York (1999)
2. Omelchenko, Y., Karimabadi, H.: Hypers: A unidimensional asynchronous framework for multiscale hybrid simulations. J. Comp. Phys. **231**(4), 1766–1780 (2012)
3. Jefferson, D.R.: Virtual time. ACM Trans. Program. Lang. Syst. **7**(3), 404–425 (1985)
4. Carothers, C.D., Perumalla, K.S., Fujimoto, R.M.: Efficient optimistic parallel simulations using reverse computation. ACM Trans. Model. Comput. Simul. **9**(3), 224–253 (1999)
5. Perumalla, K.S.: Introduction to Reversible Computing. CRC Press Book, Boca Raton (2013)
6. Yokoyama, T., Glück, R.: A reversible programming language and its invertible self-interpreter. In: Ramalingam, G., Visser, E. (eds.) Proceedings of the 2007 ACM SIGPLAN Workshop on Partial Evaluation and Semantics-based Program Manipulation, 2007, Nice, France, 15–16 January 2007, pp. 144–153. ACM (2007)

7. Schordan, M., Oppelstrup, T., Jefferson, D.R., Barnes Jr., P.D.: Generation of reversible C++ code for optimistic parallel discrete event simulation. New Generat. Comput. **36**(3), 257–280 (2018)

8. Yokoyama, T., Axelsen, H.B., Glück, R.: Reversible flowchart languages and the structured reversible program theorem. In: Aceto, L., Damgård, I., Goldberg, L.A., Halldórsson, M.M., Ingólfsdóttir, A., Walukiewicz, I. (eds.) ICALP 2008. LNCS, vol. 5126, pp. 258–270. Springer, Heidelberg (2008). https://doi.org/10.1007/978-3-540-70583-3_22

9. Schordan, M., Jefferson, D., Barnes, P., Oppelstrup, T., Quinlan, D.: Reverse code generation for parallel discrete event simulation. In: Krivine, J., Stefani, J.-B. (eds.) RC 2015. LNCS, vol. 9138, pp. 95–110. Springer, Cham (2015). https://doi.org/10.1007/978-3-319-20860-2_6

10. Schordan, M., Oppelstrup, T., Jefferson, D., Barnes, Jr., P.D., Quinlan, D.: Automatic generation of reversible C++ code and its performance in a scalable kinetic Monte-Carlo application. In: Proceedings of the 2016 ACM SIGSIM Conference on Principles of Advanced Discrete Simulation. SIGSIM-PADS 2016, pp. 111–122. ACM (2016)

11. Holder, A.O., Carothers, C.D.: Analysis of time warp on a 32,768 processor IBM Blue Gene/L supercomputer. In: Bruzzone, A., Longo, F., Piera, M.A., Aguilar, R.M., Frydman, C. (eds.) Proceedings of the European Modeling and Simulation Symposium (EMSS), pp. 284–292 (2008)

12. Barnes, Jr., P.D., Carothers, C.D., Jefferson, D.R., LaPre, J.M.: Warp speed: executing time warp on 1,966,080 cores. In: Proceedings of the 2013 ACM SIGSIM Conference on Principles of Advanced Discrete Simulation. SIGSIM-PADS 2013, pp. 327–336. ACM (2013)

13. Perumalla, K.S., Park, A.J.: Reverse computation for rollback-based fault tolerance in large parallel systems. Cluster Comput. **17**(2), 303–313 (2013). https://doi.org/10.1007/s10586-013-0277-4

14. LaPre, J.M., Gonsiorowski, E.J., Carothers, C.D.: LORAIN: a step closer to the PDES "holy grail". In: Proceedings of the 2nd ACM SIGSIM Conference on Principles of Advanced Discrete Simulation. SIGSIM-PADS 2014, pp. 3–14. ACM (2014)

15. Vulov, G., Hou, C., Vuduc, R., Fujimoto, R., Quinlan, D., Jefferson, D.: The Backstroke framework for source level reverse computation applied to parallel discrete event simulation. In: Proceedings of the Winter Simulation Conference. WSC 2011, Winter Simulation Conference, pp. 2965–2979 (2011)

16. Pellegrini, A., Vitali, R., Quaglia, F.: Autonomic state management for optimistic simulation platforms. IEEE Trans. Parallel Distrib. Syst. **26**(6), 1560–1569 (2015)

17. Cingolani, D., Pellegrini, A., Quaglia, F.: Transparently mixing undo logs and software reversibility for state recovery in optimistic PDES. In: Proceedings of the 3rd ACM SIGSIM Conference on Principles of Advanced Discrete Simulation. SIGSIM PADS 2015, pp. 211–222. ACM (2015)

18. Pellegrini, A.: Hijacker: Efficient static software instrumentation with applications in high performance computing: poster paper. In: International Conference on High Performance Computing and Simulation (HPCS), pp. 650–655. (2013)

19. Santini, E., Ianni, M., Pellegrini, A., Quaglia, F.: Hardware-transactional-memory based speculative parallel discrete event simulation of very fine grain models. In: IEEE 22nd International Conference on High Performance Computing (HiPC), pp. 145–154 (2015)

Reversible Computation in Wireless Communications

Harun Siljak[⊠]

CONNECT Centre, Trinity College, The University of Dublin, Dublin, Ireland
harun.siljak@tcd.ie

Abstract. This chapter presents pioneering work in applying reversible computation paradigms to wireless communications. These applications range from developing reversible hardware architectures for underwater acoustic communications to novel distributed optimisation procedures in large radio-frequency antenna arrays based on reversing Petri nets. Throughout the chapter, we discuss the rationale for introducing reversible computation in the domain of wireless communications, exploring the inherently reversible properties of communication channels and systems formed by devices in a wireless network.

1 Introduction

Wireless communication systems come in different shapes and sizes: from radio frequency (RF) systems we use in everyday life, to underwater acoustic communications (UAC) used where RF attenuation prevents use of radio communications. These two examples are of interest to this case study, as we explored the potential role of reversible computation in improving modern wireless communications in the RF and acoustic domains.

In the RF context, we examine the concept of distributed massive MIMO (multiple input multiple output) systems. The distributed massive MIMO paradigm will have an increasing relevance in fifth generation (5G) wireless systems and post-5G era, as it will allow formerly centralised base stations to operate as a group of hundreds (thousands) of small antennas distributed in space, serving many users by beamforming the signal to them, operating using distributed algorithms hence providing reduced power consumption and reduced computational overhead. Our aim is to explore the application of reversible computation paradigms in such systems to contribute in additional reduction of power consumption, but also to help in fault recovery and meaningful undoing of algorithmic steps in control and optimisation of such systems.

In the underwater acoustic context, we recognised the wave time reversal scheme as a physical example of reversibility, a physical method waiting for its reversible circuit implementation. The mechanism of wave time reversal is analogous to reversible computation as we know it, and as such it admits elegant and simple circuit implementation benefiting from all reversible computation advantages. With this inherent reversibility in mind, we take the question of wave

I. Ulidowski et al. (Eds.): RC 2020, LNCS 12070, pp. 208–221, 2020.
https://doi.org/10.1007/978-3-030-47361-7_10

time reversal in underwater conditions a step further, and ask about realistic models of such systems using reversible computation paradigms, and investigate the options of controlling the environment in which this process is used for communication.

Communication is inherently reversible: the communication channel changes direction all the time, with the transmitter and the receiver changing roles and transmitting through the same medium. Modulation and demodulation, coding and decoding all these processes aim for information conservation and reversibility. Hence the motivation for this study is clear: can reversible computation help in achieving goals of modern wireless communication: increasing access, decreasing latency and power consumption, minimising information losses?

In this chapter, we present results on optimisation schemes for massive MIMO based on reversing Petri nets, reversible hardware for wave time reversal, and some preliminary thoughts on our work in progress on modelling and control of wave time reversal in reversible cellular automata, as well as control of these automata in general.

2   Reversing Petri Nets and Massive MIMO

2.1   The Problem

In the distributed massive MIMO system described in the previous section, not all antennas need to be active at all times. Selecting a subset of antennas to operate at a particular time instant allows the system to retain advantages of a large antenna array, including interference suppression, spatial multiplexing and diversity [16] while reducing the number of radio frequency (RF) chains and the number of antennas to power [13]. The computational demand of optimal transmit antenna selection for large antenna arrays [11] makes it impractical, suggesting the necessity of suboptimal approaches. Traditionally, these approaches were centralised and based on the knowledge of the communication channel between every user and every antenna in the array; one widely used algorithm is the greedy algorithm [12] which operates iteratively by adding the antenna that increases the sum rate the most when joined with the set of already selected antennas. In decentralised algorithms similar procedures are conducted on much smaller subsets of antennas [21], leading to similar results in overall performance. Our approach here is decentralised, and it relies on Reversing Petri nets (RPN) [17] as the underlying paradigm. As this chapter focuses on applications, the reader interested in details about reversing Petri nets used in this example is advised to see [18]. The presentation here is based on [22].

The optimisation problem we are solving is downlink (transmit) antenna selection of N_{TS} antennas at the distributed massive MIMO base station with N_T antennas, in presence of N_R single antenna users. We maximise the sum-capacity

$$\mathcal{C} = \max_{\mathbf{P},\,\mathbf{H}_c} \log_2 \det \left(\mathbf{I} + \rho \frac{N_R}{N_{TS}} \mathbf{H}_c \mathbf{P} \mathbf{H}_c^H \right) \tag{1}$$

where ρ is the signal to noise ratio (SNR), $\mathbf{I}$ a $N_{TS} \times N_{TS}$ identity matrix, $\mathbf{P}$ a diagonal $N_R \times N_R$ power distribution matrix. $\mathbf{H}_c$ is the $N_{TS} \times N_R$ channel submatrix for a selected subset of antennas from the $N_T \times N_R$ channel matrix $\mathbf{H}$ [10].

In the case of receiver antenna selection, addition of any antenna to the set of selected antennas improves the overall sum-capacity, as its equivalent of Eq. (1) does not involve scaling by the number of selected antennas (i.e. there is not a power budget to be distributed over antennas in the receive case). This problem is submodular and has a guaranteed (suboptimal) performance bound for the previously described greedy algorithm. The greedy algorithm does not have performance bound for the transmitter antenna selection, as the case described by Eq. (1) does not fulfil the submodularity condition [24]; the addition of an antenna to the already selected set of antennas can decrease channel capacity.

As done in [21,24], we optimise (1) with two variables, the subset of selected antennas and the optimal power distribution over them successively: first, $\mathbf{P}$ is fixed to having all diagonal elements equal to $1/N_R$ (total power is equal to $\rho N_R/N_{TS}$), and after the antenna selection $\mathbf{P}$ is optimised by the water filling algorithm for zero forcing.

Figure 1 illustrates the proposed algorithm based on RPN: the antennas are Petri net *places* (circles A–G), with the *token* (bright circle) in a place indicating that the current state of the algorithm asks for that place (that antenna) to be on. The places are divided into overlapping *neighbourhoods* (N_1 and N_2 in our toy example) and each two adjacent places have a common neighbourhood. *Transitions* between places move tokens around based on the sum capacity calculations, with rules described below:

1. A transition is possible if there is a token in exactly one of the two places (e.g. B and G in Fig. 1) it connects. Otherwise (e.g. A and B, or E and F) it is not possible.
2. The enabled transition will occur if the sum capacity (1) calculated for all antennas with a token in the neighbourhood shared by the two places (for B and G, that is neighbourhood N_1) is less than the sum capacity calculated for the same neighbourhood, but with the token moved to the empty place (in case of B-G transition, this means $\mathcal{C}_{AB} < \mathcal{C}_{AG}$, sum-capacity of antennas A and B is smaller than that of A and G). Otherwise, it does not occur.
3. In case of several possible transitions from one place (A-E, A-D, A-C) the one with the greatest sum-capacity difference (i.e. improvement) has the priority.
4. There is no designated order in transition execution, and transitions are performed until a stable state is reached.

The algorithm starts from a configuration of n tokens in random places and converges to a stable final configuration in a small number (in our experiments, up to five) of iterations (passes) through the whole network. As the RPN conserves the number of tokens in the network, and our rules allow at most one token per place, the algorithm results in n selected antennas. Executing the algorithm on several RPNs in parallel (in our experiments, up to five) allows tokens to traverse all parts of the network and find good configurations even with a relatively small number of antennas and users. The converged state of the RPN becomes the physical state of antennas: antennas with tokens are turned on for the duration of the coherence interval. At the next update of the channel state information, the algorithm proceeds from the current state.

The computational footprint of the described algorithm is very small: two small matrix multiplications and determinant calculations are performed at a node which contains a token in a small number of iterations. As such, this algorithm is significantly faster and computationally less demanding than the centralised greedy approach which is a low-complexity representative of global optimisation algorithms in antenna selection [11]. The worst case complexity of the RPN based approach is $\mathcal{O}(N_T^{\omega/a})$ (here, N_T denotes the number of antennas, and ω, $2 < \omega < 3$ is the exponent in the employed matrix multiplication algorithm complexity). The parameter a is related to the relative size of the neighbourhood as a reciprocal exponent, assuming that a neighbourhood of $N_T^{1/a}$, $a > 1$ suffices for RPN algorithm (as $\sqrt{N_T}$ suffices in our case, we went for $a = 2$). The constant factor multiplying the complexity is small because of few computing nodes (only those with tokens) and few iterations.

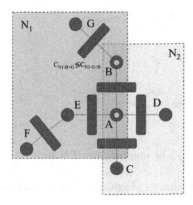

Fig. 1. A toy model of antenna selection on a reversing Petri net

2.2   Results and Discussion

The algorithm was tested using the raytracing Matlab tool Ilmprop [9] on a system composed of 64 omnidirectional antennas randomly distributed in space shown in Fig. 2(a). In all computations, channel state information (CSI) in matrix **H** was normalised to unit average energy over all antennas, users and subcarriers, following the practice from [10]. 75 randomly distributed scatterers and one large obstacle are placed in the area with the distributed base station. The number of (randomly distributed) users with omnidirectional antennas varied

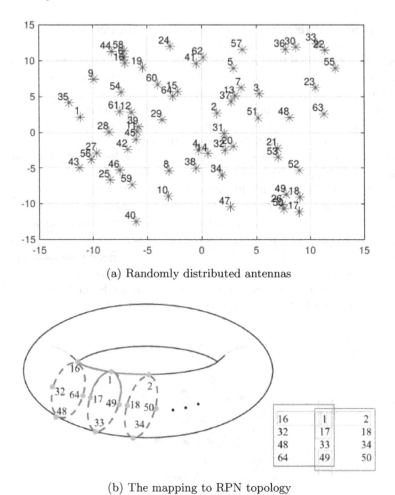

(a) Randomly distributed antennas

(b) The mapping to RPN topology

Fig. 2. Antennas in physical and computational domain

from 4 to 16, and we used 300 OFDM (orthogonal frequency-division multiplexing) subcarriers, SNR $\rho = -5$ dB, 2.6 GHz carrier frequency, 20 MHz bandwidth. Antennas are computationally arranged in an 4×16 array folded into a toroid, creating a continuous infinite network, as shown in Fig. 2(b), e.g. antenna 1 is a direct neighbour of antennas 2, 16, 17 and 49. Immediate Von Neumann (top, down, left, right) neighbours can exchange tokens, and overlapping 8-antenna neighbourhoods are placed on the grid: e.g. for antenna 1, transitions to 16 and 17 are decided upon within the neighbourhood {16, 32, 48, 64, 1, 17, 33, 49} and the transitions to 2 and 49 are in {1, 17, 33, 49, 2, 18, 34, 50}. In Fig. 3 we compare greedy and random selection with two variants of our RPN approach: the average of five concurrently running RPNs, and the performance of the best RPN out of those five. The performance is comparable in all cases, and both variants of our proposed algorithm tend to outperform the centralised approach as the number of users grows. This in practice means that a single RPN suffices for networks with a relatively large expected number of users.

The inherent reversibility of this problem and its solution generalises to the common problem of resource allocation in wireless networks, and sharing any pool of resources (power, frequency, etc.) can be handled between antennas (and antenna clusters) over a Reversing Petri Net. At the same time, such a solution would be robust to changes in the environment, potential faults, sudden changes in the mode of operation, and could operate on reversible hardware.

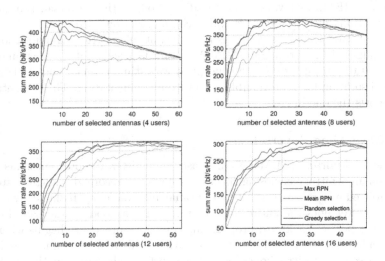

Fig. 3. Achieved sum rates for 4–16 users using the proposed algorithm vs random and centralised greedy selection

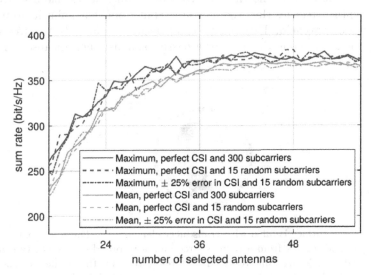

Fig. 4. The effects of imperfect CSI and random selection of subcarriers on optimisation

In [21], it has been shown that the distributed algorithms are resistant to errors in CSI and that they perform well even with just a (randomly selected) subset of subcarriers used for optimisation. Results in Fig. 4 in the case of 12 users confirm this for the RPN algorithm as well.

3   Reversible Hardware for Time Reversal

The technique called wave time reversal [6] has been introduced in acoustics almost three decades ago, and has since been applied to other waves as well–optical and RF. In our work, we focused on acoustic time reversal, thinking of its applications in acoustic underwater communications. However, it is worth noting that wave time reversal plays a significant role in RF communications as well–conjugate beamforming for MIMO systems is based on it. In the remainder of this section, we introduce the concept of wave time reversal and explain our proposed solution for its reversible hardware implementation. The presentation here follows the one in [20].

3.1   Wave Time Reversal

Time reversal mirrors (TRMs) [6] are based on emitter–receptor antennas positioned on an arbitrary enclosing surface. The wave is recorded, digitised, stored, time-reversed and rebroadcasted by the same antenna array. If the array on the boundary intercepts the entire forward wave with a good spatial sampling, it generates a perfect backward-propagating copy. The procedure begins when the source radiates a wave inside a volume surrounded by a two-dimensional surface with sensors (microphones) along the surface which record the field and its normal derivative until the field disappears (Fig. 5). When this recording is emitted back, it created the time-reversed field which looks like a convergent wavefield until it reaches the original source, but from that point it propagates as a diverging wavefield. This can be compensated by an active source at the focusing point cancelling the field, or a passive sink as a perfect absorber [3].

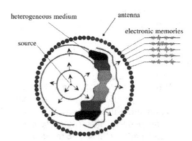

Fig. 5. A closed surface is filled with transducer elements [7]. The wavefront distorted by heterogeneities comes from a point source and is recorded on the cavity elements. The recorded signals are time-reversed and re-emitted by the elements. The time-reversed field back-propagates and refocuses exactly on the initial source.

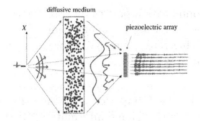

Fig. 6. Time-reversal experiment through a diffusive medium [7]

This description asks for the whole surface to be covered with the TRM transceivers, and for both the signal and the derivative to be stored: for practical purposes, less hardware-demanding solutions are needed. First, we note that the normal derivative of the field is proportional to the field in case the TRM is in the far field, halving the necessity for signal recording. Second, we note that a TRM can use complex environments to appear as an antenna wider than it is, resulting in a refocusing quality that does not depend on the TRM aperture [4]. Hence, it can be implemented with just a subset of transceivers located in one part of the boundary, as seen in Fig. 6.

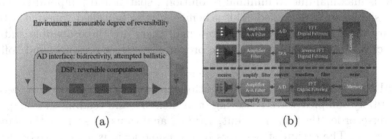

(a)   (b)

Fig. 7. (a) The three realms of reversibility, (b) The classical (top) and the reversible solution (bottom) for the classical time reversal chain

3.2   The Design

Figure 7 illustrates the challenge of designing a reversible hardware solution for a TRM:

1. The environment is reversible to an extent (we will return to this question later in this chapter). The physics of wave propagation in water is reversible, but issues arise as we lose information in the process.
2. The analog computation part of the TRM loses information due to filtering and analog-to-digital/digital-to-analog conversion (ADC/DAC), amplifiers accompanying the filters and the converters themselves, at the transition to the digital domain.

3. Finally, the digital computation part of the TRM is reversible and no increase in entropy is necessary: writing in memory and unwriting, in the fashion of Bennett's trick, enabling reuse of memory for the next incoming wave, while not increasing the entropy.

Analog Processing. The real amplifier is an imperfect device with a limited bandwidth, hence prone to losing signal information. By definition, it takes additional energy for the signal, so it asks for an additional power source. At the same time, the analog to digital and digital to analog converters both lose information because of the finite resolution in time and amplitude, preventing full reversibility. However, a single device can be both an ADC and a DAC depending on the direction [14]. In this solution, we assume bi-directional converters placed together with bi-directional amplifiers [14]. The conversion is additionally simplified in the one-bit solution [5] where the receivers at the mirror register only the sign of the waveform and the transmitters emit the reversed version based on this information. It is a special case of analog-to-digital and digital-to-analog conversion with single bit converters. The reduction in discretisation levels also means simplification of the processing chain and making its reversal (bi-directivity) even simpler. The question of the information loss is not straightforward: while the information about the incoming wave is lost in the conversion process (and the loss is maximal due to minimal resolution), spatial and temporal resolution are not significantly degraded. This scheme can also be called "one-trit" (trit is a ternary digit, analogous to a bit) reversal: there are three possible states in the practical implementation: positive pressure, negative pressure, and "off".

Digital Processing. The first, straightforward way of performing time reversal of a digitally sampled wave is storing it in memory and reading the samples in the reverse order (last in, first out, LIFO), analogous to storing the samples on the stack. The design of registers in reversible logic is a well-explored topic [15] and both serial and parallel reading/writing can be implemented. Design of latches in reversible logic is a well-studied problem with known solutions; a combination of latches makes a flip-flop, and a series of flip-flops makes a register (and a reversible address counter). In the case of wave time reversal, the recording of data is a large register being loaded serially with wave data. m bits from the ADC are memorised at the converter's sample rate inside a $k \times m$ bit register matrix (where k is the number of samples to be stored for time reversal). In the receiving process the bits are stored, in the transmission process they are unstored, returning the memory into the blank state it started from (uncomputation). We utilise Bennett's trick and lose information without the entropic penalty: the information is kept as long as it is relevant.

When additional signal processing, e.g. filtering or modulation is performed, it is convenient to reverse waves in the frequency domain: there, time domain reversal is achieved by phase conjugation, i.e. changing the sign of the signal's phase. The transition from the time to the frequency domain (and vice versa) in the digital domain is performed by the Fast Fourier Transform (FFT) and its inverse counterpart, which are reversibly implementable [23]. The necessary phase conjugation is an arithmetic operation of sign reversal, again reversible. Any additional signal processing can be reversible as well: e.g. filter banks and wavelet transforms. These processes remain reversible with preservation of all components of signals [2].

Figure 8(a) gives a comparison of the bit erasures in different implementations of the digital circuitry: frequency domain (FFT) and time domain reversal performed by irreversible circuits, compared to reversible implementations. The number of erasures changes depending on two parameters: bit resolution of the ADC and the waiting time–the length of the interval in which samples are collected before reversal starts, equivalent to the number of digitised samples. The increase in both means additional memory locations and additional dissipation for irreversible circuits. The irreversible FFT implementation has an additional information loss caused by additional irreversible circuitry compared to the irreversible time domain implementation. Our implementation has no bit erasures whatsoever. The price that is paid reflects in the larger number of gates used in the circuit: the number of gates has only spatial consequences, information-related energy dissipation is zero thanks to information conservation.

On the other hand, Fig. 8(b) shows the information loss in the analog part of the system, and we differentiate two typical environments, the chaotic cavity and the complex (multiple scattering) medium. The chaotic cavity is an ergodic space with sensitive dependence on initial conditions for waves. In such an environment there is little to no loss in the information if the waiting time is long enough and the ADC resolution is high enough. In the complex media, the difference is caused by some of the wave components being reflected backwards by the scattering environment, hence not reaching the TRM. Again, more information is retained with the increase in the ADC resolution. However, as reported in [5], the information loss from low-resolution ADC use does not affect the performance of the algorithm. The analog part of the scheme remains a topic of our future work, as it leaves space for improvements of the scheme.

4   Reversible Environment Models and Control

Time reversal described in the previous section is an example of a reversible process in a nominally reversible environment. While dynamics of water subject to waves are inherently reversible, most of the sources of the water dynamics do not reverse naturally: e.g. the Gulf stream or a motion of a school of fish. Hence, even though it would rarely be completely reversed, the model for UAC should be reversible. We discuss the questions of reversible models following the exposition in [19], and the work in progress on control of reversible cellular automata (RCA).

RCA lattice gas models are cellular automata obeying the laws of fluid dynamics described by the Navier-Stokes equation. One such model, FHP (Frisch- Hasslacher-Pomeau) lattice gas [8] is simple and yet following the Navier-Stokes equations exactly. It is defined on a hexagonal grid with the rules of particle collision shown in Fig. 9. The FHP lattice gas provides us a two-dimensional

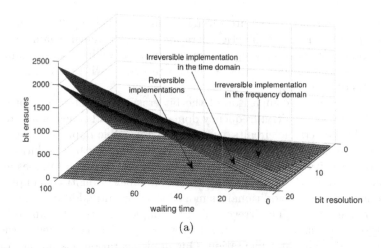

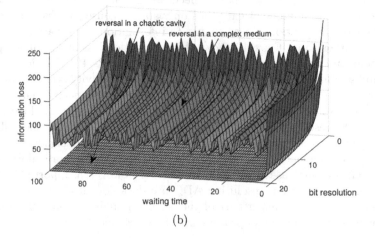

Fig. 8. Information loss in (a) the digital and (b) the analog part of the system. Units are omitted as the particular aspects of implementation are not relevant for the illustration of effects. Plot (a) is obtained by counting operations, plot (b) by simulation of back-scattering.

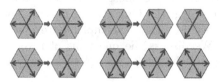

Fig. 9. FHP rules

model for UAC, easily implementable in software and capturing the necessary properties of the reversible medium.

Following the exposition in the previous section, we observe a model with an original source (transmitter) which causes the spread of an acoustic wave, the original sink (receiver) waiting for the wave to reach it, as well as scatterers and constant flows (streams) in the environment. The constant stream and the loss of information caused by some wave components never reaching the sink will result in an imperfect reversal at the original source. The measure of returned power gives us a directivity pattern (focal point). The amplitude of the peak will fluctuate based on the location of the original source and is a measure of reversibility, akin to fidelity or Loschmidt Echo. For us, it is a measure of the quality of communication, but in a more general context it can measure reversibility of a cellular automaton.

From the control viewpoint, it is interesting to ask the following: if a certain part of the environment is controllable (i.e. a number of cells of the RCA does not obey the rules of the RCA but allows external modification), how can it be used to achieve better time reversal? This is a compensation approach where we engineer the environment to compensate for effects caused by sources of disturbance out of our control. The approach we take is one of control of cellular automata [1], and it is expected that RCA are easier to control than regular CA, with easier search strategies and the ability to calculate control sequences.

5   Conclusions

In this chapter, we provided an overview of results obtained in the case study on reversible computation in wireless communications. Some of the presented work, such as optimisation in massive MIMO and reversible hardware for wave time reversal is finished and subject to further extensions and generalisations; other work, mainly the parts focused on RCA and modelling of reversible physics of communication, is still ongoing and more results are to come. This has been a pioneering study into reversibility in communications, and the results obtained promise a lot of space for improvement and applications in the future. We hope these efforts will serve as an inspiration and a trigger for the development of this field of research.

Acknowledgements. The work presented in this chapter was supported by the COST Association through the IC1405 Action on Reversible Computation, as well as a grant from Science Foundation Ireland (SFI) co-funded under the European Regional Development Fund under Grant Number 13/RC/2077 and European Union's Horizon 2020 programme under the Marie Skłodowska-Curie grant agreement No 713567. I am grateful to my collaborators, Prof Anna Philippou, Kyriaki Psara, Dr Julien de Rosny, Prof Mathias Fink, and Dr Franco Bagnoli for making this interdisciplinary research possible, and to Konstantin Popovic for the inspiring ideas.

References

1. Bagnoli, F., Rechtman, R., El Yacoubi, S.: Control of cellular automata. Phys. Rev. E **86**(6), 066201 (2012)
2. Chen, Y.-J., Amaratunga, K.S.: M-channel lifting factorization of perfect reconstruction filter banks and reversible M-band wavelet transforms. IEEE Trans. Circ. Syst. II Analog Digit. Signal Process. **50**(12), 963–976 (2003)
3. de Rosny, J., Fink, M.: Overcoming the diffraction limit in wave physics using a time-reversal mirror and a novel acoustic sink. Phys. Rev. Lett. **89**(12), 124301 (2002)
4. Derode, A., Roux, P., Fink, M.: Robust acoustic time reversal with high-order multiple scattering. Phys. Rev. Lett. **75**(23), 4206 (1995)
5. Derode, A., Tourin, A., Fink, M.: Ultrasonic pulse compression with one-bit time reversal through multiple scattering. J. Appl. Phys. **85**(9), 6343–6352 (1999)
6. Fink, M.: Time reversal of ultrasonic fields. I. Basic principles. IEEE Trans. Ultrason. Ferroelectr. Freq. Control **39**(5), 555–566 (1992)
7. Fink, M.: From Loschmidt daemons to time-reversed waves. Philos. Trans. Roy. Soc. A Math. Phys. Eng. Sci. **374**(2069), 20150156 (2016)
8. Frisch, U., Hasslacher, B., Pomeau, Y.: Lattice-gas automata for the Navier-Stokes equation. Phys. Rev. Lett. **56**(14), 1505 (1986)
9. Del Galdo, G., Haardt, M., Schneider, C.: Geometry-based channel modelling of MIMO channels in comparison with channel sounder measurements. Adv. Radio Sci. **2**(BC), 117–126 (2005)
10. Gao, X., Edfors, O., Tufvesson, F., Larsson, E.G.: Massive MIMO in real propagation environments: do all antennas contribute equally? IEEE Trans. Commun. **63**(11), 3917–3928 (2015)
11. Gao, Y., Vinck, H., Kaiser, T.: Massive MIMO antenna selection: switching architectures, capacity bounds, and optimal antenna selection algorithms. IEEE Trans. Signal Process. **66**(5), 1346–1360 (2017)
12. Gharavi-Alkhansari, M., Gershman, A.B.: Fast antenna subset selection in MIMO systems. IEEE Trans. Signal Process. **52**(2), 339–347 (2004)
13. Hoydis, J., Ten Brink, S., Debbah, M.: Massive MIMO in the UL/DL of cellular networks: how many antennas do we need? IEEE J. Sel. Areas Commun. **31**, 160–171 (2013)
14. Mirmotahari, O., Berg, Y.: Pseudo floating-gate and reverse signal flow. In: Recent Advances in Technologies. IntechOpen (2009)
15. Nayeem, N.M., Hossain, M.A., Jamal, L., Babu, H.M.H.: Efficient design of shift registers using reversible logic. In: 2009 International Conference on Signal Processing Systems, pp. 474–478. IEEE (2009)
16. Ozgur, A., Lévêque, O., Tse, D.: Spatial degrees of freedom of large distributed MIMO systems and wireless ad hoc networks. IEEE J. Sel. Areas Commun. **31**(2), 202–214 (2013)
17. Philippou, A., Psara, K.: Reversible computation in petri nets. In: Kari, J., Ulidowski, I. (eds.) RC 2018. LNCS, vol. 11106, pp. 84–101. Springer, Cham (2018). https://doi.org/10.1007/978-3-319-99498-7_6
18. Philippou, A., Psara, K., Siljak, H.: Controlling reversibility in reversing petri nets with application to wireless communications. In: Thomsen, M.K., Soeken, M. (eds.) RC 2019. LNCS, vol. 11497, pp. 238–245. Springer, Cham (2019). https://doi.org/10.1007/978-3-030-21500-2_15

19. Siljak, H.: Reversibility in space, time, and computation: the case of underwater acoustic communications. In: Kari, J., Ulidowski, I. (eds.) RC 2018. LNCS, vol. 11106, pp. 346–352. Springer, Cham (2018). https://doi.org/10.1007/978-3-319-99498-7_25

20. Siljak, H., de Rosny, J., Fink, M.: Reversible hardware for acoustic communications. IEEE Commun. Mag. **58**, 55–61 (2020)

21. Siljak, H., Macaluso, I., Marchetti, N.: Distributing complexity: a new approach to antenna selection for distributed massive MIMO. IEEE Wireless Commun. Lett. **7**(6), 902–905 (2018)

22. Siljak, H., Psara, K., Philippou, A.: Distributed antenna selection for massive MIMO using reversing Petri nets. IEEE Wireless Commun. Lett. **8**(5), 1427–1430 (2019)

23. Skoneczny, M., Van Rentergem, Y., De Vos, A.: Reversible Fourier transform chip. In: 2008 15th International Conference on Mixed Design of Integrated Circuits and Systems, pp. 281–286. IEEE (2008)

24. Vaze, R., Ganapathy, H.: Sub-modularity and antenna selection in MIMO systems. IEEE Commun. Lett. **16**(9), 1446–1449 (2012)

Error Reconciliation in Quantum Key Distribution Protocols

Miralem Mehic[1,3(✉)], Marcin Niemiec[2,3], Harun Siljak[4], and Miroslav Voznak[3]

[1] Department of Telecommunications, Faculty of Electrical Engineering,
University of Sarajevo, Zmaja od Bosne bb, Kampus Univerziteta,
71000 Sarajevo, Bosnia and Herzegovina
miralem.mehic@ieee.org
[2] AGH University of Science and Technology,
al. Mickiewicza 30, 30-059 Krakow, Poland
[3] Department of Telecommunications, VSB-Technical University of Ostrava,
17. listopadu 15, 70800 Ostrava-Poruba, Czech Republic
[4] CONNECT Centre, Trinity College Dublin, Dunlop Oriel House 34 Westland Row,
Dublin 2, Ireland

Abstract. Quantum Key Distribution (QKD) protocols allow the establishment of symmetric cryptographic keys up to a limited distance at limited rates. Due to optical misalignment, noise in quantum detectors, disturbance of the quantum channel or eavesdropping, an error key reconciliation technique is required to eliminate errors. This chapter analyses different key reconciliation techniques with a focus on communication and computing performance. We also briefly describe a new approach to key reconciliation techniques based on artificial neural networks.

Keywords: Error reconciliation · Quantum key distribution ·
Performances · Reversibility

1 Introduction

QKD provides an effective solution for resolving the cryptographic key establishment problem by relying on the laws of quantum physics. Unlike approaches based on mathematical constraints whose security depends on the attacker's computational and communication resources, QKD does not put a limit on the available resources but limits the length of the link implementation [1]. A QKD link can be realized only to a certain distance and at certain rates since it involves usage of two channels: quantum/optical and public/classical.

This work has been partially supported by COST Action IC1405 on Reversible Computation - Extending Horizons of Computing, and partly by the European Union's Horizon 2020 Research and Innovation Programme, under Grant Agreement no. 830943, the ECHO project. This work was also supported by the Ministry of Education, Science and Youth of Canton Sarajevo, Bosnia and Herzegovina under Grant No. 11/05-14-27719-1/19 and partly by the Horizon 2020 project OpenQKD under grant agreement No. 857156.

I. Ulidowski et al. (Eds.): RC 2020, LNCS 12070, pp. 222–236, 2020.
https://doi.org/10.1007/978-3-030-47361-7_11

Quantum cryptography focuses on photons (particles of light), using some of their properties to act as an information carrier. Principally, information is encoded in a photon's polarization; a single polarized photon is referred to as a qubit (quantum bit) which cannot be split, copied or amplified without introducing detectable disturbances.

The procedure for establishing a key is defined by QKD protocol, and three basic categories are distinguished: the oldest and widespread group of discrete-variable protocols (BB84, B92, E91, SARG04), efficient continuous-variable (CV-QKD) protocols and distributed-phase-reference coding (COW, DPS) [2,3]. The primary difference between these categories is reflected in the method of preparing and generating photons over a quantum channel [4–6].

A quantum channel is used only to exchange qubits, and it provides the QKD protocol with raw keys. All further communication is performed over a public channel, and it is often denoted as post-processing. It includes steps that need to be implemented for all types of protocols [2], exchanging only the accompanying information that helps in the profiling of raw keys. The overall process is aimed at establishing symmetric keys on both sides of the link in a safe manner.

The initial post-processing step is called a sifting phase, and it is used to detect those qubits for which adequate polarization measurement bases have been used on both sides. Therefore, user B, typically designated Bob informs user A, usually named Alice in literature, about bases he used, and Alice provides feedback advising when incompatible measurement bases have been used. It is important to underline that information about the measurement results is not revealed since only details on used bases are exchanged. Bob will discard bits for cases when incompatible bases have been used, providing the sifted key.

Further, it is necessary to check whether the eavesdropping of communication has been performed. This step is known as error-rate estimation since it is used to estimate the overall communication error. The eavesdropper is not solely responsible for errors in the quantum channel since errors may occur due to imperfection in the state preparation procedure at the source, polarization reference frame misalignment, imperfect polarizing beam splitters, detector dark counts, stray background light, noise in the detectors or disturbance of the quantum channel. However, the threshold of bit error rate p_{max} for the quantum channel without the presence of eavesdropper Eve is known in advance, and this information can be compared with the measured quantum bit error rate (QBER) p of the channel. The usual approach for estimation of the QBER in the channel (p) is to compare a small sample portion of measured values. The selected portion should be sufficient to make the estimated QBER credible where the question about the length of the sample portion is vital [4,7,8]. After estimating QBER, the obtained value can be compared with the already known threshold value of p_{max}. If the error rate is higher than a given threshold ($p > p_{max}$), the presence of Eve is revealed which means that all measured values should be discarded and the process starts from the beginning. Otherwise, the process continues.

Although the estimated value is lower than the threshold value, there are still measurement errors that need to be identified, and those bits need to be corrected or discarded. The process of locating and removing errors is often denoted as "error key reconciliation". As shown in traffic analysis experiments [9, 10], error key reconciliation represents a highly time demanding and extensive computational part of the whole process. Depending on the implementation, a key reconciliation step may affect the quantum channel and considerably impact the key generation rate.

In the following sections, we analyze the most popular error reconciliation approaches. Cascade protocol is discussed in Sect. 2, overview of Winnow protocol is given in Sect. 3. Section 4 outlines LDPC approach while the comparison is given in Sect. 5. We introduce the new key reconciliation protocol in Sect. 6 and provide conclusion in Sect. 7.

2   Cascade

The most widely used error key reconciliation protocol is cascade protocol due to its simplicity and efficiency [11]. Cascade is based on iterations where random permutations are performed with the aim of evenly dispersing errors throughout the sifted key. The permuted sifted key is divided into equal blocks of k_i bits, and after each iteration and new permutations, the block size is doubled: $k_i = 2 \cdot k_{i-1}$. The results of the parity test for each block are compared, and a binary search to find and correct errors in the block is performed. However, to improve the efficiency of the process, the cascade protocol investigates errors in pairs of iterations in a recursive way.

Instead of rejecting error bits in the first stage, information about the presence of an error bit in the block is used in the further iterations to detect errors that have not been detected due to the measurement parity. For any error detected in further iterations, at least one matching error can be identified in the same block of the previous iteration which was previously considered as a block without errors. Using a binary search, a deep search for errors in such a block is performed, and the masked errors can be recursively detected. Two passes of cascade protocol are illustrated in Fig. 1.

The length of the initial block k_1 is a critical parameter which depends on the estimated QBER. The empirical analysis described in [11] proposes the use of value $k_1 = 0.73/p$ as the optimal value, where p is the estimated QBER. Sugimoto modified the cascade protocol to bring the cascading protocol closer to theoretical limits [12]. Besides, he confirmed that four iterations are sufficient for the effective key reconciliation as originally proposed in [11]. However, due to the dependence of the initial block's length on the estimated QBER, it is advisable to execute all the iterations (as long as the length of the block k_i is not equal to the length of the key). In [4], Rass and Kollmitzer showed that adopting block-size to variations of the local error rate is worthwhile, as the efficiency of error correction can be increased by reducing the number of bits revealed to an adversary [13].

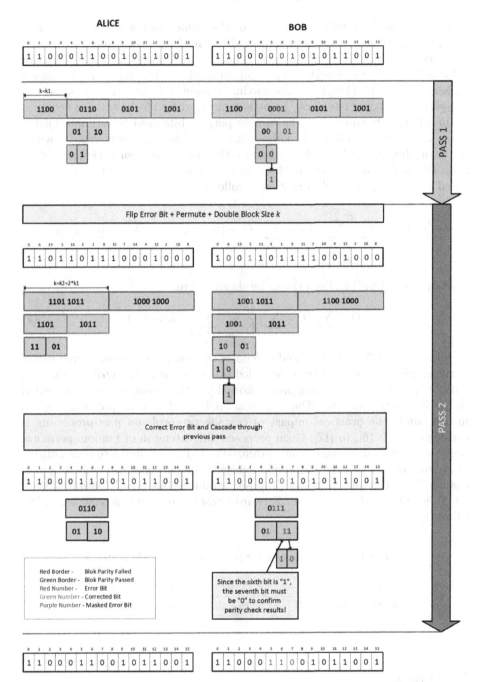

Fig. 1. Illustration of the first two passes of reconciliation using a Cascade protocol.

Cascade protocol relies on the use of the binary search to locate an error bit. The binary search includes further division of the block into two smaller subblocks for which the results of parity check values are compared until an error is found. For each block with an error bit, in total $1 + \lceil \log_2 k_i \rceil$ parity values are exchanged since $1 + \lceil \log_2 k_i \rceil$ is the maximum number of times that block k_i can be splitted, and only one parity value is exchanged for blocks without errors.

In addition to discarding the sample portion bits used to estimate QBER value, it is advised to discard the last bit of each block and subblock for which the parity bit was exchanged to minimize the amount of information gained by Eve. The maximum number of discared bits denoted as D_i can be calculated based on k_i value in the ith iteration as follows:

$$\sum D_i = \sum_i (\sum_{\substack{initially \\ even \\ blocks}} 1 + \sum_{\substack{initially \\ odd \\ blocks}} (1 + \lceil log_2 \ k_i \rceil) + \sum_{\substack{other \\ errors \\ corrected}} \lceil log_2 \ k_i \rceil) \quad (1)$$

As proposed in [14], Eq. (1) can be shortened to:

$$D = \sum D_i = \sum_i (\frac{n}{k_i} + \sum_{\substack{errors \\ corrected}} \lceil log_2 \ k_i \rceil) \quad (2)$$

where $k_i = 2 \cdot k_{i-1}, k_i < \frac{n}{2}$ and n denotes the amount of the measured values in sifting phase. The number of discarded bits depends on the QBER value and initial block size. However, Sugimoto showed [12] that most errors are corrected in the first two iterations. The empirical analysis of cascade protocol is given in [15], while the practical impact of cascade protocols on post-processing is considered in [9,16]. In [17], Chen proposed the extension of random permutations using interleaving technique optimized to reduce or eliminate error clusters from burst errors. Nguyen proposed modifying the permutation method used in cascade [18]. Yan and Martinez proposed modifications based the initial key's length in [19,20] while the use of Forward Error Correction was analyzed in [21] (Table 1).

Table 1. Error correction per passes using Cascade protocol

Iteration	1	2	3	4
Corrected errors (%)	54.522%	45.347%	0.451%	0.002%

3   Winnow

In 2003, Winnow protocol based on Hamming codes was introduced [22]. The aim was to increase the throughput and reduce the interactivity of Cascade by eliminating the binary search step.

Both parties, Alice and Bob, divide their random keys M_a and M_b into blocks of equal length (recommended starting size is $k = 8$) and calculate syndrome values S_a and S_b based on a Generator matrix G and a parity check Matrix H where $H \cdot G^T = 0$. For each block of size k, based on his key values M_b, Bob will generate and transmit his syndrome $S_b = H \cdot M_b$ to Alice, which will calculate the syndrome differences S_d. If S_d is non-zero, Alice will attempt to correct the errors with the fewest changes leading to syndrome zero values.

$$S_a = H \cdot M_a^T = \begin{bmatrix} 0\,1\,1\,0\,1\,0\,1 \\ 1\,0\,1\,1\,0\,1\,0 \\ 1\,1\,0\,0\,1\,0\,1 \end{bmatrix} \cdot \begin{bmatrix} 0\,1\,1\,0\,0\,1\,1 \end{bmatrix}^T = \begin{bmatrix} 1 \\ 0 \\ 0 \end{bmatrix}$$

$$S_b = H \cdot M_b^T = \begin{bmatrix} 0\,1\,1\,0\,1\,0\,1 \\ 1\,0\,1\,1\,0\,1\,0 \\ 1\,1\,0\,0\,1\,0\,1 \end{bmatrix} \cdot \begin{bmatrix} 0\,1\,0\,0\,0\,1\,1 \end{bmatrix}^T = \begin{bmatrix} 0 \\ 1 \\ 0 \end{bmatrix}$$

$$S_a \bigotimes S_b = \begin{bmatrix} 1 \\ 1 \\ 0 \end{bmatrix}$$

$$1 \cdot 2^0 + 1 \cdot 2^1 + 0 \cdot 2^2 = 3 \ (\textit{bit on position 3 is the error}) \tag{3}$$

The Hamming distance d_{min} between codewords limits the number of errors that are suitable for correction where a code word with the number of errors greater than $\frac{d_{min}}{2}$ may closely resemble different code word then correcting the considered code word. Due to reliance on Hamming codes, the Winnow protocol may actually introduce errors, which is the main disadvantage of the shortly described approached. Its efficiency is lower when compared to Cascade for QBER values below 10% that are useful for practical QKD [23].

To achieve information-theoretical secrecy, Buttler suggested discarding an additional bit of each block of size k in the privacy maintenance phase [22].

4   Low Density Parity Check

With terrestrial links, Alice and Bob are usually not limited to execution time, computation and communication complexity. However, with satellite links, the parties need to consider significant losses in the channel, limited time to establish a key due to periodic satellite passage where communication and computation complexity puts additional constraint. Therefore, in previous years, researchers have turning to the application of Gallager's Low Density Parity Check (LDPC) codes that have recently been shown to reconcile errors at rates higher than those of Cascade and Winnow [24–26]. LDPC provides low communication overhead and inherent asymmetry in the amount of computation power required at each side of the channel.

LDPC linear codes are based on a parity check matrix H and a generator matrix G where a decoding limit of the code is defined with the minimum distance. The dimensions of H and G are $m \times n$ where $m = n \cdot (1 - r)$ and r is defined as code rate in range [0, 1]. The code rate value is usually defined beforehand; it defines the correcting power and efficiency. The reconciliation algorithm based on LDPC includes following steps:

- An estimation of QBER of the communication channel is performed,
- Based on estimated QBER, Alice and Bob choose the same $m \times n$ generator matrix G and parity check matrix H,
- For each sifted key, Bob calculates syndrome S_b and send it to Alice,
- Alice attempts to reconcile sifted key, assuming that Bob has the correct sifted key. Her goal is to resolve Bob's key vector x, based on her key vector y, received syndrome S_b, the parity-check matrix H, and estimated QBER value. Alice can use several techniques to decode LDPC such as belief propagation decoding algorithm (also known as the Sum-Product algorithm) or Log-Likelihood Ratios which significantly lower computational complexity [4, 16, 23].

Decoding LDPC code requires larger computational and memory requirements than either the Cascade or Winnow algorithms. However, it has a significant advantage due to the reduction of communication resources since only one information exchange is required. In networks with limited resources (bandwidth and latency), such tradeoff provides potentially large gains in overall runtime and secrecy. In the context of QKD, LDPC was firstly used as a base for the BBN Niagara protocol in DARPA QKD network [27].

5   Comparisson

For testing purposes, Cascade, Winnow and LDPC code were implemented in C++ programming language on servers Intel (R) Xeon (R) Silver 4116 CPU @ 2.10 GHz with 8 GB, and 512 GB HDD. For each value of QBER, 10.000 random keys were tested with the same random seed, which allowed repeating scenarios for different protocols used (Cascade, Winnow and LDPC). In total, 870,000 tests were performed.

The total number of leaked bits is defined as follows:

- Cascade: For each exchange of parity value, one bit is discarded.
- Winnow: For each block k, one bit is discarded.
- LDPC: Total length of syndrome S_b value exchanged.

Figure 2 shows that for small values of QBER (up to 0.05%), Cascade quickly finds and removes errors resulting in a small number of iterations. However, as the QBER value increases (up to 0.10%), LDPC shows better efficiency in terms of overhead and information exchanged.

Figure 3 shows that the overhead efficiency has its price in terms of execution time. Due to the simplicity of algorithms, Cascade and Winnow codes have almost fixed execution time, while in LDPC, the code execution time varies, and gradually increases with the QBER increase.

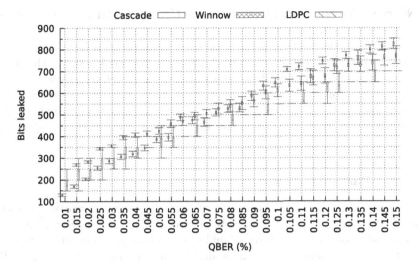

Fig. 2. The number of bits leaked (discarded) for different QBER values. Due to its simplicity, the binary search within Cascade protocol can locate errors in a short time for lower values of QBER. However, for more significant QBER values, binary search requires deeper checking of the sifted key, which increases communication. In the case of Winnow, syndrome message per each block of length k is exchanged which can be used to detect errors in early stages.

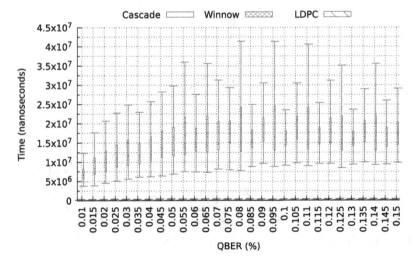

Fig. 3. The execution time for different QBER values. LDPC predominantly requires more time to execute key reconciliation tasks while due to its simplicity, the execution time of the Cascade and Winnow protocols is almost constant. LDPC based on the belief propagation algorithm was used for decoding.

6   Error Correction Based on Artificial Neural Networks

Using artificial neural networks for error correction during a key reconciliation process is a new concept, introduced in [28]. This proposal assumes the use of mutual synchronization of artificial neural networks to correct errors occurring during transmission in the quantum channel. Alice and Bob create their own neural networks based on their keys (with errors). After the mutual learning process, they correct all errors and can use the final key for cryptography purposes.

6.1   Tree Parity Machines

Tree parity machine (TPM) is a type of artificial neural networks (ANN) – a family of statistical learning models inspired by biological neural networks [29]. It consists of artificial neurons (analogous to biological neurons) which are connected and are able to transmit a signal from one neuron to another [30]. Neurons are usually organized in layers: the first layer consists of input neurons which can send the data to the second layer (called hidden). The last layer – called the output layer – consists of output neurons. TPM contains only one hidden layer and has a single neuron in the output layer. It consists of KN input neurons, where K is the number of neurons in the hidden layer and N is the number of inputs into each neuron in the hidden layer. An example of TPM is presented in Fig. 4.

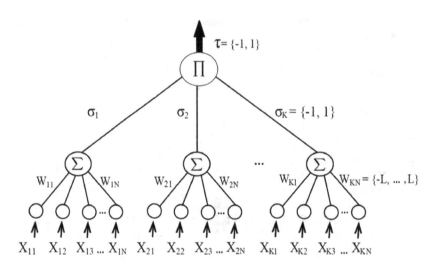

Fig. 4. Structure of TPM machine [28]

TPMs have another important feature: connections between neurons can store parameters (called weights) that can be manipulated during calculation.

Each connection between the input layer and hidden layer is characterized by its weight, which is an integer from the range $[-L, L]$. The output value of neuron k in the hidden layer depends on input x and weight w and is calculated as:

$$\sigma_k = sgn(\sum_{n=1}^{N} x_{kn} * w_{kn}) \tag{4}$$

where signum function is:

$$sgn(z) = \begin{cases} -1 & z \leq 0 \\ 1 & z > 0 \end{cases} \tag{5}$$

The output value of the neuron in the output layer is calculated as:

$$\tau = \prod_{k=1}^{K} \sigma_k \tag{6}$$

When Alice and Bob build their own TPMs with the same structure (K, N and L), they can synchronize these artificial networks after mutual learning [31]. At the beginning of this process, each TPM generates random values of weights, however after the synchronization process both users have TPMs with the same values of weights. Therefore, Alice and Bob can use this phenomenon to correct errors occurring in the quantum channel.

In order to synchronize neural networks, Alice or Bob generates random inputs and both users compute outputs from each TPM. If the outputs have the same value, they start the learning process, but if the outputs are different, a new string of bits must be generated. Alice and Bob can choose any learning algorithm; however, the generalized form of Hebbian method is the most popular in practical implementations [32]. This algorithm strengthens the connections which have the same value as the TPM output. The new weights are calculated by means of the following formula:

$$w_{kn}^{*} = \nu_L(w_{kn} + x_{kn} * \sigma_k * \Theta(\sigma_k, \tau)) \tag{7}$$

where:

$$\Theta(\sigma_k, \tau)) = \begin{cases} 0 & \text{if } \sigma_k \neq \tau \\ 1 & \text{if } \sigma_k = \tau \end{cases} \tag{8}$$

and function ν_L limits values of connections to the range $[-L, L]$:

$$\nu_L(z) = \begin{cases} -L & \text{if } z \leq -L \\ z & \text{if } -L < z < L \\ L & \text{if } z \geq L \end{cases} \tag{9}$$

After the appropriate number of iterations, the synchronization process ends, and the weights of both TPM machines are the same. However, synchronization of TPMs requires public channel for communication between Alice and Bob where Eve can eavesdrop and try to synchronize her own TPM machine with Alice and Bob. Fortunately, if the output of Eve's TPM machine is different than the outputs of Alice and Bob's machines, the learning process cannot be performed. Therefore, the synchronization of Eve's TPM is much slower than the synchronization of the TPMs belonging to Alice and Bob. An example of the synchronization process is presented in Fig. 5 (TPM machines with parameters: $N = 8$, $K = 6$, $L = 2$ and Hebbian learning algorithm). Alice and Bob synchronized neural networks before 200 iterations, but the attacker was not able to do it for 1000 iterations.

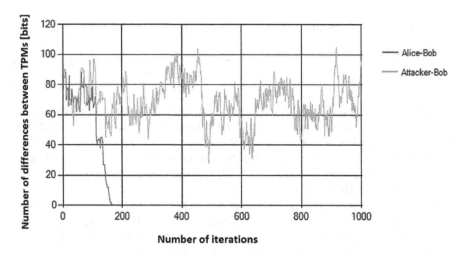

Fig. 5. Example of TPMs synchronization: Alice's TPM and Bob's TPM, Bob's TPM and Attacker's TPM (TPM machines with parameters: $N = 8$, $K = 6$, $L = 2$ and Hebbian learning algorithm)

6.2   Error Correction Based on TPMs

We can use the presented synchronization of the TPM machines to correct errors in the quantum cryptography. In the beginning, Alice and Bob create their own TPM machines based on their own strings of bits. The users change the string of bits into weights in their own TPM machines (bits into numbers from the range $[-L, L]$). Values $\{-L, -L + 1, ...L - 1, L\}$ become weights of connections between the input neurons and the neurons in the hidden layer. In this way, Alice and Bob construct very similar neural networks – the TPM machines have the same structure, and most of the weights are the same. The differences are located only in the places where errors occurred: for example, if QBER $\approx 3\%$, it means that $\approx 97\%$ of bits are correct. After this, synchronization of the

TPM machines begins and continues until all weights in both machines become the same. When each random input is chosen (input strings have KN length), the users compute outputs and compare the obtained values. When the TPM machines are synchronized, the weights are the same in both neural networks. Therefore Alice and Bob can convert the weights back into bits because both strings are now the same. All errors have been corrected.

Importantly, Alice's binary string is very similar to Bob's string of bits. The typical value for QBER does not exceed a few percent; therefore we must correct only a small part of the whole key. This means that the TPM machines are close to synchronization and the learning process will finish much faster than in the case of synchronization of random strings of bits. Of course, this increases the security level significantly.

It is worth mentioning that this idea – using the mutual synchronization of neural networks to correct errors – is a special case when this process makes sense. In general, TPM machines cannot be used for error correction of digital information because we are not able to predict the final weights after the learning process.

7 Conclusion

In this chapter, we analyzed techniques of implementing the key reconciliation using Cascade, Winnow, Low-density parity-check code and the application of neural networks with a focus on communication and computing performances.

Our previous results [9] showed that key reconciliation process takes the dominant part of QKD post-processing. With increasing interest in satellite and global QKD connections, minimizing the duration of key establishment process is becoming an increasingly attractive area. It is necessary to take into account the possibilities of asymmetric processing, which simplifies the requirements for computing power budgets as well as requirements for minimizing the exchange of packets to reduce overhead and the ability to work in networks with weaker network performance (bandwidth and network delay).

Since the development of metropolitan QKD testbed networks [33–39], LDPC is increasingly being considered as an adequate basis for the key reconciliation process in QKD, and there are noticeable variations in how this protocol is implemented. However, techniques of reversibility or on artificial neural networks can significantly improve the process to reduce communication and computing resources and represent areas of great interest for further research.

References

1. Bennett, C.H., Brassard, G.: Quantum cryptography: public key distribution and coin tossing. In: Proceedings of IEEE International Conference on Computers, Systems and Signal Processing, New York, vol. 175, p. 8 (1984)
2. Scarani, V., Bechmann-Pasquinucci, H., Cerf, N.J., Dušek, M., Lütkenhaus, N., Peev, M.: The security of practical quantum key distribution. Rev. Mod. Phys. 81(3), 1301–1350 (2009)

3. Assche, G.V.: Quantum Cryptography and Secret-Key Distribution. Cambridge University Press, Cambridge (2006)
4. Kollmitzer, C., Pivk, M.: Applied Quantum Cryptography, vol. 1. Springer, Heidelberg (2010). https://doi.org/10.1007/978-3-642-04831-9
5. Dodson, D., et al.: Updating quantum cryptography report ver. 1. arXiv preprint arXiv:0905.4325, May 2009
6. Dusek, M., Lutkenhaus, N., Hendrych, M.: Quantum cryptography. In: Progress in Optics, vol. 49, pp. 381–454. Elsevier, January 2006
7. Niemiec, M., Pach, A.R.: The measure of security in quantum cryptography. In: 2012 IEEE Global Communications Conference (GLOBECOM), pp. 967–972, December 2012
8. Mehic, M., Niemiec, M., Voznak, M.: Calculation of the key length for quantum key distribution. Elektron. Elektrotech. **21**(6), 81–85 (2015)
9. Mehic, M., Maurhart, O., Rass, S., Komosny, D., Rezac, F., Voznak, M.: Analysis of the public channel of quantum key distribution link. IEEE J. Quantum Electron. **53**(5), 1–8 (2017)
10. Mehic, M., et al.: A novel approach to quality-of-service provisioning in trusted relay quantum key distribution networks. IEEE/ACM Trans. Netw. **28**(1), 168–181 (2020)
11. Brassard, Gilles, Salvail, Louis: Secret-key reconciliation by public discussion. In: Helleseth, Tor (ed.) EUROCRYPT 1993. LNCS, vol. 765, pp. 410–423. Springer, Heidelberg (1994). https://doi.org/10.1007/3-540-48285-7_35
12. Sugimoto, T., Yamazaki, K.: A study on secret key reconciliation protocol. IEICE Trans. Fundam. Electron. Commun. Comput. Sci. **E83-A**(10), 1987–1991 (2000)
13. Lustic, K.: Performance analysis and optimization of the winnow secret key reconciliation protocol. Ph.D. thesis, Air Force Institute of Technology (2010)
14. Ruth, Y.: A probabilistic analysis of binary and cascade. math.uchicago.edu (2013)
15. Calver, T.: An empirical analysis of the cascade secret key reconciliation protocol for quantum key distribution. Master thesis (2011)
16. Pedersen, T.B., Toyran, M., Pearson, D., Pedersen, T.B., Toyran, M.: High performance information reconciliation for QKD with CASCADE. Quantum Inf. Comput. **734**(5–6), 419–434 (2013)
17. Keath, C.: Improvement of reconciliation for quantum key distribution. Ph.D. thesis, Rochester Institute of Technology, February 2010
18. Nguyen, K.C.: Extension des protocoles de réconciliation en cryptographie quantique. Université Libre de Bruxelles, Travail de fon d'études (2002)
19. Yan, H., et al.: Information reconciliation protocol in quantum key distribution system. In: Proceedings - 4th International Conference on Natural Computation, ICNC 2008, vol. 3, pp. 637–641 (2008)
20. Martinez-Mateo, J., Pacher, C., Peev, M., Ciurana, A., Martin, V.: Demystifying the information reconciliation protocol cascade. arXiv preprint arXiv:1407.3257, pp. 1–30, July 2014
21. Nakassis, A., Bienfang, J.C., Williams, C.J.: Expeditious reconciliation for practical quantum key distribution. In: Donkor, E., Pirich, A.R., Brandt, H.E. (eds.) Quantum Information and Computation II, vol. 5436, p. 28, August 2004
22. Buttler, W.T., Lamoreaux, S.K., Torgerson, J.R., Nickel, G.H., Donahue, C.H., Peterson, C.G.: Fast, efficient error reconciliation for quantum cryptography. Phys. Rev. A **67**(5), 052303 (2003)
23. Elkouss, D., Leverrier, A., Alleaume, R., Boutros, J.J.: Efficient reconciliation protocol for discrete-variable quantum key distribution, June 2009

24. Gallager, R.G.: Low-density parity-check codes. IRE Trans. Inf. Theory **8**, 21–28 (1962)
25. Elkouss, D., Martinez-Mateo, J., Vicente, M.: Information reconciliation for QKD. Quantum Inf. Comput. **11**(March), 226–238 (2011)
26. Elkouss, D., Martinez-Mateo, J., Martin, V.: Analysis of a rate-adaptive reconciliation protocol and the effect of leakage on the secret key rate. Phys. Rev. A - At. Mol. Opt. Phys. **87**(4), 1–7 (2013)
27. Elliott, C., Colvin, A., Pearson, D., Pikalo, O., Schlafer, J., Yeh, H.: Current status of the DARPA quantum network (Invited Paper). In: Donkor, E.J., Pirich, A.R., Brandt, H.E. (eds.) Quantum Information and Computation III. Proceedings of SPIE, vol. 5815, pp. 138–149, May 2005
28. Niemiec, M.: Error correction in quantum cryptography based on artificial neural networks. Quantum Inf. Process. **18**(6), 174 (2019)
29. Kanter, I., Kinzel, W.: The theory of neural networks and cryptography (2007)
30. Hadke, P.P., Kale, S.G.: Use of neural networks in cryptography: a review. In: IEEE WCTFTR 2016 - Proceedings of 2016 World Conference on Futuristic Trends in Research and Innovation for Social Welfare (2016)
31. Chakraborty, S., Dalal, J., Sarkar, B., Mukherjee, D.: Neural synchronization based secret key exchange over public channels: a survey. In: 2014 International Conference on Signal Propagation and Computer Technology, ICSPCT 2014 (2014)
32. Kriesel, D.: A brief introduction on neural networks. Technical report, December 2007. www.dkriesel.com
33. Elliott, C., Yeh, H.: DARPA quantum network testbed. Technical report July, BBN Technologies Cambridge, New York, USA, New York (2007)
34. Alleaume, R., et al.: SECOQC white paper on quantum key distribution and cryptography. arXiv preprint quant-ph/0701168, p. 28 (2007)
35. Korzh, B., et al.: Provably secure and practical quantum key distribution over 307 km of optical fibre. Nat. Photon. **9**(3), 163–168 (2015)
36. Sasaki, M.: Tokyo QKD network and the evolution to secure photonic network. In: CLEO:2011 - Laser Applications to Photonic Applications, vol. 1, JTuC1. OSA, Washington, D.C. (2011)
37. Dixon, A.R., Yuan, Z.L., Dynes, J.F., Sharpe, A.W., Shields, A.J.: Continuous operation of high bit rate quantum key distribution. Appl. Phys. Lett. **96**(2010), 2008–2011 (2010)
38. Salvail, L., Peev, M., Diamanti, E., Alléaume, R., Lütkenhaus, N., Länger, T.: Security of trusted repeater quantum key distribution networks. J. Comput. Secur. **18**(1), 61–87 (2010)
39. Shimizu, K., et al.: Performance of long-distance quantum key distribution over 90-km optical links installed in a field environment of Tokyo metropolitan area. J. Lightwave Technol. **32**(1), 141–151 (2014)

Author Index

Printed in the United States
by Baker & Taylor Publisher Services

Printed in the United States
by Baker & Taylor Publisher Services